NURTURING DADS

NURTURING DADS

SOCIAL INITIATIVES FOR
CONTEMPORARY FATHERHOOD

WILLIAM MARSIGLIO AND KEVIN ROY

A Volume in the American Sociological Association's
Rose Series in Sociology

Russell Sage Foundation • New York

Library of Congress Cataloging-in-Publication Data

Marsiglio, William.
  Nurturing dads : social initiatives for contemporary fatherhood / William Marsiglio and Kevin Roy.
      p. cm. — (American Sociological Association's Rose series in sociology)
  Includes bibliographical references and index.
  ISBN 978-0-87154-566-4 (alk. paper)
  1. Fatherhood. 2. Parenting. 3. Fathers—Psychology. 4. Father and child. I. Roy, Kevin, 1966- II. American Sociological Association. III. Title.
  HQ756.M3447 2012
  306.874'2—dc23
                                        2011039569

The paper used in this publication meets the minimum requirements of American National Standard for Information Sciences—Permanence of Paper for Printed Library Materials. ANSI Z39.48-1992.

Text design by Suzanne Nichols.

RUSSELL SAGE FOUNDATION
112 East 64th Street, New York, New York 10065
10 9 8 7 6 5 4 3 2 1

The Russell Sage Foundation

The Russell Sage Foundation, one of the oldest of America's general purpose foundations, was established in 1907 by Mrs. Margaret Olivia Sage for "the improvement of social and living conditions in the United States." The Foundation seeks to fulfill this mandate by fostering the development and dissemination of knowledge about the country's political, social, and economic problems. While the Foundation endeavors to assure the accuracy and objectivity of each book it publishes, the conclusions and interpretations in Russell Sage Foundation publications are those of the authors and not of the Foundation, its Trustees, or its staff. Publication by Russell Sage, therefore, does not imply Foundation endorsement.

═══ Previous Volumes ═══
in the Series

Social Movements in the World-System: The Politics of Crisis and Transformation
Jackie Smith and Dawn Wiest

They Say Cut Back, We Say Fight Back! Welfare Rights Activism in an Era of Retrenchment
Ellen Reese

Trust in Schools: A Core Resource for Improvement
Anthony S. Bryk and Barbara Schneider

═ Forthcoming Titles ═

Embedded Dependency: Minority Set-Asides, Black Entrepreneurs, and the White Construction Monopoly
Deirdre Royster

Family Consequences of Children's Disabilities
Dennis Hogan

Family Relationships Across the Generations
Judith A. Seltzer and Suzanne M. Bianchi

Global Order and the Historical Structures of Daral-Islam
Mohammed A. Bamyeh

The Logic of Terrorism: A Comparative Study
Jeff Goodwin

The Long Shadow: Family Background, Disadvantaged Urban Youth, and the Transition to Adulthood
Karl Alexander, Doris Entwisle, and Linda Olson

Repressive Injustice: Political and Social Processes in the Massive Incarceration of African Americans
Pamela E. Oliver and James E. Yocum

The Rose Series in Sociology

THE AMERICAN Sociological Association's Rose Series in Sociology publishes books that integrate knowledge and address controversies from a sociological perspective. Books in the Rose Series are at the forefront of sociological knowledge. They are lively and often involve timely and fundamental issues on significant social concerns. The series is intended for broad dissemination throughout sociology, across social science and other professional communities, and to policy audiences. The series was established in 1967 by a bequest to ASA from Arnold and Caroline Rose to support innovations in scholarly publishing.

DIANE BARTHEL-BOUCHIER
CYNTHIA J. BOGARD
MICHAEL KIMMEL
DANIEL LEVY
TIMOTHY P. MORAN
NAOMI ROSENTHAL
MICHAEL SCHWARTZ
GILDA ZWERMAN

EDITORS

With much love and gratitude, we are honored to dedicate this book to our five wonderful children, who challenge us to discover how to be nurturing dads.

Scott Michael Marsiglio
Phoenix Jesse Marsiglio
Owen Flynn Roy
Liam Flynn Roy
Gabriel Flynn Roy

Contents

About the Authors

William Marsiglio is professor in the Department of Sociology and Criminology & Law at the University of Florida.

Kevin Roy is associate professor of family science at the University of Maryland, College Park.

═ Preface ═

SINCE THE 1980s, American fathers, like their counterparts in many industrialized countries, have received increased scrutiny from academics, policymakers, social activists, and the general public. Numerous father "types" have been targeted beyond the normative resident biological father who works outside the home: teenage and older fathers, stay-at-home dads, doting fathers, nonresident fathers, "deadbeat" dads, stepfathers, single dads, gay fathers, fathers of special needs children, incarcerated fathers, and others. Acknowledging fathers' diverse experiences makes sense, especially when the everyday realities of families have shifted in sync with higher rates of delayed marriage, divorce, remarriage, and children born to unmarried couples.[1]

Those who pay attention to fathers have done so primarily because they want to improve children's lives, foster gender equity at home and in the workplace, or inspire men to enhance their own well-being by taking a more hands-on approach to childrearing. For many years, these motives have guided our own research agendas. They also came into play when we accepted Michael Kimmel's invitation on behalf of the Rose Monograph Series and the Russell Sage Foundation to develop a forward-looking book to explore the relationship between social policy and fatherhood. With *Nurturing Dads: Social Initiatives for Contemporary Fatherhood*, we seek to shape public discourse about fathering as well as influence how public and private initiatives are tailored to promote an engaged, nurturing style of fathering. Our title, "Nurturing Dads," underscores two related themes: the vital notion that dads can and do nurture their children, and our call for collective action to assist or "nurture" dads to become more attentive to and engaged with their children in ways that extend well beyond financial breadwinning. Most fathers face challenges in expanding their parenting to include lots of nurturance, partly because there is only limited government support for making a close father-child relationship a priority and the strategies to achieve this goal are not well established. We find, even with our own children and partners, that we as fathers tend to "make it up as we go."

We interpret the phrase "social policy" broadly. Put simply, we consider all types of social initiatives that can foster a more nurturing style of fathering. This broad approach reflects our own extensive experiences with federal and state policymakers, community-based fathering program staff, local and national advocates and media groups, and think tanks and research organizations. Ultimately we seek to refine, expand, and integrate our visions of how interested stakeholders can enhance father-child relations and bring about better outcomes for children, fathers, and mothers. Those outcomes include greater gender equity at home and in the workplace. As we see it, our primary challenge is to bridge the divide between academics and those who either craft social policies or develop and run programs that focus on men as fathers. Throughout we also share ideas about existing policies and programs and at times suggest new perspectives and projects. Nurturance can offer a new and effective framework for policy and intervention for men in families.

We relate our insights to a unique set of in-depth interviews we conducted with men from diverse backgrounds. They talk about all sorts of issues related to making babies and caring for their kids. Most important, many carve out, by accident, strategy, or perseverance, a place for themselves with their children. These stories deepen our understanding of American fathers' hopes, joys, and struggles as well as the complexities that define their everyday lives. No doubt, too, our sensitivity to nurturance as a process is sharpened by insights we have personally garnered from fathering five children. In other words, we have learned about nurturance firsthand as well as from listening to and interpreting other fathers' stories about their sons and daughters. Our moments of paternal self-reflection and our scholarly work on fathers have mutually shaped each other.[2] Theoretical frames are seldom far from our interactions with our own children. From these personal and scholarly experiences a fundamental lesson has emerged: to apprehend the breadth and depth of fathering, we must explore the full gamut of men's experiences with reproductive health, conception, pregnancy, fathering, and children more generally. We must also consider how the larger familial and social networks, as well as institutions, enhance or constrain fathers' involvement with their children.

Our book's message about the virtues of a nurturing style of fathering comes at an intriguing historical moment when public discourse is as invested in the attentive father who tends to his child's daily needs as it is in the father who has neglected his breadwinning and caregiving responsibilities. In changing economic times, millions of fathers find themselves unable to meet even revamped expectations to be providers, and they do not want to be separated from their children as a result. Fortunately, the activity list of what constitutes contemporary fathers' caring is much more in line with actions once viewed as mothering. It appears, too, that more men talk about wanting to be better fathers, and more resident fathers are making an effort to spend more time with their kids. Yet many men are dissatisfied with at least some aspects of their experience, and many children remain disappointed in some respects about the kind of fathering they receive. Part of the allure of a nurturing style of fathering is that it could produce healthy changes in men's personal development as well as benefit children and mothers.

Any consideration of how men can nurture children in more meaningful and effective ways has deep implications for how, as a society, we care for families and how such care work is distributed equitably. Thus, we add our voice to the ongoing debate about social change and gender equity.[3] In so doing we challenge others to consider personal, political, and structural implications of men's enhanced nurturance. We hope to push the stakeholders who have begun to see fathers in this more progressive light to reaffirm their commitment to support creative initiatives that help more men see the value of nurturance and to help them become the kinds of fathers they would like to be.

Our journey with this project has spanned several years and has been influenced by numerous colleagues. We were delighted with the response we received from those who attended our presentation of our first book draft at the Russell Sage Foundation in New York City in December 2010. The participants—Diana Baldermann, Suzanne Bianchi, Kathleen Gerson, Michael Kimmel, Timothy Moran, Suzanne Nichols, Naomi Rosenthal, Michael Schwartz, Judith Seltzer, and Gilda Zwerman—provided us with detailed and invaluable feedback as well as a large dose of encouragement to polish our argument and to finalize our project. Michael Kimmel, the lead contact person representing the Rose team, astutely helped us to frame our argument while encouraging us to accentuate the gendered aspects of fathers' experiences. We also appreciate comments shared by two anonymous reviewers in the spring of 2011 that enabled us to refine our manuscript in its final stage.

═ Chapter 1 ═

The Landscape

EXITING the school building on a sunny afternoon, Dwight's eyes find his adorable six-year-old son fidgeting next to his mother, Dwight's wife, as he waits for "daddy time." Dwight, a family man with a steady paycheck, has just completed his interview about working in this alternative school for "problem" kids as a teacher's aide. Beaming an infectious smile, the boy's face glows with joy—the kind that marks a child's attachment to a loving, caring parent. He lunges at his dad to give and get a hug. Clearly, Dwight's conviction to be an involved father is paying huge dividends. In his words:

> [My son] needs me as much as I can give. Work is important, I enjoy work, but you know I gotta make sure I take care of my family first. And I need to kinda be all ears to just listen to him, or help with homework, or we going out and play ball, or whatever.

This thirty-six-year-old African American father draws inspiration to be an engaged father from lessons his hardworking father ingrained in him many years ago. Earlier, sitting in his office reminiscing about his "great" childhood, Dwight spoke fondly of his father's imprint.

> Being around him and listening to the different stories that he had to tell, it taught me about being respectful and having respect for others as well as myself. And one of his main things was that if you do right no matter what the situation is, if you do right then good things will come to you.

Aside from reaping the long-term benefits of the loving attention he received from his parents and neighbors while growing up in a small neighborhood, this lower-middle-class father realizes that his own work with disadvantaged youth in an alternative school has made an indelible impression on him. Witnessing his students' daily dilemmas, Dwight sees that love and parental time are critical for child development. Dwight is convinced that the kids he teaches receive little, and very poor, parental supervision. Consequently, Dwight is determined to spend lots of quality time with his son. That's why he signed his son up for Cub

1

Scouts and has faithfully attended the various meetings and events during the past two years.

Dwight is often reminded that many of his students turn to him as a father figure because their own fathers are unsupportive, unavailable, or both. But even though he says that his job is sometimes "stressful" it also

> brings tears of joy to your eyes just to be able to step into a child's life that doesn't have a father and just show him some of the basic things, just a little time that we have together here, and that carries on for years. . . . Some of 'em would call me Daddy right now. . . . And to build that relationship with [a] child and to still see them from time to time and see what they've grown into, I mean it's just like being a father.

This story reminds us that fathers in contemporary society have increasingly complex values and desires. In part, they aspire to be acknowledged for all of the successes that mark "good" fatherhood. For decades, "good" fathers have been defined as men who provide for and reside with their spouses and children. Dwight has a stable job with good wages, and he can support his family—this is one measure of a good father. He is also married to his son's mother. As a member of a committed couple, Dwight represents a role model for his son and for the boys in the alternative school.

Images of "good" fathers have been etched onto the public consciousness through Hollywood movies, documentaries, and news stories and by other means.[1] For decades, policymakers have defined successful fathers as those who are married breadwinners and coresiding with a wife and children.[2] Nicholas Townsend refers to this bundle of elements as the "package deal."[3] He states that most men in the United States aspire to a related set of experiences, as husbands, worker-providers, homeowners, and fathers. Among these varied dimensions Townsend associates with fathering, emotional closeness and intimacy with their children was the dominant theme that came up in his interviews with middle-class fathers living in northern California. Policymakers assess successful fathers against these yardsticks, with "good" or responsible fathering being equated most clearly with the ability to provide a reasonable paycheck while living with wives and children. The vast majority of fathers, regardless of their economic status, their education, or their marital status, aspire to provide for and reside with their children.

But increasingly, the diverse family landscape of the United States has generated a kaleidoscope of fathering. Identifying the typical father has become more challenging. Men in many different parenting contexts—family men, divorced and remarried fathers, unwed fathers, fathers who work and live apart from their children—have pushed the boundaries of the basic provide-and-reside definitions of "good" fathering.[4] As Dwight illustrates, men want more out of fatherhood than being a breadwinner or a spouse. Many have worked to redefine "good" fathering to include hands-on care of their children.[5] Men like these embody the "growing spirit among new dads to be accepted, both at home and in the workplace, as whole persons."[6]

Efforts to redefine fathering in this way have come with costs. Some recent commentators suggest that men are grappling with a "new male mystique"[7]—the male version of the "feminine mystique,"[8] the term coined by Betty Friedan in the early 1960s. Friedan reasoned that assumptions about women's finding fulfillment in traditional domestic roles created conflict for those who wanted to pursue and psychologically invest their identities in meaningful paid work. Now, traditional assumptions about the father-as-wallet mentality increasingly coexist alongside of and conflict with newer ideals of men participating more actively in family life.[9] Because workplace culture and public policy fail to support men sufficiently in their attempts to balance these competing expectations, more men feel pressure to do it all. Indeed, whereas in 1977 only 35 percent of fathers in dual-earner couples reported work-family conflict, 60 percent of fathers did so in 2008.[10]

What some researchers and popular media have coined "new fatherhood" may not be as modern as we perceive.[11] But the choices that contemporary fathers (and mothers) have made are clear: their visions of successful fathering must include strong, close relationships with their children over the life span. What is striking is that the dual ideal of providing and caring that exemplifies "new fathering" is not just a middle-class vision.[12] Fathers, regardless of income, marital status, or education, value these priorities, although those with good jobs can more readily achieve them. In the United States and in many countries in the world today, high status is often accorded to men who can both provide financially for their children and care for them in close relationships. Some commentators even suggest that nurturance is a core value for cultural definitions of masculinity in many societies.[13] In addition, men and families increasingly sense that fathers' nurturance is not only beneficial to children and mothers, it is also viewed as enriching men's own development.

In this book we consider this important shift in the view of "good" fathering: from a focus on material contributions and a presumption of marriage to a focus on relationships that include a close father-child bond, as well as a new style of coparenting in which fathers and mothers negotiate how care is to be provided for their children. The shift to relational engagement, toward nurturance, is relevant for all fathers in contemporary society. We show how our agenda for changing the institution of fathering is connected to initiatives that promote opportunities for all fathers to nurture their children.

Using an assortment of men's firsthand accounts we've collected over the years, we highlight how practical and cultural forces often complicate men's visions of themselves as fathers and their ability to nurture their children. The examples focus on diverse fathering contexts and constraints, particularly those that deviate from a mainstream model of fatherhood: the biological dad who is heterosexual, married, resident, and working full time. By incorporating a broad sampling of fathering circumstances outside this mainstream vision, we position ourselves to examine shortcomings of fatherhood policy more generally. Our approach also assumes that much can be learned about fathering by studying men who are challenged by atypical fathering circumstances. It may be that the most critical innovations take place in the lives of fathers who use nurturance to transform their roles, thereby altering conventional perceptions of fatherhood in the United States.

Lest one think that this book is primarily about disadvantaged fathers struggling to be involved with their children, our message is relevant to all fathers and to those anticipating fatherhood. The four frames that anchor our analysis—fatherhood as a social arrangement, paths of fathering over time, trust building, and the notion that place matters to how fathers see themselves and interact with their children—touch every father and the families that claim them. In the appendix we describe how our previous theoretical work and our joint assessment of men's stories for this project led us to develop these key frames. The resident father of minor children living in a two-parent household is perhaps only one lapse of infidelity away from being uprooted from his routine of fathering at home. Or, the single man with no immediate thoughts of having children may find himself unexpectedly enthralled with a romantic partner who comes packaged with children from a previous relationship. Or, the middle-class army reservist who has never been away from his children may, once deployed, quickly learn the challenges of fathering from a distance. Or, the successful businessman who operates as the family's sole breadwinner may suddenly find himself an unemployed, anxious father. So even though many of our examples depict fathers outside the mainstream images of fatherhood, common threads of the human, fatherly experience transcend any specific setting.

Nurturance

By no means are we the first scholars to champion the idea that fathers can and should express more nurturing relationships with their children.[14] We embrace the legal scholar Nancy Dowd's recommendation that the definition of fatherhood be flexible and linked more directly to the fundamental concept of nurturance than is the case in the mainstream vision of fatherhood.[15] We concur with her call for fatherhood to be defined in terms of social qualities so that hands-on caregiving will typically be considered more central to the definition of fatherhood than biological or legal status. Dowd works to change expectations about who fathers are and what they do, and we believe her concept of nurturance reflects the real lives of the men we interviewed and observed in our own research. Thus, this approach does not tie a definition of fatherhood simply to biology, marriage, or financial support. In Dowd's words:

> Nurture means care—physical, emotional, intellectual, spiritual—gauged by one's conduct and the consequences for children's positive development. It is responsive to the different needs of children at different ages. Thus nurture is not a static conception. It means more than simply doing; it also means the manner in which things are done, and their results for children.[16]

In particular, we stress that care should be viewed as a human experience rather than a woman's responsibility. Men's capacity to care for children will be deepest when they are able to nurture their children's well-being and development in a holistic fashion.

A cultural and policy shift that significantly elevates the relative value of fathers' nurturance compared to financial provisioning would reshape what is known as fathers' conditional commitment to children.[17] For decades, men have linked their participation in fathering to their participation in marriage. In effect, fathers' commitment to their children was contingent on their romantic involvement with the mothers of the children. An emphasis on fathers' nurturance problematizes this commitment, calls it into question. In a society in which fathers competently practice nurturance, there is an unconditional commitment of men to children—a commitment that does not depend on a marital or romantic relationship, but one that depends solely on the quality of the close bonds between fathers and children.[18]

To be a nurturing father a man presumably must recognize some of his child's specific needs. Responsiveness—the degree to which a man recognizes and responds to his child's and the mother's needs—varies and can have implications for the child and family.[19] Although gender norms, power dynamics and partner influences, work schedules, and emotional tradeoffs can affect a father's responsiveness, we suspect that progressive social initiatives could help some men develop this interpersonal skill as well. A more attuned and responsive father is likely to express nurturance in timely, developmentally appropriate, and effective ways.

For most fathers, the decision to become engaged in more intimate, responsive relationships with their children seems to be a personal choice. But fathers' decisions are often shaped by less obvious social, economic, and political circumstances not necessarily under their immediate control.

In figure 1.1 we begin to highlight the policy implications of this larger context by sketching how conventional and more progressive

Figure 1.1   Transforming Expectations for Current Fathering Policies and Programs

	Conventional Approach Breadwinning and Marriage (Material Expectations)	Progressive Approach Nurturance (Relational Expectations)
↑ ⋮ Provider fathers (family men, married and residential) ⋮	Lack of current policies	Nurturance and healthy relationships as direct goals
⋮ Nonresident provider fathers ⋮	Single targeted policy to secure financial support	Nurturance, financial support, and healthy relationships as direct goals
⋮ Nonprovider fathers (unmarried, nonresident fathers, tangential links to jobs) ⋮ ↓	Multiple targeted policies to encourage employment and marriage	Nurturance, employment, and healthy relationships as direct goals

Source: Authors' figure.

approaches frame public interest in fathering. Conventional expectations for fathers stress material contributions, and the interventions differ for fathers according to how far removed they are from the traditional notion of the married, coresident father. In the public's eye, men who are clearly good providers, "family men" who are married and live with their kids, have typically been viewed as successful fathers. Although in many countries the idea of new fatherhood has been the driver of new laws and policy initiatives, in the United States a policy "silence" surrounds breadwinning fathers who already live up to cultural expectations as "good" fathers.[20] Existing policies and programs are scarce and too limited in scope.

Increasingly, though, fathers, mothers, and children expect more from family life and the institutions that touch their lives. The cultural narrative surrounding child care still portrays it as largely "women's work," but recent evidence shows that contemporary fathers not only value more involvement with their children, they are also getting more involved.[21] One national survey in 2007 indicates that 59 percent of men and 62 percent of women think that being a father today is more challenging than in the 1970s and 1980s.[22] Many resident as well as nonresident fathers are frustrated that they have to choose work over family.

Are there policies that could more readily support these men's efforts to be close to their children? Remarkably, the United States is out of step with most advanced countries around the world in not having a federal policy on parental leave. Elsewhere—in Canada, Germany, and Sweden, to name just three countries—policymakers recognize the need to support paternal caregiving by offering incentives to take time for family relationships.

In contrast, wide-ranging public debates and initiatives in the United States target men who do not fulfill expectations of provision or residence with their families.[23] Reactions emanate from across the political spectrum, varied academic disciplines, activist organizations and social movements,[24] and myriad sources of pop culture. Professionals who direct community-based programs offer their own proposals enriched by their firsthand experience working with men—fathers especially— and families.[25] Researchers for their part have contributed a wide range of empirical analyses to shed light on how fathers might make a difference in children's lives.[26] Conventional strategies for nonresident provider fathers and nonprovider fathers tend to emphasize either a one-size-fits-all policy or multiple policies that stress employment and marriage. Most important, the conventional approach has produced few initiatives that promote nurturance for fathers irrespective of their breadwinning efforts.

The right side of figure 1.1 depicts our proposal for a more progressive approach that highlights the value of nurturance and relational expectations. To a large extent, expectations about nurturance augment the conventional approach. Ideally, a progressive approach would transform the way fathers, regardless of social class, race/ethnicity, or sexuality, interact with their children. Although marriage would still be valued, efforts to foster healthy relationships between resident or nonresident parents irrespective of marital status would be more critical than marriage per se. Initiatives to enhance all parents' ability to become and remain effective coparents are key ("coparents" refers to parents who negotiate parenting responsibilities in either a cooperative or contentious manner). Our progressive view is also premised on the assumption that attempts to realize a more engaged and nurturing style of fathering need to be coupled with more comprehensive efforts to establish a cultural narrative that stresses men's commitment to all children.[27]

In 2001, the federal government's Department of Health and Human Services (DHHS) provided a detailed "guidance" document, "Meeting the Challenge: What the Federal Government Can Do to Support Responsible Fatherhood Efforts," that outlined organizational and individual responses that could enhance father involvement.[28] It emphasizes that fathers are very different from one another, noting that their needs must be linked to differences in residence, marital, and relationship status; experience with incarceration; and age (including teen fathers and grandfathers). Clearly, there is no one model of engagement and training for fatherhood programs. The summary statement also encourages policymakers and practitioners to recognize that "the whole family" should be engaged in any effective program or policy aimed at supporting responsible fathering.[29] In the past decade, the Department of Health and Human Services, as well as related federal fathering initiatives (such as the National Responsible Fatherhood Clearinghouse created by the Bill Clinton administration), have been informed by the principles articulated in the 2001 document that echo the inclusive range of fathering experiences (see chapter 8 for further discussion).[30]

However, the history of initiatives aimed at disadvantaged fathers shows that policymakers have chosen a different strategy than that suggested by the DHHS guidance document. Policymakers who conceptualize federal policies intended to affect these disadvantaged fathers and children seek to transform disadvantaged fathers through marriage and employment opportunities.[31] Recent federal initiatives for low-income fathers emphasize ideals and legal implications related to marriage promotion, the establishment of paternity, financial responsibility, and child custody.[32] At the national and state levels, assistance to fathers is usually guided by short-term fixes, such as job training and placement or a marriage course, to shift outcomes quickly. This approach contrasts sharply with a sustained investment of social services and financial resources that may lead to real, lasting change in father involvement.

Thus far no specific recipe has emerged outlining a coherent set of promising practices for working with this diverse set of men. Recent initiatives were broadened by the George W. Bush administration to prioritize "healthy marriages" and to use marital and relationship education programs.[33] The Responsible Fatherhood and Healthy Families Act of 2007 was introduced with the diverse aims of restructuring child support laws, expanding Earned Income Tax Credit programs to fathers, and providing additional funding for domestic violence.[34] In the 2011 budget, the Barack Obama administration replaced funding for marriage promotion programs with the Fatherhood, Marriage, and Families Innovation Fund. This initiative prioritizes the need for state and local program collaborations that lower obstacles to finding work and that enhance family well-being and best parenting practices.[35]

Evaluations of the federal initiatives have produced diverse findings related to fathers' nurturance. Interventions have taken the form of couple relationship programs or father intervention programs. Unfortunately, in the absence of random controls and experimental designs, few have been systematically evaluated as model programs. Findings are also limited because the interventions have distinctly different goals. Some aim to improve work skills, self-sufficiency, or employment; some attempt to encourage marriage or coparenting skills; and others are designed to reduce incarceration and drug or alcohol use.[36] Each of these goals, researchers and policymakers assume, may indirectly affect the quality of the father-child relationship.

At this point, results from efforts to promote men's nurturance in close father-child relationships are mixed, though promising.[37] Fatherhood intervention programs tend to foster increased child support payments, particularly in low-income families. A few of the more systematic evaluations report that father-child relationship quality was improved by the interventions, although mostly for middle-class fathers. Only one recent program for low-income Mexican American and European American families has demonstrated significant changes in father-child relationship quality. In contrast, relationship skills interventions have been shown to improve couple relationship quality, coparenting skills, and fathers' engagement in parenting. However, evaluations have identified that fathers increase their nurturance only in couple interventions with middle-class fathers and mothers.[38]

Some research indicates that there is promise in bridging these distinct programs by integrating healthy families, responsible fatherhood, and domestic violence services.[39] Thus far, the competing aims of these programs have discouraged federal initiatives, or even local initiatives, from pushing for programs that would target fathers' nurturance of children. If the goals of employment and healthy relationships do not result in positive father-child relationships, nurturance may offer an alternative model for intervention and family policy.

Fathers' Choices in Constrained Circumstances

Cultural discourses and social policies that accentuate only fixed images of father types—such as the "provide and reside" father or the "deadbeat dad"—distort men's lives as fathers. Fathers are likely to exemplify many different types of fathering over the course of their lives, and eventually most will face formidable challenges to living up to the new ideals of fatherhood. Despite growing public concern over a wide range of fatherhood issues, all too often formal strategies for dealing with them are tied to conventional frameworks, thereby providing only a partial response to the assorted needs of fathers, children, and families.

We move beyond a focus on father types and focus on policies and programs that are more responsive to fathers' daily experiences. How are the threads for men's orientation toward nurturing children sewn into the fabric of their boyhood years? What are men's vulnerabilities, needs, challenges, and opportunities as fathers? How do fathers' interpersonal networks that include coparents, family, friends, coworkers, and adults charged with monitoring children in the community affect how fathers perceive and relate to their children? How do men manage critical transitions that affect their fathering? In our own research we have talked to a wide range of fathers who are in constrained circumstances. We focus on these circumstances to get a better understanding of how men's lives are disconnected from policies and programs that might help them become more nurturing fathers.

Roughly twenty-five years ago scholars writing about fatherhood and social change stressed the importance of considering how four types of conditions or factors affect father involvement: motivation, skills, social supports, and institutional barriers.[40] These four conditions are salient in each of the three paths of fathering that we touch on in chapters 2, 3, and 4. For example, within a discussion of the meaning of fatherhood, we find that personal motivation is a critical factor in promoting men's involvement with children and that policies and programs may focus on how to shape men's motivation as fathers. We extend the typology to examine how specific skills, possibly gained through fathering programs, can support father-child bonds so that men become more nurturing, engaged fathers in diverse fathering contexts. These conditions also influence how fathers acquire human capital (credentials, knowledge, financial resources, and interpersonal skills), access social supports, and navigate transitions when confronted by institutional barriers.

The theoretical insights we use to frame our policy-relevant analysis of social fatherhood highlight the value of understanding how social structures intersect with men's volition and ability to act. In other words, men often grapple with making choices in constrained circumstances[41] that sometimes limit their visions of fathering or impede their options to interact with or provide for their children in particular ways. Thus, the framework of constrained circumstances is closely linked to the four-factor model of father-child relations. We selectively use the framework of constrained circumstances, initially designed to inform debates about gender and health, to show how modes of fathering are shaped by decisionmaking processes at multiple levels: the nation and state, community, workplace, family, and individual. Our analysis of these processes, then, underscores how the socially constructed worlds of fathers and families are embedded within larger cultural, historical, political, and physical contexts. Like Dowd, we stress men's gendered experiences as fathers while noting how conditions associated with race and ethnicity, class, and sexual orientation intersect with gender to shape the fathering landscape.

Alongside cultural ideologies that define caregiving as women's work, we recognize that structural forces in a stratified society help produce scores of men who represent the "not-so-good father."[42] Today, of most concern to policymakers are the men who are not sufficiently involved in their children's financial support or are involved in abusive ways. For many fathers, limited educational opportunities, employment struggles and poverty, and restricted sexual and reproductive education increase the probability that men will be involved with unplanned pregnancies and births and thus place many in precarious situations to which they never adequately adapt. Add to the equation, as we do, concerns about men who may be involved with their children but do little in the way of nurturing them. By creating conditions that often result in fathers spending less time with their children, large-scale forces also tend to hinder fathers' chances to develop a nurturing style of fathering.

Again, the fathers represented in this book have a great deal in common with fathers in every community in the United States. In order to understand how fathering actually unfolds, we focus on daily challenges American fathers face as providers and caregivers. Contentious negotiations arise in the throes of divorce and remarriage; job loss and job change; health problems; and fathering at a distance, in the military or in correctional facilities. In these contexts, men must on a daily basis work and rework to make themselves into the fathers they want to be. Insights can be gleaned about how all men strive to nurture their children when they are faced with these challenges, whether they are family men who want to have more time to care for children or nonresident unwed fathers who want to provide loving care as well as to financially support their children. Most important, lessons about fathers' daily lives can inform policies that are too often disconnected from fathers' real-world experiences.

Men's Stories

Ultimately, a systematic analysis of how men are, and can be, affected by policies in their everyday lives must take account of all three inter-related layers of the process—policy creation, program implementation, and individuals' reactions to the real-world application of a policy—while considering the full range of procreative and fathering experiences.[43] The intimate effects, or projected consequences, of policy and programmatic processes reveal themselves in the powerful stories of the individuals most directly touched by the presence or absence of particular initiatives. They play out even in the lives of fathers such as Andy, whose story reflects the aspirations and challenges of generations of hardworking men who believed that fatherhood was primarily about being good providers for their families.

At age thirty-two, Andy, a tall, quiet, white man with boyish looks, has already spent thirteen years working blue-collar jobs. His ten years as a shipping manager and supervisor on a line assembly for industrial plating follows the long line of manufacturing work in his family; his father has just finished twenty-five years as a maintenance worker at the largest production plant in the small Midwestern community. Andy does not see the demands of his workplace as anything uncommon or stressful, stating, "I never run myself down as far as a lot of hours. I mean, fifty-five, sixty hours a week ain't really a whole lot. I was always at home with the kids, and I've always worked overtime, from day one." However, he began to drink five years ago, and his increasing addiction to alcohol began to overwhelm his day-to-day life with his wife and three preschool-age children.

> Things started changing about the time when our first little girl came. My responsibilities became more, to where I took it upon myself to start working more hours and stuff with a kid . . . to try to make sure there was always enough money, so she would have nice things. I fell into that mode. That's what I always thought it was like to raise a kid.

Five months ago, after a string of charges of driving under the influence, Andy was taken into custody and sentenced to a work-release facility.

He admits that the first few months demanded that he do some soul searching and come up with a plan to change his life. "Being locked up is easy," he laughs, in comparison to the tough decisions he must make about his addiction and the rocky relationship with his wife. In spite of this, Andy is committed to having close relationships with his children. The promise of reuniting with them drives him to make positive changes in his life.

> I call my kids every night from the pay phone there, but I've never been one of those guys who can really talk through a phone. My three-year-old daughter, she don't talk a lot and it's hard—the emotions may come up down the road with her. My five-year-old daughter knows that Daddy says he's done drinking this time, and can't drink no more. She said if she sees me have a beer, she's gonna kick me in the shins. I'll have a lot of eyes watching me.

Andy's interaction with the courts, and the work-release guidelines that limit contact with his children, are policies that have directly affected his fathering. However, if policies had been in place to support parenting and working families these circumstances might have been avoided. For example, wage supplements to "make work pay" could have eased Andy's drive to work overtime and secure enough money to support his family. Resources to return to school and earn a college degree or a skilled training certificate could have promoted his efforts as a provider. There were no paternal leave policies available at his job, which in part led to his wife's taking on all caregiving for their children, although the family needed her financial contribution. Finally, social policies that support fathers and families in navigating transitions are also lacking. Reentry, or "second chance," programs for incarcerated parents only received initial federal funding in spring 2008. Andy attends Alcoholics Anonymous meetings, but an effective health-care system with a substance treatment program as well as access to mental health services to address early signs of depression for young parents who struggle with stress over employment could form the basis of a proactive prevention strategy. Ideally, the goal should be to stop family crises from developing in the first place.

Andy and Dwight are two of the 317 men who shared their personal stories with us between 1997 and 2006. Our pooled sample includes men who participated in one of the seven qualitative studies we conducted separately. Of these, 229 are fathers or stepfathers and another 15 have pregnant partners and are expecting to become fathers for the first time. A large percentage of the fathers can be characterized as either disadvantaged in terms of human capital or more likely to live apart from their children and have less regular contact than the average father.

Although some may have little motivation to be "good" fathers, our studies include men who are doing well for themselves and some who display either moderate or high levels of motivation and involvement as fathers. We also tap into the experiences of seventy-three men who are neither fathers nor expecting a child but who have thought about what this transition would mean for them. Unfortunately, our data have limitations as well. For example, the interviews were not designed to explore the experiences of abusive fathers or fathers with special needs children.[44]

Generally speaking, our earlier research has examined the context, process, and meaning of fathering with men of varied ages and social backgrounds on the basis of family structure, sexual orientation, race and ethnicity, and social class. More specifically, our writings have explicitly dealt with the growing diversity of fathering models, including biological fathers and stepfathers; resident and nonresident fathers; men with children in multiple families; straight and gay fathers; low-income, working-class, and middle-class fathers; and men in correctional facilities and in military deployment.

Our seven data sets enable us to explore a wide range of issues relevant to understanding the negotiated and transitional aspects of fathering that are conducive to policy and programmatic interventions. Although we describe each data set in the appendix as well as in other publications, several general points warrant mention here in order to place our analyses in perspective. First, two of our data sets, Young Males' Procreative Identity (YMPI) and Social Supports for Young Fathers (SS), are particularly helpful in highlighting how teenage and young adult men thirty or younger think about their ability to procreate, describe their degree of readiness to become fathers, and discuss their handling of the challenges of being young fathers. Second, the SS study and the Responsible Fathering Program (RF) offer a sense of what men aged seventeen to forty-two who are involved with community-based fathering programs think about specific interventions. Third, the Incarcerated Fathers (IF) project, and to a lesser extent the Fathering in Communities (FC) study, serve as useful resources for exploring how fathers cope with serving prison time. Fourth, the Stepfathers (SF) study uniquely extends our ability to consider features of the father-child bonding process that are not tied to DNA. Fifth, we use the Male Youth Workers (MYW) study to expand our vision of fathering and men's mentoring while linking family activities to community-based settings. By integrating these seven projects, we position ourselves to work with a unique qualitative data source to explore and illustrate numerous aspects of fathering that, collectively, touch the lives of most fathers.

We make liberal use of men's stories as fathers and use a modified case study approach to shed light on the expanding array of demographic, cultural, political, and economic changes affecting men in families. When appropriate, we also reach beyond our own qualitative studies to discuss other evidence that reveals insights about fathers' motives, joys, struggles, and aspects of involvement related to initiatives that could enhance outcomes for fathers and families.

The accounts we highlight vary and include descriptions of things fathers have done with and for their children as well as comments about what the fathers would like to do. Ultimately, our view of men's lives is shaped by what they tell us because we seldom directly observe them acting as fathers. Our studies use qualitative methods (in-person interviews and life-history techniques) that have the advantage of generating insights about meanings, contexts, and processes associated with men's unique experiences—observations that could not emerge from more common survey research. Although we do not present men's comments uncritically, we generally assume that the fathers reasonably portray the types of things they do as fathers with and for their children.[45] We recognize, too, that some fathers may never realize their visions either because they lack the motivation or they struggle against external circumstances. Nonetheless, we explore men's hopes and dreams because they are central to how many men express their expectations and desires as fathers. Much can be learned about fathers by paying attention to what men envision for themselves, even if their visions do not match their everyday realities.

Among the many issues our participants touch on, they are best positioned to do the following:

- Describe how they become aware of their ability to procreate and then manage their identity while navigating their fertility-related interactions with partners

- Explain how they manage the transition to adulthood as teenage fathers and how they rely on kin networks as sources of social capital for children and as social support systems to help them with their fathering

- Discuss how they secure employment and manage involvement with mothers and children in low-income communities

- Describe how they manage transitory involvement with multiple children across separate families and with families separated by national borders through immigration

- Discuss how they enter into a stepfamily situation; develop identities as stepfathers; and negotiate their relations with the mother, stepchildren, and biological father

- Explain how they have been engaged in volunteer and work-related activities with kids in the community (teachers, coaches, youth ministers, Big Brothers) and, for some, interact with their own children

- Reflect on their experiences with fathering while residing in correctional facilities, with an emphasis on strategies to build family relationships at a distance and to craft new identities as men who put "the difficult past" behind them

Those interested in a more elaborate discussion of our separate samples and methodologies can review our appendix or consult our selective publications that report that information.[46]

Framing Our Analysis

As mentioned, we rely on four broad frames—fatherhood as a social arrangement, fathering paths, trust building, and the role of place in shaping fathers' experiences—to set men's stories in perspective and advance our social-change agenda for creating a more engaged, nurturing style of fathering. We use these frames to dissect the opportunities men have or might have to be nurturing fathers while taking into account the varied constraints they face. In doing so, we show how understanding fathers' life circumstances enhances efforts to design more effective social initiatives to promote nurturance.

As men, fathers' experiences are tied to both their male bodies and the gendered social landscape that help define their actions at home and in public settings—most notably, work. Initiatives are appealing that assume that fathers and mothers have comparable potentials to nurture their children and that fathers can improve their nurturing capacities if given the chance irrespective of their social location—their social class, race and ethnicity, or sexual orientation. However, the gendered realities of everyday life and the institutions and ideologies that structure the expectations, rhythms, and resources associated with family life continue to create an uneven parenting landscape that privileges female, motherly nurturance.

Despite women's advances in the labor market, prevailing cultural norms continue to single out fathers—because they are men—as having more primary breadwinning responsibilities than mothers. In the public eye, and in the minds of many men, family breadwinning represents a "manhood act" that gives working fathers the chance to express their masculine self and claim membership in the dominant gender category.[47] Generally speaking, breadwinning in the United States enables fathers to claim privilege, elicit deference, and exert control over their own lives in ways that nurturance does not.

Consequently, initiatives to promote fathers' nurturance are more likely to succeed when they are informed by an awareness of how the interpersonal and structural threads of gender and masculinity influence fathering and are woven into the four broad themes we emphasize.[48] Noteworthy are men's gendered approaches to the body (their own and others'), health (their own and others'), caregiving, coparenting, kin work, friendship, community networks and social support, paid work, and father-child bonding. Efforts to facilitate fathers' nurturance also need to take into account the relationship between the ways men in more privileged positions construct their images of fatherhood and masculinity as compared to those in less privileged positions.

Fathering as a Social Arrangement

Fathering is inherently a social arrangement that begins with fathers themselves but that usually requires an array of critical partnerships between fathers and other concerned adults (see figure 1.2). These partnerships comprise a network of coparents, family and extended kin,

Figure 1.2   Fathering as a Social Arrangement

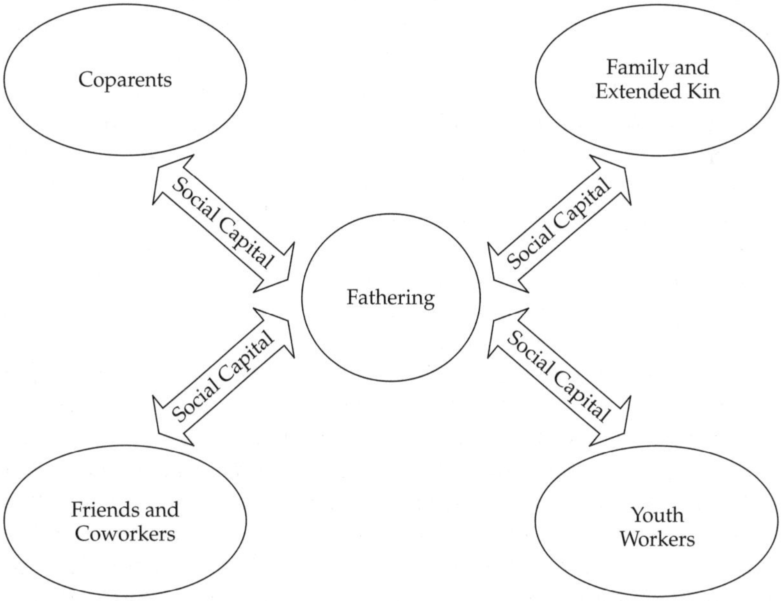

Source: Authors' figure.

friends, and youth workers who supervise children in public settings. How others treat fathers and their children can influence men's fathering, including their level and style of nurturance. Similarly, men's actions as fathers can affect how others think, feel, and act.

The diverse set of relations fathers have with family, kin, friends, and community youth workers provides them opportunities to build social capital that can benefit their children's cognitive and social development. Fathers can "expose their children to healthy dyadic interaction processes, bring about closure in their children's social networks, and act as a liaison to valuable community resources for their children. Social capital can be viewed broadly, then, as a product of families, communities, and the connection between the two."[49]

Any attempt to make policy more responsive to individuals' needs must account for the larger social matrix in which activities promoting social change are embedded. Helping men to realize their full potential as fathers often draws attention to the intimate interactions between parents and children in their everyday family lives, but these activities are also shaped by conditions related to race, class, gender, and sexual orientation; the political economy; economic restructuring; and national policy regimes.[50] Such regimes include policies such as welfare reform, child support and maintenance laws, social grants to limit poverty, and efforts to eradicate histories of discrimination and racism.[51] State intervention has directly shaped the rights and duties of fathers, although at times social policies have run counter to gender equity and have discriminated against African American and poor men.[52]

But policy stakeholders need to reach out to those involved in father- and family-based organizations, activists and social movements, and media enterprises to develop alliances that enrich and reinforce the cultural narrative celebrating high-quality fathering. Social policies lacking the cultural and social mechanisms that reinforce the message of engaged, positive fathering are likely to have little impact.

Paths of Fathering over Time

With an eye toward transitional, developmental, and negotiation processes, we highlight critical circumstances that define men's everyday fathering realities across the life course, from adolescence to adulthood. All sorts of conditions shape both the meanings men assign to their potential fatherhood as well as their actual experiences as fathers. One such condition is time. Men grow older and gain insight into how to be better fathers as they move through significant transitions in their lives. In effect, they are constantly becoming different fathers with new needs and skills.[53]

Fathers' experiences are also related to the experiences of previous generations, including their own fathers' and mothers', as well as their peers' experiences—men of similar age who struggle with many of the same issues as fathers.[54] Relationships with older generations and with peers indicate how important historical time can be, as expectations for fathers shift over decades because of changes in the economy, social norms and values, or even life expectancy and health. "No man is an island" applies especially to fathers who define their lives by how they are linked to their children's lives. Father development in large part demands that men notice how their decisions about marriage, work, and health ripple directly into their children's daily routines. In this way engaged fatherhood encourages men to support and nurture coming generations of children—their own biological children as well as other youth.

To understand the social psychological dimensions of men's lives as fathers over time, we turn specifically to a model that captures how men construct their father identities, express themselves in a fatherly way, and manage their most immediate familial relations.[55] Figure 1.3

Figure 1.3   Model of Fathering Trajectories Over the Life Course: Social Psychological Domains

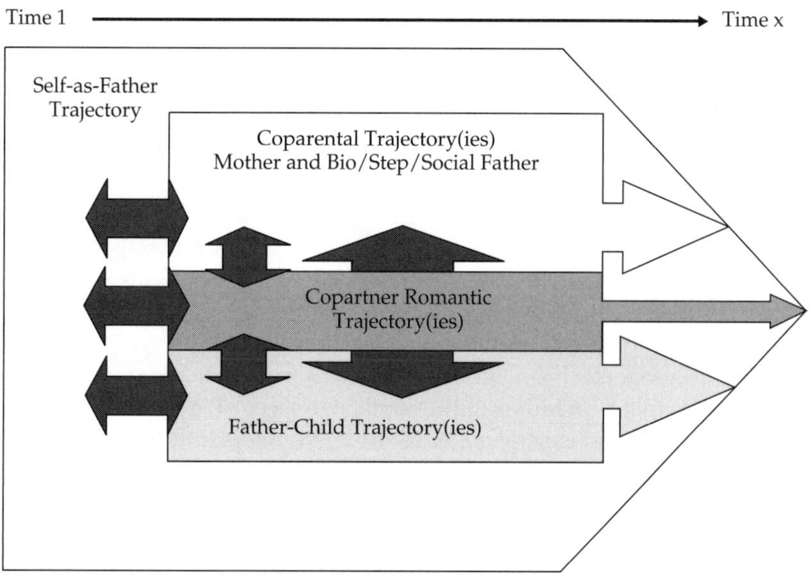

Source: Authors' adaption of Marsiglio (2009b).

highlights the complexity and negotiated elements of fathers' subjective experiences by focusing on four overlapping paths or domains of activity that mutually influence one another over time. That fathers are parents whose male bodies evoke gendered responses from children, coparents, and others adds another dimension to understanding fathers' experiences. Perceptions of men's size, strength, physical capacities, sexuality, and so forth can shape a wide range of fathers' social interactions.[56]

A man's desire and intention to have a child, his readiness to become a father, his visions of being a father, and his fathering philosophy are the principle features of the self-as-father path (discussed in detail in chapter 2).[57] These expressions do not imply any particular child or coparental and romantic relationship. A man with or without biological or social children can experience this domain so long as he imagines himself relating to a child in a fatherly way. As a man ages he is likely to consider how fathering could enable him to experience different possible selves; for example, the doting, roughhousing dad; or the successful breadwinner well positioned to provide his child with intriguing travel opportunities and expensive gifts; or the man of faith committed to raising his child in a Christian way. With more years and maturity he is also likely to shift his sense of readiness to be a father. Once a man becomes a father, his everyday experiences with his child, as well as with the child's mother or another parent figure or romantic partner, are likely to influence to varying degree his broader sentiments about what it means to be a father. Being a parent can enhance a man's personal development as he copes with new responsibilities that are tied to managing intimate relationships.

Any discussion of men's fathering philosophy and nurturance of children should also include the process of generativity. Conceptualized as a form of adult caring focused on helping future generations thrive, generativity is typically associated with a stage of middle adulthood, but aspects of it can be expressed at earlier ages.[58] The generative spirit is captured in efforts "to pass on valued traditions, to teach key skills and viewpoints, to communicate wisdom, and to help younger generations reach their full potential."[59] Generativity is also associated with a "widening concern for what has been generated by love, necessity, or accident."[60]

When we focus on father-child bonds, we recognize that many adult men's first and most central generative experience is linked to caring for their first-born children.[61] Fatherhood researchers note that as men come to know and understand their children their capacity to be generative includes "nurturing the growth of another person."[62]

Generativity is expressed in multiple forms: biological, parental, technical, and social-cultural generativity.[63] Fathering offers men opportunities to partake in each of these ways of "giving back" through pro-creation, positive parenting, and engagement in the larger community that includes children and their peers as well.[64] Although generativity emerges from a personal commitment, it is also shaped by cultural demand. The social need for fathers' nurturance is evident in the range of initiatives and men's stories we highlight in this book. Generativity, however, is also a matter of cultural permission that points to fathering as a social arrangement. Fathers without access to basic resources and skills are hard-pressed to "give back" to their children.[65] In chapter 7, we focus on how public and private initiatives can target human-capital resources during critical transitions in men's lives in order to promote their nurturance. These initiatives are especially relevant for fathers challenged by constrained choices resulting from their disadvantaged social location.[66]

Generative expressions are also associated with the second path in the figure, "father-child," which identifies a man's connection to a par-ticular child that evolves over time. We focus on this path primarily in chapter 3, where we discuss father-child bonds. Viewed broadly, the interpersonal bond may begin at varying points during the respective overlapping life courses of a man and child owing to the timing of paternity confirmation, stepfathering, and adoption.[67] For the man who develops a father identity for multiple children, the father-child relationship will be complicated by his ability to compare and contrast how his real-life fathering experiences are affected by processes involving genetic ties, family structure, gender, age, personality, health, and so forth. Each relationship may be complicated further because of multiple-partner fertility and fathering. A key aspect of this path involves a father's iden-tity, his perceived level of commitment to his child, and his ability to real-ize his particular fathering philosophy. Thus, although it is impractical for social initiatives to accommodate all the idiosyncratic features repre-sented in the countless father-child paths, developing initiatives that can account for varied circumstances is ideal.

A third fathering path, "coparental" (discussed in chapter 4), is rep-resented by a man's efforts to navigate the shared or contested parent-ing rights and responsibilities that go along with having another parent figure involved in raising a child. The other parent can be the child's mother or the child's biological father, stepfather, or social father. The coparental path can be viewed as having four main interrelated components: "support versus undermining in the coparental role; dif-ferences on childrearing issues and values; division of parental labor; and management of family interactions, including exposure of children to interparental conflict."[68] The conventional view of coparenting is that it corresponds to dyadic processes among heterosexual pairs raising biological or nonbiological children, or both.[69] However, recent efforts have also highlighted the need to explore the experiences of stepfathers who serve as allies to the biological father in stepfamilies[70] and gay men's shared parenting with other men and birth mothers.[71] Parental gate-opening and gate-keeping experiences affect a man's opportunities and constraints for navigating father-child trajectories.[72]

Because the worlds of being a coparent and romantic partner are intertwined we also examine in chapter 4 a fourth path: men's co-partnering experiences. The history of men's relationships with the mothers of their children often precedes any negotiations they have about coparenting. How individuals relate to each other as romantic partners can set the tone for how well they work together as coparents. In addition, unmarried couples who become parents prior to a commitment to a long-term relationship often face more significant challenges with communication and developing trust.[73]

In sum, we see men's lives as unfolding along the four paths without passing through specific stages or heading toward a definitive endpoint. The paths are intertwined, can affect one another, and sometimes occur simultaneously. Stakeholders interested in prompting a more engaged style of fathering can fine-tune their efforts by learning how these paths come into play and helping fathers define their identities, maximize opportunities, and respond to constraints that impinge on their ability to be engaged, nurturing fathers.

Trust Building

By viewing fathering as a social arrangement in which men navigate four interrelated paths throughout their life course as fathers, we underscore the need to understand and enhance trust building in diverse settings. Situated in families, fathers of every ilk must manage relationships with their children and usually relationships with coparents, extended kin, youth workers, and others as well. Specifics about trust and respect vary because of a child's age, gender, the father's status as a biological father or stepfather, and the father's coresiding or not coresiding with the child. Yet concerns about these matters are crucial to the father-child bond. They are especially relevant to expressions of nurturance and intimacy. Furthermore, because coparenting is often influenced by how individuals experience their romantic partnership, the full and powerful assortment of emotions that define romantic involvements will color how coparents construct, deny, and redefine trust.

In the four decades since the early 1970s, increasing rates of childbearing outside of marriage and parents' uncoupling from serious romantic relationships have generated a burgeoning array of complex households that provide the contexts within which individuals try to negotiate trust. For many men, the greatest challenge involves the fears and obstacles associated with nonresident fathering. Large numbers of poor, middle-income, and rich fathers alike find themselves wrestling with the prospects and realities of fathering without coresiding.[74] The other face to this situation is often represented by the stepfather who attempts to establish himself in a preexisting family dance of a mother and her children. Whatever the circumstances, managing trust across households and in nontraditional settings is likely to pose a challenge for all involved. Nonresident fathers who provide stable financial contributions may engender more trust because others recognize them as competent breadwinners. Of course, parents in conventional two-parent families also have to negotiate trust in the face of complications arising from the intersection of work and family life, family tragedies, geographical moves, and more.

Trust issues permeate many activities and decisions in the public arena as well. Fathers' opportunities to be more nurturing sometimes hinge on good-faith efforts by policymakers, activists, program coordinators and youth workers, researchers, and parents. Policy and programmatic decisions relating to paternity establishment; paternal leave; child custody, support, and visitation; access to children's personal information; gay fatherhood; and other similar issues are often contentious, creating winners and losers. Consequently, some groups will have to compromise and work to trust one another if they are to collaborate effectively.

Place Matters

Most fathers have coped with the challenges of parenting from a distance. Fathering often occurs when men are not in the home; they may be at the workplace (which may be many hundreds of miles from their households), traveling, deployed in the military, or serving time in a correctional facility. We emphasize the need to attend to issues of place and space when developing initiatives to help fathers become more positively engaged.[75] Far too often policymakers and others neglect to see how fathers' options and constraints are fundamentally influenced by aspects of the physical sites where men do their fathering. These sites include both public and private locations associated with commerce, criminal justice, education, faith, home, recreation, and work. The sites shape men's parenting, but men can also reshape the sites to better fit their expectations and desires for engaged fathering. Fathers advocate with their children's teachers, take on leadership roles in coaching or mentoring positions, and request paternal leave policies for the workplace.[76] In addition, sentiments about fathering from a distance and the valuing of "being there" for one's children reflect gendered and practical realities associated with place. Whether the father is a traveling business executive or long-haul trucker, deployed soldier or prisoner, the practical and symbolic dimensions to place are likely to affect fathering. Men working in predominantly male occupations may find far less support for being nurturing dads than men working in more female-oriented settings, such as primary schools.[77]

Although our analysis is firmly grounded in our data, we also move beyond empirical findings to suggest possibilities for how a wide array of public stakeholders might effectively disseminate images of and frame policies that relate to fathers, children, and families. We examine how different conventions of communication that shape messages about commitment, involvement, entitlement, obligations, and change are promoted to different target audiences. Nonresident fathers, imprisoned fathers, military fathers deployed to a war zone, long-haul truck drivers, and abusive fathers may all struggle with their limited access to their children, and strategies to assist these men must be sensitive to the special circumstances of their particular situations.[78] We consider how specific strategies can be best implemented to ensure they will be well received by men and fathers, women and mothers, children, representatives of various groups and organizations, and others.

Policymaking and Men's Family Lives

The mismatch of ordinary family life and policy initiatives is the starting point for our discussion. To be fair, fatherhood has been on the radar screen of politicians and advocacy groups. Since approximately 1990 it has been a prominent topic of discussion. In policy, practitioner, and advocacy circles rhetoric is often driven by some version of the controversial and muddled question: Are fathers "essential" to children's healthy development? Some vehemently defend the use of the "essential" term to express the idea that fathers "make a contribution to child development that is essential [irreplaceable], unique, and uniquely masculine."[79] Yet because available rigorous research fails to support this hypothesis some scholars advance a less gender-specific alternative perspective: "Good fathering makes an *important* contribution to development."[80] We side with the latter view and add that good fathering should ideally include elements of nurturance.

So far, the policy focus has been on men's personal motivation (or lack thereof) to be involved parents. President Clinton and Vice President Al Gore spoke of the need for "a change of heart" among fathers. Organizers of the Million Man March in 1995, and recently President Obama in one of his Father's Day speeches, declared that men need to "step up and take responsibility" for their involvement as parents. In 2011, Obama launched the Fatherhood and Mentoring Initiative, a partnership between the White House, the National Responsible Fatherhood Clearinghouse, and the Administration for Children and Families in an effort to link families across the country via website updates.[81] He encouraged individual fathers to visit a website where they could pledge to be a positive and supportive figure for their children to help them reach their full potential.

But in the daily challenges that families face, fathering depends on individual men as well as their family and friends. Our discussion of nurturance frames fathering as a social arrangement, not just an individual choice. It begins with men's personal commitment, but it does not end there. We envision an agenda for social change that encourages fathers to care for their children in ways that challenge gender inequalities. Initiatives that promote nurturance are progressive because they challenge the narrow breadwinner stereotype and they can change father-child relationships in positive ways. Moreover, they can transform family relations, making them more trusting and productive.

As social scientists we can make valuable contributions to the formal policy process as well by documenting how social policies have not kept pace with the dramatic changes in families that have unfolded over the past several decades. Fathers and mothers marry later in life, divorce more frequently, cohabit in larger numbers, have more children outside marriage, and manage multiple families (through remarriage and repartnering) more frequently than ever before. These family shifts have emerged alongside a dramatic transformation of the political economy. Globalization has left its imprint on local communities and income inequality has increased the gap between the poor and the wealthy in the United States. Women's increasing entry into the workforce has radically changed the workplace, and men's wages (controlling for inflation) have remained stagnant for three decades. Cultural expectations for fathers have evolved in response to these family and social changes. That the trajectories of men's family lives are now more complex adds to the challenge of forging a policy agenda—informed by social science insights—to promote more positive fathering.

Instead of viewing policymaking as the limited arena of traditional policymakers, we expand our perspective to see that there are many distinct stakeholders who try to affect fathering by working through diverse types of social entities, what we call platforms—federal agencies, work sites, local community-based groups, grassroots advocacy networks, non-profit organizations, the media, state clearinghouses, and courtrooms. Each platform offers an infrastructure and communication medium as well as stakeholders who are affiliated with the platform.

With this broader view, fatherhood policies are better defined as initiatives that involve specific efforts, ideologies, and activities to shape men's parenting. An initiative might include the efforts of a specific platform with one type of stakeholder, or it might involve collaborative efforts across platforms with multiple stakeholders. The scope of an initiative varies as well. An initiative to provide technical assistance and supports to stay-at-home fathers would be limited to a single issue or group. In contrast, an initiative to promote "responsible fatherhood" by a national media organization would be much more inclusive in scope, addressing religious values, child support payments, marriage, and advocacy for federal policies that define men's family roles.

In the United States, fathering initiatives that receive the most public attention and funding typically focus on a specific population of disadvantaged, nonresident fathers. Few initiatives offer much to other populations of fathers, such as men with more resources who could still benefit from federal support for paternity leave. Contemporary initiatives do not stem from a comprehensive fatherhood agenda to support fathers across class, race, and sexual orientation. In part, broad-based initiatives have not emerged in the United States because stakeholders have not coordinated their efforts across platforms. Federal agencies, court officers, and state child support officials have not benefited from systematic collaboration with individual fathers and communities who might be invested in their success. As a result, we are left with a limited set of policies that focus primarily on lack of residence, marriage, or financial contribution, rather than the promotion of fathers' nurturance and responsiveness.

Promotion of nurturance through collaboration happens in other contexts, however. In the United Kingdom, Prime Minister Tony Blair's commitment in 2001 to eradicate child poverty by 2020 corresponded to an emerging focus on the role that fathers can play in child well-being. Groups like the Fatherhood Institute, a U.K. think tank, have drawn attention to breaking the cycle of deprivation for vulnerable fathers in what the government terms "high cost–high harm" families.[82] Similarly, social policy commitments to redress inequality in post-apartheid South Africa have been instrumental in creating the Fatherhood Project.[83] Funded by Save the Children Sweden, the Fatherhood Project works to provide information and enhance dialogue about fathers' experiences and to encourage public and private actors to tailor services to male parents in order to improve families' well-being. Canada has developed the Father Involvement Research Alliance (FIRA) of fathers and families, community-based programs, government agencies, and universities to develop knowledge about father involvement and to create research partnerships between communities and universities.[84] In these three national contexts, policy actors are trying to better coordinate efforts at multiple levels of government to target father involvement and promote nurturing relationships between men, women, and children.

As advocates of these international programs have discovered, promotion of nurturance faces formidable political obstacles. In the United States, the call to promote more and better fathering is reasonable, but the real debates about what that should entail are fraught with points of friction. For example, spokespersons involved with either wing of the Fatherhood Responsibility Movement are often connected to policy-making streams of activity in the pro-marriage or the so-called "fragile families" camps.[85] Pro-marriage groups emphasize efforts to increase marriage opportunities as the cornerstone to a successful strategy to improve fathers' commitments to their children. Spokespersons for the fragile families network stress policies designed to remove the barriers to securing a quality education and good job. Such policies are designed to build the human capital low-income fathers need. Neither of these networks of policy actors has accorded a close father-child relationship a higher priority than marriage or employment.

Nevertheless, it is evident that those who participate in contemporary culture are ready to question and critically examine the consequences of promoting a breadwinner ideal for fathers and families. The image of Don Draper from the *Mad Men* series does not reassure parents; instead it conjures up the painful realization of the limits of men's devotion to the workplace that compromises their everyday involvement with their families. The series offers men and women a way to better understand the mandates of past eras and realize that we need to transform those scripts.

The shift to a relational approach to fathering requires that we recast the father-as-wallet model and take gender equity more seriously. Unfortunately, the goal of promoting nurturance can be quite threatening to policy actors, community activists, and even family members who are invested in conventional fatherhood models. For all of the productive outcomes of the child support system in recent decades, we still have not discovered how to structure payments in a way that fathers and children develop close and responsive relationships. Leaving it to an individual father to feel a "change of heart" is not enough. Broad-based initiatives must empower individual fathers while generating institutional and community-based innovations to accommodate individuals' needs in different settings.

Policymakers have invested in stereotypes of what successful fatherhood is and what fathers' everyday lives are really like. We rely on a unique set of men's firsthand accounts to show how they perceive their own lives as fathers. Our joint data provide us considerable leverage in highlighting a wide range of policy and program initiatives that can affect men in diverse settings. In a number of instances we use concepts we developed in earlier research and show how they can inform policies and programs to bring about a more nurturing and productive form of fathering. Our studies primarily have focused on men who were motivated to be positively and productively engaged with their children. They do not provide the same depth of insight into the experiences of fathers who neglect their children or who are violent with their partners and children.

The set of narratives we have provides rich data for the men affected most directly by fatherhood policies and programs as they currently exist. Across the country, in all sorts of circumstances, men increasingly are striving or at least are open to providing more nurturance. Unfortunately, they are doing so in the absence of family-friendly policy and in the face of policies promoting only marriage or employment.

A broad and deep change in fathering will require concerted efforts on numerous platforms. In the book's final chapter we argue that stakeholders must account for men's daily experiences and promote nurturing relationships between fathers and children for all fathers. If the realities of men's daily lives are ignored, policies will be misguided and inadequate. They will too often conflict with families' interests and overlook assets fathers can bring to relationships with their children. Our theoretically informed framework challenges policymakers to think in more complex and creative ways when they imagine what they can do to inspire and enable fathers to deepen their commitments to their children while providing them with more nurturance. More specifically, we inject theoretical insights into our interpretation of "federal guidance."[86]

We support initiatives that ultimately enhance children's well-being. The viability and public support for fathering initiatives will be greatest when positive child outcomes can be documented. However, the initiatives that interest us will also foster men's personal development, their desires to nurture their children, and their capacities to be active members in care networks. In addition, mothers who struggle to provide the more significant portions of daily care for children should benefit from the initiatives we envisage.

Our thematic approach encourages stakeholders in the policy world to think in new ways and more systematically about the expansive terrain of fatherhood. Instead of organizing our discussion primarily around subgroups of fathers, services, or specific outcomes,[87] we explore how consequential threads of meaning and experience pervade different subgroups of fathers' lives (prospective, resident biological, step, divorced, single, gay, deployed military, in-prison, low-income, married and unmarried). We emphasize the complexity of men's lives over time and focus on them as individuals capable of creating and caring for human life with its multiple, sometimes overlapping trajectories. We also highlight how our insights about men's experiences as fathers can be enriched by gaining an appreciation of the larger social mosaic that includes men's orientation toward and interactions with children in public settings via their volunteer and paid work.

We extend Dowd's approach by developing seven analytic themes to anchor our recommendations for a coordinated set of fatherhood policies that reflect and respond to the ways structural inequalities shape the lives of fathers and families in diverse contexts:[88]

- How men develop and express father identities
- Bonding processes associated with fathers and children
- Partnering and coparenting processes that shape fathering
- Alliances fathers can forge with extended family members through kin work
- Social capital fathers can build for their children with community-based child advocates
- Strategies to improve men's opportunities to develop human capital that can enhance their fathering options, especially during critical transition events and processes that challenge fathers
- Suggestions for constructing a broader cultural narrative supporting a more nurturing and collective form of fathering

Our approach is not fundamentally related to particular demographic segments of fathers. Because our objective is to promote a nurturing, engaged form of fathering in its fullest sense, we stress the seven analytic themes noted that cut across different fathering types and settings. Thus, we offer data-driven insights as to which strategies might bring about positive change for which fathers.[89]

Our starting point for discussing fresh, collaborative initiatives begins with males' procreative and father identities as well as their views of children. We explore the underlying social psychological processes that shape fathers' self-images and commitments to fathering. In the long run, developing strategies that touch both the hearts and minds of boys and men should increase the chances for encouraging fathers to be more engaged and nurturing.

Chapter 2

Constructing Meanings

TWO MONTHS prior to the projected birth date for his first child, twenty-year-old Francisco openly talks about his impending unplanned paternity. He feels comfortable with his chosen path, even though he only started to date his girlfriend a few months prior to her becoming pregnant.

> I can sit down and say right now I've done, we've doing the right thing. . . . I've been preparing myself and I'm not scared of the challenge or, I don't doubt that I'd be a bad parent 'cause I know I'll be a very good parent, but . . . I don't have the child with me in front of me right now, so I don't know if that is going to change once I see the child.

Francisco, a Hispanic, unmarried college student who had already completed two years at a major state university, spent the most recent months of the pregnancy getting his bearings. He anticipated his upcoming new responsibilities with heightened self-awareness. In the throes of a critical identity shift, Francisco set the stage for his account of his pre-pregnancy days:

> It's like I really wasn't in school. I was partying with my friends, all I did was party and drink and doin' drugs and, just being a kid I guess, but being, just goin' a little too fast and when this happened, I guess I see it as a blessing, because if—not to say that if this wouldn't have happened I wouldn't have stopped what I was doing, it's just that it would have taken a little longer for me to realize what's important in life and that I shouldn't take what I have for granted.

Now seeing himself as a "totally different person," Francisco awaits the birth of his child with his cohabiting partner. He is still working on casting aside his partying lifestyle in favor of becoming a devoted family man. His more mature orientation surfaces again during the follow-up interview several months later. He has solidified his transition to assuming a full-time father identity, even though fleeting moments occur when he has to remind himself that he is indeed a new father.

Francisco's description of his subjective reality illustrates the complexity of some men's procreative and father identities.

Like many boys, Francisco first became aware of his ability to procreate when he was roughly fourteen or fifteen. Although he reports being scared as a teenager by the thought of getting someone pregnant, prior to getting his partner pregnant he was more concerned about contracting HIV or a sexually transmitted disease. Francisco recalls being nonchalant about contraception with his girlfriend despite his concerns about pregnancy and disease.

> She kind of surprised me one day when she said that she wasn't on the pill because I thought she'd mentioned she was. But from there on, for some reason, we both didn't really. . . . We weren't careful. And it's odd because I've always been careful before, but this time we just weren't careful. It just—we just went with the flow.

Francisco even muses about whether his partner may have actually wanted to get pregnant. Like many couples, Francisco and his partner drifted into their current predicament. Unwilling to ask candid questions, too hesitant to state their preferences explicitly in a new romantic relationship, they ended up having unprotected sex multiple times not long after they started seeing each other.

As the national unplanned pregnancy rate hovers around 50 percent, other men and women like Francisco and his partner often find themselves on the path to parenthood without ever having a "what if" talk.[1] When men and women fail to activate their procreative consciousness prior to conception, it jeopardizes their chances of making a smooth transition to fatherhood and motherhood.

Francisco's tale offers us a glimpse of what it means for men to conceptualize "possible selves" in the procreative and fathering realms. Scholars define this concept as the

> cognitive manifestations of enduring goals, aspirations, motives, fears, and perceived threats. Because "possible selves" provide a relevant way to relate the meaning, organization, and direction of these dynamics to the self, they also provide the essential link between the self-concept and motivation.[2]

With an eye toward social change, we focus on the notion of possible selves to explore the diverse meanings men assign to fatherhood. Altering men's ideas about fatherhood, especially their motivations to embrace certain styles of fathering, is a critical step in promoting more positive fathering.

Francisco's story also highlights the challenge of developing social initiatives that leave a significant imprint on men's perceptions, motivations, and commitments related to different aspects of fathering. Whether it is men contemplating fatherhood prior to conception, prospective fathers preparing for their upcoming responsibilities, or fathers deciding how to treat the children they already have, the meanings men attach to being fathers and how they navigate each of the fathering trajectories we outlined in chapter 1 can affect their decisions in many areas. Men's vision of themselves as fathers can also inform their own development over time. To begin, we examine the personal path that reveals men grappling with their self-images as fathers, often separate from any specific relationship with a child.

The most basic choices men face that have policy and programmatic implications involve avoiding or pursuing a conception, acknowledging or contesting paternity, getting or remaining married, coresiding or living apart from children, taking paternity leave if it is available, attempting to be an adequate financial provider for resident or nonresident children, and committing to being an active and effective caregiver. Many of the frustrations that men experience as fathers stem from their efforts to balance expectations—their own and others'—about the "good dad" as breadwinner and caregiver.

For Francisco, as for many others, expectations about fathering are still connected to ideological beliefs about what mothers as women and fathers as men should do that are shaped by reproductive physiology. In a follow-up interview several months after his daughter's birth, Francisco asserts that women should stay at home with their child for at least a few years immediately after birth. In rationalizing why he wouldn't stay at home, he says, "Well, I didn't give birth to, to her. If I had given birth to, to that child, I'd want to stay home, I think it's part of me." Although traditional views like these may be in decline, a semblance of this gendered idea can minimize some fathers' potential anxiety about meeting competing demands and can give them cause to believe that they are less nurturing by nature.

Meanings and Visions of Fathering

A critical step toward designing social initiatives to help men develop or sustain an engaged, nurturing style of fathering is to explore how men assign meanings to fathering when faced with constrained choices. Our approach emphasizes the self-as-father domain, and we turn to the procreative identity framework for guidance as well.[3] The framework defines fathering in the broadest terms but highlights processes that enable young and not so young males to become more mindful of their ability to procreate (to develop a procreative consciousness), fashion visions of individual children and fathering activities, assess their sense of readiness to become a father, and negotiate identities as persons who can create and care for human life. Generally speaking, then, initiatives must encourage men to be more attentive to their procreative abilities, lower the rate of unplanned pregnancies, and ensure that more men are ready to assume their responsibilities as fathers when the time comes.

Some pregnancy prevention programs, including those labeled male responsibility initiatives, target young males.[4] The proactive strategies that guide these programs are designed to improve men's chances for making smart decisions about their sexual and reproductive health. Ideally, the programs are meant to improve the quality of men's future fathering by avoiding childbearing before men are financially and emotionally ready to assume fatherhood responsibilities.

Interviews with a diverse sample of young men sixteen to thirty years of age generated several core insights that can help inform the kinds of approaches reproductive health specialists and service providers might use to increase males' awareness of their prospects for becoming fathers. Generally speaking, initiatives should encourage males to reflect critically on their self-knowledge, relationships, and various facets of fathering.

Policymakers and social service professionals increasingly believe that men as well as women have a responsibility to prevent unplanned pregnancies.[5] As a result, a stronger conviction has emerged in recent decades to channel more resources toward enhancing young men's personal awareness and knowledge about sex and reproductive matters. One program opportunity suitable for reproductive health clinics, community centers, or schools challenges teenage and young adult men from all walks of life to reflect on their life goals and dreams. In addition, participants in groups or one-on-one sessions can be asked to think about how their life ambitions mesh with their current approach to sex and contraception. Ideally, men should consider how they have expressed their procreative consciousness in relation to specific romantic partners, sexual encounters, and procreative identities over time. Because the Obama administration favors comprehensive sex education rather than the use of abstinence-only approaches, progressive school-based efforts that incorporate young males and females are much more viable now than during the George W. Bush administrations.

Young men can be prompted to reflect systematically on how they perceive and treat women in their lives, especially those who might become sexual partners. For instance, do they directly ask their partners if they are using birth control or what they would do if they were to get pregnant? How would an unplanned pregnancy affect their partner? Which qualities do they want the future mother of their child to possess? Issues of respect, trust, and control can also be explored.[6]

Trust is always something couples negotiate. Arthur, a twenty-one-year-old white rural truck driver who characterized himself as a working man with a "nice" house and a couple of "nice" cars, calmly describes his previous cohabiting partner from four months back as someone who was "always faithful to me. Never, never had a problem with worrying about where she was. . . . She's a good woman." But his mood quickly shifts as he fights back tears recalling how this woman told him that she was pregnant with his child and then several weeks later aborted the pregnancy that would have made him a first-time father. Despite his attempt to reassure his former girlfriend that he would stand by her during and after the pregnancy, she had the abortion without consulting him. When Arthur heard the shocking news it sent him into a rage like none he had ever experienced. Arthur's brush with gender distrust also represented a turning point for his procreative identity:

> I'm gonna start, if I want to get to know somebody a lot better, it's for what they're geared towards, you know, what moral kinds of things they believe in, what kinds of things they, 'cause I'll never, ever date anyone who, any kind of pro-choice support at all. That will pretty much end it right there. I'll never make that mistake twice.

As he shares the tumultuous aftermath spanning the time between that infamous revelation and the present, it is clear that his former girlfriend's deception and abortion heightened his procreative consciousness and strengthened his commitment to control his fate as a potential father. Arthur insists he will always have pointed conversations with those he dates, asking them directly what they would do if they got pregnant: "Any kind of pro-choice support at all. That will pretty much end it right there."

In referring to his behavior prior to the conception, Arthur asserts that he used condoms faithfully and his partner used contraceptive foam. Despite the pregnancy's being unplanned, Arthur did not act completely irresponsibly. He had talked with his partner about the prospects of having a child someday even though he neglected to distill her views on abortion. In fact, according to Arthur, prior to her aborting the pregnancy, he had perceived his girlfriend as a "good woman." She apparently had some of the same qualities his mother possessed and he wanted the future mother of his children to be like his mom.

But at twenty-one, Arthur is not yet ready to become a father. He prefers to wait until he is in his late twenties and financially secure. Arthur remembers his childhood and his parents' struggles all too well.

> When I grew up my dad, he didn't have nothin'. [Laughs] They had me when they were like eighteen. . . . We drove ol' beat-up cars, lived in an old mobile home, and I just don't want to be like that for the rest of my life. . . . We made it. [Laughs] And that was about it. There wasn't ever an extra fifty bucks left over at the end of the week or anything. . . . When I have kids, I want to be able to go to the store and buy 'em a Nike shirt, be able to afford it. Not just shop Kmart.

Supplementing his comments about being an adequate financial provider, Arthur's story is packed with references to a third set of father-related issues that program facilitators should address: positive and negative experiences with one's own father or surrogate, current paternal role models, philosophies of fathering and fatherhood readiness, and visions of the children men may eventually or already have. To make male responsibility exercises seem more realistic men can be asked to detail their vision of a "good father" and what they hope to accomplish as a father. Professionals are likely to be most effective if they get young men to think about the feasibility of achieving their plans in realistic situations. Attention should be given to both the practical realities of family, home, and neighborhood and the formal social policies relating to custody, visitation, and child support. Because most men without children have a distorted view of parenting challenges, even in the best of circumstances, young men typically do not comprehend the struggles unwed fathers face who try to be involved with their nonresident children. Consequently, programs should emphasize how opportunities to nurture children through bedtime stories, morning and evening cuddle time, baths, feedings, and so forth are shaped by parental control over time and place. Also, young men often underestimate the financial side of fathering and the extent to which their limited education and earning power will hinder their fathering. By getting men to think about these issues, program facilitators can encourage men to be practical when assessing their fatherhood readiness. They can reflect on how they think about their self-interest versus the consequences of an unplanned birth for their partner and future child. Together, these types of exercises can enhance young men's self-awareness and encourage them to develop a better understanding of their own views and desires.[7]

Fortunately, even without the aid of a male responsibility program, Francisco learned to see himself as having the potential to move beyond his partying ways to become a responsible father, coparent, and romantic partner. That said, had he been more conscientious prior to impregnating his partner, the couple would have spared themselves the anxiety of reorganizing their personal priorities on short notice. Of note, too, is that Francisco was willing to forge ahead with his transformation because he did not challenge his girlfriend's claim that he was indeed the father. In fact, as with Arthur's story, nothing in his story suggests that he ever doubted or questioned his partner about the paternity of the child.

Although identities are often viewed as distinctly personal features of the self, they are closely tied to social conventions that provide individuals with opportunities to define and redefine themselves and to accept or refuse to see themselves as others often see them. For example, Arthur is frustrated by his workmates' insensitivity to how the abortion stripped him of his emerging identity and left him feeling emotionally drained.

> Well, most of my buddies at work are pretty much scum. . . . They don't care. Two or three of 'em are paying child support to three different women. [Playing like he is one of his buddies] . . . "Well you ought to be glad. Now you ain't gotta pay for that kid." . . . They pop off with something like that. It just gets me going all over again. I'll get on the four-foot [forklift], drive to the other side of the warehouse and just sit there for ten minutes, calm down, and go about my work. . . . It amazes me that they just don't care. "Oh, I got ten kids. I've gotta pay for 'em." Oh well. . . . They don't seem to care that they're not being a parent. That they're just making kids and letting them go out in the world. . . . I don't see how somebody can do that.

His exposure to these types of negative remarks encourages Arthur to reaffirm his views on responsible fathering. Although he is not yet a father, he has a clear vision of the kind of father he would like to be and the conditions that would make that possible. He is also apparently driven by a different image of masculinity than his workmates. In this case, the traditional all-male work environment seems to have provided an impetus for Arthur to strengthen his conviction to be an involved father, but these types of work environments could easily sway men with less conviction to be less committed to their children.

Learning to Be a Dad

A number of initiatives have been launched in recent decades to help men make the transition to fatherhood. In 1990, Greg Bishop, a father of four and brother of twelve, launched Boot Camp for New Dads, which has been named a best practice by various organizations, and in 1995 he augmented this grassroots effort by forming Dads Adventure, Inc.[8] Roughly 200,000 fathers-in-waiting have graduated from Boot Camp workshops, which have been conducted in 260 communities in 43 states, in varied settings including hospitals in low-income neighborhoods; Family Resource Centers; health clinics; black churches; Jewish synagogues; Head Start programs; and United States Air Force, Army, and Navy bases. The program has also been featured at state Summits on Fatherhood, by the National Governors Taskforce on Fatherhood, and at the National Fatherhood Initiative's Summits on Fatherhood. With at least 400 coaches who are veteran fathers, this mainstream program does not target high-risk fathers; rather it attempts to support all new fathers irrespective of age, race, or social class. By teaching men practical caregiving skills this program enables them to see themselves more fully as competent, attentive fathers.

A wide range of community-based pregnancy prevention and responsible fatherhood programs have also emerged in the two decades since 1990. These are aimed at low-income, unwed, and often young fathers and their families in an effort to provide job training and linkages, educational referrals, and other wrap-around services. Fathers are both mandated to attend the programs by judges in child support court and drawn voluntarily by the rare offer of support and resources for poor men interested in helping their children.

Responsible fatherhood programs also present a unique setting for young men to craft their visions for fathering. Through required parenting classes, these programs begin not simply by modeling good fathering but also by getting young disadvantaged men to examine how being a parent is related to their own maturity and engagement in adult roles. Men often feel frustrated trying to achieve personal success in school, work, and relationships. Some young fathers are prepared to shift their focus to become a generative adult. Kevin, a nineteen-year-old father, remembers how often he felt, while doing the program, that he "couldn't get out of bed."

> My mother, my grandmother, no one thought I was going to complete this program. But I was trying to do something with my life. It made me see beyond what I usually see for myself. They say if you can be for yourself, somebody can be for you, too.

Lamont, a twenty-four-year-old community college student, echoes this sentiment. He returned from four years of military duty in Somalia and Europe to face the four-year-old daughter he had had with his former girlfriend. Juggling classes with jobs at a local chicken shack and a parcel service in the suburbs, he is unable to free up much time to spend with his daughter. So Lamont sets aside blocks of time on the weekends to "let me get to know her, and let her get to know me." He volunteers to attend the responsible fatherhood program to meet other fathers; he realizes how important it is to take care of his own needs before assuming responsibility for another's' well-being.

> You can't concentrate on a child thing if you yourself are spiraling down. If you can't help yourself, how can you help someone else? No matter how much you try to help, if you're not together, it's not going to work. So that's the conflict: Can you raise a child, if you can't raise yourself? Are you prepared for life?

Evaluations of fathering programs report a consistent finding: peer support is one of the most effective aspects of community-based curricula.[9] In large part, fathers find a supportive context to try on new identities, accept challenging responsibilities, and confront past mistakes that would deter many young parents from becoming involved with children. A twenty-seven-year-old father in the Indiana program, Earl, notes,

> I wouldn't say this was just something to do. It put me in the right direction. People are interested in you and care about you. It was different than I had in the past. It gave me a lot. I can truly say that it's one of the turning points in my life.

The combination of peer support and practical information is offered in a context in which fathers could come to grips with past mistakes, including incarceration, substance abuse, domestic violence, and gang activity. Participants find that the advice of an all-male discussion group allows them to understand that their own mistakes are common among their peers. They feel more comfortable accepting responsibility and making commitments for better decisions when they are not required to respond to mothers and female partners in the group setting. Moreover, many programs offer a compelling mission statement that encourages even non-residential fathers to move beyond past mistakes. It is not enough to acknowledge having a child; fathers are expected to forge a relationship with the child.

Rich, aged thirty-five, raised four children with his wife and worked as a medical technician in Chicago. After seven years of using alcohol and marijuana, he fell out of his family, living on the streets. As he completed his treatment to get clean, he began a series of discussions with his wife. He acknowledges the difficult job that she had as a single mother, and for a few days each week he goes back home to reengage with his children. It isn't easy, as his children have grown to resent him, but he persists, helping them with homework, trying to provide more discipline within the household. The fatherhood program provides Rich with a reliable set of neighborhood fathers who can relate to his experiences of reestablishing relationships with children after many years of being disconnected.

> I'm through with the disappointments and resentments that I caused back in those days. This program is awesome. It helped me get in touch with myself. To be a parent, not just a daddy, but a father. Guys here have not turned their back on me. Just like the addiction, you go in, go out, go in, go out. But they're always there, like real fathers, saying, "What's up, brother?"

Unfortunately, many fathers do not have the opportunity to learn about fatherhood through firsthand family experiences and supportive role models prior to becoming fathers themselves. Their vision of being a father is primarily guided by impressions cobbled together from diverse sources: the life dramas and hearsay endemic to a particular community, varied media images, and public policy discourses promoting men's financial responsibilities for their children. For Kareem, a young father from Indianapolis, residential instability—including multiple guardians and time in the state foster care system—resulted in a patchwork arrangement of family members. He feels compelled to be a different kind of father, a family man who is consistently involved in his children's life. Fatherhood offers Kareem a more inspirational identity than those available to him through his scattered kin network.

> My relationships with other family are not real close. Nobody is really at the center. I was going through lots of moves and stuff like that when I was young: guardian's home, foster care, my mother's, my grandmother's. They don't stay in contact with each other. I just want to provide a new background for my kids and break the chain. My life's been kind of rocky. I feel like I have a new opportunity or something.

The lack of father involvement or other male role models in their families leaves many young fathers feeling, "I'm depending on my own damn self." This is a common task for young men—to carve out a unique identity, on their own terms, and relative to their own strengths. The young men, often frustrated because they can not anticipate the challenges that await them, learn about being a father through day-to-day experiences, through trial and error. Otis, an African American father, struggles with his sense of being a real man as well as a father.

> If I can take care of my kid's food, clothing, shelter, I might feel good for the rest of the week, or the rest of the month. But it's not guaranteed. I'm making it up as I go. Nobody taught me this. I never had a father, and my brother doesn't have any kids. One of my daughters lives with my mother, and I'm struggling to take care of both of them, and I can't do it. So, to be honest, I do not think that I am really a father yet. I don't think that I am what I want to be as a father yet.

Many young men feel that what is expected of them as fathers does not fit the constraints that they face in low-income communities. Mainstream markers of successful fatherhood—and manhood, for that matter—are out of their reach. Policies, programs, and even their own families offer few alternative options for being a good father, such as the chance to find jobs paying a family-supporting wage, or the opportunity to secure their own lease on a residence. The status of "just" biological father does not afford them the respect they seek. Their identities are shaped by their own internal negotiations, reflected in a vague sense of "the right thing to do" and a personal commitment to "be there" in their children's lives as much as in their own hearts and minds.

This model of programming for fathers need not be limited to poor communities or tailored to young fathers. Although the responsible fatherhood programs target economically disadvantaged fathers, many other fathers with more resources also stand to benefit from programmatic interventions that provide parental education, couples counseling, legal advice, and peer support. Middle-class fathers who are financially stable also strive to understand who they are as fathers and how to become more involved parents. This may be particularly true if they are in a committed relationship with a woman who has children from a previous relationship or if they live apart from their children because of separation or divorce. Simply put, policy interventions that promote nurturance of children and effective coparenting are rare and invaluable for all fathers, irrespective of social class background or age.

Pathways to Fatherhood

Although men's mindfulness about both their ability to procreate and their responsibilities as fathers can be shaped by diverse pregnancy prevention and fatherhood initiatives, many men never participate in such programs. Yet plenty of other cultural and social conditions shape how men over the life course experience and perceive themselves in relation to the procreative realm and fathering.

Father identities, in their many forms, cannot be separated completely from their surroundings.[10] They are embedded in dynamic cultural, historical, political, and social contexts. As institutional norms change and technologies such as DNA fingerprinting and sonograms come online, new images of fatherhood and fathering enter the public domain. Consequently, men may encounter different options and constraints that affect how they develop their self-images. These self-images may hinge on how they and others view and experience their male bodies. An earlier discussion in the book *Procreative Man* outlines how social, legal, and medical processes influence the varied ways men establish a paternal identity through one of the following major paths: having genetically related offspring, use of donor sperm, adoption or foster parenting, and stepfathering.[11] Social initiatives may be relevant to the different aspects of social bonding that unite men with the children they claim (see chapter 3 for a detailed discussion). In some instances these bonding processes implicate others and can encompass preconception, prenatal, and postnatal experiences. Of course, irrespective of whether men claim a fetus or a child as theirs, or develop a strong commitment to being a father, this does not mean that men will treat children or the mother in any particular way. However, when paternity is formally established, the government does affirm its legal right to insist that men at least provide financially for their children.

In this book we focus primarily on men's prenatal and postnatal experiences related to fathering, but a progressive national fatherhood agenda must also deal with men before they ever impregnate someone. Initiatives should heighten men's procreative consciousness long before conception occurs in order to amplify the often neglected physiological dimension to the father-fetal connection. Heightened procreative consciousness should lead to men's greater awareness of the importance of their own health status. This is necessary to improve men's contribution to fetal life and children's health outcomes.

The debate as to the importance of paternal health as a contributing factor in fetal health is far from settled, but a growing body of research on animals and humans points to patterns of male-mediated reproductive harm from toxicity at work, at war, and in the environment as well as from men's behavioral choices to smoke, drink, and use drugs.[12] In her provocative book *The Science and Politics of Male Reproduction*, the political scientist Cynthia Daniels argues effectively that a scientific bias is embedded in the cultural discourse that reinforces how conventional ideologies of masculinity are related to reproduction. It has, in her view, helped to perpetuate the public's disproportionate interest in how the "bad behavior" of women increases fetal health risks while largely ignoring how men's preconception experiences can negatively contribute to fetal and children's health. She suggests that research has "slowly extended the bridge from men to their babies from the moment of conception, across pregnancy, and now beyond birth."[13]

Here again the notion of possible selves takes center stage. The concept offers a lens to think about productive ways to educate different groups of men to make them more conscious of their health and fecundity and of ways they might protect the quality of their unique contribution to creating life. One practical strategy involves partnerships between public health departments and selective male-oriented work sites that are most likely to involve exposure to toxins that can compromise reproductive health. Although one can anticipate considerable resistance from business owners, information needs to be shared with management as well as the male workers about the possible hazards men and their children face. The irony, of course, is that many men take risky jobs because they want to be a good provider for their families. This pattern may be even more troublesome during an economic downturn. To the extent that men become more educated about work-related risks, they will need to reconcile identity conflicts stemming from their desire to be a good provider with incorporating health concerns into their assessment of their readiness to have a child as well as the issue of whether they will be a good father.

Another option is to develop public-service announcements and workshops for different audiences that attempt to increase both men's and women's awareness of how smoking, drinking, and drugs can alter the quality of sperm production. These messages must combat boys' and men's tendencies to engage in risky behaviors as a way to prove their manhood. The challenge is to convince all males to pursue the more long-term benefits that go with contributing to healthy pregnancies and healthy children even if such behavior brings little immediate masculine recognition of the traditional sort. Ultimately, the goal is to fashion cultural messages and institutional supports that assign new meanings to how boys and men can build "masculine capital"—socially valued markers of manliness. They need to receive credit for valuing their own health while protecting their future children's health before they are conceived.

Fathers-in-Waiting

As we saw with Francisco, a father's initial efforts to construct his identity as a father do not necessarily depend on a child's being born. In recent years the growth of childbirth preparation classes, availability of ultrasound technologies, and doctors' willingness to have a prospective father involved in prenatal visits have altered men's worlds. Now, the average man generally has numerous opportunities to develop his paternal identity and shape it before he ever hears, sees, touches, or smells his baby.

But a poor man is less likely than his middle-class counterpart to have the same kind of access to ultrasounds, childbirth preparation classes, breastfeeding workshops, and so forth. Being poor and uninsured may present especially difficult obstacles. Public and private efforts to extend these types of prenatal options to every prospective father, irrespective of his financial means, can do much to help improve a man's procreative consciousness during and after a pregnancy.

A man can also get involved in numerous ways by lending a helping hand to his pregnant partner. He can encourage her to attend prenatal visits regularly, accompany her to various workshops for expectant parents, monitor her exercise and diet, support her breastfeeding decision, and provide her with practical help with household chores. Each of these gestures may enhance the woman's quality of life as well as produce positive outcomes for the child.

Various conditions—including personality characteristics, the nature and quality of the relationship with the expectant mother, social class, and employment status—can influence the extent to which a man gets involved prenatally. As we show more fully in chapter 3, some measures of a man's prenatal involvement are apparently related to his subsequent involvement with his child.[14]

Unfortunately, aside from childbirth preparation classes, American society has few formal mechanisms to enhance a man's identity as a prospective father or promote his involvement with activities that produce socially and physically healthy outcomes. However, there may be ways to increase a man's likelihood of adopting prenatally an identity that emphasizes nurturance. Efforts to make this happen should account for the complex matrix of identity processes that can unfold before the birth of a child. A man may base his identity on the bond he feels with the fetus directly, or he may ground it in his experience as the nurturing, romantic partner of the expectant mother. A man's reaction to his partner may largely position her as coparent, copartner, or both.[15]

The legacy of *Roe v. Wade* adds yet another layer of complexity to how a man constructs his father identity, especially if he's involved in an unplanned pregnancy. We support a woman's right to an abortion; nonetheless, this legal precedent coupled with the gendered nature of reproductive physiology creates unique challenges for men. A prospective father can find himself in a precarious position in a society that legally protects a woman's reproductive rights because whatever identity he constructs can be nullified if a pregnancy is terminated without his consent. How can one sponsor initiatives that cultivate a man's psychological and emotional investment in a pregnancy, especially during the early months, if the resolution of the pregnancy is ultimately outside his control? It would seem that if a woman's reproductive rights are honored, no policy could have prevented Arthur's partner from having an abortion. Abortion notification laws, especially those that target pregnant married women, receive fairly broad support by the American public, even though some vehemently oppose such laws.[16] Unfortunately, no one really knows how often a notification law would substantially alter a man's procreative consciousness and father identity.

Men's efforts to construct a father identity are not simply a personal matter. Institutional, community-based, and interpersonal forces either enable or constrain men from developing self-images as fathers, based on their own or others' perceptions of them. A critical aspect of this process involves men's tendencies to develop their attachments to children as a result of their romantic ties to their children's mothers. Much has been written over the past few decades about conditional commitments many men make when they hitch their fleeting child-specific father identity to their romantic interest in the child's mother.[17] Policies and programs must therefore work to undermine the tendency for men to construct their father identities indirectly through their partners.[18] Fathers should be encouraged to bond with their children directly.

Establishing Paternity

Like many men's, Francisco's willingness to accept responsibility for his actions and claim the pregnancy and child as his rendered moot the need for a formal fertility test and court ruling to establish legal paternity. However, not all unplanned pregnancies proceed as smoothly as Francisco's did.

Men sometimes come into direct contact with agencies and institutions that manage and even challenge paternal identities, in particular through policies governing paternity establishment. Presidents since Ronald Reagan have pushed to increase the rate of paternity establishment by providing funding incentives and administrative tools to state governments.[19] A systematic paternity establishment process has been implemented in hospitals and courtrooms throughout the United States.[20] Many of the state-based programs support hospital registration efforts that attempt to capitalize on the euphoria surrounding many births and encourage fathers to sign paternity papers while their children are in the hospital. Some of these men may be uncertain that they are the biological father or are at least ambivalent about becoming a dad. Concerned with the high rate of unmarried and low-income fathers who do not establish legal paternity for their children, policymakers target young fathers in hospital settings at their child's birth. Of the roughly 1.5 million children born to unmarried parents, about 75 percent have men step forward to sign affidavits of paternity on their behalf, and about 80 percent of those men sign the papers in the hospital at the time of the birth.[21]

In recent years, advances in medical technology have further allowed men and their children to be linked biologically to a near certainty. About 280,000 DNA paternity tests are performed annually, and one review of paternity lab findings indicates that the man's paternity is confirmed about 72 percent of the time.[22] The tests are costly (up to $800), but they have become a policy tool to secure a father-child relationship, which is then linked to child support awards. Paternity establishment policies, buttressed by compulsory DNA testing, have been an asset to state budgets by increasing child support orders and reducing welfare payments to single mothers.[23] Nevertheless, the child support program in general has lost more money for states than it has saved since 2000.[24]

The business of doing DNA testing to validate paternity has entered into pop culture via the syndicated TV show *Maury* and numerous publicized court cases adjudicating paternity fraud accusations. Since 1998, the talk show host Maury Povich has run provocative theme shows called "Who's Your Daddy?" wherein he discloses DNA test results to mothers and the men who have subjected themselves to testing to determine if they are in fact a baby's father. These segments, with their distinctly scripted feel, have exposed a mass audience to the concept and personal drama of paternity testing.

Outside of reality TV, many fathers are motivated to carve out a relationship with their children prior to establishing paternity through testing. On one level, then, paternity establishment in its broadest sense includes the experiential form of knowing that "confirms" a biological relationship between fathers and children, and this relationship in many ways shapes the identity that men take on as parents. Fathers we spoke to frequently noted that they did not need to establish paternity through a DNA test because they "already knew" that babies were "theirs."

DNA testing links final authority about paternity to a high-tech, scientific measure. Although not as clearly defined, paternity was previously and sometimes still is negotiated among parents and family members—an environment more familiar to our research participants than the medicalized process of DNA testing. The potential of the new technology also leads some fathers to doubt their biological connections with their children.

Nineteen-year-old Brian left his basketball scholarship at a small, historically black college in the South and returned home to Indiana to be closer to his family and to begin a business management internship. He met Sarah, who was still in high school, and she gave birth to their son during that first year after his return home. Brian had high hopes for having a son but his dreams for a healthy baby were challenged when he learned his newborn had serious medical problems. Brian's son was born with a low platelet count, and he underwent two weeks of testing prior to being released from the hospital. As a young father, Brian marveled at the strength of his son to be born despite these challenges.

My girlfriend had no prenatal care, and it was miraculous that [my son] made it through all that—it gave me a glitter of "Wow, this is kind of unique, this child of mine making it through this drama just to get into the world." I'm glad something of mine can make it, it's a proud thing to be connected with him initially.

But Brian was unclear about the complicated blood test results and how they were related to establishing paternity:

> I'm not biological, I'm not medical, but it would seem to me if he wasn't my son or if there wasn't a correct blood match then maybe that test wouldn't have went right. That has led me . . . into thinking all this time that what if there was a complication, if the blood tests didn't match up then maybe the doctors would have found out that maybe I wasn't the father.

Brian was also counseled by friends and family that he would forgo his right to deny paternity if he signed the birth certificate in the hospital. Due to this advice, his confusion over blood tests, and the ambiguity of his biological linkage to his son, he waited nine months to pursue paternity establishment, at which point he had to pay the full cost of a DNA test himself.

Other fathers were not hesitant, and they stepped up to "do what I gotta do" as parents when their infant children needed support. Isaiah is a forty-one-year-old father of two young adult children from previous relationships, but he also has two preschool-age daughters. He is self-employed, running his own pest extermination business in the Chicago housing projects. He realized that he could not rely on his daughter's mother, who was unable to care for the baby because of substance abuse. "I just knew she was my child, I was keeping her every weekend, I buy her clothes and food. I've been taking care of her since she was a year old." Without formally establishing paternity, however, Isaiah could not obtain legal custody of his daughter. Unfortunately, after the DNA test he learned that he was not her biological father, and he lost custody of her to the state foster care system. A year later Isaiah was also contesting the paternity of his younger daughter, whom he had raised as his older daughter's sister. His sacrifices and hard work resulted in a sense of vindication when the DNA test showed that he was biologically the parent of his younger daughter. He said, "When I got my paternity test back and it said 99.97 percent chance of her being my child, my chest stuck out. There was no way . . . anyone in the world could dispute that I was the father." In effect, after years of behaving as a father and yet being challenged on his biological identity, Isaiah had achieved a peace of mind as a father.

Just as some men pursue paternity tests in hopes of confirming their genetic tie to a child, others eagerly seek scientific evidence that would prevent them from being wrongfully identified as a particular child's biological father. When paternity is contested, government agencies often step in to establish paternity, especially for children born outside of marriage and those whose mothers are requesting financial assistance. In either case, the existence of DNA testing presumably shapes how some men in recent years psychologically wrestle with their projected image of being a father or not. The anticipation that goes along with testing adds another layer of complexity to how men construct meanings related to what it means to be a father.

Straight Versus Gay

One important development in the new millennium of fathering involves the relationship between sexual identity and fathering. From a cultural perspective, Francisco's path to paternity as a straight man was facilitated by heteronormative assumptions about relationships and parenting, some of which are codified into law, such as the selective state laws precluding gays and lesbians from adopting children. In addition to the practical matter of being able to impregnate his partner, Francisco was quickly recognized by his family, friends, associates, and health professionals as being a father-in-waiting and then later a full-fledged father.

Throughout history gay men have had children while in heterosexual relationships—often marriage.[25] In recent years, however, men who are "out" and claim a sexual identity other than heterosexual are increasingly recognizing that they can pursue their paternity interests outside of a heterosexual relationship and are choosing to do so.[26] These situations introduce a unique set of conditions that shape how nonheterosexuals juggle their sexual and father identities while managing their romantic partnerships. Consider Clark, a gay college student who, after initially bemoaning the fact that his parents are never going to be grandparents because he's gay, asserts a more positive outlook toward fathering.

> I always had plans, before I came to the realization that I was gay, I planned to have a wife and kids just like my parents and their parents before them. And then, after I kind of made that realization that I was gay, I tried to keep my plan as intact as possible. You know, maybe have a husband and two-point-five kids.[27]

Nico's story further illustrates the changing times in which many gay men are integrating concerns about their future identities as fathers into relationship negotiations.[28] Nico entered into a serious relationship with Drew, a gay man who had previously donated sperm to a lesbian couple. Although Nico and Drew, a well-off couple, lived hours away from the lesbian couple, they saw the two women and Drew's genetic offspring fairly regularly. This form of "fathering" with limited responsibility was fine for Drew, but Nico desperately wanted his own children.

After trying to raise the subject numerous times, Nico presented Drew with an ultimatum: "If you don't want to do this, then maybe this relationship isn't going to work out because this is something I really want." After Drew went "back to the mental drawing board" and assessed whether he could be without Nico's relationship, he decided to become a father, and Nico and Drew later became parents through surrogacy.

National trend data are not available that would permit a careful analysis of how gay and bisexual men's views have changed over time. Nonetheless, some crude observations can be made on the basis of the 2002 wave of the National Survey of Family Growth (NSFG). This survey asks respondents aged fifteen to forty-four the question "Looking to the future, would you want to have a child at some time in the future?" Among childless men, 57 percent of gays and 71.4 percent of bisexuals report that they desire a child, compared to 87.6 percent of heterosexuals.[29] Not surprisingly, in statistical models that control for a range of background factors, straight men are significantly more likely to desire a child than gay men. What is perhaps surprising is that so many gay and bisexual men do state a preference for having children. Presumably, a large segment of gay men under age forty-five are open to having children and may very well view fathering as part of a possible self they would like to realize. Although gay men who want to be fathers are handicapped by the realities of reproductive physiology, many gays have overcome these obstacles.

Another question on the NSFG survey asks "If it turns out that you do not have any children, would that bother you a great deal, some, a little, or not at all?" Among straight men, 32.4 and 31.2 percent indicate that they would be bothered either "a great deal" or "some," whereas the percentages are 12.1 and 26.2 for gay men, and 28.2 and 17.4 for bisexual men, respectively. That a full 38 percent of gay men would be at least somewhat bothered by not having a child suggests that the landscape of parenting in the twenty-first century is likely to be quite different from that of the twentieth. Overall, gay men's desires for children outside heterosexual relationships may exceed their opportunities to fulfill their dreams—a reality that seems inevitable if innovative policies and programs are not implemented to make gay adoption and fathering through surrogacy more feasible.

The survey results indicate that identity issues associated with fathering are likely to touch a sizable segment of men who do not identify as heterosexual. But these data say nothing about how gay and bisexual men subjectively and interpersonally negotiate their procreative, fathering, and family identities. How do men who are not having sex with women come to think about their ability to procreate and see fatherhood as a possibility for them? How do men manage their dual identities of being gay and wanting to be a father? For insights into these important issues, we turn to a qualitative study that expands the procreative identity framework to gay men.[30] It explores how nineteen childless gay men and twenty gay fathers, primarily living in Florida and New York, came to discover their procreative consciousness and develop their father identities.

Unlike their heterosexual counterparts, gay men do not deal with typical sexual and fertility-related issues that prompt their procreative consciousness. In other words, gay men have no need to discuss birth control options with their partners, nor do they deal with pregnancy scares, miscarriage, abortions, or a copartner pregnancy. They may, of course, still be involved with a partner who, like Nico, requests that they ponder the idea of raising a child together, but that child would be adopted or created through a surrogacy arrangement. In many instances, gay men learn of their practical opportunities to become fathers through their associations with lesbian mothers, gay fathers, informal caregiving experiences with children, and contact with organizational policies and practices involving children.

Like a heterosexual man, a gay man follows no standard path to develop a procreative consciousness and father identity. However, a gay man is forced to be more deliberative than a heterosexual man in his pursuit of fatherhood. A gay man doesn't produce an accidental pregnancy. In most cases a gay man must interact with different service agencies, fertility clinics, and child welfare organizations to make the transition from being a gay man with no child to being a gay father. Thus, a gay man's interaction with state policies and with the organizational culture of relevant sites such as foster care facilities or fertility clinics can alter his inclination and opportunities to become a father.

Becoming a father outside of a heterosexual encounter is clearly linked to having money. Though circumstances and prices vary, many adoptions and especially paid surrogacy arrangements are realistic options only for gay men who are relatively well off. Gay men looking to adopt are often steered toward children perceived by other prospective parents as the least desirable—children with special needs, older kids, and minority youths.[31] In these cases, money may be less relevant. For some, then, becoming a gay father involves confronting the challenges of developing an identity as a father of a special needs child or a father who has missed out on many of the precious early years of bonding with an infant and toddler. Clearly, the practical realities associated with gay fathers' day-to-day experiences that enable them to see themselves as fathers are multilayered and quite complex in most instances.

Although the mainstream cultural narrative of marriage and parenting in the United States may never fully incorporate gay men as fathers, conceivably the proportion of gay men who cofather children in a committed relationship is likely to increase. In the past few decades the cultural war over gay marriage reflects a slow but incremental shift toward greater public acceptance. Despite key setbacks, states like California, Connecticut, Hawaii, Massachusetts, New York, and others have each taken noteworthy steps toward social change that is akin to what happened over forty years ago when social forces finally led to the Supreme Court's 1967 ruling in *Loving v. Virginia.* That ruling overturned Virginia's antimiscegenation statute and ended race-based legal restrictions on marriage.[32] If formal recognition of gay marriage eventually becomes the law of the land, or if gay marriage is advanced through a plethora of court or legislative processes at the state level, gay men will be able to tap into an expanded set of institutionalized resources to construct their personal stories. In doing so, gay men will have an easier time creating identities as "family men" that encompass their involvement with raising children. More genuine public support should also make it easier for gay fathers to openly engage in a nurturing style of fathering in and away from home. Eventually, the public and policymakers may be swayed by research indicating that children raised by gay and lesbian parents are as well adjusted as those raised by heterosexual parents.[33] Essential public support is likely to come not only from the mainstream heterosexual society but from those who represent the gay and lesbian faces and voices of the neighborhood. Today, the stigma of betraying the "gay lifestyle" by having children, though real for some, is far less prominent for gay men and lesbians than in previous eras.

Prior to a transformation in how the public views and treats gay men as possible or real fathers, gay men and their allies must lobby for progressive policies and programs to address gays' paternity-related needs. Obviously, legislative efforts that extend adoption and surrogacy rights to gays and lesbians in all states would give some gay men more options. Ultimately, having laws on the books is not sufficient. The laws need to be reinforced locally by the various organizational policies and practices of adoption agencies, foster homes, and fertility clinics that most directly enable gay men to become fathers or discourage them from doing so. So the push to help gay men grapple with their constrained choices must occur on both a cultural front, to transform public opinion, and on an organizational level, to encourage key decisionmakers to recognize gay men as legitimate fatherhood candidates.

Beyond Biology

Much has been written about the power of genes in shaping both public policy related to family and parenthood and individuals' perceptions about their own parental identities.[34] Despite the increase in individuals' personal experience with stepfamilies and the expanding openness among professionals and families about adoption, biology still usually trumps familial ties based on behavior and interpersonal sentiments. Yet in people's everyday lives, and even in American courts, men without a DNA link to children can sometimes win respect, privileges, and even legal rights that exceed what is offered to nonresident biological fathers. Those who receive this recognition often earn it by being a steady, parental force. Nurturing behavior is not uncommon in these cases.

Nonresident fathers—assuming they are alive—are the other side of the family equation that defines nonbiological parenthood. Nonresident fathers sometimes know about their children but choose to keep their distance, others may drift apart after being involved prior to the dissolution of their romantic relationship, and some may not have known that they had impregnated someone or may have been duped for a period of time as to their paternity and thus kept in ignorance. Without the convenience and symbolic value of sharing residential space with their children, many nonresident fathers, especially those who once lived with their children, grapple with identity shifts.

Contemporary culture has begun to acknowledge the ambiguous expectations for some men who have never met their children. This is particularly true for men directly affected by recent technological advances in sperm donorship and DNA testing. In the 2010 film *The Kids Are All Right*, the teenage children of a lesbian couple (played by Annette Benning and Julianne Moore) decide to contact their father (played by Mark Ruffalo) who donated his sperm to the women decades earlier. They develop a close bond with their father, although he is unprepared for his deep desire to be a parent and to accept the responsibilities that he had not assumed when he was absent from their lives. This character's discovery of his desire to be a father, even decades after his children's births, reinforces a public discourse that encourages men to develop their procreative consciousness and father identity based on the belief that biological parentage is the norm and superior to other ties.

Few boys or men grow up anticipating and planning to become social fathers without a genetic tie to their offspring. Because social recognition and support for fathers can be consequential, going against the trend and claiming a committed father identity without a genetic tie is challenging for most men. This is no trivial matter because plenty of men express themselves in a fatherly way once they become stepfathers, adopt children (some of whom were not born to the men's romantic partner), serve as foster fathers, or use donor semen. In-depth interviews with a diverse sample of thirty-six stepfathers show that some men are perfectly capable of being engaged as a "father" to their stepchildren.[35] Terry, middle-class and white, saw his full commitment to his six-year-old stepson,

Zack, as the only way he could manage his venture into a stepfamily. Referring to a period of his life when he was in his mid-thirties, he recalls the sentiments he shared with his future wife, Zack's mother, when they discussed the prospect of getting married:

> I'm either going to be an all husband and an all father or nothing at all. I can't have half a relationship. I can't be half a father. Where do you draw the line? At what point do you stop and say, "Oh well, I'm being a little bit too harsh here." Or, "I can't tell you [that] you can't go to base-ball tonight. Only your mother can do that." If I'm going to love you, I'm going to be your father. I'm going to be there all the way.

To a large extent, Terry was able to carve out a fathering niche because Zack's biological father lived in another state and was barely involved. In contrast, Eddie, a thirty-five-year-old African American, found him-self growing close to Rhendy, his eight-year-old stepdaughter, even though her father, Eddie's coworker at a bookstore who helped Eddie land his current job, remained active in her life. The father's involvement challenged Eddie to find a way to make sense of his muddled identity.

> Sometimes I feel like I'm on the outside looking in because—sometimes I wish she was mine. I guess because we're just that close. Sometimes we can just have that right chemistry. We just . . . smooth. . . . That's the time I'm actually—that kin, that father, just right, because she's happy, I'm happy, everybody's happy. When everybody's happy, everybody is doing their job. I'm doing the job as a father, doing the job as a step-father, and my wife's doing a job as mother—everybody's happy. . . . In my heart, I feel like I'm her father. In my heart. I know in reality, I'm not, but, I'm going to give her all the benefit that a father should. I'm going to make sure she gets those benefits. Even though her dad is giv-ing them to her, she is given a little extra and I figure that extra go a long way. That holds a lot of truth.

Eddie has a sharp mental map of Rhendy's habits and idiosyncrasies, similar to how he thinks about the two daughters and son he has with other mothers. He describes Rhendy as needing ten to twelve hours of sleep or else she'll be very difficult. Eddie says he's also learned to ignore some of the things she says because she'll be okay in ten to fifteen min-utes. Otherwise, if he says something or confronts her, things get ugly. At his interview, Eddie revealed his responsive and nurturing style of father-ing by commenting that Rhendy was feeling down that day because she wasn't able to go to some program with her mother. To brighten her day, he planned on buying flowers and taking them home to her.

The compelling stories Terry, Eddie, and many others share are grounded in men's orientation toward family and children as well as their emotional exchanges with romantic partners and their kids. Although men vary considerably in their approach, many stepfathers develop some semblance of a father-like identity that is consequential, for the men and the stepchildren.[36]

Paternal claiming—the process of a man's perceiving and treating a child as his own—tends to occur most often when the mother is supportive, the biological father is not actively involved, the stepchild is relatively young, and the stepfather feels some affinity with the child's personality.[37] When a man puts some effort into claiming a child he does so by invoking strategies and routines that enable him to manage his orientation toward the stepchild. An analysis of the stepfathers generated ten properties that help to clarify the paternal claiming process.[38] Three properties are particularly relevant to our efforts to link identity issues with social initiatives. Although this list of properties was developed while studying stepfathers, most also shed light on how biological fathers construct their identities and practice fathering.

A basic way of differentiating one stepfather from another is to assess how firmly each man holds his identity beliefs. When a man is frequently placed in situations that require him to express himself in a fatherly way it is likely to intensify his conviction, though it is by no means determinative. For example, spending lots of time monitoring and fostering a stepchild's daily activities may prompt a man to embrace his identity. Also, a man may strengthen his conviction if he is asked or expected to advocate for a child or assume important responsibilities related to school, health care, the criminal justice system, and the like.

In a related vein, the paternal role range represents how widely the man tends to express himself as a father toward his child. One man may engage in fatherly behavior that involves affection, discipline, financial provisioning, play activities, homework support, and basic child care, whereas another may only assume the breadwinner role and some basic child-care responsibilities. Each man may perceive himself to be a fatherly figure, but each has a distinctive way of thinking about the borders of how he expresses his identity. Claiming a child, then, can be interpreted differently by the stepfather, child, and mother.

The extent to which and how a biological father is involved with his child can have implications for whether a stepfather perceives himself as having a unique fatherly identity or an identity that he shares with the father. In the United States, mainstream family discourse leans toward defining both fatherhood and motherhood as unique—there can be only one father and mother—even though some family members and others outside the family may recognize stepparents informally. Some children distinctly believe that they have multiple fathers or mothers. American legal institutions as well as education and health-care facilities have been slow to accommodate a multiple-father or -mother model, so it is the rare stepfather who in these service environments is routinely treated like a father, though some clearly are. Without that kind of reinforcement, a stepfather must swim against the current of public sentiment to develop a father identity.

Fairly recently, however, in both the United Kingdom and the United States, a series of innovative policy and legal initiatives have expanded stepparents' rights, which in the long run may alter how some stepfathers construct their identities.[39] In general, these efforts acknowledge that some stepparents deserve to be treated as parental figures—they've paid their dues. The Children Act of 1989, which became law in 1991 in the United Kingdom, provides a template for how other countries might permit resident stepparents to establish a legal relationship with a stepchild by petitioning for a residency order if they have been married to the biological parent for at least two years. The parents retain their legal rights, but the stepparent is given some of the same rights.

In the United States, a proposal has been circulated for a new parental legal category, "de facto parent,"[40] which could legitimize stepfathers' relationships to their stepchildren because it would

> legally recognize stepparents as parental authorities but not cut off the rights of nonresident biological parents and not continue indefinitely in the event of a divorce. The concept of de facto parent is currently used loosely in the law with respect to those caring for children, but it has not taken on full form, with clearly delineated rights and obligation. Moreover, there is not consistency in the courts as to its use.[41]

Careful thought should be given to providing incentives to urge and enable stepfathers and stepmothers to become and, in case of divorce, remain more invested in their stepchildren's lives. Such an innovation is likely to make a difference for how some stepfathers develop and manage their father identity. We explore in chapter 3 how a deeper commitment to a stepfather identity might influence the stepfather-child relationship.[42]

Although most stepfathers do not formally adopt their stepchildren, a large proportion of stepfathers do construct their father identities as stepfathers who formalize their identity and commitment to their partner's children by adopting them. About 2.3 percent of all men and 3.8 percent of ever-married men aged eighteen to forty-four in 2002 had adopted a child during their lifetime.[43] In contrast to the parallel comparison for women, men who have already fathered a biological child are more likely than men without children of their own to have adopted a child. The pattern is mixed as to whether men's biological paternity occurs before or after their adoptive fathering.

One key policy issue, particularly in terms of child support, involves a stepfather's willingness to commit to a stepchild in certain ways if the biological father is still involved. In some cases, stepfathers and biological fathers can reach agreements to tailor their financial responsibilities—a complicated transfer across multiple households—to different children in a way that also allows time for care and interaction.

Lucas, a thirty-six-year-old small-machine operator, pieced together a string of short-duration manufacturing jobs through a temp agency in Indianapolis. He put two years in prison behind him, staying clean and living with his wife and his stepdaughter. His two biological children lived across town in another neighborhood. He talked repeatedly about bringing his children to visit with his stepdaughter, although he had not seen his biological children in over two years. At the same time, Lucas welcomed the involvement of his stepdaughter's father, who could contribute little financially but offered to spend time and care for his daughter.

> I'll take my kids in the summer, I'll supply school uniforms, whatever they need. But their mother feels that my wife is going to hurt them. My kids say, "Why can't I go to my dad's house?" My stepdaughter, she there by herself, and she's always asking me, "When your kids going to come over?" She wants to be the big sister, but she's not given that opportunity. And her father says to me, "I don't want you to feel that I'm disrespecting your house." I said, no, that's your child, you want to come see her, you're more than welcome, I'll be the one to open the door for you.

Multiple-Partner Paternity and Father Identity

Increasingly, men and women have or raise children with multiple partners. The way this transpires for most middle-class adults is that they have children in a marital context, then divorce, and then either remarry or cohabit with someone else. It also happens with low- and middle-income unmarried partners who break up and then take up with new partners. Some men, in all social classes, have biological children with different women; in other cases men may have a biological child with one or more women and act as a stepfather, foster father, or adoptive father to another child. Across the board, all of these fathers must develop identities related to children of different mothers. As noted earlier, these situations can provide fathers with distinct opportunities to compare and contrast how they see and express themselves as fathers. The condition of multiple-partner fathering also gives men a practical basis for evaluating their level of commitment and style of fathering in terms of breadwinning, discipline, monitoring, affection, and intimacy.

Crafting multiple identities as a father proves to be a complex negotiation. It requires almost constant daily identity "work" as men try to maintain their commitments amid shifting concerns and expectations from families and former or current partners. Becoming a father does not simply occur as a result of having a stable partner relationship, coresidence, or a steady job. For young, disadvantaged men the transition to fatherhood is often unsuccessful. Young men may have to manage their hopes and expectations as nonresident fathers if their ideas conflict with the sentiments held by the mothers of their children. When they become fathers with a subsequent partner, their tenuous identities as fathers are again open for examination. What may prove most challenging is the lack of control that these aspiring men confront, as their obligations to adults and children multiply quickly across families. Remy, a Native American father in Indiana, felt that this can happen "when you ain't got a stable home for no kids. . . . I was excited [about my second child], but I was also kind of down about 'cause here I'm about to have another child and already can't take care of one I've got." Measured by normative expectations of providing for his family, a second family seemed to be another impossible burden. For Chris, having a second son made him realize that he "felt like I couldn't support my children. If I couldn't do this, I didn't want to have much contact. Like I didn't deserve to see them, which of course now I know is dumb. The least I could do was to be in their lives."

As young men grew older and found stable jobs, however, they also learned how to be an involved father despite these barriers. Acknowledging the challenges of being a father in multiple families, fathers were still often ready "to try again." As a twenty-four-year-old father with two sets of children from different partners, Bradley discusses the process of maturing through trial fathering, which left him better prepared—and even excited—about becoming a father again.

> At first I was upset. I wasn't wanting any kids at that age [eighteen]. I had a lot of other things on my mind other than kids. But it turned me around from doing a lot of things that I used to do. I settled down for a long time when I found out I was going to be a father. My second child went a lot easier. I was a little older, I already knowed what to expect. I was just ready for it, looking forward to it.

Perhaps most important, these men were better prepared to be fathers and to accept their identities as involved fathers. Many young disadvantaged men sought to return to their older children and work to develop better relationships, with a better understanding of what was expected of them as parents. Without role models, however, men were hard-pressed to envision what it meant to be a father in different ways with different children. They did realize, however, that such an identity needed to be flexible and dynamic. Gil, a thirty-year-old food services chef in Chicago, uses the metaphor of a pivot player on a basketball team to illustrate how he has remained active in the lives of multiple children in multiple families. He envisions himself as being at the center of the action, able to see all the players as they spread out to different sides of the court. "I'm only one man, many children, and we could do so many things," he says. "I could play the pivot point, in the middle of the court, and we could make it work."

Aspirations for Being the New Father

Although social policies and programs have generally equated men's role with children to that of an economic provider, men and women are increasingly challenging this narrow vision. The scripts for "new fatherhood" have expanded how men can legitimately express themselves as fathers, even though the contemporary models usually refer to middle-class, European American, heterosexual experiences.[44] Most significant, the normative change melds expectations for provisioning and caregiving.[45]

To create a more relevant and meaningful sense of who they are as fathers, men have struggled in the absence of social initiatives that have promoted identities distinct from that of the breadwinner. Middle-class men in dual-earner families have made tradeoffs with partners to care for children, thereby expanding their sense of responsibility and achievement as parents.[46] In a global economy in which companies are downsizing their American workforces, fathers lose good jobs with family-supporting benefits and wages. These losses can lead men to struggle with their failure as breadwinner-fathers and at times to withdraw from their children and partners.[47] In these and other constrained workplace circumstances, even "successful" fathers find themselves lacking in their capacity to nurture their children in ways of their choosing.

Commitment to an enhanced version of fathering, however, may come at a price, as workplace policies across the board typically do little to recognize the pull that some men feel to be hands-on parents on a daily basis. At best, employers and public policymakers have been pushed to consider family-friendly policies in order to attract or retain employees. What is lacking is a broader public discussion of how engaged fathering may motivate or curtail men's commitment to a specific job, and how to craft workplace policies in which employers and employees could both benefit from fathers being more motivated to take an active role in their children's lives.

Some men see strength in numbers when promoting an engaged father identity. They have sought out like-minded committed fathers to create social movements in local communities. These local initiatives with a broad focus recognize the social and family contributions men make as fathers. For example, Ecodads, cofounded in 2009 by Michael Leifer and Craig Fox, is an environmentally responsible parenting movement that is spearheaded by a California-based group of entrepreneurial fathers.[48] Ecodads's mission is to foster opportunities for men to serve as positive role models for children by building community programs that support conscientious consumption patterns and sustainable economic, social, and environmental development. The programs are part of a campaign that integrates online and offline training activities and tool kits that can be implemented by local chapter directors to help fathers connect with their children and the natural world. Recent programs focus on getting fathers, children, and families to work together to improve the environment in settings such as oceans and beaches, playing fields, schools, gardens, garages, and so forth. Linking their identities as stewards to both the environment and to their children is a means for these fathers to achieve their fathering ideals on their own terms.

Policy and program initiatives aimed at disadvantaged fathers often explicitly equate fatherhood with the provision of financial support. However, in communities in which low-income men face barriers to full-time employment with good wages, families develop a broader set of expectations for men's parenting. Families and fathers may negotiate men's roles as providers and caregivers informally, guided by a sense that men can contribute "whatever they can offer at that time." Only through a tailored set of interventions, with staff who are cognizant of the ways in which providing and caregiving are related, can policies and programs begin to support men who struggle with barriers to finding a stable job or who may not be valued by others for their caregiving efforts. Initiatives must also recognize that for some fathers, receiving support from family and friends for their nurturing ways may matter little if they are unable to be a provider as well. For example, Rollie, a part-time library clerk in Chicago, coped with the legacy of using drugs by living apart from his children. After spending many months with a community-based fathering program, funded by both public and private agencies, he reflects on how his experiences helped him develop a new understanding of what it means to be a good father.

> Before the program, I thought the only way I could approach my kid was with a job in hand. And I never had that. I learned that it's okay if I'm not working. I mean, I know I need a good job. But I can still be a father for my kids. I'm not a failure if I just spend time with them, if I help them with their homework and love them. That was a huge realization for me.

Can Social Initiatives Target Father Identities?

Clearly, social policy and community programs have been created in order to influence directly what men "do" as fathers. Although initiatives that influence the meanings men assign to who they "are" as fathers are less pervasive than those that target behaviors like providing child support, they too are critical. Thus, stakeholders committed to helping fathers adopt a more engaged style of fathering should do more to tap into how men think and feel about themselves as fathers and their responsibilities toward their children.

Policies and programs can increase men's awareness of the consequences of their parenting and lifestyles while heightening their sense of new opportunities to become more nurturing fathers. The efforts must, of course, take into account the constrained choices many men face in their daily lives at home, at work, and in their communities. Initiatives must also take into account the wide range of circumstances that affect men's identities as fathers, including young men at risk of an unplanned pregnancy, married and cohabiting heterosexual fathers, gay men contemplating adoption or surrogacy, stepdads, single fathers, and nonresident dads.

As alluded to earlier, a range of activities in the public and private sectors can help men understand more clearly the special role they play in their children's health even before a child is born. Public-service campaigns promoting a health-conscious style of fathering can urge men to forgo drugs, alcohol, and chemical exposure in order to demonstrate how these choices can affect a fetus, infant, or older child. Likewise, fathers can be encouraged to participate more often in prenatal care and early postnatal pediatric visits as well as be persuaded to make healthy choices in exercise, nutrition, and physical care that will model desirable behavior for their children. A critical challenge is to target pro-health messages to men who, despite being fathers, embrace risk-taking behaviors such as having multiple sex partners, substance abuse and smoking, fast driving, gun use, and so forth as a way to compensate for their inability or unwillingness to accumulate more conventional forms of masculine capital that stem from formal education and legitimate employment. Unfortunately, risk-taking behaviors typically elicit highly valued respect from male peers but jeopardize relations with partners and children.[49]

Men's identities as fathers—whether they are linked to messages about health, education, work, the law, spirituality, or the like—may be strengthened by policies and programs that promote behavioral changes. Men may come to see themselves differently if they receive assistance to raise and interact with their children in specific ways. Fathers may be receptive to signals that a specific kind of fathering is prioritized in new initiatives. For instance, on-site visitation guidelines for flexible interaction of incarcerated men and their children can encourage fathers to hang on to their sense of themselves as active parents even at a distance. Such guidelines imply that offenders are still viewed as valued parents. Similarly, the use of communication technologies to allow military personnel to maintain regular contact with children can ensure that men who work halfway around the world from their children do not lose a sense of their importance as fathers. These initiatives would emphasize that engaged fathering is critical for children's well-being; it requires regular sharing between fathers and children and opportunities to nurture, even without a physical presence. Unfortunately, these efforts face significant obstacles in settings where "hypermasculine" behavior is pervasive and the code of conduct reinforces stoicism, physical toughness, and even violence.

Although diverse initiatives can introduce men to fatherhood or encourage men to act as fathers in new and creative ways, their effects on how men think about themselves as fathers, as men, and as developing adults may be quite relevant. Men in contemporary families struggle to expand their vision of parenthood after decades of social policies guided by implicit assumptions that fathers are defined almost exclusively by their capacity as providers.[50] Moving beyond the breadwinner assumptions that ground too many initiatives will open up a new vision for men's nurturance of children. If men are to see themselves as engaged fathers, they must be given and seek opportunities to do much more than contribute to their children financially.

Chapter 3

Building and Sustaining Bonds

MONTY, a hardworking man of twenty-seven at the time, found himself enthralled with Sue, a thirty-four-year-old mother of four who had a six-year-old daughter, Beverly, and three teenagers. It was an accelerated romance—within two months of starting to date Monty and Sue were cohabiting in Monty's small apartment. Beverly's father was in jail, again, and was due to be released in a few months. Monty felt that the other father, of the teens, was an "abusive alcoholic."

Monty entered into his new informal family arrangement with Sue optimistic that he could prove to her and her children that not all men are "jerks." He was confident, despite the practical obstacles posed by the fact that his two-room apartment was too small to accommodate the entire stepfamily. In addition to Sue, some of her kids came immediately and stayed; others came then left, only to return when Monty bought a bigger place shortly thereafter; and some coresided for a while in the newer house and then left for good. For the first four and a half years, Beverly split time between her father's home and Monty's but eventually came to live full time with her mother and Monty when her father suddenly moved, presumably to take a job out of state.

Six years into his relationship, Monty painfully reconstructs his memory of the early period and the aftermath of his turbulent stepfamily life. After describing how he expected to be the teenagers' friend, Monty asserts that he thought he could be a "daddy" for Beverly.

Whether she [Beverly] called me Dad or not didn't matter that much to me. But whether she was close to me, like you know had a father-daughter relationship, that was important to me, and that never happened. Which is why I'm so bitter now. It's like I'm punishing her for being, for liking her father basically. To me it's like a slap in the face; I'm always there; I'm always providing for her, and at one point was willing to listen and be a father figure. And he never did any of that, and he got all the credit and I got nothing. I just couldn't stand that; I still can't stand it. . . . I['d] like to see her go live with her father. She loves her dad so much, go be with him . . . nothing would make me more happy . . . just have her gone.

Monty's sarcasm highlights his bitterness. Even though they continue to live under the same roof, Monty has ignored Beverly for so long that his indifference to her is now second nature. He has long since abandoned the fantasy of being a father for Beverly, even though he still financially supports her. Their relationship has deteriorated to the point where they avoid each other when the newest addition to the household is around—Monty's and Sue's ten-month-old son, Beverly's half brother.

Was Monty doomed at the outset to fail in his quest to be both a friend to the older children and a daddy to Beverly? Not necessarily. If we are to believe Monty, his motivation to establish a fatherly bond with Beverly was genuine and was not the source of his problems with her. He mostly attributes things not working out to Beverly's disrespectful personality and unconditional love for her father. Monty's interpretation may be partially accurate, but in a separate interview Sue portrays Monty as cold and detached from her children from the start.

The full story most likely should include Monty's lack of responsiveness,[1] interpersonal skills, and inadequate social supports as well as the presence of institutional barriers that contributed to Monty's constrained choices.[2] Prior to his involvement with Sue, Monty had interacted with kids very little and had never lived with them. Though lacking insights about the ways of children, he was still expected to make sense of the children's needs and moods. He also apparently received no formal or informal support to manage his new familial arrangement. By his own account, he failed to appreciate fully both how fearful the children were about trusting another man and their anxiety about having someone disrupt the chemistry of their "tight-knit group, the five of them." Furthermore, the messy circumstances of his partnering with Sue contributed much to his stepfather difficulties—a matter we say more about in the next chapter.

Unlike Monty, Miles has started laying the groundwork for a closer and better relationship with his biological sons. He grew up in the housing projects in Chicago with his mother, stepfather, and brothers, and although he did not excel in school, he was good at sports and popular with his peers. But Miles turned to selling marijuana and fighting in high school and was kicked out. His first son was born when Miles was eighteen and was working at a gas station. His girlfriend, Diana, was living with her parents. They eventually lived together for two years with their infant son, but stress and limited work options led Miles into a fleeting affair with another woman, and at age twenty he had a daughter with her. After this relationship ended, Miles returned to live with Diana from time to time. At twenty-two, he had a second son with her, but poor communication fueled their romantic demise.

In the early years with his children, Miles developed a lucrative business selling drugs and he owned multiple apartments and cars. When he was twenty-five, Miles's mother, brother, and aunt all died. He grew depressed and eventually began to "slip up"—make mistakes that led to arrests and his serving six separate prison sentences in as many years.

During his most recent stay in a work-release facility in Chicago, Miles committed himself to getting clean, obtaining a GED (general equivalency diploma), and finding a mainstream job with a paycheck. He also wanted to renew his relationship with his children and work with their mothers to coparent and provide for them. Locked away when he was in his late twenties in prison, he had been separated from his sons for two and a half years. He had had plenty of time to reflect on the day-to-day care he once provided for his babies, putting them to sleep on his chest each day. Now, Miles seems attuned to their personalities and developmental needs. After getting back in touch with Diana, who has remarried, he spends a number of weekend afternoons with his sons. He bonds with his twelve-year-old son through computer games and completing online school reports—of this son Miles says, "He is the bookworm." Miles's eight-year-old son requires a more hands-on approach, with more discipline and structure. He feels:

> I have to stay on Little Miles because he's just like me, and it took me this long to change. I know it will be hard for him. I have to give it to him straight, the things I've done, without trying to sugarcoat it. That's why I'm trying to stay in school and get close to a job I really want—to model that for him. So he doesn't end up in the penitentiary.

When he contemplates what, despite his absence, he has done right with his sons, Miles speaks about "being there."

> What makes me a good father is being there. . . . I would be a better father to my kids if I was there more, but for someone else it might not be the same case. Answering their questions, and talking to them when they need that, and trying to teach them a lot of things about life. Be there with them and teach them right from wrong and having control of yourself and themselves, and stay focused on stuff. A good father has a lot of love. The deepest feelings for your sons. I care and spend a lot of time with them, as much as I have. Because if you don't spend no time there is nothing there, period. And being the man, a man's image in their life, you are a role model and you want to be that. They need that manly role model.

Miles's vision of "being there" is complicated. He can only get permission to leave the work-release program every two weeks to visit his sons. His sentence wraps up in five weeks, and he is excited to become a part of their daily lives. However, Miles stresses that he has a quality relationship with his sons even without the frequent contact and physical presence that such closeness often requires. He realizes, too, that being incarcerated, and the setbacks he faced from not seeking a mainstream job or education, will shape his life and fathering for many years. To interact regularly with his children Miles knows he has to remain clean, find a good job, and "get straight."

> For me to tell my kids right and wrong, I have to be at least trying to do things that are right. And if I don't keep myself focused, how can I ask somebody else to be focused. I can't lie to my kids, I can't lie no more. I owe this to my sons. I owe them more than five years of their life when I was gone. I owe them a lifetime of love. If I can give that to them and they accept that I will be one of the happiest men on earth. I want to be there when my kids go college. I want to be at their games if they play a sport, or be there and read their book, or if they are a teacher I want to be sitting in one of their classes while they teach. I want to be there, I don't care what they do. I just want to be there.

As this example illustrates, father-child bonds can develop despite physical separation, despite negotiation between multiple unmarried couples, and despite inconsistency in contact and interaction. Somehow, Miles and his sons are establishing an emerging sense of "we-ness" as they persevere through difficult times.

Writing over a hundred years ago, the esteemed American sociologist Charles Horton Cooley (1864–1929) captured the essence of this type of interpersonal connection while discussing the meaning and value of primary groups:[3]

> The result of intimate association, psychologically, is a certain fusion of individualities in a common whole, so that one's very self, for many purposes at least, is the common life and purpose of the group. Perhaps the simplest way of describing this wholeness is by saying that it is a "we"; it involves the sort of sympathy and mutual identification for which "we" is the natural expression.

Despite his difficult circumstances, Miles longs to reassure himself and his sons that it is okay for them to share a dream of solidifying their "wholeness" as a family.

Policy initiatives need to recognize that the search for "we-ness" unfolds in myriad ways. This search evolves in all types of families: those that reside together on a daily basis as well as those coping with divorce and separation, incarceration, or deployment. When men live apart from their children they are not necessarily absent from their lives. Families facing these circumstances often find ways to promote nurturing relationships, and these strategies can be supported and even augmented through explicit policy measures.

Stories like Monty's and Miles's underscore both how complex many fathers' lives are today as well as the need to explore how initiatives can enhance fathers' nurturance of children in diverse settings. Prior studies and existing policies and programs often emphasize men's involvement as fathers. For many, father involvement is viewed as behavior *for* children, through providing, caregiving, or simple interaction. Our vision of father-child relations also highlights fathers' behavior *with* and affinity for children, through creating and maintaining close bonds with them. With this added emphasis, initiatives designed to shape men's nurturance would by definition strive to embed involvement in the context of a close bond, a feeling of we-ness shared by fathers or other men and children that develops and deepens over time. Interpersonal bonds are the foundation that enables fathers and children to feel more at ease and ready to reach out to each other in displays of vulnerability, intimacy, and nurturance. Whereas these diverse bonds with children generate a joint emotional sentiment reinforced by shared activities, nurturance reflects fathers' special behavioral style of caregiving.

Father-Child Bonds

Efforts to promote healthy relations between fathers and children must take into account several issues related to interpersonal bonds and intimacy. The bonds of interest to us emerge from the basic trust fathers create with their children and signal an emerging sense of attachment. Key aspects of these bonds are similar to what has often been defined in popular culture as mothering.

Because bonds arise and grow as a result of men's behavior *with* children, we pay close attention to how fathers and children share daily life; how they communicate through established exchanges and language; and how they respond to each other's temperaments, quirks, and emotions in familiar ways.[4] A related phenomenon is that fathers and children who do not share a sense of "us" exhibit fragile bonds that can be marked by distrust, as well as a limited capacity to share or anticipate emotions.[5]

Types of Bonds

The essence of a father-child bond is expressed in many different forms.[6] The most basic and common types of bonds, deserving of special emphasis, are behavioral, cognitive, emotional, and spiritual or ethical.[7] While building and living these bonds, a father often taps into his desires to be the companion, teacher, caregiver-nurturer, or protector for his child. At times, a father may even achieve a sense of bonding by fulfilling his expectations for being a breadwinner. In other words, to the extent that a man incorporates a consumption ethic into his perception of being a good father and perceives that his child recognizes this, the father may see himself as sustaining a valuable interpersonal bond.

Although we discuss four expressions or forms of father-child bonds, all of the connections we highlight include an affective dimension that differentiates them from father involvement more generally. For our purposes, then, a bond represents at minimum a "feeling state" from the father's perspective.[8] Ideally, for the bond to produce the most good, the child will recognize and share this bond in whole or in part. A key aspect to the child's affective reaction is some form of trust appropriate to the child's developmental stage. In short, does the child trust the father to be responsive to his or her feelings and needs? In addition, even though we highlight varied moments and contexts in which bonds manifest themselves, healthy bonds transcend any given occasion or setting. Ultimately, bonds represent enduring sentiments that motivate a father to want to be involved with his child and to embrace certain parental obligations while committing his time, energy, and resources to enhance his child's well-being.

Behavioral Bonds   Behavioral expressions involve a father and child's participating in some shared activity, such as playing catch, riding bikes, making cookies, playing music, or working on a yard or school project.[9] The companionship that comes with doing a shared activity can foster a cooperative spirit and sense of togetherness. Talking is more or less crucial to the flow of particular activities and may be quite variable across father-child pairs. But the process of a father and child coordinating their lines of action to pursue a task represents the core of the behavioral bond. Most of these expressions require the father and child to be in the same physical location; however, communication technologies are evolving so that a father and child, especially those in the middle class, can readily have behavioral experiences in cyberspace through texting, photo sharing, video imaging, gaming, and so forth. Thus the definition of "being there" is increasingly flexible and open to multiple interpretations.

Cognitive Bonds   Some shared activities may involve a clear cognitive component in which members of the pair teach and learn from each other. A father may teach a child how to do math, cook an egg, paint toenails, shoot a basketball, play guitar, or any number of skills. Likewise, a child can show his or her father how to play a video game, send text messages, learn a second language, and the like. Learning from each other can be empowering and rewarding. In some instances, the teachings the father offers may take on added significance if they include a legacy component. For example, passing on knowledge about running the family farm or a family-owned small business can give a father and child a special opportunity to share in the generative spirit of handing down valuable personal insights and resources.

Emotional Bonds   Emotional expressions often go hand in hand with each of the other bonds, but some rituals embody a distinct, nurturing element.[10] Bedtime stories, baths, homemade pizza dinners and desserts, and special picnics come immediately to mind. Such rituals provide a father and child an opportunity to express physical and verbal intimacies in places that have powerful symbolic value (the bedroom and the bed, the bathtub, the kitchen, the park or beach). The bedroom, for example, offers a father (or mother) the chance to be the person who helps a young child transition from the wide-awake reality of the day to the more vulnerable sleep state of the night. A father who reassures a child not to fear the dark, that he—the father—will be there in the morning, plays an active role in earning a child's trust. Similarly, a father can elevate his standing in a child's eye if he is available throughout the night to ease the fussy child back to sleep.

Emotional bonds may also emerge from more isolated crisis events that bring family members together, such as mourning a family member's death or dealing with complications associated with being forced from a home by a natural disaster or an eviction notice. Bonds are formed or solidified when a father and child share these moments and assign sentimental value to them. For the infant or toddler, sentimentality may be less clearly defined and articulated but the affinity with the father can exist nonetheless. In the throes and aftermath of a crisis, the pair is likely to embrace a sense of we-ness that reinforces claims about time, commitments, energies, and affections.

Some mundane child-care activities are probably best labeled as a mix between a behavioral and emotional expression. Going shopping for school clothes or taking a child to the dentist may have little special emotional significance for a child, but a father may value his chance to provide these types of services. In return, the child may on some level appreciate the concern he or she is receiving from the father.

Ethical and Spiritual Bonds   A father and child can also develop a connection imbued with spiritual or ethical overtones if they actively talk about and share similar values and life perspectives. Faith-based ties are probably the most obvious source for this type of bond. These ties commonly emerge from religious rituals or activities with moral implications (picketing an abortion clinic, helping out at a homeless shelter, devoting time to a rescue pet shelter). Because men are less actively involved in practicing a faith than women, it might be important to expand men's involvement with their children in settings with a faith dimension.[11] A father and child might also develop a spiritual or ethical bond that is based on their commitments to environmentalism, feminism, or veganism. A father and child may reinforce their mutual respect and bond by doing things together or simply by knowing they share similar values. Of course, talking about values and sometimes acting on them usually entails some type of cognitive effort as well as emotional energy, but it's worthwhile to single out how bonding over shared values may be unique in and of itself. Bonds reinforced by shared values may provide fathers with openings to communicate with their children about sensitive matters and nurture them more effectively.

Ideally, irrespective of family structure, initiatives to support fathers will try to foster holistic father-child bonds that combine behavioral, cognitive, emotional, and spiritual ties. Relationships are more likely to be enriched and bonds will be reinforced if men and children express an affinity for one another in multiple ways. An interpersonal chemistry that is sustained by a complex set of exchanges may also provide fathers with more fulfilling opportunities to nurture their children.

A father and child's bonding experience will be affected by their overlapping life trajectories. Although the typical biological father is involved in his child's life from the prenatal period and birth, it is quite common for a stepfather or adoptive father to meet a child sometime after the child's early childhood. Furthermore, a man who becomes a father for the first time when he's eighteen is likely to experience fathering quite differently should he become a father at forty-nine. The older father may well be more willing to devote time to "being there," may have more life lessons to teach, may have a deeper reservoir of emotions to draw upon, and may have a stronger spiritual center. Of course, a young father can be actively engaged, but he is generally more restricted in the human and social capital he can access and share. At the same time, the young father is less likely to have as many life complications and potential constraints resulting from multiple-partner fertility.

The child's developmental stage and evolving personality represent the other side to the matching of life courses for the father and child. Obviously a developing child will have different needs over time, and these needs draw on the extent and quality of the father's responsiveness. Generally speaking, a man who has relevant experience with children of a particular age, gender, personality type, and cultural background will have a better chance as a biological father, stepfather, or adoptive father to respond well to a child with similar characteristics at a given life stage (infancy, preschool, preteens, and early to middle or late adolescence).

People in policy circles, social service agencies, and any number of organizations that deal with men need to evaluate how social and organizational structures as well as daily practices enable or constrain fathers from bonding with their children in the ways described. Part of this analysis must recognize how bonds are fostered or eroded in the context of larger social and physical environments, just as fathers' identities are fostered or eroded in different contexts. In other words, various conditions influence how fathers and children relate to one another and bond in specific ways.

Men's fatherly bonds with children often stem from a genetic tie, but men nurture children who are not theirs biologically as well. In recent decades, the rise in single-parent families and stepfamilies has altered the circumstances under which increasing numbers of men develop familial commitments to children. Some of the men may be extended kin to the children, others not. Either way, the men's efforts represent a major commitment of love, time, and resources.

The most common version of a nonbiological father figure is the man who is romantically involved with a woman who has had a child with another man. Typically, he lives with the woman and the stepchild, but this is not necessarily the case. In-depth interviews with stepfathers reveal that men develop all sorts of ties with stepchildren and in many instances claim them as their own in their hearts and through their wallets.[12] Thirty-year-old Brandon, a stepfather of two children, compares his feelings for his stepchildren with those he has for his own child.

> I thought initially when we first, we all moved in together that maybe—
> I was a little worried, how am I going to feel towards them? But now. . . .
> I consider them my kids even though I'm not the biological father. I don't
> really try to step in to take—for them to call me Dad or anything like that—
> but I don't really see them as any different. I mean. . . . I'll do my best to
> protect them and treat them fairly.

He explicitly adds that he's capable of "loving" his stepchildren in all aspects just as he does his son.

Ethnographic studies with African American fathers have also identified the importance of godfathers, uncles, brothers, grandfathers, cousins, and community elders—"ol' heads"—as significant male parents in communities and kin networks that support men's flexible options as caregivers.[13] Compadres, or godfathers, in many Latino families occupy a valued fatherly role in children's lives, alongside a similar set of uncles, brothers, grandfathers, and cousins.[14]

How do relationships between nonbiological father figures and children differ from the relationships fathers have with their own offspring? The former may rely more on men's sense of commitment arising from family or partner obligations to children rather than a personal commitment to specific children. Nonbiological fathers may see their bonds as trial "fathering" experiences, or they may accept the responsibility to be involved but not to be nurturing. However, as more men take on diverse family roles and are motivated to care for children for reasons independent of their romantic involvements with the children's mother, the bonds these different types of fathers forge with their children may become more similar in form, content, and spirit. If children adopt new ways of looking at family, they could play an important role by expecting and calling forth the same commitment from father figures as they do from their biological fathers. At the same time, stepfathers, especially those with stepdaughters, must grapple with the powerful public discourses that depict men in general as potential child predators and single out stepfathers as being particularly worrisome.[15]

Recent policy changes, public discourse, and community reactions to committed father figures suggest that it may become commonplace to expect that nonbiological father figures and children will establish close bonds. In addition, the evolving culture of fatherhood, including the meanings assigned to biological and social bonds between men and children, continues to be muddled by the litany of court cases that rely on DNA evidence to confirm or disconfirm genetic paternity.[16] Ironically, as scientific advances unravel the mysteries and significance of shared DNA, and elevate the significance of the gene in some circles, social realities accentuate individuals' uncanny ability and passion to nurture others irrespective of blood ties. If stakeholders are to develop effective initiatives to enhance fathers' bonds with their children they must adapt their strategies to accommodate this changing cultural landscape.

As we examine how father-child relationships are shaped by public and private initiatives, we need to account for four things that have been shown to shape paternal involvement: motivation, skills, social supports, and institutional barriers.[17] We extend this vision of involvement by examining additional dimensions of father-child relationships, including interaction, consistency of men's involvement, the centrality of men's monitoring and protection of children, promotion of health and well-being, and the urge to be generative and leave a legacy over time through relationships.

Motivation to Create and Maintain Bonds

What motivates a father to establish and maintain a close bond with his child? This is an obvious and vital starting point. As we discussed in chapter 2, a father's sense of motivation may surface in tandem with his changing identity as a father. Motivation may emerge from the reflections and cognitive maps that parents have of their children. A kind of "emotional responsibility" for children's growth is often relevant to this endeavor.[18] One specific form of mental activity that comes into play involves parents' reflecting on and evaluating their childrearing efforts. This thinking typically occurs before or after parents interact with their children and is a form of indirect care.[19] Others refine this notion by suggesting that there are five types of thinking attentive parents do when they contemplate how they can (1) manage their children's development and respond appropriately to their children's needs, (2) prevent adverse situations, (3) monitor influences that can affect development, (4) mentor that development, and (5) model appropriate behavior.[20] As we note elsewhere, men have the capacity to reflect regularly on how to be nurturing, intimate, and responsive to their children.[21] To what extent and under what circumstances they think about their children in this way are empirical questions. For new fathers and mothers in particular, the transition to parenthood is filtered through social images of "good" fathering and mothering that are gender specific. Not surprisingly, fathers tend to have a less active "parental consciousness" than new mothers and are less likely to feel ultimately responsible for a baby's care.[22] Although there are no data that clearly document a historical trend, it seems clear that fathers in recent years increasingly have thought about their newborn babies' needs and have become more attentive to them.

Research suggests that at the birth of a child, even an unmarried man in a fragile low-income family can be committed to being an involved father.[23] Often, early indicators of motivation to have a child and establish a close relationship are evident prior to birth. Studies suggest that a man's prenatal involvement with a fetus, as well as with a partner, can elevate a father's sense of attachment and ensure his continued involvement over time.[24] These findings support efforts that push for paternity establishment programs in hospitals. If a man embraces his father identity at the child's birth, the reasoning goes, he is more likely both to act like an engaged and committed father and to establish a positive relationship with his child.

The motivation to be a nurturing parent may also be linked to how attached fathers are to their own parents and grandparents. Listen to a handful of men share their fondness and respect for key family members who shaped their identities and, presumably, their approach to fathering.

[I] had a father who was very tender, loving. . . . Number one life lesson that my father shared with me was to be decisive, to be able to look at . . . what's going on, and make a decision and then support it. . . . I'm very proud to say that I'm just like my father 'cause he would always get that input from everybody but then make a decision and move forward. With my mom, I think that probably the main thing that I got from my mom was, she was willing to do anything with me. . . . My mom nurtured [my fascination with the Civil War]. . . . That's one of the things that's kind of probably influenced me a lot with my own kids, is that we try to find what are those things that really excite them, that really interest them and how can you nurture that to grow too. (*Matthew, forty-eight, white, CEO of his own company, married with two biological children and two stepchildren, was raised youngest of five*)

My father, there was nothing he wouldn't do for us [children]. . . . [My father's life-threatening work accident when I was sixteen] made me realize how much I loved my father, because I feel like I had never prayed like I prayed before then, because I was like on my knees constantly, it seemed like every ten or fifteen minutes I was praying and asking God, please don't take him away, because I didn't know how to function, or know what to do. I want him to be able to see me when I get older and having kids and he can play with his grandkids. (*Emmit, twenty-eight, African American, exercise specialist, married with a six-year-old stepson and a five-month-old biological son, grew up fairly poor; his father was a church deacon*)

My grandfather taught me how to do everything. I was, like, reading in preschool. He had me reading newspapers, and the teachers didn't want me in class, because I already knew how to read. I would ride with him to pick up my grandmother from work, and he would have me up in the passenger's side, reading the newspaper and counting money. He taught me how to ride a bike. He was that father figure. See, I didn't really miss out on life. I saw my grandfather in his daughter, my mother, too. It's like they're the same person to me. As a little boy, you can't tell the difference, you just know that they love you. (*Jordan, nineteen, African American, grew up in St. Louis and moved to Indianapolis at fifteen; not working or going to school, he is the unmarried father of an infant boy two months old*)

I've always had a very close connection with my father. You know, he's the man; he's the coolest guy ever. Just unbelievably so. I still kind of idealize or really look up to my father. He's a good friend of mine. (*Ben, thirty-one, white, minister, married with two small children, raised in the upper-middle class*)

[My mom taught me not to be] selfish. She also taught me to treat everybody the way that you would want to be treated. . . . I just got, you know, total respect for her. Everybody that knows her, loves her. . . . She is . . . always willing to you know give, lend a helping hand to anybody that needs it, so I try to [help] too. If they [family or students] need me, and I can do it for them, I am going to do. (*Vince, forty-two, African American, team leader at alternative school, married with two stepchildren, raised in poor rural area as the fourth child of nine*)

My father. Well, it was a very close relationship, because I was the first child. . . . My father was, like, a nice guy, he always enjoyed being with you, he always [pause] was there. Life lessons . . . let me see. You know, the fact of being a friend, the importance of the truth, take it easy that we are going away, anyway. (*Santiago, forty-five, Hispanic, landscaping supervisor, married and living with his two children, grew up in Colombia on a ranch with four siblings*)

[My father] was what I lived to be. He told me something when I was six which makes a lot more sense now that I'm older that "you wear my name," you do wrong, I look bad. So it's something that stuck with me forever. . . . I remember I was going to kindergarten and he was working four or five jobs a day to try to make ends meet for our family. . . . He was my hero. . . . We [Darnell and his sisters] wanted to do everything to make him happy, because he did everything that he could, you know, to make us happy. (*Darnell, thirty-seven, African American, high school teacher, married with three children, grew up in the lower-middle class*)

Clearly, these stories about family members capture only some of the many cultural and social forces and personality characteristics that contribute to fathers' desire to be attentive and involved with their children in loving ways. Although the media often portrays men as bumbling parents, role models of attentive fathering pervade contemporary popular culture as well. For instance, in the 1991 movie *Boyz in the Hood,* the strong hand that the character Furious Styles (played by Laurence Fishburne) takes with his son Tre conveys a father's need to protect and monitor his children in the midst of the violent street life and often deadly challenges associated with becoming a man in South Central Los Angeles.

Research on the biological and social origins of our need to be attached to others, and to care for others, is generating an impressive set of findings that will shape perceptions about fathers' motivation to be nurturing parents.[25] Both mothers and fathers are primed to care for their children by physiological and behavioral changes that occur prior and subsequent to birth.[26] Children are biologically predisposed to become attached to stable figures in their immediate surroundings and are likely to activate such bonds with fathers during rough-and-tumble play.[27]

Fathers are also inspired because they love their children and they have a need to love. Unfortunately, researchers and policymakers seldom discuss familial love. Yet such deep and complex feelings ground most fathers' conviction to invest time, energy, and resources into helping children develop and navigate their worlds.

Finally, fathers may seek to create a strong bond with a biological child because of their previous experiences with other children who meant a lot to them. For example, men who were caregivers for their younger brothers, sisters, or cousins may have felt the power of attachment at an early age and seek out such close relationships with their own children. Or men may have played the social father role with a partner's child from a previous relationship. These trial "fathering" bonds may have revealed the allure of being attached, or they may have raised expectations about a child's needing a father—which some of the men may have ultimately been unable to fulfill. Some of the fathers, however, may end up channeling their time and energy into being good providers and as a result may forgo the chance to develop close, nurturing ties with their own child.

Men's efforts to establish affinity and we-ness through intimate relationships with their children are connected to their own experiences of familiarity, trust, self-disclosure, emotional vulnerability, and physical affection. But nurturing fathers, presumably, must recognize some of their children's specific needs as well. The key questions, then, are: Can initiatives influence how men recognize and respond to their children's development and well-being, particularly if bonds are constructed because of children's desire for their fathers' attention? Furthermore, to what extent can policies, programs, and other initiatives be used to change or reinforce what men believe, how they feel, and what kind of father they want to be?

Fathering Skills and Competence

Eager to take part in a close, intimate relationship with their child, many fathers learn to be nurturing and responsive to their child as he or she ages. More responsive fathers are likely to express nurturance in timely, developmentally appropriate, and effective ways. But learning to be a nurturing dad takes more than an urge to act in an involved manner. Policies and programs that promote men's involvement with their children must not assume that more involvement is always better involvement. If fathers act irresponsibly, say, by neglecting to monitor young children or by using inappropriate physical or verbal discipline, children will not be nurtured in a productive fashion and they are likely to suffer negative consequences. A close bond with a child requires men to develop skills and competence in relationships. They must be attuned to what works to promote their children's well-being over many years and in many different contexts. By definition, then, when competent fathers attend to their children in a developmentally appropriate way they are less likely to expose their children intentionally or unintentionally to harmful circumstances.

For younger children, the first skills fathers need to acquire are those of basic child-care tasks: changing diapers, bathing, and feeding. These caregiving skills are more complicated if fathers have special needs children who require specific exercises, medication regimes, or extensive monitoring.

Fathers often distinguish themselves as teachers of their young children. Many men feel comfortable with promoting language as a skill by frequently discussing things with their children, even when the children are young. Fathers who engage in regular interaction with children in their homes have been shown to have a greater impact on language learning skills than mothers in low-income families.[28] These educational activities can form the basis for a close emotional bond that is distinct from other close relationships in children's lives. As Kareem, a young father in an Indianapolis fathering program, asserts, "I spend time with my daughter, and that's mostly teaching her. It's different when she comes to my house. She can run around and be bad at her mother's house, but at my place, it's like going to school."

Although some fathers may just be learning about children's developmental capacities themselves, they are often motivated to push their children to learn in ways that make sense to them. For example, some men choose to immerse their young children in an environment saturated with books and reading activities. Fenton grew up on the South Side of Chicago and struggled to put himself through community college while holding down part-time work building backyard decks. He notes that he did not have anyone to push him to succeed in school, but he is set on pushing Sheila, his own three-year-old daughter, to do so. Although Fenton does not know when exactly to expect his daughter to be developmentally prepared to read, he encourages her nonetheless.

> Since I've been around Sheila, she's started school. She loves school. I've started to work with her as far as her schooling goes. It's not just fun and games anymore. I'm stressing education. She's enjoying it right now, though. I don't hang out. I spend my time reading. I don't watch TV when I'm alone. I read to my kids . . . I want to have Sheila reading by second grade. I know that's asking for a lot, if she catches on so fast, who knows?

Some low-income fathers recognize that the public schools are not providing opportunities for their children, and they see it as their responsibility to stress education at home. Kelvin and his partner made concerted choices about spending their time in educational activities with their daughters.

> I make sure that they have all of the things and support that they need. Like the educational system is starting to lower their standards and let the kids graduate not knowing as much as they should. So, as a parent I take the responsibility to get them many books so that they will know what the school is not teaching them. Math was always my thing, and my two oldest are math whizzes.

Fathers also turn to bonding with their children through athletic activities, promoting development of musical skills, teaching basic computer skills, and so forth. For example, Terry, a forty-one-year-old middle-class stepfather, recalls how easy it was for him to develop a bond with his stepson, Zack.

> Within that first year I started staying over at her [the mother's] house and we [Terry and Zack] just hit it right off. He was five years old then and he's nine now. . . . He's a little jock, very very sports-athletic. I was All State in three sports in Massachusetts growing up. I've been physically active all my life, so we were very similar in nature.

This athletic connection offered Terry all sorts of opportunities to spend time with Zack and to be a part of his life by being regularly involved with his friends and recreational activities.

Terry's experience highlights the way many fathers and sons, sometimes daughters, are seduced into seeing sports as a means to get closer. Adult males frequently reminisce with delight or describe with frustration how they sought as youngsters to achieve intimacy with their fathers by playing sports and sharing sports talk.[29] During their youth, they sensed that their fathers would value them more and spend more time with them if they devoted their time and energies to athletics. For many, sports-based exchanges and the rituals that often go with them provide a familiar and safe means to connect with fathers who may be emotionally distant or otherwise too busy.

Some fathers may feel especially competent sharing information and teaching their children about other things that, like sports, often are perceived as manly pursuits, such as automotive and house repair, camping, wood working, computer technologies, and finance. Although these areas may be less distinctively defined as part of a masculine domain in today's world, they continue to be associated with the "male experience." Consequently, fathers are more apt than mothers to use these areas as opportunities to bond with their children. In addition, as definitions of gender-appropriate behavior have evolved in recent decades, fathers appear increasingly more likely to share this information with their daughters as well as their sons.

Gender norms, partner influences, work schedules, emotional trade-offs, and physiological conditions can affect fathers' responsiveness. And we suspect that social initiatives can also help men develop this interpersonal skill. In the innovative program Boot Camp for New Dads mentioned earlier, experienced fathers with their infant children in tow train soon-to-be fathers in basic child-care techniques such as burping, changing, wrapping, and, if the babies are crying, calming babies and bonding with an infant. This program also presents other issues such as forming a parenting team, child safety, preventing child abuse, and dealing with relatives. The hands-on man-to-man orientation workshops rely on sports and military traditions to reinforce messages about active fathering. In addition, the website associated with Dads Adventure includes a magazine for fathers, a blog, how-to videos, an "Ask a Dad" section, and print resources relevant to new fathers.

In community-based fathering projects that work with low-income fathers, program facilitators typically try to improve fathers' awareness of child development and their competence in dealing with children's needs. Sometimes a simple message about being attentive to a child opens up an understanding of how fathers can make important contributions to their children's well-being. One program participant, Parrish, had children when he was a teenager. When he was twenty-four his interaction with his newborn daughter seemed qualitatively different from those when he was younger. Partly his new confidence stemmed from his acquiring some basic care skills, but he also heard a vital message for the first time, as he put it:

> And the program told us: Check the crying. That's one of my main things, get her to stop crying, check to see if her diaper's wet, if she's hungry, if she wants to be played with, if she's sick. Finding out about all those things at once I get to know my daughter on a day-to-day basis. If I can take care of her for twenty-four hours, I can do it for a week. I feel like that.

Programs offering a comprehensive overview of children's development give fathers a context to absorb the complicated and overwhelming aspects of their relationships with their children. We see this with Xavier, a father of ten children with multiple partners whose main focus was bringing in enough money to contribute to their support. The program curriculum's details accumulated in his mind, and he began to forge a broader vision of how he could be attuned to each of his children's needs, at different ages. Xavier attributed his strength as a father to this insight:

> It just opened me up more with kids, what a kid needs. All I knew about was fixing things. I wasn't working about school stuff, hospital visits, you got to stay here, you got to go there, take the child on this field trip, all this volunteering for the school. I wasn't thinking about it. You got to be there to show your kid "I'm here with you. I'm gonna be there." It depends who got the strong-enough mind. Most don't have it. Most can't handle taking care of themselves.

Again, many fathers in these programs homed in on education as a vehicle for their children's progress. However, it was a challenge for unmarried, nonresident fathers to try to teach their children in a context of relationship conflict, exposure to violence, and other environmental stressors. As Marcus notes, he knew what he "should" do, and he felt he had the skills to be a catalyst for his daughter's education, but he was fighting an uphill battle:

> [You need to] check up on them, go to school, make sure that their head is on the right track when you're having a conversation with them and get a reply. It is up to me to do it, exactly. . . . She don't know how to count change. She's seven years old; all she knows is how to count dollars. If you watch the cents, the dollars will come. I show her the difference and how to put it together. She should learn that way before you get to school, so you can excel, so you can become above, go to more things. That's what you're supposed to do with kids, teach them before they get there.

Many young fathers struggle to bond with their children during the first few weeks of their life because they are distracted by state agencies pressuring them to get a blood test as well as their conflicts with the mothers. The closeness some fathers feel with their children can be jeopardized by men's hesitancy to commit to a relationship that they negotiate with the mothers, maternal and paternal kin, and state agents.

Program staff members often serve as advisers in courtroom matters for fathers involved in the paternity establishment process. These personnel encourage men to build close communication with their children. They also help men to cope with frustration that can obscure important interactions with courts, state agencies, and mothers. However, at times staff members can find themselves enmeshed in unanticipated legal and family dynamics, with few skills or program resources at their disposal to help men strengthen fragile ties with their children.

Partnerships between local programs and fathers can also help fathers deal with circumstances in which biological paternity is not an issue. Not surprisingly, stepfathers typically receive even less guidance than biological fathers. Family professionals have done little programmatically to assist stepfathers, and researchers have generally ignored studying interventions that include stepfathers. Thus, efforts are clearly needed to help stepfathers appreciate more fully the dynamics of stepfamily life and navigate the unique challenges associated with developing meaningful bonds with stepchildren.

One innovative study that targeted couples who had been married for less than two years used a randomized control experimental design to assess how the Parent Management Training—Oregon model (PMTO) influenced stepfathers' parenting skills.[30] It also considered early symptoms of depression in elementary school stepchildren and their levels of noncompliance. This multimethod study included videotaped observations of different combinations of interactions between stepfathers, mothers, and individual stepchildren. Two years after the intervention, the researchers detected positive changes in the quality of stepfathers' parenting and improvements in stepchildren's outcomes.

Turning to the self-help literature, the therapist Dr. Carl Pickhardt outlines numerous tips in his book *Keys to Successful Step-Fathering* to help stepfathers manage stepfamily life and create healthy relationships with their stepchildren.[31] His insights can inform programmatic efforts to assist stepfathers. Pickhardt's objective is to "help the stepfather keep his choices constructive, his expectations realistic, his contributions significant, and his returns rewarding."[32] Pickhardt encourages men to express "positive authority" with their stepchildren and notes various ways this can be done.

Men can provide a positive influence for their stepchildren by acting as their protector, interceding for them, and opening up opportunities. Forty-four-year-old Doug, a technician for vending machines, did this exceptionally well when he personally confronted the high school principal and teacher about Sammy, the stepson he formally adopted. After learning of Sammy's school troubles and his apparently poor chance of graduating on time, Doug immediately came to his son's rescue and marshaled educational resources on his behalf.

As positive decisionmakers stepfathers give permission, make exceptions, and assert leadership. In a situation requiring a special decision a stepchild can see the stepfather as someone who is capable of taking charge, making reasonable decisions, and rendering desirable outcomes for the stepchild, such as allowing the child to stay out later for a special occasion. This strategy is more feasible when the mother is unavailable at times because the man has a chance to gain his stepchild's trust and establish his unique connection with the child. Unfortunately, some men, when left in charge to make their own decisions, make poor first and subsequent impressions with their future or current stepchildren and the children's birth mothers.

Stepfathers can endear themselves to stepchildren by controlling resources effectively. They can give money directly to their stepchildren, financially support their special interests, and give them rides to school or other places. John, disabled and unemployed at twenty-seven years of age, gave his teenage stepdaughter, Harmony, daily rides to and from school. Such occasions can provide stepfathers with opportunities to establish their own line of communication with stepchildren separate from the mother. Seizing or creating opportunities such as these can influence the bonds stepfathers build with their stepchildren.

Passing on positive knowledge—such as teaching a child how to play a musical instrument—confirms for many stepchildren that their stepfather can provide help, give advice, and teach them about important matters. Exchanges such as these are often viewed as "affinity-seeking" gestures, in which the stepfather strives to make himself likable and establish a connection with the stepchild.[33] Such encounters are valuable not only in the early stages of stepfather-stepchild relations but also later, when "affinity-maintaining" strategies can be important after rapport has already been established. Unfortunately, some stepfathers may take their stepchildren for granted and neglect to sustain their affinity beyond the initial phases of a relationship. Stepfathers also need to be attentive to kids when they ask for help, advice, and information, because the kids may want to establish or sustain affinity. Stepchildren may be drawn to specific stepfathers because they have unique experiences and insights or are able to teach them different things.

Finally, stepfathers can work toward earning their stepchildren's respect through positive evaluation in the form of being supportive, giving praise, and rewarding their stepchildren's good behavior. Certainly confirming kinds of statements made in private can be uplifting to a child. But even more, when stepfathers praise their stepchildren in the presence of their friends, family members, the stepfather's friends, and even complete strangers, they go a long way to reassure the kids that they value them and are interested in securing a meaningful bond.

Much more could be done within these partnerships between local programs and fathers to raise men's self-awareness of how and why they should display positive authority with their stepchildren. Men who express themselves in this way during the early phases of their relationships with their partner's children may position themselves to engage in more effective coparenting with the birth mother, assume a more constructive disciplinary role later on, and possibly enter into a cooperative cofathering relationship with the biological father. Those who practice positive authority do not seek to control children. Rather, they try to provide a supportive environment and have children see them as assets. Compared to meting out discipline, positive authority is more closely associated with a nurturing style of interacting with children.

Enabling "We-ness"

Interpersonal chemistry is likely to figure prominently in fathers' and children's tendency to develop and sustain a sense of we-ness, but other conditions may also affect the likelihood that healthy, productive, and close relationships will develop. Public and private initiatives may be able to do little to alter individuals' personalities or the fit between them. However, initiatives can address some of the constraints that hinder fathers and children from creating and maintaining meaningful bonds.

Fathers who end up not living with their children, whether by choice or circumstance, will often face significant hurdles in spending quality time with their children in an environment conducive to developing mutual respect, understanding, and a deep bond.[34] Perhaps the best-known hurdle involves the turmoil that follows the uncoupling process when a parenting couple breaks up. Many men eventually find themselves as nonresident fathers, often disappointed with visitation schedules that in effect restrict the amount of time and the type of activities they can share with their children. Those who are granted joint physical custody have more options than their peers who are not, but they, too, are challenged to preserve a special sense of we-ness with their children, because they have fewer chances to sustain meaningful everyday rituals.

In recent decades, fathers' rights groups in the United States, the United Kingdom, and elsewhere have been quite vocal about reforming child custody, visitation, and support policies.[35] A common theme among the varied activist groups is that fathers' bonds with their children are inexcusably negated when courts have, these groups say, expressed an unjust bias against fathers. They echo observations made by child development scholars: if children form attachments with parents, they are best served if given the chance to sustain active relationships with nonresident fathers. This is best achieved by fostering extensive, meaningful interactions that require ample overnights, extended stays, and, for very young children, frequent transitions when custody is shared across residences. Some countries have embraced the standard of joint custody, but the United States is not one of them unless unusual circumstances suggest children's health would be compromised by not doing so. Various jurisdictions across the United States have tried to minimize the adversarial nature of divorce and the child custody process. Some have implemented mediation sessions as a key component, particularly when children are involved. Whether these sessions enhance fathers' bonds with their children is not yet known.

Visitation policies also structure the development and maintenance of close relationships. Younger children with regular visitation may begin to share ideas and communicate honestly with their fathers about the challenges of living apart, and consistency can promote a sense of trust. For older children, these regular visits may allow for reciprocity and exchanges with fathers to unfold, as both children and fathers learn to depend upon each other, to appreciate differences and shared interests, and to manage living apart. But children may have a harder time trusting their fathers if there are long stretches of time between visits.[36] These relationship barriers may be exacerbated when children feel torn by competing loyalties between, for example, their mother and her new partner and their father and his new partner. A tenuous attachment may also make personality clashes between fathers and children more explicit. In these contexts, formal program initiatives and court decisions could collaborate to minimize the already adversarial nature of child custody and visitation during divorce.

Organizations associated with physical sites such as schools, health-care facilities, and child-care centers can provide incentives or disincentives for fathers and stepfathers to solidify a nurturing relationship with their children. Although school staff sometimes treat nonresident fathers as members of a student's parental support team, some are excluded. Stepfathers often face even more stringent limits to their assumed role with children in school settings, as school staff members are confused about and distrustful of the actual relationship dynamics between stepfathers and children. If stepfathers are encouraged to participate in parent-teacher meetings, administrators and teachers can help inspire them to see themselves as a vital part of a coparenting team that is expected to help a child succeed at school. This image can solidify stepfathers' impressions of and commitment to their sentiment of we-ness as it relates to important matters in a child's life. Efforts to support stepfathers and promote their familial sense of we-ness should be done mindfully so as not to alienate responsible, caring biological fathers.

Increasingly, systemwide educational initiatives have begun to encourage men's involvement. For instance, many urban school systems across the country sponsor a "Father's Day to School" early in the school year, a day when men bring their children to school; come into the classroom; and help out with reading, math, or other volunteer and tutoring activities. These initiatives may set the stage for fathers to feel at home in school and for children to feel proud of their fathers' commitment to their education.[37]

Health-care facilities also present a set of formal and informal rules regarding fathers' interaction with children. Often staff's resistance to men's involvement begins with the contested presence of unmarried fathers at the birth of their children. Over the past decade, training programs have been established to encourage hospital staff to appreciate and nurture men's motivation to "be there" for their newborns and their partners, and their older children as well. Knowledge of men's promotion and monitoring of children's health is limited, but hospitals, clinics, and doctors' offices are promising sites to develop new understanding and to encourage men's relationships with children. As children witness their fathers' presence and concern about their health, they may grow emotionally closer to them.

Social institutions can also support informal initiatives that facilitate close interaction and a sense of we-ness between fathers and children. These initiatives may be cost effective and involve crafting meaningful rituals in everyday interaction. For example, staff at schools, hospitals, community centers, recreation centers, and churches may simply shift the timing of children's activities to make it easier for fathers to participate. This time accommodation might open up opportunities for fathers to participate in important rituals. These institutions may also set aside activities for fathers or target fathers as guests or volunteers. Children and fathers can share experiences at school when fathers are incorporated into special lunch functions and invited to work with their children to paint murals or refurbish classroom facilities. By not limiting these types of activities to a one-time "Father's Day" in June, communities also take more responsibility for fostering positive father-child bonds.[38]

Modern technologies, sometimes with the support of formal institutions, can provide fathers opportunities to communicate with their children about sensitive topics via email, cell phones, and text messages, each of which can accommodate mobile lifestyles.[39] Simple texts such as "I love you" or "I'm thinking about you" can remind children and their fathers that they share an intimate bond. Although middle-class fathers currently are better positioned than less affluent fathers to purchase and use these technologies, this class-based imbalance should dissipate over time as communication technologies permeate all levels of our society. And modern communication techniques are likely to become more commonplace during the transition to adulthood, when fathers and their children are less likely to live in close proximity but still seek to retain close ties or even develop closer ones.

Monitoring and Protection of Children

Most research on monitoring children for their safety is focused on what mothers do for their young children. However, being a protector of one's children has been a traditional role that fathers have embraced for centuries, even though it is less common today and fewer media sources mention its importance. Men's efforts to establish a safe environment for their families can convey a strong intimate bond with their children.

Modern communications technologies, in addition to opening up new moments to express intimacy, also offer parents novel tools to keep track of their children and supervise their exposure to inappropriate media content.[40] Today, a father equipped with adequate resources can, among other things, watch a monitor to keep an eye on his young child, place programs on a child's computer to restrict access to adult content, download movie reviews from the Web to ensure that his child does not watch age-inappropriate films, or monitor the GPS in a car or cell phone to keep tabs on his teenage child's physical whereabouts. To the extent that a man is intrigued by technological gadgetry, he may take a special interest in these high-tech methods of parental monitoring.

Again, the class divide affords the more affluent man greater opportunities to use some of these technologies to supervise and monitor his children.

Fathers' more conventional strategies for protecting their children are probably most evident in neighborhoods in which families confront daily violence and conflict. In these contexts, men may build close relations with their children in different ways than women. Like mothers, fathers may monitor their children's activities through constant supervision and "keeping tabs" on their whereabouts, as well as restriction of specific activities, such as using playgrounds. Fathers also commit to keeping their younger sons and daughters physically close to them as they move through risky environments. Fathers may assess their own presence as a threat to children's safety—for example, in circumstances where fathers try to avoid contact with gang members and police—and then take themselves out of the picture to ensure safe passage for their children.[41]

Moreover, fathers can offer distinctive ways of educating their children about survival tactics in dangerous neighborhoods or strategies to deal with conflict, often drawing on their own experiences as young men in these very neighborhoods.[42] Fathers may also advocate for their children's safety outside the household by confronting troublemakers and becoming active in community affairs. In resource-strapped communities, they may play a pivotal role in protecting their children from being involved with or even targeted by the police and work to clean up unhealthy housing and streetscapes that lead to asthma, injuries, or accidents.[43]

For children, this proactive and engaged fathering serves as a model for protecting family members and promoting their health. Studies suggest that monitoring and protection may lead to different types of bonding for sons and daughters. Fathers sometimes try to shield their daughters by closely monitoring their friendships, daily routines in neighborhoods, and interpersonal strategies to avoid conflict.[44] Their efforts to raise boys through educating them about survival tactics, by contrast, are attempts to protect their sons from deadly personal violence.

Fathers' efforts to monitor and protect are sometimes intimately connected to mothers' attempts to protect their children. For example, many low-income mothers facilitate a process called "kinscription" in which they actively recruit nonresident fathers to begin building a closer bond with their children. They must balance the advantage of fathers' attention and commitment to being protectors with the disadvantage of fathers' possible risky or inappropriate behavior, such as drinking, drugging, or running with peers in the streets, which can jeopardize the benefits of close father-child bonds.[45]

Policies and programs that acknowledge families' daily struggles to monitor and protect their children might provide leverage to foster collaborations between community agencies. These collaborations can offer a central role to men who are familiar with the risks posed by dangerous neighborhoods.

Bonding Despite Distance

Men's involvement in the workplace is often seen as the culprit that keeps fathers apart from their families and, more specifically, prevents the formation of more intimate bonds with their children. Because fathers aspire to be providers as a way to be successful fathers, they commit much of their time to responsibilities at work and to securing income. A breadwinning orientation can give men a strong sense of accomplishment and pride. If children appreciate this orientation, it can be the basis for a shared appreciation for men's family commitments, even though they are often away from their families. But such a time commitment can lead to fathers spending sporadic time with their children, limited to time after school, late nights, and a few hours on the weekend.

What can policymakers and employers do to help reduce conflict between the need to develop close relationships with children and the need to work hard and earn a living? Workplace policies are perhaps some of the most explicit and visible initiatives that potentially can promote bonding by encouraging flexibility in work schedules. Although public support for such policies seems to be relatively high, only a small number of businesses in the United States provide paternity leave and flextime to fathers.[46]

The United States clearly lags behind many European countries, particularly the Scandinavian countries of Denmark, Iceland, Norway, and Sweden, in providing appealing paternity leave around the time of a child's birth and paternal leave options to care for young children. A majority of European countries offer some type of paid entitlement for fathers to be with their newborns or young children. Documenting how often these options are used and making sense of how particular programs influence fathers' and children's experiences is difficult because the mix of policy provisions geared to fathers and mothers separately as well as joint provisions vary greatly among countries. Some schemes include programs that target fathers in the form of "daddy days" or a "father's quota" of leave time, and others do not.[47] Some strategies promote leaves that include reimbursement at various rates, whereas other leave programs are completely unpaid. Moreover, for various reasons countries do not keep accurate records of rates of

workers' utilization of maternity and paternity leave. One recent esti-
mate suggests that fathers in European countries take on average nine
days of paternity leave and that "increasingly, younger generations of
European men are approaching this time away from employment as
an important component of family togetherness and personal identity
formation."[48] This observation may be most consistent with trends in
Iceland and Sweden, where in 2005 fathers took roughly thirty-three
and twenty-one paternity benefit days, respectively, compared to three
and fourteen in 2000. Fathers increase their use of paternity leave when
they are paid for this time at a level of at least two thirds of their regular earnings.

Although studies have not yet systematically assessed the possible
benefits to children's well-being that result from fathers taking paternity leave, some emerging evidence indicates that "paternal leave taking
has the potential to boost fathers' practical and emotional investment in
infant care."[49] One large cohort study of eight- to twelve-month-old
infants in the United Kingdom found that fathers who took any paternity leave after the birth were "25% more likely to change diapers, 19%
more likely to feed the baby, and 19% more likely to get up at night
when the child is age 8 months to 12 months."[50] In addition, research
with young American children shows that fathers who take more paternity leave are more involved nine months later in child-care activities
than those who take no leave.[51] Unfortunately, while policies that
encourage fathers to spend time with their infants and young children
appear to promote men's commitment to fatherhood and may possibly promote children's well-being, such policies are generally more
accessible to persons working in larger, public, and white-collar companies than to others.[52]

Giving fathers the flexibility to tailor their work schedules around
care for their children might result in men's having more hours to
develop close relationships. At the very least, the availability of paternity leave would maximize the chances that fathers can stay at home
for a considerable amount of time to care for their newborn infants.
Lack of universal support for flexibility in fathers' work schedules
also means that as children grow, fathers are less able to take time
from the workday to attend teacher conferences and school trips, to
provide support for school work and social activities, or to develop
playful routines that on a daily basis form the foundation of close and
trusting interaction.

Many fathers also travel for work, whether flying to meet clients on
international business or driving goods across the country in a truck.[53]
Fathers are challenged to sustain bonds with children when they cede
control over their physical environments as well as their time to work

demands. Although they may be dedicated to spending as much time as possible with their children, fathers who work at a distance from home often travel for weeks at a time. The accumulation of trips can foster a hands-off approach to fathering and restrict opportunities for communication, sharing, and the physical expression of affection that come with trusted daily interactions.

Fathers and families who have struggled to make it through multiple deployments to Iraq and Afghanistan are some of the best and more urgent examples of the effects of distance and lost time on bonds.[54] Soldiers try to nurture their children from halfway around the world by using email, cell phones, and video cameras. They deal with large time differences, waking up at odd hours to talk to children about their latest recreational event, school reports, or problems with siblings and friends. Unfortunately, limited communication capacity in specific deployment areas often results in unreliable connections. Members of the military, confined in public space, also struggle to secure privacy so they can disclose to and hear intimate details from their children. When they return home, many are frustrated if their high expectations for close interaction with their children are not met because the children feel estranged and distant from them. Although today's deployed military and support personnel are better equipped technologically to maintain contact with family than their counterparts in earlier eras, it is unclear how effective this sporadic communication is in promoting trusting relationships between fathers and children. That said, the military in collaboration with private business should be encouraged to develop creative solutions to improve the quality of these communications. Sustaining tight bonds between military fathers and their families can protect children's well-being as well as prove critical for men's continued commitment to military service.

Traveling, migrant, military, or nonresident fathers make a relatively free choice to live apart from children. In contrast, incarcerated fathers live in facilities that both enforce separation from children and families and require men to yield control over their time and physical place completely.[55] Physical interaction with children is limited to fathers' visitation schedules and the facilities available in prisons for these visits, which can consist of an uninviting room with benches and vending machines. The public space of a prison provides at best a limited moment for telephone contact for children to "hear my daddy's voice." Sometimes fathers can transcend these boundaries, such as when they are permitted to be active outside correctional facilities in local communities, such as in a work-release program, and can interact with their children. Even in these programs, however, it is common for fathers to succumb to doing "hard time" by shutting down emotionally and cutting off communication with family and friends. Both fathers and their children acknowledge that the result of months in prison or jail may be a falling out of contact and ultimately children's confused reaction to their fathers: "Who are you? I don't know who you are."

Yet there are valuable opportunities to promote father-child closeness in correctional facilities. Initially, time spent away from their homes and communities can afford men a chance to get clean from substance or alcohol use and to develop new understandings of their conflicted relationships with partners. Programs can use resources to build developmentally appropriate rooms with books and toys where men can spend time with their children. Some prisons have developed other innovative ways to foster more intimate interaction. It is common for minimum-security work-release programs to allow inmates to earn passes to leave the facility.[56] Fathers can opt to visit their children and partners at home or to take their children to a restaurant or a movie. Correctional officers and policymakers have begun to understand how the promotion of continued father-child interaction gives ex-offenders a clear reason to stay out of prison once they return to civilian life.

Initiatives that promote consistent bonds must acknowledge the long list of challenges to men's interaction with children. Employment takes men away from children, through long hours of work commitment and often great distances for traveling. Other social institutions, such as the military and correctional facilities, house hundreds of thousands of fathers apart from their children and partners. Each of these contexts reduces control over the time and space that fathers need for sustaining bonds with their children. As discussed in chapter 2, men's control over their immediate environments fundamentally affects their identities and sense of being fathers. Moreover, decisions about time and place shape the bonds fathers can create through reliable interaction with children. Formal initiatives can provide fathers with options to reclaim some control over important aspects of their interaction with children, even in prison or during military deployment.

Promoting Health Through Father-Child Bonds

All things being equal, a father's establishing a loving bond with his child is likely to enhance the child's well-being in varied ways over time. Whether it's a bond with a newborn, a toddler, an early adolescent, or a teenager on the cusp of adulthood, a father can directly and indirectly leave an imprint on a child's health broadly defined. Bonds forged through one or more of the forms described earlier—behavioral, cognitive, emotional, and spiritual-ethical—can translate into opportunities for a father to secure his child's attention, trust, and admiration. When a child feels an affinity for his or her father and respects him, the child is more likely to listen to his advice and model his behavior.

How fathers view their bodies and roles as caregivers is as consequential as the nature and quality of the bonds they form. The big picture for American men's health is rather bleak. About one third of men are obese and about 10 percent will become alcoholics during their lifetimes.[57] Men are more likely than women to smoke, to eat fatty foods, to drink and drive, to use guns, to play violent sports, and to get inadequate sleep. Men even use seatbelts less often than women. Finally, men are less likely to seek medical attention for routine physicals or when serious health problems arise. A key force underlying these patterns is the way boys and men seek to earn masculine respect, especially from other males, while avoiding being labeled feminine and weak.[58]

Men's attitudes toward their own and others' health have broader implications when they become fathers. Research shows that fathers with poor health habits are more likely to have children who are overweight, smoke, abuse drugs, eat poorly, and experience other negative health outcomes.[59] That link may be partly attributed to genetics, but there's also a notable social dimension. The challenge is to encourage and enable men to be nurturing role models and teachers who make healthy choices for themselves and their children.[60]

To achieve this goal, we need to transform public and policy discourses so that "definitions of 'good fathering' will summon fathers to pursue a healthy lifestyle while cultivating the same for their children."[61] We need to do more than simply prod fathers to talk to their children about healthy alternatives. Incentives need to enhance the chances that fathers will engage with their children in health-promoting activities, such as organized individual or team sports and other activities such as hiking, biking, shopping for healthy food, growing a garden, and cooking together.

For those living in poor inner cities and rural areas, political commitments are needed to improve health-enhancing infrastructure. Parents and children need greater access to fresh food markets, health-care facilities, recreation sites, and organized sports. Flexible workplace policies, more father-friendly corporate cultures, and more convenient evening and weekend hours at pediatrician offices and other health-care facilities can also help fathers solidify their convictions to be more responsive to their children's health needs.[62] Social programs should strive in particular to enhance the likelihood that fathers will play an active role in their children's prenatal assessments and early care. Creative prenatal and early fatherhood programs should coordinate efforts to curb smoking, drinking, and drug use. Success in these areas may foster fathers' own health consciousness and willingness to monitor their children's health-care needs and to manage acute and chronic care issues.[63]

Extending Bonds Through Generativity and Advocacy

Policymakers, researchers, and even the public at large tend to frame father-and-child relationships as interactions with young children, even though men nurture and provide for children over many years. Positive bonds formed when children are quite young often have long-term consequences. Research and policy have increasingly come to meet at this common point: promotion of close bonds is a policy investment in immediate as well as long-term positive outcomes for children, and sometimes their fathers, too. New research on children's brain development in the first years of life has led to a push for infant and even prenatal involvement of fathers.[64] Promoting attachment at birth, in the hospital, and enticing a father to nurture and support his child during infancy may set bonding patterns for years to come.

What are the ripple effects of fathers and children having closely bonded, linked lives over the life course? Few researchers have tracked how intimacy and nurturance among older fathers and adult children unfold.[65] Many argue that the transition to fatherhood for the first time is the most significant moment in which men embrace generativity, or "giving back" to the next generation. A bond between fathers and children symbolizing closeness may become a commitment to promote continuity over time in the form of a shared family legacy. In other words, a close relationship may lead to the sharing of skills and knowledge about commitment to work in farming communities or family businesses. It may imply that fathers feel compelled to serve as guides or counselors as their children navigate their first steps into the workforce or into family life or as they navigate job loss and relationship dissolution as well.

Although we focus primarily on how fathers influence minor or young-adult children, the life-course approach to father-child relationships suggests that social interventions should acknowledge the importance of reciprocal nurturance. In addition, initiatives designed to generate tighter bonds between fathers and children should facilitate social supports for a relationship that changes and grows over decades. Thus, efforts should take into account how children respond to and nurture their fathers as both generations age.[66]

These relationships can grow of their own accord and positive consequences may result. However, fathers need basic resources and skills in order to be effective at generativity.[67] Feeling a commitment to being generative is not enough; having the social and material capital to sustain close bonds is challenging, especially for low-income and working-class fathers who are unmarried and have few family relationships that tie them to their children. This raises the question of when and how fathers should become the targets of initiatives to foster close bonds with their children and to maintain them during crises and transitional periods. To some degree, policies and programs aimed at securing employment opportunities and job training for men may indirectly be doing just that. When fathers feel they can contribute something of value to their families they are more comfortable pursuing a relationship with their children, and others who control access to nonresident fathers' children are more likely to accommodate fathers' overtures.[68]

Father-child bonds may deepen and expand when men not only act generatively but also act as advocates for their children in contexts outside of daily family life. When children witness their fathers promoting their interests and skills with teachers and coaches, or when they observe how fathers navigate networks of friends and employers to help secure jobs and opportunities for them, a new sense of trust and intimacy may emerge. As noted earlier, this strategy for building a close bond may be uniquely valuable to nonbiological fathers, who often must do more to earn children's trust. In partnership with youth workers in sport leagues, scouting programs, or churches, stepfathers can fashion a public role that can signal a long-term commitment to their stepchildren's development.[69] Thus, developing close bonds with children can become a subtle but important part of men's everyday activities connected to work, leisure, and networks of friends and families.

Finally, public and private initiatives may be useful in helping fathers and children reconcile relationships damaged by neglect, abuse, estrangement, and so forth. Although it would be unwise to try to repair some father-child bonds because it would not be in a child's best interest, other situations call for good-faith interventions.[70] Some efforts will seek to rejuvenate father-child bonds that were once strong and intimate; others will confront the prospects of establishing feelings of trust and nurturance that were previously lacking. In many instances, policies and programs will need to enlist the support of the child's mother and perhaps other caregivers. The success of some initiatives is likely to hinge on how interpersonal dynamics are addressed that implicate the (ex)partner, coparent, and other possible alliances relevant to fathering.

Chapter 4

Negotiating Trust
as Partners and Parents

RUSTY is no stranger to family complexity and drama, after thirty years of life experience and three unique partnerships, with Miranda, Kristy, and Kim, resulting in a total of six children. In Rusty we can see how the self-as-father, father-child, and coparental paths can define men's fathering, and we also learn how experiences with trust and communication in romantic relationships can alter how fathers feel, think, and act. A close look at the history of Rusty's intimate world reveals much about the challenges public and private initiatives sometimes face when they try to foster an attentive, nurturing style of fathering.

Rusty, a jack-of-all-trades, and Miranda have been together as a couple for nine years. They are busy raising Amanda, five, Gabrielle, three, and Luke, one, into preschoolers and kindergarteners. Rusty likes to say that they are engaged to be married, but he admits that nine years of promises are too long. He is at risk of losing his relationship with Miranda, and with it, his children. For the past five years, Rusty has been in and out of correctional facilities on a variety of charges, most related to his passion for smoking marijuana. "When I'm out of incarceration, I live with them [Miranda and children] all the time. We're still together, but we're having some problems right now because of me being in a work-release program," Rusty says. "She's real upset that I'm locked up again. Which I can't blame her. I've been in and out of jail almost the whole time I've known her. But we're talking, like just yesterday, and she said, 'I love you and I can't wait to see you.' "

But jail is not the only thing that keeps Rusty from seeing his wife and children. They currently live in Tennessee, and Rusty is locked up in Indiana on a drug charge. A while ago, he and Miranda tried to make a new start, to get away from past mistakes. They made that new start by moving out of his mother's house and to Tennessee. Now, after months of separation, Miranda has hinted that she would move the family back to Indiana to be closer to him. "I'm actually kind of excited they're talking about moving back," Rusty admits at first, but then recants. "But really I don't want them to. I'd rather they stay in Tennessee because it's a lot nicer town. They're in church, they're in school, there is a whole list of reasons. But I would have time to see them every now and then if they moved up." Rusty also realizes how things are changing quickly for his children, even as Miranda stays committed to the vision of him as a family man. For example, Miranda took the kids to see him the day after he was arrested and still housed in Tennessee. When she told his oldest daughter, Amanda, about the arrest, she said "Well, looks like we got to go out and find a new dad." "That was upsetting," Rusty says, "but my older daughter is more understanding of what's going on. She has a better idea of things than the younger two. Luke, I don't even think Luke knows who the hell I am."

Fathers like Rusty have histories that mark their aspirations, images, and identities as fathers in general as well as their actual relationships with specific children. These two types of histories, or fathering trajectories, are linked to a third type of path in which men negotiate coparenting relationships over time with the mothers of their children.[1] Coparenting relationships are uniquely complicated by the degrees of commitment to trust, communication, and intimacy that define them. For Rusty, the commitment he shares with Miranda allows their children to stay connected to him despite his incarceration and the physical separation it demands.

But Rusty's relationship with Miranda and their children represents only one piece of his life as a father. Nine years earlier at the age of twenty-three, just before he met Miranda, he met and lived with Kristy for three months. He had been working odd jobs, and smoking, but had not yet gotten entangled with the criminal justice system. It was a quick and seemingly easy relationship. Kristy soon revealed that the purpose of that relationship was not what Rusty himself expected. When she discovered she was pregnant, he recalls, "She packed up all my stuff and set it out on the porch. And she said, 'Thanks, that's all I wanted.' " Nioka was born during the same year, but Rusty couldn't recall her exact birthday, noting, "I got to see Nioka one time, and that was in passing. I ran into Kristy about four years ago, and I asked if it was possible to see my daughter, and to get to know her. Kristy just smiled and said, 'No, her new daddy wouldn't like that too much.' "

Many fathers have multiple coparenting relationships that, like Rusty's, differ from each other dramatically, in terms of both their parenting and their romantic dimensions. In the tenuous and short-lived romantic involvements, men often find that they have little hope of developing a close bond with the children those involvements produced. Rusty feels some regret but probably realizes that he would not have been able to contribute a paycheck or to care for his daughter Nioka in the way that perhaps her new father could. This fleeting relationship was too weak; neither Rusty nor Kristy was prepared to develop the trust and invest the time, energy, and resources necessary to achieve a stable family life. Marriage was clearly out of the picture.

In fact, Rusty knew this from his own bitter marriage and divorce experiences as a young man with Kim. That relationship shaped his views of every subsequent intimate relationship and involvement with his children. Rusty met Kim when he was eighteen, not long after he had lived with another girl and her mother for a year. Prior to that first cohabiting experience, his youth had been spent in foster care under child welfare supervision. He left his last foster home when he was sixteen. Looking back on his time with Kim, Rusty acknowledges first and foremost his problems with alcohol:

> Look I was a heavy drinker then. When I first met Kim, I didn't pay a whole lot of attention to mentality. She was a nice-looking girl, she had a nice body, I was drunk, she was willing. That's how our relationship started. I was drunk clean up until I found out she was pregnant. I felt like I should do the right thing and marry her, but I can't honestly say I ever really loved Kim. I care a lot about her, she's a very sweet girl. I'll always care about her. But I never paid attention to how smart she was or how mentally evolved she was until after I stopped drinking.

Rusty recalls his days with Kim and how he cried at the birth of his first child, William, who is now eleven years old. Richard, his second son, was born two years later. "I watched both of them come out, it was just amazing. When they put them in my arms for the first time, it was definitely . . . something . . . I don't get to see my sons much now." As a twenty-year-old father of two boys, Rusty was at a loss to talk to Kim about what was missing in their relationship. Yet he worried as she sat and watched Mr. Rogers on TV and played with baby toys. He urged Kim to go to parenting courses or to go back to school and get some kind of vocational training. He even turned to outside help.

> I got us into marriage counseling because we weren't getting along. That was why I went on the road with the carnival, because I couldn't deal with it anymore. I told her, "Kim, I can't stay with you. I got to have a divorce." But I think I could have . . . I could have dealt with it because she was maturing. She was trying to. A lot of Kim's problems come from her mother, who didn't want her to grow up, and treated her like a child all her life.

Almost retracing the steps he took with Miranda a decade later, Rusty related how he had moved the family to Tennessee. After Rusty left a good job, Kim's mother told her, "It's time to come home [to Indiana]. I'll come pick you up in a few days." It seemed that every other month Rusty pressed Kim not to move back in with her mother.

> If I wanted to be with my family, either I lived with her mother, or I wouldn't be with them. So I'd end up giving up my place and moving. If Kim and I had a disagreement, it was really me and her mom's disagreement. Now, her mom tells me when I [can] see my sons. I can't deal with it anymore.

Rusty's history with Kim—from teen pregnancy to five years of marriage to divorce—is yet another distinct relationship path, in contrast to his short-lived affair with Kristy and his long-distance but stable non-marital relationship with Miranda. Their effect on Rusty is that each set of linked lives is intertwined with another set of linked lives.

Situated in the present, but burdened by twelve years of complicated personal history, Rusty's dilemmas are substantial. His two eldest boys live with their grandmother, who does not trust Rusty after years of inconsistent jobs and the perceived betrayal of her own daughter. So in addition to trying to get clean and leave prison, he has been trying to raise money to hire a lawyer to pursue custody of his first-born sons but has been unable to do so. He sees them once a year, even though they live in town next to the prison—ironically, much closer than his current partner and their young children. "Me and my ex-wife, we get along great, we like each other," Rusty asserts.

His current stay in work release is not related to drug use. Past arrears on child support landed him back in jail. Rusty was hit with a class D felony for owing thousands of dollars in back support for his older sons; he also owed $2,000 for his youngest daughters, payment that was due to the state of Indiana to collect reimbursement for Miranda's reliance on welfare payments when Rusty was incarcerated in recent years.

Rusty's convoluted history as a father presents a number of challenges to policy assumptions about the centrality of intimate relationships, even marriage, to men's parenting. The assumptions that drive many social policy initiatives targeting fathers often begin and end with the couple relationship. Federal and local guidelines that shape paternity establishment, child support, marriage promotion, the Family and Medical Leave Act (FMLA) of 1993, and other family policies define good fathering largely as marriage, shared residence, and provision. Each of these aspects of fathering points to fathers being in coupled relationships with mothers as they jointly raise children.[2]

In offering her compelling thesis on nurturance, Nancy Dowd presents a different vision of fathering, one that directly challenges the primacy of couples to men's parenting. What would it take, she asks, to promote father-child relationships apart from father-mother relationships?[3] Can social policy make such a transition? How would this shift lead to reforms in family law, welfare policy, paternity establishment, and child support systems?

We begin our search for answers to these questions by identifying some of the most explicit and systematic policies and programs directed at men's parenting, usually focusing on the couple relationship between a mother and father. However, we extend our attention beyond the immediate status of a relationship, be it marital, cohabiting, or friendly. Because relationships are dynamic we want to identify the critical moments when they change over time. We examine nonmarital and nonresident relationships that are located outside the purview of many policies and programs. The increasing pervasiveness of young unmarried couples, gay fathers, divorced parents, and multiple-partner parenting in extended family networks encourages us to examine the contexts for new coparenting processes.

Figures 4.1, 4.2, and 4.3 show how a father's family and household context can evolve from a residential arrangement to a simple nonresident fathering scenario to a more complex arrangement that includes two new sets of romantic partnerships and additional children in both households. Figures 4.2 and 4.3 highlight the reality that the transition to becoming a nonresident father involves a readjustment period in which fathers and families must decide how to distribute time and resources among both resident and nonresident children. We explore part of the readjustment process later by considering how fathers do kin work in order to remain productively involved with their children.

Figure 4.1   Residential Fathering in a Couple-Focused Household

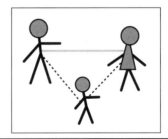

Source: Authors' figure.
Note: —— lines represent adult ties within family and kin network from fathers' perspective. ----- lines represent ties between adults and children.

Figure 4.2   Nonresident Fathering

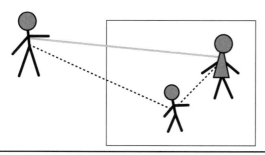

Source: Authors' figure.
Note: —— lines represent adult ties within family and kin network from fathers' perspective. ····· lines represent ties between adults and children.

These more complex family networks challenge us to create flexible programs that are responsive to the full range of dynamic coparenting that occurs outside of marriage or coresidence. In particular, we examine communication patterns and how trust is negotiated in intimate relationships so as to understand how these practices shape men's involvement with children.[4] Policies and programs already directly influence coparenting relations, but they could play an even more constructive role in

Figure 4.3   Fathering Across Households in Complex Networks

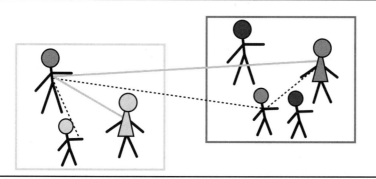

Source: Authors' figure.
Note: —— lines represent adult ties within family and kin network from fathers' perspective. ····· lines represent ties between adults and children. ☐ and ☐ boxes represent new households for the father and mother and, in this example, new partnerships as well. Stick figures shaded the same color represent original family groups.

coparenting trajectories if supportive resources can foster better couple communication and trust.[5] Such resources might be connected to fatherhood programs, stepparenting workshops, mediation sessions for divorcing couples, or specific coparenting interventions designed to help new parents adjust to their more demanding lives or assist experienced parents navigate a difficult family transition.[6]

The Back Story: Relationships Prior to Children

Perhaps the earliest moment in a long-standing coparental relationship is the beginning of a couple's joint history. Prior to their emergence as mothers and fathers committed to their families, prospective partners work together to sort through the baggage of prior intimate relationships and to build a new story of who they want to become as a couple. In practical terms, before negotiating the coparenting demands of raising a child, those who become parents typically have a sexual relationship and establish some sort of intimate bond as a couple. For straight men, a pregnancy and baby can result from all sorts of involvements, some of which

> are fleeting, some endure years of special moments, sentimental rituals, heated arguments, difficult negotiations, and life-course transitions. Some involvements with particular partners evolve without interruption for decades. Some are monogamous and intermittent, here one moment, gone the next. Some are concurrent involvements with several women and may be defined by similar or different boundaries. . . . The spectrum of involvements evokes a potpourri of emotions from men, ranging from the wonderful feelings of love, respect, and passion to the darker sides of anger, jealousy, and sadness.[7]

In our interviews, men describe all sorts of involvements whose qualities are captured by the terms they use to label their partners, such as fiancée, serious girlfriend, best friend, casual friend, female, fuck buddy, and one-night stand. In a few cases, men resort to derogatory phrases like "hi and bye," "bend 'em and send 'em," "sperm buckets," and "sperm dumpsters." Although it is rare, some men become fathers in situations in which they have little or no respect for the mother of their child. Not surprisingly, it is challenging to implement effective strategies that promote engaged fathering in men who despise their child's mother.

A first-time father's intimacy backstory usually predates his efforts to figure out what it means to be a father, but in some critical ways it is a key factor in successful fathering. Even the man who has had children with another woman and has already developed a father identity may forge distinct and vacillating impressions of what it will be like to raise a child with a different woman (or man). In either case, the type of romantic involvement a man has with his partner—the future coparent of his child—can affect the type and level of social support a man receives and his ability to reciprocate commitment and care to his partner and child.

Todd, a poor, twenty-seven-year-old high school dropout, reflects on the miserable relationship he has with his two-year-old son's birth mother, a woman who has six other children from a previous relationship. Currently his son lives with his parents because a child protection agency had concerns about the quality of supervision the boy was receiving from Todd and the mother, who were living apart. While in the mother's care, the boy was hit by a car, was burned, and was not taken to the hospital. Todd asserts that his son's mother, during her pregnancy, exhibited poor judgment by smoking, drinking, and doing drugs. Ironically, while Todd pleaded with her to curb her extensive drinking and smoking, he "strongly suggested" that she take LSD and psychedelic mushrooms during her pregnancy because, he thought, it can "totally . . . make children smarter." Responding to a question about whether he thought about being a father during his partner's pregnancy, a disgruntled Todd illustrates the power of a romantic partnership in shaping a man's orientation toward fathering.

> I sure did—we wanted this baby to go away. It wasn't right or whatever, it didn't seem right. And, then, when that wouldn't happen, . . . I started thinking about it, what it would be like to be a father, what it's gonna entail, you know, once she started leaving me and all this crap while she's pregnant, that's just the way she is, she's really, like, capricious, and if one of her friends or something tells her . . . that I'm a piece of shit, she's gonna believe them, whether she feels that way or not, or whether its true or not. . . . I had to go through thinking about what it's gonna be like to have her raising the kid, or me raising the kid that we both have, stuff like that, and then it went back to, okay, now we're going to do this together.

Sadly, it may be in the child's best interest that his parents didn't get along because his well-being is probably enhanced by living with the grandparents. Although not impossible, it is a tall order to expect that any initiative can help couples like Todd and his partner redirect themselves to become healthier, more focused parents while developing trust in a close relationship. Sometimes the best family policy is to minimize the destructive influences that particular fathers and mothers can have on their children.

Contrary to Todd's circumstances, some fathers' and mothers' relationships emerge through many years of sharing intimate thoughts, gaining trust, and working together to overcome life's challenges. In the world of middle-class couples who are well integrated into their communities, conscientiously use highly effective contraception, and have a reasonably harmonious relationship, partners often find themselves together for a number of years, established in their jobs, and cohabiting or married prior to a planned pregnancy. Such couples tend to have an established understanding of how they incorporate extended family and friends into their lives as a couple. This foundation facilitates the next step whereby couples, as coparents, weave others into their lives and their children's routines in new ways.

But some men become fathers in far less conventional circumstances. Parrish is a twenty-year-old African American who expected many of the things that young men have desired for decades: a good job, marriage, and home ownership. Coming from a poor community in the Midwest, however, he had grown up in a foster home and had only a few community college courses and part-time work to show for his efforts. He tried to track down family members in his old neighborhood in recent months, only to find "nothing but broke people, the whole family doing bad. You can't get help from nobody."

Parrish's relationship with Erika was one of the only "good" and consistent things that marked years of change and difficulty. They met in eighth grade and Parrish remembered her as the only person "who was real while I was in a foster home. She always said, 'How you been doing?' " They grew together as a couple, culminating in her expecting their first baby. Having an established relationship full of trust steadied him during this transitional time. "She's a keeper, and she's smart. I've known her for seven years, but I still don't know her well enough to marry her. But it's a deeper bond now. Nothing will break us up. It's like, that's my blood now."

Other nascent relationships lack the foundation of years, or even months, of casual, friendly interaction. They become trial learning experiences for men and women. These precursors to coparenting relationships represent critical personal moments to examine values about procreation and bonding through shared commitments to others. As young men become aware of their potential to create human life, and as they begin to project a future identity based on the promise of being a parent (as discussed in chapter 2), they have the opportunity to ground their visions in responsible sexual decisionmaking with their partners.[8] Decisions about how and when to have children are embedded in very specific relationship contexts. As we saw with Todd, romantic partners play a pivotal role in shaping whether or not and how men enact their wishes to be involved fathers or supportive partners. Premarital education curricula may also be an effective means to encourage healthy relationships.[9]

The complex history of couple intimacy emerges in different ways for every set of partners. Weighty matters, such as how and when a person wants to become a parent and with whom, are negotiated alongside other mundane experiences. Men and women learn more about each other over time, and as they disclose and experience more with each other, partners may either learn to trust each other or grow more tenuous about committing to a shared future. For example, Arthur, the young man whose partner had an abortion behind his back, was surprised to learn that his partner was pro-choice. Unbeknownst to him, her values took on immediacy during her pregnancy, and his discomfort with her clandestine abortion forced him to acknowledge that he did not want to ever again be in a romantic relationship with a pro-choice woman.

A conception, especially an unplanned one, accelerates many relationships by forcing couples to grapple not only with their commitment to each other as romantic partners but also with their suitability as coparents. Men who express their fatherly conviction prenatally tend to display a stronger commitment to their partners.[10] Care for their partners' and unborn children's health, shared doctor's visits during pregnancy, and support for their pregnant partners' mental health struggles as they transition to the role of mother also have long-term effects. Prenatally involved male partners are more likely to act like fathers during their infants' first years of life.[11] Even more important than prenatal involvement, however, is the change in residential circumstances. Recent studies have shown that what may matter most for young men transitioning to fatherhood is a parallel transition into cohabitation with a partner. It is even more important than whether they have a high-quality relationship with the future mother of their child.[12] In other words, sharing a residence before and after conception clearly shapes men's experience of fathering. It is less clear how varying patterns of trust and communication between partners become a strong thread in the father-child trajectory over time.

Our initial commentary on fathers' backstories to fatherhood assumes that the men are heterosexual, but what about gay fathers? The backstory of a gay man's relationship is not linked to a child's conception; rather it is linked to the man's conviction of wanting to become a father. Presumably, the intimacy pattern that unfolds for the gay man who becomes a father is less varied and more likely to be a serious one because gay men don't have unplanned pregnancies.[13] Furthermore, the social and financial obstacles that a gay man must surmount to become a father through adoption, foster care, surrogacy, or an extended-kin care arrangement tend to lead to the self-selection of individuals who are involved in trusting, long-term partnerships. Thus, policies and programs targeting gay fathers and couples are more likely to focus on tensions between individuals and elements of the larger community than are those that deal with heterosexual couples. Generally speaking, public discourse and institutions encourage straight men to procreate and act in fatherly ways, whereas public sentiment is very mixed about gays doing the same.

Despite recent efforts to explore aspects of being a gay father in an era that has become more receptive to fathering outside of a heterosexual relationship than earlier eras, precious little is known about how a gay man's romantic relationship with another man influences his transition to fathering or his experience as a father over time. Stereotypical portraits of the gay male party scene imply that the majority of gay men, even those in committed relationships, will scoff at the prospects of forgoing gay parties, cultural events, and dining out to accommodate a child's needs. But Ben and Peter, a gay couple in their late thirties, represent a growing breed of gays who challenge that premise.[14] They describe how their exposure to models of gay fatherhood altered their life visions and openness to fathering as a couple. For Ben the turning-point experience came when they were at the Amsterdam airport after "fourteen days and fourteen nights of nonstop, all-out party" at the Gay Games. "We're exhausted, and we both had gotten really sick from no sleep and too much everything. . . . And across from us were two guys, and an adorable little baby whom they had adopted." Peter chimes in:

> Adorable little baby. And [Ben] was the one who expressed that like the bolt of lightning struck. Honey, look at that. And they had obviously not been into the scene of the Gay Games and the party and on and on. They were warming a bottle and changing a diaper. . . . It was the juxtaposition of what we'd done over the two weeks. It struck him first. And he was just like, look at that. The clouds cleared, and a ray of light came down.

The ray of light appeared on the heels of another positive experience Ben and Peter had while living next door to a happy gay couple who had twin girls with a surrogate. Although elements of the gay male party scene may discourage larger numbers of gay men from wanting to become fathers for the foreseeable future, a subset of gay men may increasingly long to be involved in a committed couple with expectations of cofathering. Thus, questions about coparenting may become a more common and vital part of how gay couples negotiate their romantic partnerships. These changes are likely to occur more quickly in states where gays and lesbians can legally marry.

In addition, unmarried gay men living in states that do allow a same-sex parent to adopt a partner's biological or adoptive child without terminating the rights of the first parent must grapple with trust issues when creating and navigating an adoptive family.[15] How do members of a committed gay couple decide, prior to adopting a child, which partner will assume legal custody rights for the child? The decision is critical for many because romantic partnerships often end. When they do, the man who has not secured parental rights may be left without recourse to sustain his fatherly connection to a child he nurtured, and the long-term father-child trajectory can be fundamentally altered. A nonlegal partner can also experience discomfort while his romantic relationship and fathering experience are ongoing. One gay father's feeling of distress over being the "invisible dad" or hearing others ask "Which one of you is the real dad?" is an experience likely shared by many.[16]

Though far less common than households headed by heterosexual single fathers or single mothers, gay single fathers are often confronted with the challenge of finding a suitable mate who is willing to become a gay stepfather. In some cases, having a child already may actually make a gay father a more appealing partner, but because adoption and foster agencies are more likely to direct gay men toward the "hard-to-place" children, often the gay man will be asked to become a father to a special needs child or to a child of a race other than his own.[17] Thus, the stress as well as the joys associated with these parenting circumstances will often influence gay fathers' romantic involvements, whether they become fathers to the same child simultaneously or sequentially.

Wedded to the "Package Deal"

Most of the prominent and influential policy and program initiatives on fathering are guided by men's participation in a heterosexual relationship. These programs tend to emphasize some elements of the "package deal" mentioned earlier, including residence, marriage, and provision. In this scenario, being a good husband is first and foremost about being a good provider, and work and family decisions for fathers and mothers are guided by a limited set of policies. Typically, paternal leave policies are implemented in two-parent families, often dual-career families, in large part because they are offered to workers in professional careers who have weighed their choices for allocating coparenting resources. As discussed in chapter 3, different countries around the world have created social policies and programs that support couples' efforts to take time off to care for family members, and most of the programs are implemented by a federal agency, not by individual businesses. In the United States, the principal federal policy, embodied in the FMLA, is an initiative to guarantee men's and women's jobs during medical leave to care for a family member. For fathers, this translates into a limited amount of unpaid time to care for their newborn infants and wives after childbirth. Generally speaking, social policy has most often been crafted to prioritize fathers' potential to provide for families, not to nurture and care for them.

Even in programs that promote a contemporary model of "new" fathers in which men invest time and emotion in caring for their children, sustaining an intimate relationship with the mother of one's children is seen as a required task of fathering.[18] Researchers have examined the related premise that the condition of being a good father must be embedded in a committed marital relationship. Often underlying such studies is the premise that religious values or beliefs drive men's parenting and marital relations. Belying this assumption is the fact that differences between men's parenting remain negligible across a variety of marital relationships in conservative or liberal Christian families.[19] Anyway, in 2008 only 68 percent of all children lived in married-couple households.[20] Even within this subset of households, many of the couples will divorce or separate over time, including those in conservative Christian families that appear to be most dedicated to traditional marriage and "family values." Only some of the coparenting relationships we present in this chapter reflect the prevailing ideals underlying much social policy.

A heated debate persists as to who is ultimately responsible for men's involvement with their children. Answers to this question not only drive ethical considerations of how to deal with the division of labor between men and women in families but also inform long-standing family policy initiatives that enforce specific work and family roles on men and women.

Researchers specializing in the family have debated how to conceptualize father involvement, and the degree to which mothers play a role in encouraging or enabling such involvement.[21] Mothers' caregiving is usually perceived as both direct care for children and the work needed to encourage men's interaction with children. For instance, in the course of everyday interactions, many white women in middle-class marriages work to manage the difficult emotions such as anger, frustration, sadness, fear, and disengagement their husbands and children sometimes experience.[22] So, too, mothers orchestrate fathers' and children's interest in each other's lives, their styles and frequency of communication, and their transitions into each others' worlds, such as fathers' attendance at children's basketball games or swim meets, family trips to church services, and men's participation in planning birthday parties.

Although two-thirds of children live in married-couple households, this statistic masks complexities among married couples. Children are more commonly found in married-couple households in immigrant than in nonimmigrant families. Over three-fourths (77 percent) of immigrant families in 2008 reported long-term marital commitments.[23] Research on coparenting in immigrant families is scarce, especially in terms of marital quality, communication, and the meanings and expressions of trust between coparents. Unfortunately, very little is known about how these committed-couple relationships are regularly reconfigured by the demands of jobs, migration, and cultural negotiation.

For one Mexican immigrant father in Chicago, his "traditional" marriage and commitment to family life did not live up to the ideal of "provide and reside" for good fathers as defined by many social policies. Miguel's family was disrupted by the realities of low-wage work and real-world concerns about raising children in a threatening community. He and his wife had three children, but he left them in Mexico to journey to the Midwest to find a good paying job. After eight years of living apart, Miguel and his wife were reunited in Chicago, along with their daughters and son. But this nuclear family had only finished one period of separation in order to begin another. According to Miguel, after six years of living in the United States, his wife decided to prioritize her daughters' safety and this jeopardized their marriage.

> I brought my daughters to the United States, but they didn't like it. They [daughters and wife] went back to live with my mother-in-law. One minute, my wife says both parents should be in their kids' lives, then she wants to move away and do things on her own. She says, "We have different cultures—my people are different from your people." She's more oriented to her family than our own.

Miguel found himself confused about his commitment to his wife. He held tightly to the security of marriage and family as traditional ideals, but everyday interaction and communication with his wife were constrained. His expectations as a parent and as a partner were stalled, and he remained uncertain about his relationship with his wife (and therefore his children) largely because of a poor job market, hostile immigration policies, and an unfamiliar American cultural influence for his children.

If workplace policies identified only married coresident couples, then Miguel and his wife would not consistently appear on the radar. Policymakers and employers have used jobs as a basis for intervention, adapting the FMLA, vacation and sick leave policies, and flexible work week schedules to help working fathers set aside more time for their children and spouses.[24] As an immigrant worker, Miguel was not securely attached to the job market and did not work in jobs that offered such benefits. Fathers who do not live with their families are hard-pressed to justify taking leave to care for their children or their partners.

In sum, married coresiding couples fit the public and private visions of men and women who qualify as successful parents. But these assumptions do not capture changes in marital and residential statuses. How can social policies and programs influence men's involvement in cases where married coresiding couples move apart, couples never marry, parents never coreside, or gay partners in committed couples go unrecognized as having parental rights?

Is There an "Us"? Parenting Before Partnering

In the accepted package deal, successful long-term relationships are marked by the achievement of marriage, cohabitation, and childbearing. As marriage rates have declined, cohabitation rates have risen, and increasing numbers of children have been born outside of marriage, researchers and policymakers have continued to focus primarily on relationships in which these three events co-occur.[25] These demographic changes suggest the emergence of new pair-bonding sequences, in which each event is an independent choice.[26]

To understand the range of relationships that fathers and mothers may form with each other, it is also important to pay closer attention to the process of change over relationship trajectories.[27] For example, policymakers have focused intensely on the efforts of young unmarried couples who are at the beginning of their shared experience as coparents: a moment when they are parents but not truly partners, struggling to define commitment, residence, and "we-ness" in what some have termed "incomplete" relationships.[28] Researchers have also distinguished between couples that "slide" into cohabitation without a pronounced commitment to the relationship and those that "decide" to commit to their relationship.[29] When couples slide into cohabitation, father involvement is based on a commitment to a shared child, as compared to the stronger involvement of cohabitating fathers who remain committed to both child and partner.[30]

Of course, plenty of middle-class people in their twenties and thirties also have the misfortune of being involved in an unplanned pregnancy with someone they hardly know. The premise of the 2007 Hollywood comedy *Knocked Up* is that a white, middle-class woman (played by Katherine Heigl) struggles to develop a relationship and coparental partnership with Seth Rogen, her irresponsible one-night stand. Although the pair eventually finds ways to manage the financial and emotional demands of their arrangement, not all middle-class parents are as fortunate as these film characters. Some may have vicious battles over paternity as well as child custody, support, and visitation issues.

When men and women interact as parents without clear expectations about their intimate relationship, they must first resolve the paternity question. For unmarried couples, paternity can be achieved through an informal social process of establishing trust, as family members reach consensus that a certain man is indeed the father of a newborn. While effortless at times, this process can also create stress and conflict for some couples, often as young men come to grips with being responsible for the consequences of their sexual activity.

Kelvin was an active father of three girls he had with his common-law wife, Erica. Recalling how he eventually accepted that he was the biological father of his first child, he notes that his own immaturity almost ended any hopes of a committed relationship with Erica.

> I denied the baby, I knew she was mine, but I denied it because I was living with another girl. When the baby came, I tried to sign the birth certificates, but they were gone from the hospital when I got there. The second time [we got pregnant], I denied the baby too. I knew I shouldn't deny it. . . . I was a dog. I was really bad. But Erica was still there.

When voluntary efforts to claim biological children are ineffective, low-income couples confront welfare reform policies that enforce paternity establishment. Mothers who receive public aid are threatened with termination of their benefits unless the biological fathers of their children are "smoked out."

Many researchers and policymakers have used the notion of intendedness as a means of predicting a man's subsequent involvement with his child.[31] A father's story of whether and how he planned to conceive and raise his child emerges alongside his willingness to accept paternity. We also suggest that how a father thinks about and communicates the intendedness of his child is indicative of how he interacts with the child's mother.

Oscar recently gained permission to see his daughter and girlfriend during the final months of his work-release program in Chicago. He has two daughters and is sorting out his complicated obligations to both. When he first heard that Melinda, his older daughter's mother, was pregnant, he responded "by laughing—I said, 'Girl, you better quit playing with me.' I didn't believe her for two or three days, but then her sister and mama told me, and I got kind of happy. Then I started thinking I had to get a damn job. I was working after school to midnight, in two jobs—didn't see her or the baby except at night, after work." Now, after separating from his first partner and ready to reconnect with his second partner, he reassesses what it means to be a father.

> I wish I waited a while. I love my daughters, I don't want to say but, but
> if I didn't have my kids there is no telling what I would be doing.
> Because that threw a monkey wrench into everything. I would be ahead
> of where I am at now, I would be working. Now, I have to go get me
> some Pampers, I am broke. It is so much stress to make sure she has
> food and everything. I can go a day [without eating], but she has to eat.
> I stress on her eating and her mama, and then we have to pay bills, and I
> am not even working. She is on aid—like $150 a month—but she doesn't
> get Food Stamps.

Although Oscar loves his daughters, he wonders about how his partnering relationships would have played out if he had waited longer to become a father, especially as a man living in an economically strapped community. Would he have been better established as a provider had he waited? Although many fathers clearly believe that they intended to conceive and raise their children, at least in retrospect, they are less clear about the toll that a child takes on their career interests and on their ability to work with their partners as providers for a family.

Uncommitted partners may have to negotiate their loyalties to each other in the wake of a child's birth. A baby's birth may not always ensure coparents' long-term romantic chemistry, but for some couples the urge to embrace a status as a new family is compelling, even when fathers and mothers live apart. For those who have a child prior to securing a partnership, commitment can also be much more tenuous and casual, regardless of their age or financial standing. In some ways, investing time, energy, and trust in a future with the mother of one's children seems like a voluntary relationship or the next choice in a long line of choices that extends from an emerging relationship with a child. Granted, some men view their decision to have a relationship with their child as voluntary as well.

Unwed fathers may approach the relationship with mothers of their children as an attempt to answer the very basic question "Is there an 'us'?" The unique twist for these couples is that a sense of "us" emerges primarily from their complementary roles as coparents—not necessarily through sharing intimacies and visions as romantic partners. By severing partnering from parenting, fathers and mothers give priority to their relationships with their child. The child is the impetus to build a family. Unmarried parents of a newborn have to communicate daily about numerous child-care issues and routines. Unlike established partners who can turn more easily to a mainstream template depicting what their parenting roles should be, unmarried couples who start an intimate relationship built on ties to another family member may need to be more innovative and flexible as they develop shared expectations.

A child may even be the impetus for staying together as a family. Partners can discover and share new aspects of themselves as they express love and care for a young child. This clear purpose—"We're together because of our child"—can provide its own momentum and foster family continuity even when partners are uncertain about their relationship ties. Many fathers report that their commitments are unique simply because "she's the mother of my children." Bryan, a twenty-one-year-old father, had only seen his son once, at his birth. Two months later, he continued to struggle with his ex-girlfriend's mother, who denied him the chance to be with the baby. He was further frustrated by a dismal job picture, working eight jobs in six months only to be laid off each time. Bryan could not even buy his son a Christmas present because he had tied his commitments to his child and his child's mother so closely that they became synonymous.

> We really did help each other. The love I have for her . . . it's the same love I have for my son, in a fatherly kind of way. When I see my son, I see her. So by me and my babymama having a good relationship in the future, because of my son . . . we could just be a big happy family.

Obviously, the stress of a pregnancy, birth, and parenting can also rapidly accelerate and destabilize tenuous relationships between uncommitted partners. How individuals handle these experiences is partially tied to the demographic characteristics of the woman who gets pregnant, has an out-of-wedlock birth, or opts for an abortion. In general, relationships involving persons of color and persons with the fewest human-capital resources are most likely to be affected by fertility-related experiences over a period of time. Abortion rates are related to complex attitudinal and behavioral patterns associated with contraception, pregnancy, and childbearing. Young women, unmarried women, and women at 200 percent of the poverty line are more likely to have abortions than women who do not share these demographic and socioeconomic characteristics.[32] African American and Hispanic women account for higher rates of abortions than whites, although the total number of abortions is similar across racial and ethnic groups.[33] That said, when unmarried partners develop a shared commitment to a baby it can sometimes provide the necessary family incentives that such couples need to gain stability.

One way to understand these unmarried couples' relationships is to rethink our accepted vision of the foundation of a family. Normative assumptions about the sequences of young adults' decisions—"First comes love, then comes marriage, then comes a baby in a baby carriage"—imply that a child is the end result of an established marital relationship.

However, since the mid-1970s this sequence of transitions with the birth of a child as the final event has become far less common for young adults.[34] What is the foundation of a family, if not the couple relationship? These couples' experiences suggest that commitment to partnering can be built on a shared commitment to a common family member. A specific "we-ness" as a couple might emerge from a larger commitment to a "we-ness" as a family and a related commitment to "we-ness" as parents of a child, placing a child—not a couple—at the center of family life, with an array of parents and family members distributed in a network of care and support.

Few policies or programs identify unwed-couple families in this way. From a normative perspective, "incomplete" relationships, especially those involving low-income partners, call out for intervention to move them toward marriage and coresidence. Legitimizing these couples and securing commitment, from a policy perspective, promotes stability, reduces dependence on state assistance, and can enhance health and well-being for children and families alike. The first wave of programs under welfare reform in 1996 sought to establish paternity for unwed fathers. As state policies define providing obligations, a father has "a legal bond with the child through enhanced identification and paternity establishment mechanisms."[35] Paternity is based on an assumption that the biological father of a child is the marital partner of the child's mother. In many states, husbands do not sign the paternity certificate for their wife's children. However, an unmarried father must sign the paternity certificate to indicate that he is indeed the biological father. Over the past decade, advances in DNA testing and new hospital-based programs have made it easier to identify and to obtain signatures from unwed fathers. These advances have introduced new relationship dynamics into the policy arena, as mothers and fathers must indicate clearly the intentions of their relationship, in a public way, through paternity establishment.[36]

Many fathers are quite supportive of securing a legal bond with their child. However, some resist paternity establishment because it is linked immediately to a financial support order and less indirectly to a commitment to the mother of their children. For low-income couples in particular, the hesitance to "turn yourself in" (formally acknowledge paternity) emerges from their need to maintain the mother's public aid benefits in a difficult job market and the fear that paternity would lead to a reduction in or loss of these benefits.[37] Fathers like Miles look back at their transition to first-time fathering and realize that they did not want to jeopardize their tenuous hold on income. "I don't have paternity established for Little Mike," Miles admits. "Since [my partner] wasn't working at the time, and I was working at the car wash, we didn't have enough money coming in.

To keep her [welfare benefits] coming in, she didn't say anything." Some states have created hospital and community programs to establish paternity through an administrative consensual process and to avoid the conflict-prone atmosphere in court proceedings. Although voluntary efforts to establish paternity often reduce conflict initially, they do not ensure that relationships will go smoothly. For instance, even after Tremaine agreed to acknowledge his daughter, her mother attempted to replace his name with that of another boyfriend.

> She didn't come to court proceedings. She was represented by the state, and I got the letters and went down to clear it up. I had to defend myself. She put in my name . . . something to do with paternity, she said. But she put the wrong name on it, and it didn't work out the way she thought it would.

In the rush to establish the paternity of unmarried mothers' children, many states neglect to examine all potential biological fathers among the casual intimate partners for welfare recipients on their caseloads. Some fathers have petitioned to disestablish paternity.[38]

Some unmarried fathers rely on paternity establishment to deescalate tensions with the mothers of their children. They want to guarantee a legal relationship with their child in case the mother tries to remove the child from their lives. Regardless of the conflict between the couple, this effort sends a message that men are serious about being involved fathers. Bird, a twenty-year-old former gang member, knows, "I want to establish paternity, so she can't say, 'You can't see your shorty, and I'm taking her [child] somewhere else.'" External arbitration of paternity can help to decrease the tension over coparenting expectations similar to what an older father, Curt, experienced. Curt refused to pay child support because his girlfriend would not allow him to see his daughter. He felt that he "shouldn't take care of someone I can't even see. She took me to court, and I never denied paternity. Took the test and [was happy with the result]."

A second wave of programs is aimed at low-income couples more specifically through marriage promotion and counseling.[39] Over two hundred community-based programs were funded with grants under the Healthy Marriage Initiative of the Administration of Children and Families in the U.S. Department of Health and Human Services in the mid-2000s. Some of these programs include a faith-based approach to relationship development and commitment. This approach has been more contentious than paternity establishment, because many question the government's role in promoting marriage in the first place.[40] Some programs are based on assumptions that unmarried parents do not want to be married and need to be taught traditional marital values, although research with these parents does not support these assumptions.[41] Couple-based relationship skills—and the programs that provide such skills-based training—may affect parenting relationships by increasing positive support among coparents and decreasing conflict.[42] Programs that nurture men's and women's engagement with employment and that secure good wages for unwed parents may play a significant role in moving these fragile couples towards marriage over time.[43]

But are these relationships actually "incomplete"? Is the goal of initiatives to promote nurturance through interaction with children, or to promote nurturance as a by-product of securing a coresident marital relationship? What are the consequences of the latter approach? In the wake of coparents dissolving their intimate ties, one consequence is for the father and child to have a weakened relationship or none at all.

Gatekeeping After a Breakup

Evan knew Beth when they both attended a Catholic elementary school in Muncie, Indiana. Despite their six-year age difference, they dated throughout high school, and Beth had a baby at eighteen. Evan was already a steady drinker when, by the time Evan was twenty-three, the birth of his first son prompted him to get a job at the local mill and to marry Beth. He had drunk a great deal even before this, but that did not stop them from getting married. "When she got pregnant again, we didn't even have the first one paid for at the hospital," he recalls. "Yeah, we weren't doing very good." Evan and Beth divorced when Mitchell was five and Stephen was two, as Evan continued to drink and gamble, losing jobs along the way. He paid child support for a few years, and Beth brought them to see their father "when she needed a sitter, and I was not doing things just to be with them." But when she and the boys moved to Tennessee to live with her parents, Evan stopped his monthly payments. "I didn't get to see them, so I quit paying and moved to Florida. Figured I wasn't coming back." Over the next few years, Evan was incarcerated for driving under the influence of alcohol as well as nonpayment of child support. He has not seen his sons in five years, and his ex-wife refuses to have any contact with him.

The breakup circumstances surrounding Evan and Beth's relationship reflect a common transition for many couples with children. Two people establish a sense of togetherness, a commitment to continue together as a couple and as parents. However, they decide at some point that they are unable to continue as a couple and they end their intimate relationship. Although Evan and Beth were married, committed couples who break up yet continue parenting include nonmarital cohabiting or even noncohabiting couples. In other words, our focus during this transformative moment in a couple's relationship is not on individuals' residential status but rather on a shift in these parents' commitment to continue as a couple.

A lack of trust may lead some coparents to break up. The shared sense of familial "we-ness" that holds coparents together may dissolve because of infidelity or because one partner or both partners fear that the other is having a sexual relationship with someone else. As Rusty's and Evan's relationships illustrate, mothers often anticipate that the fathers of their children may seek new partners when the novelty of marriage wears off or when men's personal struggles with employment, respect, or even simply "growing up" overwhelm a stable commitment to a family. Infidelity is complicated in that lack of trust may involve not only sexual but emotional commitments. Some fathers, for example, worry that the support that partners offer them through many difficult circumstances—job loss, depression, substance use, incarceration—will dissolve once their partners find a new boyfriend who is not struggling with these problems. Fathers refer to "the summer shake," when their partners find new romantic relationships.[44] For coparents, sharing weaknesses and managing difficult disclosures are always a challenge to maintaining healthy relationships over time. Additionally, the capacity to trust the mother or father of one's child is often linked to a sense of respect.

The concept of maternal gatekeeping describes mothers' primary roles in directing or possibly rejecting fathers' efforts toward involvement with their children after a breakup. In studies of divorce, primarily among middle-class (and usually white) couples, researchers show how mothers exercise their ability to manage and control fathers' access to their children in exchange for power within the spousal relationship.[45] Many gatekeeping studies link discouragement of paternal involvement to mothers' attitudes, but few link this to actual family processes.[46] In many married couples, mothers likely negotiate relationships with fathers in order to encourage and support nurturance as well as to direct and even separate men from their children.

In what physical locations do men interact with their children? This is an immediate concern for fathers after a relationship breakup.[47] Months and even years of daily contact and conversation often end. Both care arrangements and patterns of conflict with children begin to change as fathers and mothers struggle to redefine where and how father-child relationships can unfold. Troubled relationships turn areas that were familiar sites of memorable daily interactions—the family kitchen or living room, the backyard or park down the block, the in-laws' house, the church, or even the school—into places of tension and discomfort. Many fathers, especially those who are nonresident, feel unwelcome in these formerly receptive locations, and they cannot quickly substitute alternative places to express themselves as fathers. Many lack resources to do so, their children may resist change, and children's mothers—often justifiably—are not quick to accept new spots for father-child interaction that may be risky or unsafe. As a result, some fathers opt for public places, such as shopping malls, restaurants, arcades, or other consumer-oriented sites that reduce some of the possible tension of the more-proven intimate areas. Some of the fortunate few with plenty of discretionary income turn into "Disneyland dads," willing to buy their children whatever they want and take them wherever they ask to go.[48] However, many of these sites also curtail fathers' opportunities to express themselves in nurturing ways, for example, by discouraging private talks and snuggling.

The well-established middle- and upper-middle-class father is typically better equipped than the low-income dad to negotiate favorable terms for divorce and custody. Moreover, the affluent father can more easily create a home that provides his children with their own bedrooms and space, and he can produce a home environment that affords him a wider range of opportunities to nurture his child and share family rituals in a comfortable setting.[49] Thus, the father who has limited access to his child and cannot afford to create a cozy family-home environment is in greatest need of programs that promote physical settings that foster a father's nurturance.

Another typical challenge for a nonresident father is the need to adjust to his former romantic partner's getting involved with someone else. The mother's new boyfriend or partner introduces another layer of complexity to how a father communicates with the coparent, the coparent's new partner, and children. In some instances, the new partner or stepfather may act as a father ally and help to minimize the mother's gatekeeping, which could restrict a father's access to his children.[50] In ideal circumstances, the stepfather may reduce tension between ex-partners and help a father to feel more welcome and comfortable in public settings that include him (school functions, sporting events, birthday parties). In many instances, though, stepfathers and fathers are suspicious and jealous of each other.

Men who express themselves as some type of stepfather must confront their own set of issues with gatekeeping as their relationship unfolds with a single parent. Research with heterosexual stepfathers shows the wide variation in the ways mothers come to incorporate stepfathers into their preexisting family dance, defined by shared rituals, common understandings, and a reservoir of family trust.[51] At various points throughout the evolution of a man's relationship with a woman who has a child with another man, the mother can thwart or foster the stepfather's opportunities to develop a bond with her child. Being sexually involved with a single mother also does not necessarily mean that the mother will encourage her partner to assume a fatherly presence around her children. And the man also may not be looking for anything resembling a stepfather-stepchild relationship. Concerns about what if any role a stepfather will play in disciplining a child can be especially confusing. Moreover, when men (and their partners) develop romantic intimacy it may force some to hide or distort their feelings for a partner in order to protect the children. Some children may not even be aware that their mother is dating someone.

A number of policies are in place that shape couple relationships after breakups and also, indirectly, father-child relations. A federal child support policy was enacted alongside the Welfare Reform Act of 1996 with the purpose of extending a rigorous system of court-ordered child support and collection that stretched across state boundaries. By the mid-2000s, almost 75 percent of child support cases had support orders, with over half of the cases resulting in collection of child support awards. Child support collection rates have more than doubled, from 20 percent in 1996 to 54 percent in 2006, with a total collection of almost $25 billion in 2006.[52] These child support funds have passed through state collection agencies to children and custodial parents, who are primarily mothers. The increase in the rate of collection of child support from welfare families is lower, increasing from 13 percent in 1996 to 32 percent in 2006.

These policies benefit children and mothers, and most fathers recognize these benefits. But they also dramatically transform relationships between the couples. Policy intervention focusing on families can be a reliable protection for some mothers, but other parents perceive it as an unwelcome intrusion. If anything, child support policies call into doubt the intentions of both custodial and noncustodial parents, which can add to the sense of distrust and blame in the wake of a breakup. In contrast, policies that obligate noncustodial parents' payment of child support—sometimes through garnished wages— could be tailored to also hold custodial parents more accountable for how these funds are spent on children.

A child support system with a more rigorous accountability element— although certainly controversial—could significantly reduce the interpersonal, negotiated aspects of nonresident fathers' (or mothers') monthly payments to the resident parent. This is timely because many men claim that their former partners spend much of their child support on themselves rather than on their children.[53] Although many of these claims are false or exaggerated, others, regrettably, are true. A revamped system, perhaps restricted to fathers who fulfill their financial obligations and do not abuse their children or former partners, could enable nonresident fathers (especially those with shared custody) to have a better sense of how their child support payments are being used.

A key question frames much of the debate about a child support system with more rigorous accountability: Should fathers who are conscientious about their child support obligations be entitled to at least know that their money is actually being spent on their children?[54] One specific option is to modify the child support debit cards that have been adopted by a number of states in recent years.[55] Unlike the cards currently in use, monthly itemized statements would be sent to both resident and nonresident parents documenting the preceding month's purchases. To ensure accountability, the cards might also be structured so that cash withdrawals were not permitted. Mandatory mediation sessions could provide parents an opportunity to learn about how this card works, and modifications for its usage might be negotiated in that context.

The nonresident parent has a moral and legal obligation to pay child support, and the resident parent is morally (though not legally at the present time) obligated to use these funds on her or his children. Is it not reasonable to assume, then, that the nonresident parent should be entitled to have at least some sense of how his or her child support payments are being spent—especially if money is being automatically withdrawn from his or her paycheck?

Critics believe this type of card would represent an unwarranted intrusion into the personal affairs of the resident parent. But this view seems indefensible because it is generally expected that child support payments are to be used to provide goods and services for children anyway. Perhaps the most volatile aspect of this scheme would involve the process of adjudicating nonresident parents' complaints regarding resident parents' spending habits. We suspect that the loudest, and least valid, complaints would come from resident parents who have not been conscientious about using child support payments on their children. Although it is beyond the scope of our comments to outline a specific structure and set of guidelines in this regard, suffice it to say that it seems wise to provide resident parents with a considerable amount of discretion in their financial decisionmaking while providing nonresident parents with a reasonable method to draw attention to blatant examples of inappropriate behavior. In short, this card would have the effect of making resident parents more accountable for how they spend child support payments than they currently are, but the program should not be structured in a way that gives nonresident parents a means for harassing resident parents.

If this type of program were to be introduced on a trial basis, research should assess whether the costs associated with administering it would be offset by a comparable increase in the payment of child support.

We anticipate that the child support debit card would have little effect on fathers who are already very committed to their children financially and emotionally. It also would probably not affect the behavior of fathers who have no interest in maintaining a connection with their children. However, we speculate that such a program could have a noticeable impact on more marginal fathers who show at least limited interest in being involved with their children. In addition, it would be important to study whether this program encourages some nonresident fathers to feel more at ease about their financial responsibilities to their children, which in turn might facilitate healthier coparenting, better father-child relationships, and greater child support compliance.

To some extent, a policy that enables financially responsible nonresident fathers to know that their money (at least a significant portion) is being used to meet their children's needs could yield outcomes similar to those produced by the government serving as the enforcement agent for mandatory withholding legislation. Together, both approaches could reduce the potential animosity between former partners because they would lessen the uncertainty and negotiated aspects of the process of transferring resources from one parent to the other. No doubt tension will still exist if the mechanisms to document fathers' contributions lead women to feel as though a former partner is monitoring them or if nonresident fathers, on viewing the records of expenditures, perceive that specific types of purchases were unnecessary or otherwise inappropriate.[56]

Finally, some states have implemented mandatory mediation sessions for divorcing couples with minor children that can help couples better anticipate and understand the struggles they will face as nonresiding coparents who have severed their romantic ties. An important feature of the mediation programs would be to help both fathers and mothers see more clearly how they may be affected if their former partner gets involved with someone new.

Babymamadrama in Complex Couple Arrangements

There is no litmus test to identify individuals who make up an active "couple" in the context of coparenting. Sometimes romantic relationships for couples with children occur outside marriage and cohabitation, and over time individuals who were once part of a couple drift in and out of multiple statuses, including cohabitation, romantic involvement, friendship, or lack of contact.[57] Some fathers referred to "babymamadrama" as the daily hard work that transpires as mothers and fathers who are not committed to a romantic relationship sort out the obligations, trust issues, and communication necessary to be successful coparents. The strong policy focus on marriage as a successful achieved status has hindered efforts to identify positive relationships among unmarried parents. Thus, we focus on how social policies and programs usually misunderstand or ineffectively try to manage complex unmarried couples.

As discussed previously, child support laws are based on the identification of a biological father through paternity establishment. Men in different phases of residence, or in marital and nonmarital commitments, are liable to pay child support. For unmarried couples in middle-class communities, arrangements for subsequent financial support emerge alongside new coparenting demands and ambiguous relationship dynamics. These couples must navigate the legal system to ensure movement of resources to the custodial parent in their efforts to be good parents.

Poor fathers, in contrast, are more likely to take part in complex family arrangements, and their child support orders may be quite distinct. Fathers whose children receive public assistance are ordered to pay child support to the state as a reimbursement of state welfare assistance. For over fifteen years, since 1996, few states have allowed child support funds to "pass through" to mothers and children who receive welfare. Studies with low-income fathers find that these child support orders provide little incentive or motivation for father to make financial contributions, and they may exacerbate conflict among couples.

Corey lives in a room in a housing project on the South Side of Chicago, but he aspires to be a wrestler in World Wrestling Entertainment. In his mid-twenties, he has two preschool-age boys with a former girlfriend, he has just completed paternity establishment, and he has been served with a child support order. He and his ex-partner have different perspectives on how he was identified to pay child support, and Cory feels betrayed by her in a way that disrespects his motivation to provide and be involved with his sons:

> When I was going for child support, I had second thoughts. I was kind of mad, because I thought she put them on me. And I didn't have no job at the time, but she said that public aid did it. People try to tell her what to do and she do it. It's "he said, she said," because some say the system made her do it, or that she wanted to do it. I really couldn't tell. I was gonna take care of my kids, even with no money, I was going to be there no matter what.

Beyond these relationship dynamics, poor fathers who pay child support find that their children do not see their payments and instead the payments end up with the state. As a result, many of these fathers go underground to find "off the books" employment—seasonal jobs, earning cash in hand, and temporary services.[58] By going out of the mainstream to find work, fathers can make more money without garnishment. They can also contribute when they feel that they can and give money directly to their children's mothers, which earns them trust and credit with the mother.

After the rush to set up a system of paternity establishment in the mid-1990s, many low-income fathers in particular were pushed quickly into paying child support to recoup welfare payments. However, only about half of all fathers with noncustodial biological children who received welfare received an order, most likely because they could not be identified and located. Of these, only 30 percent reported paying child support, and child support paid by these fathers actually declined a bit from 1996 through the mid-2000s, when only $2.1 billion was recouped in child support payments.[59] The majority of unpaid child support in many states is owed by fathers who make less than $10,000 per year.[60]

Other policy initiatives with low-income unwed parents also face tremendous challenges. How can policymakers promote marriage as a solution if a father has children with three mothers? Or a mother has children with multiple fathers? The common outcome for what many call "serial parenting" is that fathers become less and less involved with their first-born children. Strategies are needed to identify and provide counseling services to parents involved in multipartner parenting. If clear service options are institutionalized in a community, individuals may flock to programs or be recruited into them through public outreach. These programs must address the formidable challenges associated with individuals' lack of trust for each other and their often limited commitments.

Incarceration is an obstacle that can complicate these tenuous and uncommitted relationships.[61] After two years of separation, Evan had begun to spend time regularly with Nick, his five-year-old son. He felt accepted by his ex-partner because "she's a bit more considerate than my [other] ex, and she's not hateful. She's got a decent new relationship. If she finds me around him or her drinking, she'll straight up call the law . . . so I know not to mess with that fire." However, the new relationship that Evan had begun with his son was jeopardized when he was incarcerated. The physical distance and the constrained times for visitation seemed to be the final straw for Nick's mother and her tolerance of Evan's efforts. Despite his pleas, she decided to move her family to Florida and start over down south.

If I get these visitation passes [I asked her] if she will bring him over. It's gonna be hard for me to do. Pay a hotel for her and her boyfriend to come here so I can see him, but I'd do it . . . And [the boyfriend] said, "Yeah I've heard that before." And then he said, "Well we'll go on down [to Florida] and when you get off, you come down there and buy you a house down the road and you can come visit."

As they drift in and out of various intimate relationships, some fathers maintain a special connection to the mothers of their children. To some extent, by having children together these couples share something that still offers a potential future—usually in the form of marriage or a similar commitment. In these "suspended" relationships coparents find that they can be nonexclusive yet retain a promise of commitment.

Children are often the impetus for relationships between unmarried parents, and they also promote the continuity of suspended relationships.[62] Unmarried parents continue to communicate with each other if they are both involved in their children's lives. Often, they consider returning to their former partners or they choose to stay in conflicted relationships to preserve contact with their children. Akida, a twenty-three-year-old father of two, struggles to make sense of his partnership and its relation to his fathering.

> I don't see us having a future. [The mother of my daughter is] struggling, I'm struggling, two people struggling can't do nothing. I'm always considering how I'd rather raise my daughter without her mother. I realize it's impossible, she's got to be in her mother's life, just like she's got to be in my life. It comes back to "it's all about her," and keeping her mother happy.

Unmarried parents cannot dismiss the persistent need for more resources that eats away at the potential for successful relationships. The sporadic nature of having steady work teases both men and women with promises of formalizing relationships, and it obscures future plans for establishing family households. Leon feels ill prepared to settle down with his common-law wife of twenty years:

> I always say she's my wife, we've been together since seventh grade, and there's nothing stopping us from getting married. We just ain't really right. I'm not working, but she's working. When I was working, she wasn't working. But I'm going to be with my kids, hoping that me and her will get married. The only thing I have to do is get my feet in the door, and we can get this thing going right.

Other unmarried parents accept the uniqueness of suspended relationships—complete with strengths, promises, and limitations. Young fathers like Amir realize that real relationships may be quite different than what they had expected.

> The more times passes, we're not in touch on no kind of level. . . . I can only look down the line to when we're forty-something. Maybe we'll only have one other relationship and we're both still around. Our lives probably won't be a nice family barbecue or nothing like that, right?

These unresolved commitments to a child's mother are increasingly complicated because more fathers and mothers have children with multiple partners. Studies suggest that 8 percent of fathers are responsible for multiple-partner fertility, with higher levels for low-income men.[63] These are complex interactions because they require us to understand what happens over time within each coparental relationship as well as across multiple coparental relationships. Because intimate partnerships with mothers of first children are frequently unresolved, tensions arise when fathers develop new romantic interests. Many men engage in what might be considered active kin work, doing the emotion work necessary to iron out bad feelings and secure a basic understanding that permits them to be involved with children of different partners. Gil, a thirty-five-year-old father of two biological children and two stepchildren, struggled over many years to have a "sit-down" and establish understanding between the two mothers of his children.

> My wife loves my other daughter. Her mother has been over here, my wife has met her, sat down and talked. There's no animosity between them. I'm married to my wife, but Jackie's mom still loves me, because I'm the father of her first child. It just works. I don't know why. I think we all have an understanding for each other. My children understand who I am, who I'm married to. They know the boundaries, my wife does, the other mothers do. They can't expect more than what I do. As long as everyone has that understanding, it all falls into place.

To appreciate more fully how multiple-partner parenting plays out over time we need to consider how mothers not only restrict but also encourage nonresident biological and social fathers to be involved with children. As we discussed in relation to father-child bonds, mothers may pursue nonresident fathers to fulfill conventional expectations as fathers and even partners, all the while protecting children from harm.[64] However, the early stages of recruiting fathers may be marked by fits and starts, competition and cooperation, guilt and gratification, trust and wariness. In large part, the consequences of mothers' recruitment are unclear for the intimate relationships with fathers. Although these mothers describe recruitment through clear-cut offers to "pay to stay," the daily process of recruitment is actually quite open-ended.[65] Most mothers heavily invest in biological fathers, so rejecting them means letting go of the chance of legitimacy with fathers as well as the promise of marriage with a partner. In practical terms, they may simply need someone to watch their children when they work.

Married to My Child?

Most popular, political, and legal assessments of a father's involvement with his child are filtered through the lens of his commitment to a relationship with his wife or partner, the child's mother. Ideally, a lifelong commitment to his child begins with and is reinforced by a marital promise to the child's mother. However, we and many others have found that couples are often unwilling and unable to uphold a lifelong commitment to each other. Instead, their real "marriage" is frequently with their children. Bird, a former gang member with an infant daughter, captures this sentiment: "When she wakes up, I'll be holding her hand. I'll be there, beside her. I feel like I'm married to my kid. Through thick and thin, rain, sleet or snow, whatever you need, I'm there."

Do public and private initiatives focus on couple relationships at the expense of dismissing or underestimating the significance of father-child relationships? As Dowd asks, how would we need to transform public and private initiatives if we redefined fatherhood as a father-child relationship that did not privilege marriage but was flexible enough to recognize the value of actual conduct within marriage or other relationships?

> The support of marital fatherhood is appealing because it suggests a commitment to a long-term relationship that accords with the developmental benefits to children from consistency of care and stability in their familial relationships. If fatherhood is understood as a permanent relationship, then marriage might arguably best support that understanding. However, the breakdown of marital patterns, as evidenced in high divorce rates, nonmarital birth rates, cohabitation rates, and men's nonmarital and post-divorce parenting, argues against a definition tethered to marriage.[66]

In line with Bird's alternative use of the marriage label, Dowd's vision of fatherhood would acknowledge that men's nurturance of children continues within and beyond traditional marriages, healthy alternative arrangements such as cohabitation, or even conflict-riddled coparenting.

Partnering and coparenting relationships affect how fathers see and respond to their children. We have stressed the value of trust and communication dynamics between a wide range of fathers and mothers, within and outside shared households, and within and apart from marriage. The capacity to share weaknesses and disclose difficult experiences and to turn trust into a strong sense of respect for one's partner can buttress men's efforts to be nurturing fathers. Likewise, emotional or sexual infidelity can undermine close relationships and shake men's sense of competent parenting. Unfortunately, crafting policies and programs that promote trusting alliances between two parents remains a challenging task, as there are few effective mechanisms by which to shape healthy relationships. Numerous local programs have tailored a range of healthy marriage counseling programs, faith-based initiatives, and mediation efforts to encourage couple formation and maintenance, with mixed results. Many of the more durable alliances must be built informally within families themselves.

When couples come together because of a lifelong commitment to children, they may find support for their romantic relationship and their parenting among their family and friends. How trust is managed in heterosexual and homosexual committed couples is likely reflected in the expectations fathers manage within a broader set of close relations. Trust is critical to a network of adults that prioritizes the well-being of children at the center of a circle of kin and friends. Or, in another sense, a couple's "we-ness" can emerge from a broader commitment to the "we-ness" they experience as part of an intergenerational family legacy. Thus, to extend our focus on couples we need to explore how men's nurturance of children is often influenced by the larger network of immediate and extended family members.

= Chapter 5 =

Kin Work and Networks of Care

[In] my family, children are everything. . . . People in the family, when it comes to the children, people gonna do what they can do. If you need some help or something, you gonna get that help. We'll rely on each other. It's like a circle. Everybody looks out for everybody. Because it takes a village to raise our children. That's how we taught, that's how it was taught to us. And my grandmother, she refused to let any child born into our family disappear [outside of the family].

Ben is lucky to be a part of a family network that helps him to be a strong father. At twenty-three, he has hustled the streets of Indianapolis and found part-time work in construction. He has also struggled with substance abuse and short bouts of incarceration. With four children from two different mothers and a spotty employment record, Ben could see himself as a failure as a partner and as a father. Instead, he remains upbeat about his ability to work with his mother, grandmother, and siblings to welcome his children into his large family. He insists that "it's not just the mother, father, and child—it's the family child." For example, his younger cousins were

> . . . in the worst state, because my aunt was on drugs. But when we have a problem, someone in the family steps up to take those kids in. Nobody outside our family has had to adopt anyone else from the family. If we had a problem, someone in the family steps up and takes them in.

Growing up in rough communities, Ben received help from his sister when no one else stepped up. When he took college courses and when he was incarcerated, "she was there, she is the backbone of our family. She takes care of me, no matter what." Now she runs a day care next door to their apartment, and her children and Ben's children participate in the center. To show his appreciation, Ben runs errands for her if she's tied up watching her own children in the child-care center. This united family front of support has allowed Ben to stand firm against the demands of his oldest child's mother. After years of absence from her son's life, and upon learning that Ben is engaged to his current partner, she insisted that Ben return their son to her. His sister has played an instrumental role in providing official paperwork on his son from the care center confirming that Ben has had informal custody of him since birth.

It is Ben's grandmother, however, who has done the most to secure Ben's status as a responsible young father. When Ben's first child was born three years ago, he was skeptical as to whether or not he was the biological father. His grandmother helped him to understand his child's mother's perspective.

> I got stories on top of stories. My baby's mama told everybody that the baby was mine, but I know she sleeps around. I ain't trying to hear it. That story got to my grandma, and she said, "Look, did you have sex with her? Did you use protection? No. What's the odds of that being your baby?" And I be like, man, the odds are there, but what's the odds of everybody else? My grandma said, "Let me see it, when the baby get here." At first, I didn't want nothing to do with [the baby]. But she pointed out, "How would you like it, a baby whose father didn't want anything to do with it?"

Family members can navigate the fragile communication between paternal and maternal kin to find a role for a young father like Ben and thereby preserve an intergenerational legacy. Some family members may play a more limited role in men's nurturance of their children, but a critical role nonetheless. Lombardo turned to his mother and father to act as caregivers while he worked through a twelve-month stay in work release that resulted from a charge of domestic violence with his wife. A veteran of the Gulf War, he dealt with severe bouts of anger, which he managed with daily medication. His job cutting trees did not provide a big enough paycheck to support his family: his wife and her two preschool-age children from a previous marriage.

Lombardo was fixated on his sporadic interaction with his twelve-year-old son, Jake, born to a girlfriend who did not stay committed to him through the course of his deployment overseas. He was ashamed that he had fallen away from his son, but with his parents' help he has begun to communicate with him regularly.

> My relationship with Jake over the past years has been slim to none. I didn't really have a relationship with him. I mean I love him to death now. It's hard to call because he lives in Delphi and it is so expensive to call from these phones. My mom and dad got me a pay phone card and I call and talk to him. I try to call once a week. Just to say hey. I don't talk very long. He knows where I'm at. He knows what's going on and he understands that it is expensive. He's just happy that I call him to say hi. When I never used to. Maybe it doesn't matter how much I say or what I even say it's just the fact that I am calling and I do care.

Lombardo's parents' farm also figures into his plans to pull all of his children together for visits outside the correctional facility. He is allowed two four-hour passes each month. Lombardo tries to schedule visits when he can pick up his wife and her two girls and then go to his parents' house to see Jake. "I'll hop on their four-wheeler, and now I let him drive it. All the kids hang out together, play games, have dinner. It's hard to do anything really, though, in the two hours I end up with, before I got to turn around and come back."

We often assume that fathers and mothers manage care for their children on their own, a belief reflected by the American values touting self-sufficiency and family privacy. However, the actual day-to-day challenges and strategies that parents employ to secure care for their children usually demand that they draw on extended kin and friend networks.[1] Most policies and programs would focus on Ben's child support payments or the state of Lombardo's conflicted marriage; few policymakers would recognize the safety net of kin members critical to these two fathers. To address this oversight, we shed light on this expanded network by examining the interpersonal dynamics involving fathers and both paternal and maternal kin. We also consider informal care arrangements with friends. The shared obligations that fathers and their family members create provide social capital for children and even a sense of legacy that nurtures children above and beyond their relationships with their fathers. Yet family support is not simply about what kin offer to fathers. We also explore the emotional and physical work men invest in family relationships that helps them express themselves as involved fathers.

Fathers as Kin Workers

As we move beyond a focus on fathers as part of a parenting couple, our emphasis on family networks draws attention to the interdependence of lives as well as intergenerational relationships between grandparents, parents, and children. Most studies that situate parenting in the broad network of family members have emphasized how women as mothers coordinate care for children, aging parents, and other kin. For decades many poor women and women of color have cultivated supportive networks of family members as strategies for daily survival, although there is a debate as to how extensive and useful such kin systems are in contemporary globalized communities.[2] Scholars suggest that the use of kin-work strategies in most families crosses racial and ethnic boundaries and is found as well in various socioeconomic strata.[3]

Generally speaking, "kin work" encompasses the myriad ways adults and older children offer their support for daily living, social mobility, and care of younger children.[4] Most family networks are child focused, guided by parental figures performing kin-work tasks "to regenerate families, maintain lifetime continuities, sustain intergenerational responsibilities, and reinforce shared values."[5] Figure 5.1 depicts this type of child-focused familial network in which various adults within and outside the immediate family have some type of obligation to a particular child. The boxes on the right represent separate households occupied by maternal kin, perhaps grandparents and an aunt, and then two of the mother's supportive friends. On the left, the paternal grandparents and a close friend are shown to have ties to the focal child. For lots of actual families, the networks that define children's lives are much more expansive than that shown in Figure 5.1.

In Figure 5.2, we shift the focus to the father to illustrate how constructing a network of supportive family members requires the father's initiative and effort. When a mother and father are both faced with demands at the workplace, a married couple may turn to their in-laws for help in caring for children. A single custodial father may likewise seek support from *compadres*, or godparents, who could spend time with

Figure 5.1   Care Obligations in a Child-Focused Network

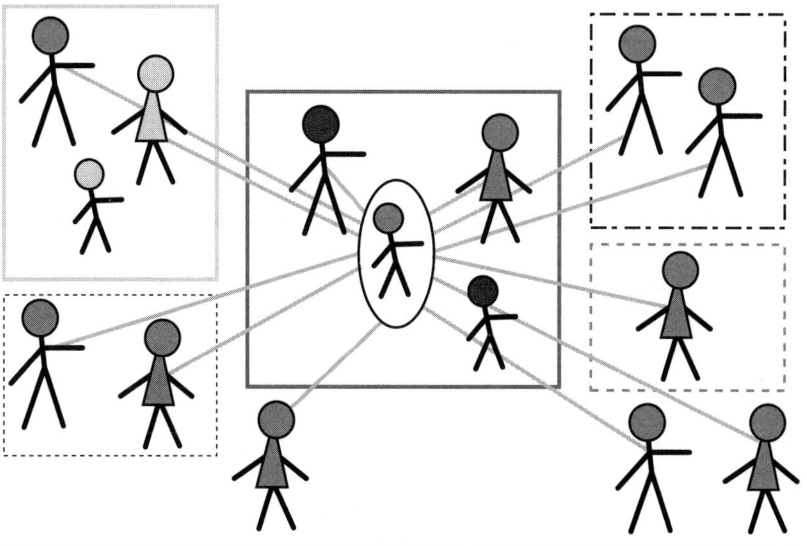

Source: Authors' figure.
Note: ——— lines represent ties between adults and children. ☐ and ☐ boxes represent new households for the father and mother and, in this example, new partnerships as well. ⌐‿⌐, ⌐‾‾⌐ , and ⌐·‿⌐ boxes represent households of extended kin. Stick figures shaded the same color represent original family groups.

Figure 5.2   Fathers' Kin Work in a Child-Focused Network

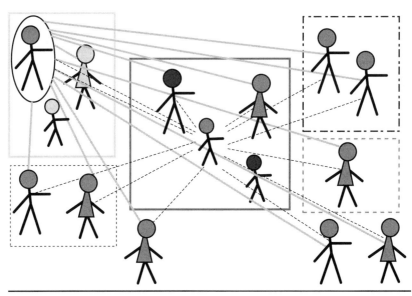

Source: Authors' figure.
Note: ═══ lines represent adult ties within family, extended kin, and friendship network from fathers' perspective. ····· lines represent ties between adults and children. ▭ and ▭ boxes represent new households for the father and mother and, in this example, new partnerships as well. ⌐ ¬ , └ ┘ , and ⌐.¬ boxes represent households of extended kin. Stick figures shaded the same color represent original family groups.

his daughter to allow him to exercise, go to church, or take a weekend trip. Figure 5.2 shows how the father is positioned in the network to manage relationships between the adults and child. In each case, the father plays a pivotal role in a system of coordinated and shared child-care responsibilities. The kin system can offer the father resources to help him forge his fatherly identity and, in some situations, secure involvement with his children.[6] For example, a mother may encourage a nonresident father to attend birthday celebrations and holiday events to spend time with his children. Ultimately, someone has to take the initiative to coordinate child-care arrangements, and this is often no simple task. To do this well, attention must be given to family dynamics that take into consideration individuals' personalities, sensibilities, and preferences.

How, exactly, do men help build and maintain a system of kin work in their extended families? In order to come together and agree on how to best nurture children in this large family group, fathers and family members must share expectations for behavior with each other. These expectations are based on trust and communication, and if someone in a family does not fulfill expectations as a caregiver, families can hold that person accountable. Parents, uncles and aunts, grandparents, or siblings who cannot be accountable to lend a hand in nurturing young children may find it difficult to garner emotional support and resources for themselves from family and friends. In this way, kin work opens up spaces in families for reciprocal parenting relationships that can be close and intimate but need not be confined to intimate couple relationships.

Social policy is often created in a vacuum with regard to what occurs informally in family networks. But outside the dictates of family law and the focus on biological coparents in family policies, fathers are active, critical players in systems of kin work that nurture their children. As we begin to account for family complexity and change over time, through recognition of divorce and separation, unmarried parents raising kids, children raised by grandparents, shifting residences, long-distance communication through new technologies, and multiple children with multiple partners, we can see that men's kin work is a common thread in all of these contexts. Recent research suggests that men in families see the "ideal" man as a successful financial provider as well as an involved father, son, husband, or partner.[7] In some sense, men want to "do it all" and are choosing to shoulder kin-work tasks that spouses previously assumed. To some extent the growing complexity of family networks calls for men to do more kin work in coordinating obligations of adults for children's well-being. But management of conflicting and reciprocal roles is not easy.

Lamont, the twenty-four-year-old military veteran of the Gulf War whom we met in chapter 2, is deeply enmeshed with his own childhood family as well as the lives of his daughter and her mother, his former girlfriend. To Lamont, being a father involves much more than his one-on-one relationship with his child or even the child's mother. Lamont feels the pull of multiple obligations and tries not to lose a sense of his own priorities.

> When I was younger, my mom always said, "You the man of the family," and that's really come true. Just to know that I was going to be a husband, a friend, a big brother, an uncle, a father, and all that in the same boat. I want to go learn, fall down and make mistakes on my own, and it's harder to do now that someone depends on you to be the benefactor in their lives. It's what my whole life is based on—family matters—and it's taking its toll.[8]

"My People": Negotiations with Paternal Kin

Paternal kin play critical roles in the lives of fathers and children. They may be the first kin members to commit to helping "the family's child," an expression of their obligations to these fathers. Although many men hold to an ideal of being self-sufficient, they quickly find that the needs of their children far outstrip what they and the mothers of their children can offer on their own.

As people live longer, paternal kin members may also be alive for many more years than in recent decades. Paternal grandparents may be active and ready to care for their grandchildren much later in life than grandparents in earlier decades. These changes in longevity and in fathers' capacity to coordinate care for their children have led to a growing number of intergenerational households in which men's parents move in with them to help care for grandchildren and receive care themselves.

For dual-income couples, paternal kin can serve a vital role by step-ping up to take care of children during transitions after school and on the weekends. As active older adults who live independently, some paternal kin embrace a more limited role of grandparent—a role that doesn't necessarily demand the challenges of disciplining children or doing housework for the family. Many grandparents admit that child care in older age is more enjoyable and more engaging for these rea-sons, as well as because of their own maturity and perspective from later in life.

Some of the men who are most precariously positioned to care for and support their children are young unwed fathers. Though they come from all kinds of backgrounds, they disproportionately are men of color and live in poverty. Often they are unemployed or underemployed and have limited education. Not surprisingly, many young fathers feel hard-pressed to achieve self-sufficiency in their own lives. Thus they turn to their own families for day-to-day help with personal challenges—which makes paternal kin a clear option when these fathers struggle to nurture their own children.

Men's own families offer them a context at a young age to learn how men care for children, how men act responsibly as providers, and how obligations to family members foster men's parenting. In poor communi-ties in particular, older siblings are valued and needed to tend to their younger siblings' needs. A shared responsibility for child nurturance in these extended families means that young men are asked to step up to shoulder responsibility for child care alongside mothers and fathers. Ironically, the adult-like actions of adolescent caregivers and off-time teen fathers provide unique opportunities to claim manhood status in the eyes of some.[9] Consistent with contemporary views on paths to manhood, young men are still more likely to construct their masculinity by acting hard as well as showing disdain for all things feminine or gay.[10] But the familial caregiving options available to some young men reinvigorate masculinity definitions pervasive in earlier centuries that emphasized distinctions between childhood and adulthood far more than perceived differences between manhood and womanhood.[11]

Men in supportive kin networks are recruited by other family members, usually their mothers or sisters, to be involved with and help care for younger children. Not only do many young fathers accept adult responsibilities at an early age, but also their mothers' and grandmothers' presence, advice, and support shape their ideas about family and parenthood.[12] Many have participated as younger men in their family's child care under these women's supervision. This socialization allows fathers to try out their roles and to learn the limits of family expectations for what male caregivers should and should not be. Ellis, an eighteen-year-old father of a newborn daughter in Indianapolis, was able to develop a strong sense at a young age of what was expected of him as a father. As he suggests, his involvement with his preschool-age nephews was not a "choice" but an imperative.

> It comes with a child, knowing what I have to do before I become a father. I had no choice but to accept that role because their daddy is not here, he's deceased. It's up to the uncles to step up and try to show them the right way. Their mama, we're not blood, she "has family," but she really don't have family, so we make her family. We've been there for her, because she still has medical bills.

Many young men growing up in poor families understand that their early socialization to caregiving is more than an opportunity for learning to be a parent. Their families rely on their additional pair of hands to help care for younger children. With relatively few men in kin networks who can offer consistent family child care, these young men make real contributions to critical child-care routines. Jordan is a young man who learned how to parent by default—he was the oldest child in a house with a single working mother.

> I was like the man of the house. At ten I was watching my little brothers. That's how I grew up, it's illegal, but I grew up faster than any other person. I was cooking at ten. I learned everything when she had to go to work, so I had to get up early and watch my brothers. I didn't have any help.

In these family contexts, young men were first and foremost encouraged to accept that men as well as women can be effective caregivers. They learned what was expected of them through experience: changing diapers, playing, reading, monitoring, and even providing discipline. Finally, they gave meaning to the roles they created as caregivers. They saw how being a father might affect them, and they could envision parenting their own children someday.

Not all men learn how to father through their own hands-on experiences with providing care for siblings and cousins. Many absorb parenting lessons and come to appreciate parenting obligations by watching family members. Eric has reached the end of his twenties after having a series of relationships resulting in three preschool-age children with three different mothers. As he struggled through a decade of hustling to make a living for himself and his children, he relied on what he had learned from his own mother about the importance of taking responsibility for one's family.

> That's how I was, my mother worked two jobs, sometimes three jobs. I remember one time it was thirteen of us in a three-room house. You know, so, my mother never turned her back on our family. . . . Big Mama, that's what they call her. Keeps all the family together. Keeps everybody in tact to make sure there's no arguing. See our immediate family, we've always been together all our life.

Living up to his mother's example has been difficult for Eric. He cannot secure the jobs that his mother had, stating, "I don't get it. . . . Am I not searching hard enough for a job, or maybe it's not meant for me to work right now." But he has been forthcoming in two different child support cases in an effort to guarantee access to his children. Navigating multiple family systems is confusing, with different dynamics and demands for each child. Eric again looks to his mother, who tells him, "Don't give up."

Needing assistance and guidance with their children, some young fathers depend on female-headed households and family networks.[13] Although they receive family support, the fathers are challenged to reciprocate in the true spirit of kin work in an extended family. Young men with children are embraced as part of a kin-work group but are just beginning to learn how to provide care for their children and others as well. Brian, nineteen, whom we introduced earlier in connection with paternity establishment and the health problems of his infant son, is trying to do the right thing by working closely with his son's mother, even though they are no longer together. Feeling overwhelmed and naïve, he struggles to manage child care for his baby in the midst of work and school demands. So Brian seeks out someone whom he trusts and is comfortable with, his cousin, to watch his son during the day while he goes to work. Realizing that his cousin also needs his support, he explains his swap of money and time:

> I've only been able to give her money when I have it. Nowhere near what normal babysitters will receive on a weekly basis, but she's been watching him for the duration of these last four or five months and that's just been a great boost for me. Whatever I can do [to reciprocate]. Being around for her kids, taking them places, or watching them, whatever, it's pretty much give and take. That's how I want to be with my relations with mostly anybody.

Paternal grandparents sometimes play unique roles in their grandchildren's lives, roles shaped by fathers' needs and capacities. Early on during the transition to fatherhood, when their sons have not established their own place to live, grandparents may provide the basics of everyday living—a room in a house, food, laundry, a telephone, a spare car to use—for fathers and their partners and children. This arrangement can benefit fathers even when they are separated from their children. Brando is incarcerated in a work-release program. He counts on his parents to provide for his girlfriend and his infant daughter; he calls them each night "out at my parents' place, just out of town. . . . My folks even have a budget that they give her, and I know about that too."

In kin networks, paternal grandmothers perform a range of kin-work roles for the well-being of their grandchildren. From the earliest interactions, mothers help their sons to establish relationships with their children. Paternal grandmothers are instrumental in defining paternity for younger fathers and in resolving conflicts between fathers and the mothers of their children.[14] Men's mothers also play key roles by keeping tabs on their grandchildren's health and well-being and by relaying that information to their sons. This link is an important family lifeline for men like Brando who live apart from their children because of separation or incarceration. Some paternal grandmothers care for children and keep them overnight, an important resource for both young fathers and mothers. They are often the trusted "bridge-care" providers during weekends, between work shifts, or on random days of urgent need.

However, depending on a shared system of kin work with men's family members is not without challenges. Some young fathers are anxious to move away from dependence; they want to assume the majority of responsibilities for their children. Jordan, a nineteen-year-old with one unborn child, describes the relationships among his family members as "very, very close-knit," but he insists that "I don't have anybody to rely on for anything like making ends meet or emotional support or taking care of me when I'm sick. . . . I'm just basically relying on myself. It's all about what I can do for myself, and my child, right now. Can't rely on my mother no more. I'm a grown man now." Similarly, Allan is careful not to burden his family with child care. At eighteen, he has two children with his girlfriend, and he has found some part-time work in spite of a short stay in jail. It is important to him to establish his independence and identity apart from his family, saying, "I'm not gonna put my burden on them. I'm not gonna have them watch my children because it's not their job. It's my job. It's my children. They raised their kids already. They already did they part, so I respect that."

The concern both young fathers and their paternal kin may have for the well-being of children may also lead to disagreement about how to best manage their nurturance. For instance, young fathers may struggle with other family members over who controls access to their children. Family members may perceive these young adults as potential risks to their children or other family members because of their lack of employment, dropping out of high school, or questionable activities with peers. They can require that young fathers relinquish control to them regarding the terms of their involvement with their children. In this scenario, men's mothers frequently act as gatekeepers, deciding when, where, and how their sons become involved with their own children. Taquan talks about how the relationship between his mother and his girlfriend has influenced his own interactions with his son. Living with his mother, he allows her to supervise his interactions, to make sure he is fulfilling his fatherly obligations, and to define the terms of his relationships.

> I'm [living] here, at my mom's, again . . . so it's really their [mother and girlfriend] arrangement and I just happen to be living here. So that's what allows me to see him [son] like that. It's not like I got my own place and that's the arrangement. So actually, I'm on someone else's time with him. I'm on my mama's time—his grandma's time—with him.

Paternal kin may also make decisions about young fathers' financial contributions to their children, within the context of what is "best" for the entire extended family network. Wesley is a young father in Chicago who completed his time in a boot camp program. As was their policy, program staff provided him with $2,200 to establish a new life, which included his girlfriend and their baby, to be born in two months. He sent the money ahead to his mother, to save it for his return. When he arrived at his mother's house, he found that "she had spent all of the money on baby stuff for my sister's baby. They were looking at me, and I was looking at them. My mama said, real soft, 'I spent that money on the baby.' I said, 'That's okay, Mom,' but I couldn't believe it."

Reliance on paternal kin can further divide fathers' commitments and strain relations with men's partners, the mothers of their children. Donnell, a young father with three sons, recognizes this conflict. He works in two fast-food restaurants and splits time between his mother's household, his girlfriend's household, and visits to the household of his former partner. He reflects, "Adriana, my girlfriend, is jealous of the bond that I have with my family. She feels like she is competing with my family for my attention, especially my mother. I would do anything for my mother. And Adriana, she ain't even my wife."

Sometimes, though, young as well as older fathers demonstrably place their partners and children above paternal kin. Thomas, a thirty-eight-year-old married stepfather with two teenage sons and a four-year-old daughter, Ginny, with his current wife, Stephanie, faced a difficult situation because his parents struggled to accept his new life as a stepfather. According to Stephanie, Thomas's parents caused a lot of trouble between them, and much of it had to do with how they treated their stepgrandchildren. Apparently, the parents always made a point of explicitly differentiating whose children belonged to whom. Stephanie recalls that this annoyed Thomas to the point that he once told his family, "This is my wife. And I love her very much. Those aren't my boys, but they are my boys. . . . And I love them very much, too. And unless you can treat them like family, then we just don't need to be around each other." Thomas even refused Stephanie's offer that he should take Ginny to see his family by himself. As he saw it, "We're a family. We're gonna go as a family or we're not gonna go at all."

For fathers who seek to establish their own independent capacities to support their children, there is both a clear benefit and a high price for the support and guidance of paternal kin. Their close family ties and, for younger fathers, the sustained committed relationships with their own mothers are concrete and have real impact. In contrast, fathers' relationships with other family members can appear to be tenuous. As with Donnell, bonds with his children's mother and her family may be quite important, but they are likely to be more ambiguous and even more short-lived than the connections to his own kin.

"Her People": Negotiations with Maternal Kin

A child's mother's family members can also validate the place a father has in his child's life or challenge his intentions and behavior as a nurturing parent. Maternal kin have considerable latitude in criticizing fathers. They are obligated to mothers and children first and foremost and to fathers only to the extent that they support mothers and children. Thus, maternal kin tend to commit fewer resources and limit their identity investment in their involvement with men's parenting. Nevertheless, when a coparenting couple sits down to arrange child care, find resources for children's well-being, or plan birthday celebrations, the couple often takes maternal kin into consideration. A man perceived as risky by his child's mother must work to gain her trust as well as her family's support. This can be difficult, as a mother's family members may have divergent views on how men can effectively nurture their children. Maternal kin may also contest how a father should enact fathering: as a breadwinner, as a caregiver, or as a quiet partner who follows the lead of the child's mother.

Young fathers in particular often work with their own paternal kin to navigate relations with the mothers of their children. Because children's mothers, like young fathers, need support and guidance, discussions of how to arrange care and provision for children often develop into a team negotiation, with maternal and paternal kin, especially grandmothers, playing leading roles. By agreeing on a step-by-step set of responsibilities that young fathers can handle—such as consistent visits, helping with an infant's physical care, and contributing small amounts of money and resources (such as the always appreciated and expensive bag of diapers)—maternal and paternal kin can cooperatively scaffold learning to be a parent.

Men embedded in maternal-kin networks often receive clear messages about responsibility and the sanctions for irresponsibility. A father's failure to understand and comply with maternal kin's desires and needs can result in a mother's limiting the time she grants him to spend with his child. Brian discusses his attempts to gain acceptance into the network of his child's mother while she was pregnant:

> I visited her at the hospital, trying to make good relationships with her family, trying to vouch for the fact that I am presently in school, I am educated, I do have ambitions, I'm not out here trying to make babies all over the place. It's just, I'm going to do the right thing, I'm going to be responsible, I'm going to handle what I can, I'm going to build the relationship I need to.

Some fathers assess their own efficacy and realize, owing to their fragile position as young men with few resources, that they must compromise with family members in order to be involved with their children. They need to learn and relearn how reciprocal relationships work, and that give-and-take is not simply synonymous with a loss of masculinity and lack of control. Such careful attention to acting responsibly, in concert with elder maternal and paternal kin, can result in shared authority over caregiving. Trust building between families pays off when young fathers need emotional support. Akida, for instance, is coping with depression after the premature death of his infant son. Fortunately, both maternal and paternal grandmothers have stepped up to care for his older preschool-age daughter to give him space to grieve.

> It's times when I have my days when I really don't . . . I kind of shut down and don't really talk to nobody. I might go out just walking at nighttime for a few hours, or I might just sit in the house all day, and drop my daughter off at my mother's. Or, Tina's mother's house, and I just sit in there . . . you know, I might sleep. I might just listen to some music or something, but, you know, I'm always thinking about him, his heart's always going to be with me.

Similarly a shared understanding between paternal and maternal grandmothers can help to diffuse conflict between young unmarried parents as well as extended kin. Joe has found that his family has earned the trust of the mother of his son. When she was incarcerated, her family chose Joe's mother to be the child's guardian.

> My son has been with my mom for the last three years. His mother knew no other people who would be able to take care of the child to her satisfaction, but she knew me and my family since she was fifteen years old. She knew what kind of people we were and she felt safe since I was the father.

However, agreement among maternal and paternal kin all too often only leads to a fragile and momentary support network. Numerous young fathers do kin work to nurture trusting, high-quality relationships among family members. They introduce their parents and siblings to the family members of the mothers of their children, and they encourage communication between the families. But fathers also protect paternal kin from maternal kin who might use or damage the mutual support arrangements. Leonard mentions that he cannot vouch for every family member or friend of his children's mother, and he wants to avoid conflict that could disrupt his fragile network.

> My mother's talking to my girlfriend, and she's talking to my best friend. They're all like really, really tight. My mom's friends with my brothers' friends, too. But I don't call people friends . . . people I call associates. I've been through a whole lot. That's why I'm careful about what I bring into the family, friends I mean.

Not all young fathers act in concert with their own paternal kin when negotiating their place as fathers with mothers and her kin. Some struggle to establish themselves as independent adults and find that their daily lives are still too chaotic to settle into a supportive role as a young father. In effect, even when mother and maternal kin communicate clear expectations for men to offer some money or clothes, to spend time with a baby, some young men limit their involvement and give priority to what they need in their own lives. Their resistance to the obligations set forward by maternal kin, or even denial of their relationship to their children, places strong barriers between fathers and children.

In many instances, maternal kin eventually give up on efforts to encourage or coerce fathers into involvement and decide to manage children in their own way. Will's noncommittal experience illustrates why maternal kin often find it easier to assert their moral authority over child care. Although his family worked in concert with the family of his one-year-old son's mother to share care, Will is hesitant to build his life around his son's need for care. He reflects,

Every couple days, I go over to my grandma's house and watch the child for a while. I'm always on the move, people can barely catch up with me. . . . I can't play father. I don't believe he's mine. It is what it is. Her family calls my mother and relays the message about him. They keep saying that boy is mine. I got a shaky feeling. I don't want to do anything. . . . I can't take him, one being that I don't got a crib [baby bed], and two being when you do come to my mom's crib [apartment], I don't got no food to feed. I'm at my mom's with my brother, and I'm scavenging myself.

In this context, it becomes easy for fathers like Will who have few resources with which to support a child, let alone themselves, to deny their fatherly role and the relationship altogether.

Not surprisingly, mothers and their family members protect children and their own interests by isolating young men who seem to pose a risk to their families. Often, the atmosphere of animosity obscures the best intentions and motivation of two sets of family members focused on a child's well-being. Sometimes, the course of events gets ugly. Marcus lives in Chicago and professes to be making changes in his life to get off the street and to move beyond dangerous friendships. By visiting his daughter soon after birth at his ex-girlfriend's apartment, he entered into disputed gang territory that was not safe for him. He watched his ex-girlfriend's grandmother at the window of the apartment pick up the phone to call the police when he arrived. Her family eventually provided information to police that led to the arrest of his friends. "My mother don't want anything to do with them. My family, theirs, everybody is at each other's throats. Her grandmother been out to get me for the longest [time]. When you go into those flats, having slept around, she's in everybody's business." Failing to get permission from maternal kin, Marcus had not seen his daughter in many months.

Older nonresident fathers may also need to reach understandings about their involvement with the family members of their children's mothers. The history of broken trust and strained communication between coparents affects maternal kin (see chapter 4). Sometimes, even if former partners can reach an amenable and secure relationship, maternal kin step in to act as parental proxies for fathers' children. As recounted in chapter 4, thirty-year-old Rusty was frustrated that his partner's mother determined when he could see his kids. In part, the accumulation of burned bridges and perceived betrayals is taken personally by maternal kin.

If mothers' family members are actively involved with their children, fathers must face up to them as actual coparents. Among unmarried low-income parents, maternal kin may be granted custody as kin foster parents. Family members may even turn on each other in an effort to gain access to vital funds from public aid. Isaiah is seeking the custody of his two daughters, whom he raised on his own when both of their mothers were on the street and in need of drug rehabilitation. To achieve custody, he has to contest in court the efforts of his daughter's aunt, who, he says, was only interested "in the aid check." He believes that "you can present yourself the same way as an attorney, but you won't have a snowball's chance in hell, going in there as a poor black father up against the state attorneys who represent the mother or [family services]."

For other groups of men, such as older fathers who live with and commit to a long-term relationship with the mothers of their children, maternal kin can still have a significant effect on fathers' opportunities to be nurturing parents. With careful coordination, fathers and mothers can piece together a place for maternal kin as much-needed caregivers. Because mothers usually have a close and trusting relationship with some members of their families, these maternal kin become obvious "go-to" adults when couples need bridge care. They provide options for whom to name as emergency contacts when children are in school or day care, and they help in managing the time demands of dual careers, especially when getting from one place to another in a timely fashion is a challenge.

Maternal-kin networks can be perceived as a strain as well as a support for these committed-couple families. Fathers in these families may have conflicts similar to the way the terms of fathers' obligations and access to their children are up for grabs for many unmarried or low-income couples. Five years ago, Carl married Lani and adopted her daughter from a previous relationship. As a college graduate and computer programmer, he brings stability to their lives, which Lani's mother appreciates. But developing trust took some negotiation on both of their parts.

> [Her grandmother] smokes and things like that that have come out over time that—I don't allow smoking in my house. Little issues like that that we've had to smooth over in some points, but over time I think Giselle has seen that I'm taking very good care of her daughter and her granddaughter . . . I think at first she might have been concerned that I was just another one of those guys, but she has not had a very good time in the past as far as husbands, so I think she was concerned for her daughter. . . . [So she] stays away from [my daughter] when she's smoking, or at least tries to keep the smoke away from her, realizing we don't like it. . . . She goes outside to smoke, and that's fine.

These fathers, having more authority as custodial parents, are in a better position to challenge maternal kin's expectations. For example, mothers may have very close relationships with their parents and own siblings who are interested in becoming active figures in the lives of their grandchildren, nieces, and nephews. But if fathers take exception to how the maternal kin behave or are uncomfortable with their values, fathers are less likely to trust them. These discrepancies can alter how the caregiving network operates, especially if the fathers care for and are devoted to their children.

Stepfather-Father Alliances

Some men's involvement in a network of familial caregiving includes the typically sensitive interpersonal process whereby fathers and step-fathers negotiate the terms of their involvement with children. Viewed broadly, a network of care encompassing both fathers and stepfathers can be marked by supportive and loving activities as well as tensions, frustrations, and jealousies. Although we can focus on the men's perceptions of and interactions with each other, these experiences are embedded in larger familial and social contexts that include other influential family members, most notably mothers and children. They cover the initial phase of new stepfathers acclimating themselves to families in which mothers and fathers have preexisting routines and perceptions of their respective parent-child bonds as well as whatever arrangements emerge over time. At the outset, and potentially through-out, mothers may be entangled in a mix of romantic and paternal jeal-ousies between fathers and stepfathers.

Previous research that draws on the stepfather data we incorporate here emphasizes the gendered process of cooperative multifather par-enting while highlighting stepfathers' supportive actions.[15] These analy-ses generated the "father ally" concept, which underscores the idea that fathers and stepfathers sometimes share a common interest—children's well-being. More specifically, viewed from the stepfather's perspective the concept captures his

> . . . conscious or unconscious expressions or gestures that could reason-ably be interpreted as supportive of the father-child relationship. These efforts include a stepfather's attempt to act directly in support of the father as well as indirectly; that is, the stepfather is not clearly motivated to benefit the father overtly. Father ally expressions can be viewed as springing from a stepfather's orientation/mindset toward children and "fathering," experiences often connected to family-related activities affected by context and time.[16]

In a society in which gendered masculinity norms continue to encour-age many men to be competitive, self-reliant, and assertive in critical family decisionmaking, men's willingness to cooperate to produce a form of shared cofathering becomes all the more impressive. To varying degrees, and in stark contrast to these norms, some stepfathers embrace the sentiment that they should downplay the competitive ethic and embrace a more cooperative orientation toward their multifather circumstances. Stepfathers are capable of expressing this cooperative spirit in diverse ways that consider fathers, mothers, and children alike. They can, for instance, go out of their way to accommodate nonresident fathers' schedules so the fathers can spend extra time with their children, or they can discourage mothers from badmouthing their former partners, especially in front of the children. They might also say supportive words directly to a child, as the thirty-five-year-old Eddy does to his eight-year-old stepdaughter when her father works late and doesn't come to pick her up as he promised.

> I guess I kind of smooth things over for him. . . . when he do bad things, whether he do it intentionally or not—I try to make him look like he—it's a mistake, nobody's perfect. . . . It's okay for Dad to make mistakes. He's human. . . . He doesn't know half the times I cleaned up his mess.

These are just a few of the many ways stepfathers can step up to the plate to make things better for fathers and their children.

What conditions lead stepfathers to adopt this type of cooperative multifather orientation? Preliminary evidence suggests that stepfathers may be more likely to go in this direction if they: experience some form of male bonding with the father; are not forced to go beyond their comfort zone in terms of how they interact with the father; feel secure in their romantic relationship; see the father as deserving respect because he takes fathering seriously enough; and have their own children, which makes it easier for them to relate to the nonresident father's experience. So, too, we suspect that more rigorous study of the father-ally experience will show that the mother can make a difference as a gatekeeper or mediator for the stepfather-father relationship, and the quality of the stepfather-child relationship may be significant as well. Ultimately, a complex mix of circumstances, including mothers' and children's sentiments, fathers' commitments and resources, and stepfathers' involvement, will shape the extent to which fathers are included in or locked out of their children's lives.[17]

The time may be right to encourage stepfathers and fathers to consider a healthier form of cooperative cofathering because men increasingly construct more open friendships that are not as steeped in stereotypical masculine norms as men's friendships used to be.[18] Even though truly cooperative cofathering appears to be relatively novel, creative counseling strategies and workshops could make them more common and effective. Evaluation studies that assess initiatives to improve stepfather-father cooperation as part of the larger stepfamily ecology would be useful.

Friends in Shared Care Networks

Fathers find themselves seeking or creating their own networks for support, leisure, and play dates for their children. One website encourages men to reach out to one another with this invitation:

> If you've been resisting finding or joining a dad's group or playgroup because you feel like you shouldn't need to go to a support group, take a deep breath and relax. Dads groups aren't group therapy, and you won't need to reveal any deep secrets or insecurities. Meeting up with other dads and their kids can be a great way to spend part of your day hanging out with people in a similar situation as yourself, and a healthy social outlet. You can also learn a lot from other dads, like what to do when your toddler's answer to every question is, "No way!"[19]

Such networks become important because family support has its limits. The vision of fathers with strollers at a local playground or at Starbucks is increasingly familiar. Men's relationships with other parents that are rooted in children's needs and development may be a new world for many fathers. Such relationships can push men to express themselves in different ways, but they also present a range of challenges for fathers.

Coordination and cooperation in networks extends beyond kin who share parenting responsibilities. Both fathers and mothers face increasing demands at their workplaces, as do other family members. The shortage of family members who can care for children leads many parents to create networks of shared care arrangements with a hodgepodge of adults, ranging from close kin to trusted friends to staff in community institutions (discussed further in chapter 6). Although fathers may plan for formal care for their children, there is a growing need for informal bridge care, for adults who can nurture children during the gaps of time between school and work. Friends are needed to pick up children, provide snacks and meals, transport them to other caregivers, and serve as emergency contacts when children are sick. Both fathers and mothers can coordinate this mosaic of care strategies by identifying members of an integrated kinlike network.[20] A network of similarly situated fathers and mothers may provide stay-at-home fathers in particular with emotional support and understanding as well as friendship.[21]

As men move into public settings as nurturing parents, they may be unprepared to establish relationships with women as well as other men that are based on talking and interacting with their children. Self-reliance is a key value for men; fathers are not apt to seek advice or assistance from others who have their own parenting challenges. Beyond these aspects, men may also have smaller social networks of friends than women. As fathers navigate their new arrangements with peer parents, they work on the borders of traditional women's child care and the emerging circumstances that enable fathers to play an active role in caring for children. Shared care encourages fathers to hone their skills of being attentive to others' needs, not just to plan and provide care for their own children but also to plan ways to provide care for all children in their local communities.[22]

Some of the resistance to men's participation in shared care networks stems not simply from their own discomfort in that role but also from gender-specific barriers to cracking networks of parents who coordinate play dates for their children.[23] A man may experience isolation in a circle of mothers as the only father who is responsible for caring for his children. Although many fathers coordinate care arrangements, or reach out to develop relationships based on their children's needs, they are often perceived as "helpers and not sharers." It may be that fathers who take on the primary responsibility for shared care arrangements are in a minority, and that in the majority of families, they are recruited by mothers to help with care work. Increasingly, though, fathers have become indispensable actors in this care network.

Networks with friends who share care may also take different forms in different racial, ethnic, and social class groupings. Middle-class dads, for example, are more likely than low-income dads to turn to their friends and participate as care providers themselves, helping children in sports and leisure activities as well as offering emotional support. In working-class networks, in contrast, men's friends tend to offer more material supports, including money, services, or goods. In past decades we have found that fathers and mothers in poor families and in families of color have pooled resources with friends in order to nurture their children.[24] But white middle-class families, too, have restructured care arrangements to allow married couples to use the extensive base of resources that friends can offer.[25]

In a mobile society in which close family members may not live nearby, fathers also create networks by turning friends into family. These "fictive kin" gather for holidays and celebrations and may have more intimate relationships with children than paternal or maternal kin. Like mothers, fathers frequently identify and cultivate relationships with their friends, who become "other mothers" and "other fathers" in trusted family circles. Gay fathers who have experienced strained relations with their families of origin may build a new network of friends with children in a community that supports homosexual couples with children.[26]

Men's individual efforts to welcome friends into a network of caring adults may guide the efforts to create a national program agenda for shared care networks. For example, Latino parents have made a place at the table for friends and relations outside of their immediate families. The National Compadres Network is an initiative to reinforce the positive involvement of Latino males in their families, communities, and society. Established in 1988, the network grew from a gathering of Latino-Chicano men who met in Jolon, California, to join in a Circulo de Amistad y Hermandad (Circle of Friendship and Brotherhood), to share stories of their achievements and challenges. This gathering is now an annual event, known as Hombres Retiros (Men's Retreat), and has reached over 1,000 men since 1990. A wide range of men have been integrated into extended family networks, as "fathers, sons, grandfathers, brothers, compadres, partners, and mentors in their families and community."[27]

To redevelop the traditional extended family system on a national level, families in this organization aspire to the principles of "Un Hombre Noble" (a noble man). The network uses public information campaigns to reduce involvement in substance abuse, domestic violence, child abuse, teen pregnancy, gang violence, and other family and negative behaviors that damage communities. A recent campaign, Respectar y Leer (Respect and Read), aimed to challenge men to provide safe and secure homes for their children, to take part in storytelling and reading with children, and to support youths to succeed in school and increase Latino children's high school graduation rate. The network has also established the National Latino Fatherhood and Family Institute, a policy, advocacy, and training organization to provide technical assistance for program implementation.

By extending care networks beyond family members, fathers are taking the first steps to introduce their children to their local communities and the broader public world. Fathers become more and more adept as intermediaries in the places where family life and community life meet. And in these places, fathers begin to seek out resources that are available for their children through networks rich in social capital linkages.

Family Social Capital: Linking Children to Friends and Kin

Fathers can nurture their children through the provision of material assets—food, shelter, educational books and toys—and services such as educational camps and health care. In media or political discussions of responsible fathering, particularly in the case of postdivorce families or unmarried couples, attention is often focused exclusively on what fathers provide their children in terms of finances or care. But the resources fathers make available to their children through the maintenance of networks of families and friends—called family social capital—might be the most profound benefit children receive from being involved with their fathers. These resources are the source of knowledge, relationships, advice, and interactions that can help children attain certain goals, such as finding a soccer team or learning about a good high school or job opening, and can help fathers identify a nearby home child-care provider.[28]

Fathers promote their children's development by advocating for them with family and friends. Although fathers are embedded in a diverse set of interconnected relationships, using this network of obligated adults is an ongoing project. Here we explore how fathers interact with a network of family and close friends as distinct from advocating on their children's behalf with individuals in community schools, day-care centers, sports teams, or other nonfamily groups and settings. We pay attention not only to which resources these family and kin networks provide but also the processes by which fathers use these networks.[29] Mainteinance of these relationships is laden with both a shared sense of purpose as well as misunderstanding and tension. Various forms of trust and love for children may be the glue that holds these adults together over time.

Maternal and paternal kin are likely to be obligated early in children's lives to commit to providing something tangible to fathers and children. Kin who give presents on holidays and birthdays, who sacrifice spare time to attend events and help with homework, or who call to check in on children are investing in children's growth and development. Children's health reflects the well-being and continuity of the family network. In fact, as we have seen, maternal and paternal kin may be more likely to contribute resources to children than to fathers, as children are young and dependent on adults, and fathers are assumed to be responsible for their own well-being.

Close friends are usually overlooked as potential contributors of social capital. Fathers rely on their friends for emotional support when relation-ships are strained with mothers of their children and also turn to them to support and celebrate their children's accomplishments. Men often become aware of activities in local neighborhoods—sports teams, church functions, county-sponsored events such as fairs or holiday celebrations, and free clinics—because this information is passed to them through a network of friends. Ultimately, children experience a greater sense of community and their role in it through the social capital that network members offer.

As caregiving networks of kin and friends grow more complex, opportunities to develop social capital for children change as well. The added complexity means that fathers are more apt to help manage the relationships between kin, so the potential for complications and tension emerge repeatedly. As many men have discovered in recent years, when married, resident fathers step out of these traditional roles they may be obliged to engage in a more proactive masculinity by orchestrating relationships, especially if they desire access to and involvement with their children. For example, stepfathers can build social capital if they can hone their abilities to act like fathers in public settings, not just in the household. They can model healthy and productive adult interactions and help to bring closure in social networks by sharing critical information with other responsible adults about children's activities, disposition, or needs. As a member of a parenting "team," stepfathers become part of children's family-based social capital. Their hands-on advocacy for their children demonstrates support for and cooperation with children's birth mothers.

A divorced father may find himself in a bewildering network of current and past partners, former in-laws, stepfathers and father figures, godparents, and his own family members. To secure his place as an involved father, he will need to tap into many of these relationships. Such a father can encourage a wide range of adults to contribute to his children's well-being. If he manages these potentially contentious relationships well, he may find network members who can offer his children a rich, complex family life, emotional and financial support for schooling, linkages to employment opportunities, and contacts with community groups. Ironically, the social capital represented by this complex network might extend far beyond what would be available in a network anchored by a conventional two-parent nuclear family.

Fathers are likely to help forge an understanding of reciprocity in obligations and benefits when they are part of a developed network of family and friends. When parents grapple with the conflicting demands of work and family schedules, fathers may help babysit or transport children of their close friends or neighbors in exchange for the same. These arrangements may be scheduled on a daily basis (one family transports children to soccer practice, and the other family picks them up), or these obligations may be mobilized during specific events. In case of an emergency such as a sick child at school or a problem at the workplace that keeps a parent over time, fathers may ask friends and family to take care of their children for a few hours.

Reciprocity may look different with intergenerational ties in kin networks.[30] Fathers may not only swap care with their siblings but also turn to their own parents for financial help with children's school tuition or with down payments on a car or a house—actions that indirectly affect children's well-being. Within families, reciprocity may only play out over the long term, when family members call on each other for a "return" on many years of investments.

Russell is an underemployed father of four teenage sons. He lives with his current girlfriend and her two sons but stays in close contact with his two sons from a previous marriage, who live a few blocks from him in Chicago. His aging mother helped to raise Russell's oldest son. Later, however, she fell ill. Not long after that, Russell moved his mother into an apartment next door to his own, where she lives with his son, a high school senior headed to the Air Force. He and his son can monitor her health and help her out with daily routines. "My father's passed, and she doesn't like to sleep alone," he said. "My son is the first grandson of my parents, and he is my mother's favorite. I had a lot of help with him, and she needs to know where he is. So it works out for everybody."

In this network, three generations of family members take part in providing emotional support, guidance, financial contributions, and physical nurturance of both young and old kin. They also offer a resource that fathers cannot provide on their own, but one that is tied to multiple generations of their own family: a sense of legacy, a clear continuity or discontinuity that locates children within a history of caring adults and children.

Creation of Family Legacies

In 2004, then Senator Barack Obama published *Dreams from My Father: A Story of Race and Inheritance.* In this book, and in subsequent speeches on race and intergenerational family life in 2008, Obama gives meaning to the experiences and history that his absent father, a Kenyan who married a white Midwestern graduate student, passed along to him. As he delves into the implications of the sudden death of his father, his relationship with this man becomes a catalyst for exploring his place in a family network that stretches across generations, racial boundaries, class lines, and global borders.

Intangibles make family networks unique contexts for fathers to nurture their children. Like Obama, who strived to manage key relationships and gather resources for children over the years, some fathers create networks that offer their children benefits beyond what the fathers can provide themselves. A well-maintained system of family and friends can give children a sense of belonging. The continuity of commitment stretches across generations within families and becomes larger than any one parent. In creating family legacies, fathers and their networks offer children a valuable and irreplaceable sense of "who we are" as a family.

Legacies may require that fathers use an intergenerational network to pass along a unique type of knowledge to their children. Detailed insights can include family histories, such as the story of how family members emigrated to the United States. Or fathers may help expose their children to an entirely different language and aspects of an ethnic identity. Or by taking part in the daily routines of a family farm, fathers and mothers teach their children distinct skills needed to maintain both land and family life. Generations are linked to the land by farming soil farmed by one's ancestors.[31] In a broad sense, men's efforts to create and sustain family businesses are legacies in which networks of family members participate. Although more frivolous, sports culture can also provide emotionally significant rituals for family members to weave threads of affinity with one another across generations. The bonds shared by fans of professional teams like the Pittsburgh Steelers and Boston Celtics, specific university sports programs, or even small town high schools often merge individuals' time-honored loyalties to family and community.

As the life expectancy of the baby boom cohort increases, opportunities to remain active as a grandfather or grandmother will likely expand, although future cohorts of grandparents will have fewer biological grandchildren. Older adults will spend longer periods of time in good health, and many will be part of an intergenerational network of care. In addition to providing care, however, fathers and their parents can work together to convey a sense of legacy for adolescents and young adults. Research illustrates that children develop cognitive skills through interaction with their grandparents, by grappling with effects of historical time and changing contexts.[32] They are also exposed to snippets of family stories that stretch their understanding about who "counts" as family and how wide and deep family networks can become.

As noted, fathers learn to be parents from numerous sources. Inevitably, most men compare their gendered parenting behaviors and attitudes with those of their own fathers.[33] Their fathers may offer a model approach on some aspects of how to be a provider, how to persevere through hard times, or how to live for fifty years in a good marriage. Fathers may also provide negative models so that their sons want to "be everything my father was not," rejecting, say, years of abuse, silence, or lack of closeness. Positive fathering behaviors may be recycled, stretching forward across multiple generations as fathers socialize their sons to be good, strong men. Antonio, the father of a two-year old son, struggles to find a career for himself as a twenty-four-year-old with a bit of college experience. His father was born in Mexico, and Antonio makes sense of his own parenting by comparing himself to his father.

My dad's parents were very abusive. My grandpa would hit my dad if he brought him the wrong pack of cigarettes. My father felt that that wasn't the right way to raise kids. So, my dad is a perfectionist. If he tells me to help him with this drywall and I don't do it right, he's like, "Ah, get out of here." He doesn't mean any harm, but that's the way he is. I'm going to make mistakes. But like me, when my son grows up, he'll say, "Well, this is what my dad did right, and I'm going to apply it. This is what my dad did wrong and I'm going to change it."

Fathers also seek out family members and other friends who can be models for how to become a good man, a successful adult, even a strong parent. Intergenerational fathering may also include father figures for men who did not have relationships with their fathers. Miguel moved from Michoacàn, Mexico, to the West Side of Chicago when he was nineteen. His father died when Miguel was five years old, but he found guidance from another man by working in his community in the countryside.

A person that I used to work with—he gave me a lot of love, he taught me respect, all of that. He taught me a lot of things to do with my hands, in a job. I was eight years old when I started working with him, and I worked with him until I was around fourteen. He worked the land, cultivating corn, raising sheep. It was like a father-son relationship, yeah. He taught me values, how to respect others.

Ultimately, being a nurturing parent likely requires contemporary fathers to mix and match. They will choose to honor and express some of their parents' attitudes and behaviors and to reject others. Thus, legacies of intergenerational fathering become dynamic stories, shaped by fathers as they struggle with new expectations for nurturance and closeness.

Some men face a more painful trial if they cannot find anyone in their network of family and friends who can provide guidance or support in their efforts to be involved fathers. Their own fathers may have passed away, or they may have lost contact with them long ago. Some men may have been raised by stepfathers who never assumed full responsibility for them. For these reasons and others, some fathers are on their own when they try to build a legacy for their children.

Latrell dropped out of high school and with a friend's help found his way into a community fathering program. He is frustrated by not finding a job, and he has a one-year-old daughter who demands his attention. He says, "Tell you the truth, I don't have a father figure, so I don't know what fathers are supposed to do. I mean, I taught myself everything I know, so I'm living like I'm stuck, I'm very stuck here."

But some men, even those lacking family legacies or models of fathers who nurture, do not remain "stuck." Their search for examples of a progressive vision of manhood that embraces a contemporary fatherhood based on providing and caregiving can come up empty. And so they start at the beginning with their own children, creating a story to build bridges to their own family members who are no longer present. Bird's father died when he was three. Although he could remember little of what happened at the funeral, he imagined who his father was and what he might have been concerned about. The story that Bird creates and passes down to his daughter—a new story that is not necessarily based in reality—motivates him to be an involved father.

> I still think about my Pops, but it's not anger anymore, more like relief. I know he was thinking, "My son is only three years old and I'm fixin' to leave him." I didn't want [my daughter] to look at me like I left her, so she grows up saying, "You ain't been in my life all this time—who is you?"

Even imagined intergenerational linkages can help children make sense of their family's contributions to their lives. In this way, fathers are key actors both in continuing ongoing legacies and in making new ones.

Children in families marked by disruption and discontinuities may long for a sense of legacy that fathers cannot create. The complex networks that emerge after divorce or in the wake of multiple partnerships are difficult for fathers to navigate. How can fathers develop continuity in relationships with adults as diverse as an aging grandparent of a former spouse, the best friend of a former girlfriend who is the mother of one's oldest child, or a stepfather who once acted like a father but who is no longer intimately involved with the mother? These "familial" ties may not fit the nuclear family model with its distinct intergenerational ties, and the adults who want to sustain relationships in these complex networks will be challenged to mesh their ambiguous roles. But they will also have new opportunities to write stories and tailor family legacies to each child.

Fathering Initiatives Based on Family Strengths

Few studies show how social policies and programs directly shape fathers' experiences in kin and friend networks. For the most part, policymakers and local programs are not as concerned with buttressing the safety net of kin members in children's lives as they are investing in fathers' human capital or the health of coparenting relationships. These networks are usually treated as informal arrangements that families are free to build—or not—depending on their needs, preferences, and circumstances. They typically exist in every family, but they do not emerge as a prominent source of support for fathers and children without extensive investment of time, emotion, and resources.

Other countries around the world have launched initiatives to support family networks in order to support children's well-being. Unlike the American legal system, many other nations' legal systems recognize de facto parenting, along with the rights and responsibilities of a range of social fathers—stepfathers as well as grandfathers, uncles, brothers, and nonbiological kin. Governments have experimented with providing custodial adults raising children with family allowances regardless of their socioeconomic status. These allowances are understood to be investments in future generations of citizens, and by focusing on children, these programs move beyond marital relationships as the means to assist families. In a similar move, South Africa has created a system of old age pensions in part to allocate funds to grandparents who may be raising their grandchildren in the absence of the children's parents.

"Intergenerational programming"—suggesting the potential of linking grandparents with grandchildren, especially as seniors retire and bring their expertise to mentoring and monitoring—has become a buzz phrase for policymakers in the United States. We suggest a different perspective: to frame fathering initiatives in a manner that incorporates intergenerational family strengths. Our view requires a shift away from prioritizing only married couples and from men's personal potential as providers through an emphasis on jobs and training for fathers.

If we acknowledge how family networks grow in complexity over the life course, we begin to recognize that much of that complexity results from fathers' central location in the networks. If, as some researchers argue, kin networks are not as robust as they may have been a few decades ago, then families need more committed adults.[34] When fathers who are no longer intimately involved with the mothers of their children reconnect, these men can link their children to an even broader network of concerned and motivated paternal kin and friends. Fathers and family members may replenish overly burdened kin networks, provide additional role models for children, and enhance a range of informal social supports for children.

Policymakers and courts have increasingly acknowledged the standing of maternal and paternal kin in the development of men's roles as fathers. Decisions about custody in child welfare cases often take into account extended family involvement, as officials seek to place children with fathers or related kin. Unfortunately, such arrangements can put the father and mother at odds with each other. Welfare reform laws formally recognized the importance of maternal kin by creating new requirements that teen mothers live with their own mothers in order to receive public assistance. Similarly, leaders of local programs have acknowledged paternal grandmothers' intensive efforts to secure their young adult sons' smooth transition to fatherhood. For example, judges often turn to the mothers of young men to ensure the stability of an established household to steady men's first steps as providers and caregivers.

Fathers, irrespective of age, class, and race or ethnicity, grow accustomed to a much more nuanced position in family networks over time. As their own relationships with the mothers of their children and with kin from both sides evolve, fathers' responsibilities to help their children manage connections to groups and individuals outside the family are transformed as well. Perhaps fathers are pulled into greater activity and a more responsible stance as "public" parents as they try to define and organize family network activities. These networks may also push fathers to embrace community responsibilities as they come to appreciate the value of moving beyond family and close friends to explore how networks in local neighborhoods and with local institutions can enhance their children's well-being.

══ Chapter 6 ══

Community Connections

DOUG, a forty-four-year-old vending machine technician, talks freely about the intense love he's developed for his nineteen-year-old adoptive son, Sammy. Sixteen years ago Doug came into Sammy's life when Sammy's mother, Patricia, accepted Doug's qualified marriage proposal—"I'll marry you, but that's my son legally. No step involved, nothing like that. That's my son." With Patricia's help, Doug claimed legal paternity status for Sammy shortly before the wedding. Since then, as Patricia confirmed in a separate interview, Doug followed through on his commitment to be a devoted, loving father.[1]

Doug confirms his strong paternal commitment when he describes how he advocated for Sammy during his senior year in high school. After learning that Sammy was in jeopardy of not graduating on time, Doug made several assertive phone calls and arranged a joint meeting that afternoon with the school principal, Sammy, and his history and English teachers. With conviction Doug recollects a defining moment early in that intense session:

> I told both his teachers, "Just let me have the floor for a second." I said, "That goes for you too, young man, be quiet too. . . . If Sammy right now at this moment, promises to get both of you full cooperation would both of yous be willing to tutor him in the mornings in the afternoons, whichever one ya'll can get to? . . . If I can guarantee it, would you be willing to tutor him? . . . He's going to graduate, come hell or high water he's going to graduate."

The teachers and principal accepted Doug's appeal for help and Doug convinced Sammy, who had been diagnosed with attention-deficit/hyperactivity disorder (ADHD) ten years earlier, to go back on his Ritalin prescription the next day and to rededicate himself to his schoolwork. With everyone honoring their commitments, Sammy graduated with his class on time. As a father Doug is proud that he was instrumental in getting Sammy back on track.

Doug's interactions with school personnel highlight the fact that significant facets of fathering can take place away from other family members. His interactions also underscore important but poorly under-stood aspects of fathering. Popular notions of fathering, as well as the research literature on fathering, stress breadwinning obligations and images of family-centered activities in homes.[2] Yet fathering, for resident and nonresident fathers alike, can and does occur away from domestic settings and clearly involves much more than financial support. One of the critical domains of a father's involvement includes what has been called "community responsibility" or "parental community social capital."[3] Responsibility of this sort includes parental effort that connects house-holds to each other and families to other social institutions concerned with children's needs. Such social capital is related to fathers' commu-nication of gender-based information about "manly" matters, such as cars, house repair, jobs, politics, and sports, which can illustrate "how the world works" and help to prepare children for experiences in their later lives. When parents reach out to or respond to those in the community who work with youths—schoolteachers, child-care workers, youth min-isters, nurses, dentists, probation officers, coaches, child psychiatrists, and others—they help establish social capital for their children.

Parents clearly vary in their attentiveness to children's emotional, physical, and practical needs and personal growth. Fathers and mothers may, on average, also be more or less invested in community-based par-enting activities related to a specific area that affects children, such as sports, education, artistic expression, criminal justice, health, youth leadership, and religious instruction. Gender stereotypes might lead us to expect fathers to be more involved in sports and mothers to be more concerned with health and religious education.[4]

To his credit, Doug noticed Sammy's declining academic perfor-mance and suspected that Sammy's "class clowning" and indifference to school was tied to his ADHD and his decision to stop taking his medica-tion. Doug was well aware of Sammy's ADHD because he had played a major role in getting Sammy diagnosed and treated ten years earlier. Thus, Doug's attentiveness to Sammy, his knowledge about his life cir-cumstances, and his commitment to helping Sammy grow positioned him to develop an action plan with key school personnel to help Sammy graduate.

Ultimately, fathers tend to be far less involved than mothers in establish-ing and managing children's growth in settings away from home.[5] Even though mothers tend to do more of the planning, worrying, and decision-making in this area, fathers are not inherently incapable of taking on these tasks, and many do an excellent job, especially in recreational sports.

If publicly and privately instigated initiatives are to engage men as nurturing fathers in the fullest sense they must enhance men's involve-ment in family-community linkages that involve children. A community responsibility perspective moves us beyond the previous notion of fathering being tied to a coparent team or as embedded within larger familial care networks. It emphasizes how engaged forms of fathering push fathers to help their children navigate their worlds away from home and their families. Viewed from a broad theoretical and public policy perspective, exploration of fathers' community responsibility reveals how the culture and conduct of fathering could be and is linked to male youth workers' involvement in children's lives more generally.[6]

Fathers must have meaningful access to the individuals in the community who are monitoring their children. Generally speaking, if fathers and youth workers are to collaborate successfully in a form of child advocacy they must be attentive to children's needs, ask questions, and share pertinent information that enables all adults to be more responsive to the child's needs. Ideally, fathers will grasp the value of different sorts of questions and be open to sharing information with youth workers that can make a difference in the care the youth workers provide. Similarly, youth workers must be committed to appreciating the parents' perspective and keeping them informed of their children's diverse needs and personal growth.

Men's Limited Community Involvement

Although Doug played a pivotal role in getting his son through high school by reaching out to school personnel, Doug also admits both he and Sammy were disappointed that his work demands prevented him from being more involved over the years in Sammy's sports activities. That fathers' work and travel schedules often hinder their ability to be more involved in managing their children's activities outside the home is well established.[7] But even when work hours do not preclude community-based fathering opportunities, fathers generally are less inclined than mothers to get involved at this level.[8] Custodial arrangements that privilege one parent's access to critical information can also make a difference in fathers' involvement in their children's lives away from the father's home. Nonresident fathers are likely to lack key information that would shed light on their children's everyday lives and personal needs, whereas single resident fathers and fathers in coresiding couples are more apt to be privy to those bits of information for resident children.

The sociologist Andrea Doucet's qualitative research with Canadian primary caregiving fathers, most of whom were single fathers and stay-at-home dads, highlights another set of conditions that constrain fathers' efforts to connect with other fathers and engage in community responsibility for their children. Her insights about men—especially their relatively sparse social networks, tendency to form competitive friendships through work and sports, and the homophobic sentiments that restrict those friendships—also apply to men in the United States.[9]

Fathers are less apt than mothers to develop and sustain friendships that are based on their parenting experiences. In part this pattern reflects the encouragement or pressure men receive to be self-reliant and autonomous. Moreover, men's less intimate and more competitive friendship styles often reduce their willingness to talk to other men about their insecurities as fathers or to focus on children's needs. The competitive nature of their friendships leads many fathers to fear their male peers' judgment and to avoid appearing incompetent or risking their image as an expert. This fear restricts some fathers' ability to develop supportive social networks in which children's needs are emphasized. It may also limit fathers' chances to develop productive partnerships with adults in the community who are involved more formally with caring for children.

Finally, organizations may shun certain types of fathers. Young unwed fathers sometimes struggle to be acknowledged at the hospital when their child is born. Similarly, nonresident fathers and stepfathers may struggle at times to gain access to the schools their children attend. Thus, otherwise supportive communities can make it difficult for some men to express themselves as fathers in public sites where they are perceived as too risky or without proper standing.

Making Community
Institutions Father Friendly

How can public and private initiatives help fathers build social capital for their children by getting them more involved in their children's public lives? Our previous discussion about conditions that matter signals the need for a multilayered approach that recognizes the value of families' and men's taking the initiative to question their assumptions and alter their habits. It also encourages policies and programs that make it more desirable and convenient for fathers to connect with those in the community who are involved with their children.

Previous research suggests that numerous resources can help fathers develop and sustain community networks that encompass their children.[10] In some cases, women close to fathers may need to step aside to let the men come forward and get more involved in reaching out to specific organizations and persons in the community who work with youths. Other men may benefit from their association with a "crossing partner," a woman who helps them to get involved with child-centered community activities, particularly those disproportionately organized by women, such as child care.

Experiences in community organizations can shape men's pathways into youth work and parenting. Early in their marriage, Luz and Martin lived in Mexico, prior to their move to the United States. Luz asked her husband to help her work with her elementary school students outside the classroom. He became involved with the parents of these students, and over many months, he found himself tutoring their high school siblings on Wednesdays and Saturdays in his own home. He recalls, "Their parents were always working, so they needed somebody to help out. We were very popular—sometimes we had twenty kids in the house." Martin makes sure to include his young daughter in these tutoring sessions, and he continues to volunteer alongside his daughter since he moved to the States five years ago.

> She was young, but she was always with us. She played with the other kids. . . . It is important for her to know that money is essential, but life is not all about money. It's about love, help, showing that you care about others. Sometimes I am involved at school, at home—with her, everywhere.

Not surprisingly, those who are well known in the community may have advantages because they are respected by others and have interpersonal connections. In a society steeped in "stranger danger" fear, men who are known, admired, and trusted can avoid the public gaze that sometimes casts suspicion on men's involvement with children in public settings.[11] This is relevant because men's investment in community responsibility for their children may place them in positions in which they are involved with other parents' children as well.

The inclusion process may be accelerated in areas where public sites afford parents a convenient chance to meet and develop connections that transcend any given rendezvous, such as playgrounds and community recreation centers. These sites, and other programs most often found in churches, hospitals, and schools, are unevenly distributed throughout urban, suburban, and rural areas. Some cities and neighborhoods simply have more financial capital to invest in facilities and programs that support fathers and mothers. Unfortunately the message of "build it and they will come" oversimplifies fathers' realities, but facilities that cater to children's recreational, educational, and health needs and also promote fathers' involvement may entice fathers to make connections with youth workers and parents.

Patrice is an unemployed father of five children from different relationships. He wants to remain active and engaged in the community during the rigors of his job search.

I'm currently enrolled in school to get my GED and everything else. I'm here [at the parenting program] on the days I'm not in school for a job search. I sometimes volunteer at the neighborhood schools to help out in the lunch room areas, you know. Just basically maintenance around in the school and you know, to spend time with my children there, and at home of course.

Work in community organizations serves many goals for fathers like Patrice. It keeps them physically close to their children, so they can monitor their progress and advocate for their needs. It also keeps fathers socially connected at times when they risk being isolated from the everyday world of work because they are out of a job.

Voluntary work may even lead to job opportunities and resources as well. Jelani, a twenty-three-year-old father of an infant son, is also unemployed. He uses his time away from his child to get involved in different community groups, with hopes that they will lead to a job.

I am involved in the church but I just started going like two or three weeks ago. I volunteer at an organization for adults to learn reading and filling out applications. I go there on Tuesdays and Thursdays. There was a guy in our neighborhood who volunteered there to get some experience. I went down there to be around people who were less fortunate than I was, and the people there are great and they are a great organization. They . . . are teaching me data entry and office type skill[s] so I could maybe get a temp job.

While working at the adult literacy program, Jelani mentioned to a caseworker that he had a young son. To his surprise, the caseworker referred him to a fathering program based in a local community college. Drawing on close-knit social service agency networks in Chicago, he has located extensive job training, parenting guidance, and education resources.

Community-Parental Alliances as Youth Work

Youth workers often perform diverse practical tasks and act as liaisons between parents and kids and various public entities such as schools and the criminal justice system. As owner of a day care and after-care center, Richard, forty-seven, picks up assignments directly from teachers (after receiving parental and school approval) for the kids in his program. This routine enables Richard and his staff, which includes his daughter, to better monitor kids' homework and give parents a detailed account of what their children's teachers expect. Brandon, a forty-one-year-old middle-school science teacher, pays out-of-pocket costs for a creative web-based grade report system that enhances his communication with parents and allows them to stay up to date on their child's daily assignments and academic progress. This is an example of how both fathers' and mothers' human capital may determine their ability and comfort level in corresponding with youth workers using the ever-expanding range of modern technologies. Presumably, computer-competent parents appreciate having direct access to Brandon via email. Both Richard and Brandon help fathers feel more connected to the organizations that influence their children while making it more convenient for the fathers to build social capital for them.

Youth workers can help parents and their children improve their joint communication. Some step forward formally and offer their services, for example, a youth minister doing group or private counseling sessions with parents and kids, or the director conducting parent-child communication workshops in a family-based diversion program for juvenile delinquents. The parent-child communication gap may be bridged best by youth workers with parenting experiences of their own.

Another strategy is for youth workers to complement parental child-rearing efforts proactively by trying to teach or model specific parental values and morals, manners, discipline, and interpersonal or practical skills. Some talk to youths about the parents' expectations. Scott, a Boys & Girls Club staff member, frames his understanding of parents this way: "Their most prized possession is their child, and, yeah, I understand that it's the most important thing in the world to them most of the time, and, I'm gonna find out what kind of things . . . they want to go on." Although Scott is not yet a father, his sensitivity to the emotional side of parenting reflects his empathetic abilities. His willingness to ask parents what they want reassures fathers that they have the opportunity to work with others to help them teach their children certain life lessons.

Lastly, youth workers can take the initiative and share information about children with their parents. Barry, a twenty-seven-year-old activities leader at an aftercare program, describes how he communicates with parents when they pick up their kids.

> And I try to interact with all the parents. And if they do talk to me, I try to let them know how their kids are doing, especially when their kids are doing well. I don't think any parent wants to come in from a hard day, pick up their child, and know that their child has been misbehaving. So, I try to give daily reports.

Barry's efforts here, similar to the other options youth workers have at their disposal to act as a resource for fathers, can lead to a solid alliance.

Ultimately, though, it requires that both fathers and youth workers be open and invested in the process.

Athletics is the obvious arena in which fathers are most likely to engage in community responsibility for their children and come into contact with youth workers. This is most visibly achieved when fathers serve as coaches for their children's recreational sports teams.[12] Recreational sports is the activity that produces the most volunteering among men, so fathers have plenty of opportunities to interact with other males when they get involved with their children's public lives. No solid estimates exist, but plenty of fathers spend some or much of the time they devote to community responsibility activities for their children by coaching their young sons' and daughters' recreational teams.[13]

Even though the man who is both father and coach to his own child faces distinct challenges, he also has a unique opportunity to be actively involved in his child's public life and social networks. He becomes a new type of resource for his child while also providing unique options for modeling by having his child observe him coaching other kids. Furthermore, a father-coach has additional options to model good health behavior and communication skills. At the same time, though, a father can reinforce stereotypically unhealthy tendencies if he shows inappropriate anger, ego, and traditional displays of aggressive masculinity.

Fathers as Youth Workers

Some men are likely to be better equipped to coordinate their fatherly interests with others if they have special knowledge and competence in, say, sports, outdoor recreation, music, or medicine or possess interpersonal skills that enable them to communicate easily about children's personal growth issues. For example, men with specific youth work experience are uniquely positioned to pursue tasks associated with community responsibility.[14] Along with their insider's view of how valuable such parental contributions can be, these men may have developed a useful skill set that includes good interpersonal skills. These attributes can sharpen their sensitivity to kids while solidifying their self-confidence as caregivers for youths. Interviews with male youth workers reveal that many believe they have become more attentive, discerning, confident, caring, and approachable through their involvement with kids in the community.[15] Many also believe their experience has made them better fathers or has the potential to do so. Kevin, a thirty-seven-year-old African American, reflects on what his vocation as a youth minister has done for him as a father to three boys.

> It gave me a vision, that I could help see where I'm trying to take my child to, what he's going through, so working in youth ministry was huge, and to this day I think, you know, it's the best parenting class for anybody. . . . Just come work in youth ministry for a little while and deal with kids, and you can see, at least help map out where you're trying to take your kids instead of just raising them randomly and hoping they all turn out well.

Similarly, Charles, a thirty-two-year-old director of a Boys & Girls Club who is not yet a father, speaks for many when he contemplates the value of what he assumes his youth work will bring to him when he does have a child.

> It's taught me to be more patient. Show me how to not take anything for granted. It's also, I think it's preparing me to be a better father, to be a good father, whenever I have kids. Cuz it's kinda like a blueprint of if you learn to work with kids so now you learn how to be a better father. . . . If you want to know how to be a good parent, learn how to be a good teacher, listen to the kids. They'll tell you how to do it.

Lessons male youth workers learn in the "field" may not always transform them into better fathers or fathers who work more productively with adults in the community on behalf of their own children. But such lessons probably give these men greater incentive and a practical edge to take on community-oriented aspects of fathering. When there's a reasonable amount of comparability between what men experience as youth workers and the types of issues they face as fathers, men are likely to feel more at ease being assertive with other youth workers who take an active role in shaping children's lives. The social networks they've established through paid work and volunteering can also make it easier for some to establish developmentally appropriate social capital for their own children.

The reciprocal partnership between fathering and youth work is evidenced in the reports of fathers who describe how their experiences as fathers influence their volunteer and paid youth work. Several of the most common themes running through fathers' narratives are that they become more sensitive to and accepting of kids' emotional well-being and varied personalities, grow more comfortable talking to kids, learn how to predict and manage kids' behavior, are concerned about kids' family circumstances and the roles that parents play, and develop a better understanding of different aspects of youth culture. In some instances, fathers are actively building alternative masculinities in contrast to more traditional notions of the emotionally detached, breadwinner-focused image of masculinity and fatherhood so pervasive for many decades in the United States and elsewhere.

The complementary relationship between youth work and fathering means that efforts to encourage more men to volunteer and do paid work with kids may have the long-term benefit of making men more mindful of the value of their taking an active role with the adults in the community involved with children.

Promoting Fathers' Involvement in Community Settings

Perhaps the most obvious strategies for helping men become more active in their children's public lives involve efforts either to alter workplace policy and work culture or to adjust child-oriented activities to accommodate parents' work schedules. Recent surveys indicate that fathers increasingly say they are frustrated with how their work schedules limit the amount of time they can spend with their children.[16] Thus, for the past few decades, the conventional thinking has been that if men had greater flexibility in their work schedules in the form of flextime and generous family leave, including paternity leave, they would be able to spend more time with their children at home and in public settings. Some of that time could be invested in activities that involved interacting with their children's teachers, pediatricians, coaches, and so forth. But this is not a given. In Sweden, results of progressive paternity leave policies are well documented and are somewhat disappointing. From Sweden's case we have learned that fathers' more limited involvement with children's activities is deeply rooted in a larger social context.[17] Gender-based wage differentials, family work histories, and patriarchal breadwinning norms are not easily swept away by shifts in public policy.

Decisions made by obstetricians, pediatricians, local schools, day-care facilities, and other sites involving children or organizations that include fathers, such as prisons, can provide fathers with more options and incentive to be involved. From a historical perspective, men's heightened commitment to the world of pregnancy and childbirth provides an excellent success story in bringing about change. Over the past several decades we have witnessed dramatic increases in fathers' participation in childbirth preparation classes as well as their involvement during labor and delivery.[18] Shifts in perceptions about men's and women's work and family roles no doubt fueled these changes in part. However, on a practical level, men's greater involvement in childbirth activities was fostered most directly by administrative decisions at local hospitals across the country to expand their services to include fathers more fully. Admittedly, our understanding of whether and how fathers' greater prenatal involvement affects their involvement with their children after birth is tenuous.

Nevertheless, it seems wise to pursue strategies that assume there's a genuine connection.[19]

At a very early age, children can benefit from their fathers' advocacy with early-childhood education programs in their communities. In the wake of the substantial expansion of Head Start programs under President Bill Clinton in the early 1990s, early-childhood researchers and policymakers agreed on the need to bring resources to children at younger ages, as it was more widely recognized that brain development is critical in the first three years of life. The Early Head Start initiative began in the mid-1990s, with a system of wraparound services to provide children with developmental supports and access to health and dental care. Parents and families also receive literacy services, access to parenting programs, and information and referrals to community agencies. Similar to the Head Start programs, Early Head Start seeks to include fathers in its approach to securing family involvement. Fathers have been encouraged to volunteer and to participate as bus drivers, story tellers, classroom aides, and event coordinators. They have also been hired as staff in the programs.

How widespread and successful has father involvement been in Early Head Start programs? Research shows that about half of all fathers with children in Early Head Start programs participate in an activity, including parent education, group socialization, policy councils and program committees, home visits, father-only activities, or dropoff childcare services at the center.[20] Instructors in these programs appear to encourage greater complexity in play between fathers and children, which can result in better cognitive and social developmental outcomes for young children.[21] Likewise, when staff integrate fathers into Head Start programs for children three to five years of age, children experience better outcomes in mathematics, and fathers' learning about positive involvement carries over into subsequent years, when their involvement remains high.[22]

Again, men's participation in early-childhood education programs depends on the relationship between youth workers and fathers. Fathers are clearly motivated to engage in these programs, but only when they are fully integrated into them. Men have not been enthusiastic about father-only programs that are segregated and in which their participation is treated as a special event.[23] As these programs are often aimed at low-income families, program staff who approach fathers with an interventionist goal—such as to transform "ineffective" fathers into responsible parents—are typically met with resistance. Instead, program evaluations suggest that program staff's work with fathers is successful when staff present themselves as competent partners concerned with enhancing children's well-being.[24] Fathers also welcome reciprocal exchanges with program staff and are receptive to staff members who take into account not only men but an entire intergenerational family network, of which fathers are a vital component.

Many fathers have also found support for their involvement with their children within their children's schools from kindergarten through high school.[25] Over half of all resident fathers attend general school meetings, parent-teacher conferences, or a school or class event, but what about the others? Unfortunately, only about 20 percent of nonresident fathers participate in these activities. Involved fathers bring another type of community social capital to bear through school involvement. For children in two-parent families, fathers and mothers who are highly involved in their children's schools are more likely to belong to community groups, churches, unions, and professional organizations as well as participate in service activities. The skills fathers use to form partnerships with community youth workers are similar across these contexts, so fathers who begin to build a network of community ties can quickly take advantage of a number of resources in their communities, with school as a central conduit of these connections.

Getting through the school doors in the first place may be difficult for fathers who themselves struggled in school as students. Unmarried and nonresident fathers perceived by school staff as risky may also face difficulties in being welcomed at school. Local community groups have tried various projects to address nonresident fathers' perceptions about the barriers that curtail their school involvement. For instance, at the beginning of every new academic year since 2004, the Black Star Project in Chicago has promoted the Million Father March.[26] They organize black fathers, grandfathers, stepfathers, and foster fathers to "march" their children to their first day of school, to demonstrate their commitment to education and to their children's futures. In 2010, the project registered 602 cities in which fathers participated in escorting their children to school, as the first step in welcoming fathers into the classroom as mentors, aides, tutors, and role models.

Incarcerated fathers can partner with local programs, in conjunction with facility authorities, to create more opportunities to interact with and nurture their children. Research suggests that parenting programs offered by correctional facilities can improve men's attitudes about and satisfaction with parenting as well as increase their sense of control over their lives.[27] Church ministries have been instrumental in creating national programs to connect children with fathers behind bars. The Angel Tree program offers prison fellowship for inmates and their children.[28] Affiliated local churches connect parents in prison with their children through the delivery of Christmas gifts. Angel Tree volunteers also help ex-offenders to find housing, provide the families of ex-offenders with assistance in buying food or paying their bills, and offer information on reentry challenges such as finding jobs.

Scout troops have also become involved in connecting incarcerated parents and children.[29] One troop, the Lone Star Girl Scout Council in Texas, established the Girl Scouts Beyond Bars program in 1992 with another troop in Maryland. The initiative, expanded to include 800 girls and 400 parents, includes a curriculum to build self-esteem and critical thinking in girls and their incarcerated parents.

Six states have been at the forefront of implementing "virtual visitation," a program that gives judges the authority and resources to mandate interaction through video conferencing, email, and other technological devices.[30] Virtual visitation with inmates is not a new concept. The pioneer for this program appears to be the state of Pennsylvania, which introduced it in 2001. Pennsylvania's Family Virtual Visitation, created by the Prison Society in partnership with the Pennsylvania Department of Corrections, provides high-tech video conferencing equipment that allows families to visit in "real time" with their loved ones who are incarcerated. For a relatively small fee of $20, families can schedule a fifty-five-minute visit once a month. According to the Prison Society, inmates, family members, and prison staff have expressed their support for this program. Correctional officers have reported that many inmates are better adjusted and seem happier after virtual visits. Virtual visitors express how important and meaningful the program is to the health and welfare of their families.

Some correctional programs have teamed with parents to use virtual technology to promote literacy as well as parent-child bonds. Florida offers a program called Reading Family Ties, which allows incarcerated fathers to read stories to their children using live video via the Internet. The program has been credited with enhancing family unity, easing inmates' transition back to society, and improving both parents' and children's literacy.[31] This emerging institutional capability has enabled states to expand what is likely the most popular program, Storybook Project, in which fathers record tapes or CDs as they read books to their children, or they video conference live with their children.[32]

Another far too common problem is that fathers lose contact with their children entirely during incarceration, especially if their children are in foster care.[33] Some local programs have begun to advocate for and develop strategies to locate fathers' children even while the fathers are serving time.[34]

In 2004, a legal decision gave a noncustodial parent outside of correctional facilities the right to have electronic communication with his or her child. A computer programmer in Utah demonstrated to judges in the courtroom the possibility of video conferencing with his daughter in Wisconsin. By 2010, Illinois became the sixth state to implement Virtual Visitation legislation. As a result of the new law, judges were granted the statutory authority to grant virtual visitation between children and noncustodial parents through use of technologies such as email, telephone, Internet, and video conferencing to protect and strengthen critical parent-child relationships. These services are supported in private homes as well as visitation centers and community agencies. By extending virtual visitation practices beyond correctional facilities, future custody law will reflect technological advances and possibly allow parents to avoid the challenges of place-based visitation conflicts.[35]

Fathering as a Series of Partnerships

As we illustrated with Doug, one of the critical challenges for some men's attempts to boost their lower level of involvement in general and their community responsibility in particular is the lack of time. Organizations could go a long way toward helping fathers assume more community-level responsibility for their children by adjusting their services to accommodate fathers' work and life circumstances and the constraints on their time; they could do this on their own and in partnership with other organizations. Pediatric practices could offer more evening and weekend hours so that working fathers would have more opportunities to attend appointments. Likewise, schools could set aside evening and weekend hours for parent-teacher meetings and provide on-site baby-sitting services that might entice both partners to attend. As in some prisons, modern communication technologies can provide incarcerated, deployed military, nonresident, or working fathers with options to be more involved. Church-based health ministries that offer parishioners resources to monitor and improve their physical health are a good example of an organizational partnership between the church and community health services. These initiatives can focus on getting men to become more involved in the church and also more committed to taking care of their own and their children's health.

   The sponsors of these and other initiatives tied to formal organizations must recognize that some fathers may be suspicious of bureaucratic structures and processes. Individual men may have had negative experiences with particular groups during their own childhood or later or a disturbing encounter with a particular organization. This might make men reluctant to trust a particular organization's motives. They may also feel uncomfortable with people involved with a specific group because those members' views may be adversely influenced by the group ideology. Estranged parents will no doubt feel uncomfortable if they sense that they are receiving only partial information about their children from those who service them.

By now it should be clear that we see fathering as much more than the one-on-one relationships men have with their children; it is part of an elaborate social arrangement. In our view, the arrangement is predicated neither on the traditional image of men being dependent on women's kin work and support nor on a sense of fathers exhibiting the profound self-confidence and "go-it-alone" mentality typical of traditional expressions of masculinity. Whether it involves a coparent, other family members and close friends, or youth workers, the fathering experience is intimately tied to trust-building efforts and is embedded in a much wider network of personal relations and organizations. In some respects, fathering can be viewed as a series of partnerships, many of which overlap in complex ways. Indeed, men's romantic partners and others can contribute to their willingness and ability to reach out beyond their families to forge and nurture productive interactions with youth workers. Men's personal attributes can also affect their assertiveness and success in establishing social capital for their children beyond the home.

A closer look at the disparities in fathers' human capital can deepen our perspective of what needs to be considered when planning public and private initiatives to engage fathers more fully in their children's lives. Recall that the primary forms of human capital include income potential, employment experiences, educational attainment, knowledge, and interpersonal skills. Some fathers are clearly more constrained than others in their ability to solidify the web of resources available to children inside and outside the home.

In addition, fathers draw on their skills and capital as they encounter risks, experience pride and shame, and develop resilience in contexts that challenge their involvement as parents. Men's experiences as youth workers are an example of using and developing human capital. Now we turn to a broader discussion of men's capacities to be generative—to promote and support future generations, either through their own biological children or other children. These capacities emerge from the wide range of experiences men have as workers, students, parents, and partners.

Chapter 7

Transitions and Human Capital

VIEWED together, the narrative snapshots we've shared give a sense of the dynamic dimensions of men's lives as fathers. The stories highlight the value of understanding the critical transitions that all fathers experience, as well as the scope of the complex dilemmas and constraints they encounter along the way. They not only raise questions about the circumstances affecting when and why fathers feel vulnerable and stressed; they also indicate how fathers try to adjust to new conditions and expectations.

Most policies and programs have lagged behind the dramatic and frequent changes in individuals' personal and family lives in recent decades. So too, some of the prominent socioeconomic changes related to patterns of education and work have negatively affected males, young and not so young, but especially those with more modest or limited means. Increasingly, men, not just fathers, struggle to establish themselves financially and to find contentment. If men lack resources, they are poorly positioned to navigate their own lives successfully, let alone make plans to be a family man or deal with the demands, if they are nonresident fathers, of fathering children across households.

To be effective, public and private initiatives must be responsive to the circumstances of critical life transitions that on a daily basis challenge fathers as well as men more generally and limit their choices. It may also be appropriate at times to intervene and initiate a transitional process for fathers. Initiatives must be geared to the wide-ranging primary transitions such as divorce, military deployment, remarriage, or a cancer diagnosis for a child as well as the cascade of secondary changes that influence men's desires, resources, and opportunities to be engaged fathers. Some of the latter circumstances include mothers taking children to live out of state, losing hours on the job, or completion of a general equivalency diploma certificate. In line with our earlier comments about the value of building fathers' capacity to create social capital for their children, initiatives should address how the human capital men possess enhances or limits their fathering potential during their transitions.

168

To sharpen our call for a responsive vision of public policy we look more closely at ways to conceptualize fathers' life transitions and human capital. This means paying closer attention to men's and fathers' critical transitions as targets for intervention.[1] Even though it remains important to manage crises resulting from difficult circumstances, efforts to help fathers avoid dilemmas should be featured more prominently in the policy mix. Instead of thinking about interventions as one-time, short-term projects, we take a long view: the provision of educational and employment opportunities may need to occur repeatedly over a person's life course. Our long view acknowledges that men's personal and family lives are unique and dynamic over the life course. As fathers, men face an array of challenges at different points in their own and their children's lives. Ideally, public and private efforts should encourage men to be nurturing, engaged fathers irrespective of their breadwinning capacity.

The transitions that interest us most are those involving men who are susceptible to feeling confused, frustrated, or anxious about their chances to be "good" fathers. The transitions also impinge on the fathering paths central to our framework: self-as-father, the father-child relationship, coparenting, and copartnering. Each of our participants has unique challenges yet shares recognizable threads in the fatherhood mosaic: whether a man is a young father—like the 20-year-old Francisco—undergoing an unexpected identity transformation as he seeks to rededicate himself to his education and future career; a committed middle-class stepfather like Terry, who negotiated the terms of his second marriage as being contingent on his being given the opportunity to be a complete father to his stepson; a nonresident father—like immigrant worker Miguel—wrestling with uncertainties of low-wage labor while coping with the consequences that go with living apart from children; or an ex-prisoner like Andy, struggling to break free of his addiction to alcohol and deal with both court regulations and work-release guidelines that restrict his autonomy. Each of these men mentioned how he wanted to transform his life through a closer bond with his children, and many of them worked to create circumstances by which they could redeem past mistakes through renewed involvement with their children.[2]

Our observations about transitions and human capital apply to all types of fathers facing constrained choices. Many of these men anticipate or undergo significant transitions that can influence their interactions with their children and partners as well as their own personal development. With an eye toward promoting social and personal changes that serve fathers well during their fathering careers, we focus on both transitions grounded primarily in men's experiences with work, education, and health as well as events tied more directly to men's initial transition to fathering and subsequent transitions within fathering.[3] Dealing with men more generally can help men prepare to be fathers beforehand, and some of the initiatives might help all men, fathers or not.

Transitions

Social scientists guided by the life-course perspective—which "looks at how chronological age, relationships, common life transitions, and social change shape people's lives from birth to death"—continue to debate how to define transitions in a meaningful way and to differentiate them from more generic kinds of change.[4] Philip Cowan noted that the "transition" concept needs to be viewed as something distinct from continual change. In his view, individual and family transitions are best viewed as

> long-term processes that result in qualitative reorganization of both inner and external behavior. For a life change to be designated as transitional, it must involve a qualitative shift from the inside looking out (how the individual understands and feels about the self and the world) and from the outside looking in (reorganization of the individual or family's level of personal competence, role arrangements, and relationships with significant others). Passing a life marker (e.g., entering school) or changing one's identity (e.g., becoming a husband or father) does not in itself signify that a transition has been completed.[5]

Thus, transitions mark the ongoing shift in men's state of mind as they adjust to a set of "before" and "after" conditions. They also represent behavioral adjustments.

One recent review of the parenting literature highlights four developmental themes associated with Cowan's and other theoretical models of transitions.[6] First, in a successful transition some form of personal growth occurs that involves a higher level of flexibility, mastery, and the ability to understand how different situations require unique responses.[7] A man finds a way to resolve the tension he is experiencing prior to a transition by adapting to circumstances in a manner that pushes him to see and experience his world in new ways. The immigrant father who leaves his wife and children to find work in a new country may make a successful transition to being a nonresident father if he accepts and is able to implement new ways of expressing his standing as a father from afar. Second, the developmental shift can be either progressive or regressive. Some initiatives can bring about changes that enable a father to enhance his nurturing connections with his children, whereas others heighten the negative outcomes a father experiences. Third, changes associated with transitions integrate the way a man thinks, feels, and acts as a father, which can change substantially. Fourth, a transition begins when some degree of disequilibrium has been reached and it ends when an integrated level of equilibrium is achieved. Thus, a father initially will sense that certain things in his life are not working as smoothly as they once did but eventually he experiences more stability in his state of mind.

Some transitions occur because of specific events at specific times; others involve less definable moments. Transitions sometimes can be anticipated; other times they happen unexpectedly. Efforts to deal with predictable transitions can take a different course than those intended to manage transitions that take fathers by surprise. Whether foreseen or not, several conditions can trigger fathers' transitional experiences. Changes in men's personal lives—a new job or a job loss, a cancer diagnosis, or a second family—can lead to dramatic shifts in parenting. Such shifts may be tied fundamentally to fathers' orientation to specific types of changes that debilitate or enhance their sense of manliness. In other words, when men believe their masculinity is dependent on achieving certain things and responding to situations in certain ways, it can affect how they express themselves as fathers. Dramatic events can also lead men to transform their views of masculinity and chart a different course for fathering.

Men sometimes feel the need to distance themselves from mistakes and disappointments in their lives, such as drug abuse, incarceration, gang activity, crime, or failed relationships. Fathering can offer hope of redemption, of a second chance at being a nurturing parent. Although challenges await men who try to "knife off the difficult past," the transition into starting over as a parent can inject a new motivation to succeed as a father.[8]

Men may also tailor new ways of fathering in response to a child's developing new needs, to his partner's return to the workforce, or to his family's enduring the crisis of losing a family business. Finally, some triggers for changes in men's fathering reflect broad social changes. Cohorts of fathers adapting to the revolution in women's roles or to a transformed global economic environment in the current recession may find different ways to interact and nurture children. As we dissect the transitions fathers experience we bear in mind their timing relative to other ongoing transitions and life-course roles and relationships.

Other insights can be generated by taking a broader view of transitions that includes changes specific to fathering or those more directly tied to men's accumulation of human capital. Many men launch transitions when they undergo changes that involve human capital related to education, work, or health status. Reflecting on our participants' varied experiences we can identify key properties of transitions that transcend the developmental themes noted earlier.

First, some transitions that are repeated over the course of a man's fathering career may influence a man's sensitivity to particular programmatic strategies in dealing with these recurring situations. Second, timing and sequencing are important issues for those experiencing multiple transitions. In many instances, transitions appear in bundles so that a father undergoes multiple shifts simultaneously. At other times, the relative timing of particular transitions can alter how a father perceives and copes with consequences. For example, both Miguel and Andy experienced critical changes in their lives in their thirties, when they had established themselves in the world of work and had over a decade of fathering experience under their belts. Forced to live apart from their families because of incarceration and immigration, they did not "head for the hills." Their measured responses helped them to sustain their central role in their children's lives. Third, the occurrence and nature of a father's transition are often responsive to his significant others' transitions. Working effectively with a father may require that services be provided to someone else. Fourth, the duration of transitions can vary widely among fathers. One father may experience a month-long layoff from work, whereas another might endure a protracted period of searching for a job after his layoff. Similarly, the consequences associated with a sudden debilitating accident may differ from a long bout with an illness. In many instances, developing strategies that move fathers through particular transitions in a timely yet healthy way is warranted. Social initiatives can benefit fathers indirectly by encouraging young men, irrespective of whether they have kids or not, to make a mature, productive transition from their formative years to adulthood.[9]

Human Capital

Of particular interest to us in terms of human capital are the aspects of jobs, education, and interpersonal skills that enhance fathers' efforts to manage transitions associated with their self-as-father, father-child, coparental, and copartner trajectories. In the world of work, what matters most is training and employment opportunities, interviewing skills, wages, and benefits. Because fathers are typically expected to fulfill breadwinning responsibilities, fathers will be better equipped to resolve most transitions productively when they have strong ties to the labor market or the potential to achieve such ties.

As for formal education, key resources include vocational-technical training, high school degrees, and advanced credentials. Although these resources can help fathers land jobs and establish careers, men acquire other valuable assets through formal or informal means that can enhance their ability to be better fathers. Child-relevant knowledge, technical competencies, emotional intelligence, and hands-on experience with children can help men be more attentive, responsive, and effective fathers.

Finally, interpersonal skills are relevant if they strengthen men's resiliency; improve risk-taking decisionmaking; and foster effective ways to manage pride, anger, disappointment, and shame. Some skills will be tied explicitly to the educational assets noted earlier. In addition, efforts to help men refine specific people skills will complement programmatic initiatives designed to dismantle the antifeminine and homophobic codes of conduct that discourage males of varying ages from being more attentive, empathetic, nurturing, and feminist-minded individuals and fathers.[10] We emphasize how initiatives should address men's capacities and opportunities for engaged fathering by focusing on helping men build human-capital resources. Those who launch and administer initiatives need to be sensitive to critical transitional periods in which the timing, intensity, and delivery format of interventions are essential and develop programs that deliver such interventions.

The "New" Transition to Adulthood

Policymakers and program staff also need to understand how historical shifts in the economic climate and gendered family roles have been building for decades. Governments the world over have responded to changes in the youth labor market over the past three decades.[11] In the United States, changes in the economy and in family life have culminated in unique ways for the current cohort of young men. In particular, men's annual earnings in adjusted dollars actually declined between 1970 and 2008.[12] Young African American men continue to experience disproportionately low wages and a high rate of unemployment. The entry of women, particularly white mothers, into the workforce has also continued unabated for three decades. In 2010, for the first time in the United States, there are more women in the workforce than men.[13] One of the many implications of this trend for family life is the easing of expectations that young men must choose to be breadwinners immediately upon marriage or the birth of their children. In fact, to a certain extent poor economic conditions have taken such choices out of young men's hands. The Great Recession of 2008 to 2011 has hit young men the hardest of all demographic groups. There are few entry-level jobs that pay enough to support one person well, much less a family.

In addition, to the extent that sexual norms have grown more flexible in many communities, young people are reconsidering the necessity of getting married in order to have a sexual partner or even to have a family. Many look at the circumstances of their own parents' divorces and decide to be more cautious about entering a marriage without some trial and error.

The combination of these trends, along with the increased life span of the general population in the United States, has led to the recent emergence of a "new" period of the life course. The transition to adulthood has been demarcated as a stage usually occurring between eighteen and thirty years of age in which young men and women now take more time to accumulate the resources that enable them to secure a viable adulthood.[14] This may mean staying in school to attain degrees, building an employment history through exploration of different types of work, and delaying marriage and parenting.

This "new" transition is more complicated than many recognize. The twelve-year span is also the most demographically dense period of the life course in the sense that young adults pass through more significant life-course transitions—five—during this period than at any other time of their lives: (1) departing from the parental residence; (2) completing an education; (3) securing employment; (4) establishing partnership and marriage; and (5) having children. For the past fifty years, however, fewer and fewer young adults complete these transitions in this sequence, despite conventional wisdom about the desired order in which adult life "should" emerge. Even as early as the 1980s, only 25 to 29 percent of young men and women experienced the transitions of completing school, finding work, getting married, and having kids, in this order.[15]

What, then, is a reliable marker for adulthood? For many, a best approximate is "when I feel like an adult."[16] For most young men, establishing a secure identity, a stable job, a network of social support, and a degree of self-sufficiency would represent success. But there is considerable disagreement as to how one becomes an adult. In addition, even when young men want to follow a particular path and timetable into adulthood, many lack the resources to complete school, find housing, and begin family life. The pathways to work for low-income and working-class men may be even more fragile, leaving young fathers unable to "close the deal" on marriage and setting up a household with their families. In spite of these limitations, most men become fathers during this new phase of the life course (21 percent of men become biological fathers by the age of twenty-two, and 56 percent by thirty).[17] By the end of the decisive decade of their twenties, most fathers find themselves on one side or the other of a great divide: settling into two-parent married households or on the periphery as unmarried, noncustodial fathers.

Set against the cultural backdrop of this prolonged transition into adulthood, young fathers grapple with how being a parent reshapes all

of the related transitions in school, work, and family. With little basis
for coordinating these life domains, they often move in fits and starts
towards synchronizing these changes. Antonio is the twenty-four-year-
old son of Mexican immigrants and father of a two-year-old son, Rafael.
He was not prepared to become a father and felt ambivalent about how
this transition would influence his future prospects.

> Well . . . I'm not going to lie. When she first told me [she was pregnant] I
> wasn't very excited. I didn't really want to have a child at the time. You
> know, I was still young, I wasn't financially prepared. I never wanted to
> have a split family, so that also crossed my mind. Young couples tend to
> split up, it doesn't tend to work out. It was definitely more negative than
> positive but I didn't want to see it that way because it wasn't his fault or
> her fault that the child was inside. . . . But as more months went by and I
> kinda got used to it and I know that I'm an intelligent person. I looked at
> my parents—they came from Mexico with absolutely nothing. My parents
> have bought two brand-new cars within their life, they own a home, two
> homes. They put me through [Catholic] school and all this with under
> thirty thousand dollars a year, so, to me they're inspiration. I thought, as
> long as I finish school I know I got their support, it's not going to be impos-
> sible. I didn't want to have an abortion, she didn't either. So . . . all I had
> to do was man up, basically, take responsibility for my actions.

Having a son speeded up Antonio's timeline for making a decision
about his relationship with Rafael's mother. He was immediately confronted with bad feelings from her family, and over the early months of his
son's life, Antonio and his son's mother have lived together in a succession
of apartments. Even with his upbringing in a traditional two-parent
Mexican family, he remains uncommitted to the possibility of marriage.

> Her father, he still doesn't speak to me to this day. He thinks I'm a bum,
> I'm a lame. I mean, granted I don't have much to offer financially, but I
> don't think that that makes me less of a man if I'm taking care of my son,
> I'm going to school, I'm working. You know. I'm doing the best I can with
> what I got basically. The rest of her family have come along, they speak to
> me, but her dad is still holding a grudge. . . . Right now I'm living at home
> and she has her own apartment but we are planning on getting an apart-
> ment together now so that I can move out of my parents' house. She
> moved out of her parents' house and she has her own apartment with him
> [my son]. . . . [I think marriage] is very important, but you've got to do it
> for the right reasons. If you're going to get married, do it because you both
> care and love each other, not just for the kid.

The transition to fatherhood has also intensified the pursuit of a viable
career that would allow Antonio to become a real "adult," which for him

means being able to "stand on my own two feet." Like many young men, he tries to make the best decisions from his limited knowledge of opportunities in the local community. Antonio struggles to coordinate his studies at community college and his part-time job with family demands, while at the same time remaining true to the dreams he harbored for many years as an adolescent.

> I work down the street at a health clinic; I am the switchboard operator. They have several kinds of offices down at the community college. I go there to get all my general electives out of the way. Then I'm going to Chicago State to study education and get a job in the public school. Either that or, you know, wherever they will take me. . . . I mean, I got a lot of ideas, man. I'd like to open up my own business. I got ideas for inventions. I want to look in the mirror and be satisfied with what I see. To me, I'm a success if I can stand on my own two feet. I can take care of Rafael, whatever he needs is his. To me, that will be successful—I have my own home, I have a car, I have money in savings, you know, things like that.

Other young fathers also acknowledge that getting a high school degree and some postsecondary education are clearly linked to better job outcomes and higher quality fathering. However, some of them never make it to postsecondary education because they do not complete high school. The goals of in-school programs are to reduce dropout rates as well as to enhance postsecondary attendance and completion. Some of the most successful of the high school programs have been evaluated, such as Multiple Pathways to Graduation (MPG), GEAR UP, Upward Bound, and Achievement Via Individual Determination (AVID).[18] These programs offer young fathers mentoring relationships; compressed timelines for graduation; and smaller, tailored learning communities in large schools. Work-based learning components geared to the needs of men who are anxious about the upcoming transition to work are a common feature and include job-shadowing, on-the-job training, and skills training. Over 2000 Career Academies across the country offer young fathers career and technical education courses as well as supplemental summer and year-round employment.

Most young men recognize that education is an indicator of success, a prerequisite for mobility in the current economy, and an asset to establishing a family at a young age as well. But sociohistorical forces, by altering the social landscapes of gender and work, have contributed to a pattern whereby fewer young men are attending or completing college than young women. All adult women and men in the United States are about equally likely to complete a bachelor's degree (29 percent to 30 percent), but since 2000, women have consistently represented about 57 percent of enrollments at American colleges.[19]

Community colleges may be the one exception to this pattern. The number of male community college students from low-income, working-poor, or minority families has begun to increase in recent years. In fact, the majority of young men of color who attend postsecondary schools are choosing to enroll in community colleges.[20] In fact, most of the growth in college attendance in the past decade has been among nontraditional students. Some expect that 85 percent of the growth in the number of college degrees in coming years will be from older adults, working parents, and minority men and women.[21] About 9 percent of all community college students are fathers (over 600,000 men), and 4 percent are single fathers.[22]

Once enrolled, young men encounter the increasing financial demands of college. Between 2000 and 2010, the average college tuition, adjusted for inflation, increased by 92 percent.[23] About half of all college students drop out before graduation, and young adult men are a substantial portion of those. They incur more and more debt if they do complete their degrees: in 2008 the average college senior had $23,000 in outstanding debt at graduation.[24] New programs established by the Barack Obama administration have simplified the student aid system and increased the number of Pell Grants and funding for community colleges, but they have done little to slow the rapid increases in tuition faced by young men and women.

More flexible college course schedules may enable more young fathers to attend college and complete their postsecondary education. Increasing options for distance learning offered by all types of educational institutions might give fathers greater control over their daily routines and perhaps allow more of them to complete coursework while working full-time jobs. An additional cost for young fathers trying to fulfill work demands and attend classes is the burden of paying for child care while they work and study.[25] Funding for on-site child care in community colleges and four-year colleges would give young fathers and mothers a valuable resource for managing their transition to adulthood.

Pursuing a postsecondary degree is a better option for many young fathers than looking for a job. Youths were the hardest hit age group during the most recent recession, and unemployment continues to grow. Roughly a third of all jobs lost between December 2007 and September 2009 (2.5 million jobs) were held by those sixteen to twenty-four.[26] By August 2010, the unemployment rate for young men and women under the age of twenty-five hovered around 19 percent, more than double the rate for the overall population of working Americans and the highest unemployment rate for this age bracket since 1948, when federal data were first collected on youth employment.[27] Over 20 percent of young men were unemployed, and the rates were higher for minority youths

(33 percent for African American youths, 22.1 percent for Hispanics, and 21.6 percent for Asian Americans).[28]

Employment is a nonnegotiable responsibility for most young fathers, and they can be hard-pressed to pursue both work and school. Full-time school attendance takes a great deal of time and money, both of which can detract from success in the workplace. Likewise, the time demands of a full-time job and caring for children can both jeopardize completion of a degree. As a result, young fathers risk falling behind in school and becoming disconnected from work. Many need support to reconnect to these social arenas.

Most communities suffer from a paucity of programs that connect colleges and training facilities with employers who can help young men make the leap to stable jobs. Federal policymakers need to develop a comprehensive youth policy that integrates school and work initiatives across departments with efforts in criminal justice, mental health, and local social services.[29] Coordinated policy efforts can offer young fathers committed to contributing financially to their children a range of options to secure work and attend school. Apart from in-school programs, mentoring activities in youth development programs like those offered by Boys & Girls Clubs and the Harlem Empowerment Zone have been shown to have a positive effect on academic, social, psychological, and behavioral outcomes.[30] Fathers in their mid- and late twenties may benefit more from Job Corps or the National Guard Youth ChalleNGe Program, which include vocational curricula, optional residential programs, and strong links to employers and businesses. Other programs such as Job Build or the Job Service and Conservation Corps are oriented toward service employment to instill civic values and provide opportunities for community engagement.[31] Although some of these programs look promising in terms of helping young men find employment with good wages immediately, they may not help with long-term employment prospects four years out after program completion. In any event, to make a difference in young fathers' lives programs must recognize young fathers' special needs as they struggle to become self-sufficient adults with parental responsibilities. Assistance with parenting and relationship challenges, life-coping skills, housing, mental health services, and substance abuse can improve the success rate of the employment outcomes that the programs for young adults are specifically created to achieve.

Embedded in the mix of men who are disconnected from school and work is the vulnerable cohort of young fathers who are incarcerated or are leaving the criminal justice system to reenter communities and family life. Fathers make up 93 percent of all incarcerated parents, and over 50 percent of all federal or state prisoners reported that they were parents of children under eighteen. Many incarcerated fathers are in their twenties, and of these, a disproportionate number are men of color.[32] Prerelease programs that encourage employment and training are one approach to helping these men, and postrelease services are another complementary strategy.

Partnerships with courts and service providers can be productive after young fathers leave correctional facilities, but creating an interface with schools and employers appears to be the major hurdle. Training programs have shown some impact on wages, and "transitional job" programs, in which young fathers receive paid employment and supportive services, do not help with the transition to public-sector jobs with good pay. They do, however, reduce recidivism.[33] Across the board, small-scale programs designed to enhance father-child interaction and to develop emotional bonds may have a similar effect in reducing recidivism when young fathers find that their children give them a new reason to stay out of jail.[34]

Young men without children or with noncustodial children have been hit the hardest in the current recession. Those who have limited access to Temporary Assistance for Needy Families or Unemployment Insurance (UI) benefits need job placement services, further education and training, and possibly subsidized jobs.[35] A comprehensive and coordinated youth policy would likely necessitate reauthorization of the Workforce Investment Act. Under this act an agency could be established to coordinate the necessary complex arrangement of actors, formula grants, and competitive grants.[36] A comprehensive policy would also place young men at the center of an emerging commitment to a new national apprenticeship program to create pathways from school to work and to the exploration of a mandatory national service program, in which youths would contribute to community development efforts and learn work skills in the process.[37] The current lack of such broader federal initiatives makes it clear that there are very limited existing structures to accommodate moving young men with families into self-sufficiency and adulthood.

Young fathers will most likely change residences frequently as they pursue their education and take on their first jobs. Many hope to establish some level of self-sufficiency and stability. Today, parents are increasingly less likely to expect their sons to leave their parental home around their twentieth birthday. Many parents assume that their sons' transition out of the household will be drawn out and will depend on their sons' capacity to support themselves (and even their own young children and partners). For most young fathers, a transition to an established residence apart from their parents' home is not a smooth process, with phases of returning back to parents, living with friends, living independently, and cohabiting alternating over a period of years. Young men's residential histories are especially complicated during the transition to adulthood.

Policies and programs that leave the door open for men's prolonged dependence on their parents can give families control over how and when to make changes in adult relationships. For example, current health-care reform legislation allows adults to continue coverage of their young adult children through age twenty-six, perhaps many years after they have left or returned home. Other critical measures are initiatives that provide incentives for young fathers and their families to settle in residential households. Tax credits for first-time home buyers, subsidized home loans, and government-backed mortgages to encourage home ownership have been available to young families in some form for over seventy years. Department of Housing and Urban Development programs have offered affordable housing options for lower income and young working-class men, but the volume of such affordable housing is extremely limited, and the recent economic downturn has reduced the economic advantages offered by such programs. In addition to providing access to subsidies and rental alternatives, programs could help young fathers make informed decisions about the best available residential arrangements in an uneven housing market.

The related changes in education, employment, and residence patterns reflect the rapid transformations in family relationships during the transition to adulthood. Young men increasingly find themselves negotiating their own independent role with their parent(s) and kin, their partners and their kin, and their children. In recent years, traditional expectations for "what young men should do" as loyal sons or proud providers in their twenties have become much more ambiguous because men's experiences as live-at-home adult sons, unmarried fathers, and cohabiting stepfathers are relatively undefined.

How might policies and programs shape families' efforts to support young men's fathering? Fluency in managing household finances may be central to independence for young fathers, and money remains a contested issue between parents, partners, and men. Public services— delivered in schools, hospitals, community centers, churches, or workplaces—can provide information and counseling on balancing budgets, establishing savings accounts, planning for retirement or college, paying taxes, and the menu of tax credits available to young families. Many community institutions and federal agencies have realized that young adults' financial illiteracy has contributed to a low savings rate, poor decisions about buying or renting homes, and lack of understanding of Social Security and retirement.

More and more initiatives focused on early education for parenting and couple relationships have emerged in recent decades. As noted in previous chapters, faith communities, some researchers, and even recent presidential administrations have viewed "relationship" literacy as a key factor in young fathers' potential to become nurturing parents. Public and private agencies are now integrating the development of relationship skills with more concrete resources, such as access to health-care services, information on welfare programs, and opportunities for job training and postsecondary education.[38]

Looking for Jobs and Hope During the Great Recession

Typical media representations of contemporary fathers often highlight men as caregivers, friends, even nurturers of their children. Although the new "male mystique" and cultural models of "new fathers" reflect these eclectic images, being a breadwinner is ultimately the foundation on which successful fathering is judged by mainstream American culture.[39] So transformations in the economy and the workplace have direct implications for men's identities as providers and for their ability to contribute materially to their families' upkeep.

Even after fathers settle into stable employment, they negotiate jobs in workplaces that are continually transforming to adapt to the demands of a globalized economy. Some men recognize the competing expectations of work and family life. Middle- and working-class parents learn to make a tradeoff between family time and work time in jobs that are less secure and pay less, whereas upper-class parents struggle to create family time while working in high-paying environments that demand more and more of their time.[40] This pressure to work compromises men's potential to nurture their children.

Families have to maneuver between the conflicting demands of child care, household tasks, and workplace demands. Parents' decisions to share care or return to work or to take jobs with flexible time schedules are typically perceived as reflecting their individual preferences or choices. Unfortunately, few policies and programs have been established to ease the stressful tradeoffs that parents must make. Widespread provision of on-site day care is a workplace policy option that could possibly facilitate families' work-versus-family choices. As some fathers take on working longer hours, on-site day care would allow fathers to fulfill work demands while remaining close to their children. They could share lunches, participate in pickup and dropoff routines, and be available for emergency care.

The shifting landscape of global and local economies is remaking men's parenting in another sense. The economic downturn since 2008 has been termed a "man-cession" because it has sharply affected the market for jobs typically held by men, primarily construction and manufacturing. About 75 percent of the jobs lost since 2007 have been held by men. Although women still lag behind men in the labor market in many respects, the declining real wages for the past three decades have increasingly left working-class and middle-class fathers with few pathways toward providing. Not since the Great Depression have fathers' prospects for being good providers been so bleak.

The key to helping these fathers is work itself. Work-based subsidies may be adapted to free up resources that keep fathers linked to a job. As policymakers try to manage the current economic recession, they encounter historically high rates of unemployment. Extension of UI benefits has been a source of contention, but they remain a lifeline for many fathers in families who struggle to weather single or multiple job losses.

Policymakers have considered ways to make training and education opportunities more responsive to the needs of the local labor market. Older fathers who lose their jobs must be retrained and often must begin again in an alternative career, especially if the prospects of their prior career paths are limited. Resources from the economic stimulus package, the American Recovery and Reinvestment Act of 2009, were channeled through the Workforce Investment Act to offer training to skilled workers in downsized industries for jobs in health care or renewable energy. However, the promise of new careers in these fields has remained fleeting for many men who have lost their places in the workforce because of downsizing and layoffs.[41] Programs such as Workforce 1 career centers in New York, No Worker Left Behind in Michigan, and Workfast in Minnesota encounter the obstacle of lack of demand for retrained workers.

The need for these programs appears more urgent when we understand how difficult it can be for working-class men to "connect the dots" and find a place in a new global economy with its demands for advanced skills. Many men struggle to fit into a workforce that continually retrains in response to the needs of relocating businesses. Without these comprehensive retraining programs, men are often left with only a vague sense of how to proceed with finding effective pathways to a good job.[42] "I've taken some general education courses—but I ain't lying— I wasn't going to go into computer engineering," admits DeQuam, sitting in a community resource center on Chicago's South Side. "I know you need to be good at math, and there are steps to get into that program . . . but I haven't went to school yet for it. I still go to the resource center and get on the computer." DeQuam is excited about a future career that includes using computers because

... computers are like a second medication for me. I just like getting on the Internet, pressing buttons, typing, and stuff like that. You can find anything you want, any information, history, whatever you want you can find. My sister got [a computer] but I want my own. I don't like to depend on nobody, cause you got to go through her, there's a lot of problems.

At home, DeQuam, twenty-seven, is under pressure to come up with a coherent plan to provide for his two stepsons, who at thirteen and eleven are not much younger than he is. He also has a twelve-month-old daughter, as well as his girlfriend's five-year-old son, who live in a nearby apartment. DeQuam's excitement about computer engineering has flavored his decisions about his baby's future as well. He admits, "I bought her a little thirty-dollar play laptop for kids. It's got games, it teaches her math, and it's like a Spanish version. Cause I want her to learn at an early age."

Longer term employment policies could begin by extending the Earned Income Tax Credit (EITC), the largest and most successful antipoverty program today, to childless working men as well as to noncustodial fathers.[43] Childless-worker credits have been proposed in federal legislation because workers without children are the only taxpayers who owe federal income tax even when their income is below the poverty level.[44] The minimum age at which a working father can receive EITC benefits is twenty-five, which eliminates many young unemployed fathers from consideration. Bills under review call for studies to examine the effect of this age restriction. Finally, for over a decade federal legislation has explored the possibility of extending the EITC to noncustodial parents, but these legislative proposals tie receipt of tax credits to full payment of child support. Because lower income fathers are most likely to be in arrears with their child support, proposals that provide tax credits to help lower child support debt will be useful to the very category of fathers who could benefit from accessing resources.[45] Policymakers should remain sensitive to this barrier and others for low-income working fathers and potentially permit the partial payment of arrearages in exchange for EITC credits.[46]

If work is the key, which solution would help fathers who have not worked in recent months? Many fathers find jobs in an informal economy, working for cash-in-hand or off-the-books jobs that are fluid. Work-based subsidies will not provide a paycheck or promote the role of being a nurturing provider for this population of men. Likewise, men who are returning to their families and communities after serving in a correctional facility need to start at square one and find a job. Policymakers have suggested a system of subsidized jobs, transitional jobs, or jobs of "last resort." For example, one popular program proposal mandates transitional jobs for men who are required to work, such as ex-offenders or those who owe child support.[47]

Realistically, though, these initiatives may fall short of filling the needs of fathers who have been unemployed for long periods of time because of incarceration or unemployment. Xavier's children—ten in all, with four different mothers—live in Chicago and in two communities in the South. At thirty-two he has found his first mainstream job, as a sales assistant at Old Navy in Chicago's Loop. He is energetic, witty, and intelligent—and in his own eyes is very successful in this job. Such service-sector jobs will likely come and go in the current recession, but he expects to parlay his job experience into a career that will ensure his children's futures:

> I was going through the dark my whole life. Once I dedicated myself to the street against all my mama's rules, I only see dark, I ain't seen light. My future is basically brightening up now. [I'm out of jail, I got my job,] I see light at the other end of the tunnel. . . . My father did like I do now—work, come home—that's it. He's a strong man, a provider, I give him that much. Sitting in his rocking chair, watching kids play. I didn't know I was going to turn out like it is now. . . . Nowadays the only thing a young man have—they don't have nothing going on for themselves. The best thing that [they] can do is get each of their kids an insurance policy. So as I was out there selling [drugs] I opened up an insurance policy. Like that rapper said, it's like that Lotto, guarantees a hit. This is better than the Lotto. If I die my kids are going to be taken care of. I wasn't born with no silver spoon. I wasn't born with no corporate mind. So I know they have something to fall back on if I leave this earth.

Men's job losses take a heavy toll on the stability of family households as well, although it is difficult to quantify how many fathers and children are currently without a stable residence. But homeless shelters have not been receptive to offering a family housing when the family includes a father. Usually males over the age of fifteen are segregated out and housed in separate facilities, apart from their children, siblings, or parents. Protecting women and children from abusive husbands is key in providing a safe residential space and managing a shelter program. However, providing more facilities for homeless fathers with children will be critical during the recession, as fathers try to hold their families together and find stable employment.

In spite of the current recession, some fathers continue to seek employment across national borders, a huge challenge to the management of work and family life. Historically many fathers have moved across substantial boundaries to manage work and family life. Over the past decade, hundreds of thousands of fathers have transitioned into active military duty and have moved thousands of miles away from their children and family routines. Although men can successfully manage this separation, the departure from and return back to children can put great stress on father-child bonds. Although running two wars was their top priority, military services have nevertheless had to reconsider scheduling of deployment in order to meet the needs of military families. Preliminary research indicates that while fathers' multiple deployments increase the stress that adolescent children feel, these kids also develop resilience by living through the challenges of their fathers' absence.[48] The military has developed an innovative online portal to support and educate personnel and their families about relocation, parenting, education, and stress. The Military One Source website archives educational materials for service members and their families to help them with a range of topics, including transitioning to fatherhood, remaining involved during deployment and returning home from deployment, and being an involved father for children at different developmental stages. The website also links service personnel and their families to immediate private and confidential counseling services offered 24/7.[49] Military personnel, their spouses, and their families can receive referrals for child care, educational opportunities, jobs, and even social programs available on and off base.

As we've seen in previous chapters, fathers in immigrant families who come to the United States to find work have to manage family life across national borders. Migration for jobs is disruptive to father-child bonds and can endanger the closeness that fathers have established with their families despite tenuous living circumstances. A long history of policy initiatives in the United States has affected father-child relations across borders. The Bracero program, which was in place from 1942 to 1964, was a program to recruit Mexican men to work in specific industries in the United States. It offered few if any provisions for men's families and specifically for facilitating father involvement from a distance.

Today, migrant workers and their families continue to face a bleak picture of substandard housing and poor wages, although local and state resources have been invested in providing education and care services for children in these transient families. Yet the policy tools to address immigration-related transitions for men's work and family lives remain limited and have grown more contested in recent years. With widespread job loss and unemployment, local labor markets and communities in the United States do not welcome immigrant workers to the same degree as they did before the recession. In many communities local residents monitor the physical sites such as street corners, vacant lots, or even busy intersections where unemployed workers queue to look for informal day-labor jobs to paint, dig trenches, pick fruit, load trucks, and the like. In Alabama and Arizona, the possible legality of police sweeps and deportation at the heart of recent legislation limits many immigrant fathers' employment prospects. These states' legislation even calls into question the citizenship of children born in the United States to non-citizen immigrant fathers. In such an environment, even well-placed education and employment resources, or education and skills-based training, can do little to stabilize immigrant fathers' fragile family life.

Health Concerns

In chapter 2 we began to lay out our argument that a man's commitment to an engaged, nurturing form of fathering should be grounded in his approach to health—his own, his child's, and his child's mother's. Some obvious targets of opportunity for public and private initiatives we listed include male responsibility programs to deal with reproductive health issues; linkages between public health departments and work sites so that program staff can talk about possible reproductive health risks associated with exposure to toxins; public-service announcements explaining how smoking, drinking, and drug use can adversely affect sperm quality; and enhanced access to prenatal health care and parenting classes that offer information on the health of one's children and partner. These efforts take on additional meaning when a man is going through transitions involving health-related concerns for him or other family members.

Health problems can influence a father's ability to be an attentive, nurturing father. Sometimes the added stress surrounding health problems or the practical limitations associated with disabilities can prevent a father from doing certain things. But some types of health challenges may actually heighten a father's sensitivity to issues that positively affect his relationship with his child. We see both of these patterns in Randy's account of his experiences with his wife and nine-year-old stepson, Jamie. A former paramedic, Randy is a severely obese fifty-year-old who has been disabled for roughly twenty-one years. Among other misfortunes, he has had his leg amputated and had gastric bypass surgery. Despite his physical setbacks, he has committed himself during the past seven years to being an active stepfather for Jamie. Most recently, he has contemplated adopting him.

Some time ago, on the eve of yet another surgery, Randy absorbed one of his most powerful transitions when his life perspective fundamentally changed.

> The first time I had an operation and I had a family, I was a basket case. I was really worried. I took out—they hit you with all this advance directives [bank account authorizations]—boy was I listening . . . it wasn't just

a case of signing papers. . . . All of a sudden, I wasn't just worried about me. I was worried about other people and what happened to me. Now if I get sick it affects two other people, so I damn well better take care of myself. I better listen to the doctor. I better do what I got to do, even though I've probably screwed it up to this point. I've got to start doing what I need to do because other people are depending on me. And I think it's more so with Jamie than as if we were just married. Molly's able to cope on her own without me, basically. I'm not sure Jamie can. . . . It makes you have to stop and take stock of—okay, you can't do this. . . . I can't run around and go drinking with my friends anymore, because then I have to explain to him why it's okay for me to do it and I don't want him to do it.

Randy's health difficulties clearly took hold of his mind and heart. He began to alter his self-perception about his health status and started to see himself more fully as a family man who had clear and important mentoring responsibilities as a father. Thus his identity transition joined his perceptions of his health and family responsibilities.

Ironically, the same physical challenges that left Randy feeling helpless at times because he could not be more active physically with Jamie helped him be a more responsive father by developing a better sense of how Jamie felt about contracting and living with Crohn's disease.

I think I had a lot to go through mentally after I got injured and realized that up to that point I could have made my body—if I didn't do something it was because I just didn't push myself. Okay. Well, I finally hit the wall to where it didn't matter how hard I pushed, it wasn't going to happen. That's a real hard thing for you to have to face. But once you face it you can grow up and get on with things. I think in some ways he [Jamie] may be, to him it's the first time his body ever broke on him and he couldn't really—not that he was in any point where he can't do what he wants to do—but the first time it wasn't easy to do and his body did something he didn't want it to do. It sure has made him grow up a little. . . . You can't tell a kid what to do. You think you are, but it's—you're just guiding him and if he still goes down the stream, you gotta make sure you guide him but you don't have a hundred percent control over him. You just got to push him the right way and hope that you're going to be there when he crashes or be there to help him not crash and go the other way.

Randy's disability insurance provides him some measure of comfort in that he knows he can contribute something to his family's financial needs. Of course, not all fathers are as fortunate. Some men with little or no health or disability insurance face a difficult transition if their own health fails them. They find themselves incapable of providing for themselves as well as their children. Similarly, many fathers with inadequate or no insurance are confronted with a disturbing transition when their child encounters a serious, costly health problem. Even those with seemingly good insurance may face tough decisions as their child's medical bills mount. For those with multiple children, spending huge amounts of money on one child can leave fathers uncertain about the sacrifices their other children are enduring.

The recent health-care reform bill passed into law during the summer of 2010 offers some hope to low- and middle-income fathers because the bill extends health coverage to an estimated 32 million individuals who earn above 133 percent of the poverty line and are currently uninsured.[50] Once the law is in effect in 2014, many of these newly insured fathers and mothers are likely to feel more connected to the health-care system as a regular part of their daily life. Parents may feel less isolated and helpless when they or their children undergo a personal health-care crisis. Similarly, fathers who lose their job will still have protections to make sure their children's and their own health care are not forfeited.

Money, of course, matters a great deal when bills need to be paid. But having the flexibility to take paid time away from work to care for a sick, disabled, or injured child is also valuable. In the United States, options for extended periods of paid leave to provide care for a child are few and far between. At the very least, a father is relatively well off if he can rest easy that his job is secure while he responds to his child's health needs even if he does not have access to paid leave. The Family and Medical Leave Act, signed into law by President Bill Clinton, provides most parents who are federal employees access to up to twelve work weeks of unpaid leave during any twelve-month period to care for a newborn child, a child who has a serious health problem, or themselves if they have a health condition.[51] Unfortunately, recent cross-national research in twenty-one high-income countries on parental leave packages around the time of a child's birth or adoption reveals that the United States and Australia are the only two countries that grant no paid leave, and the United States ranks twentieth in the number of weeks provided for protected job leave.[52] This research does not address family leave in a broad sense. The expansion of such policies could contribute to health-related outcomes for fathers, mothers, and children alike. If fathers are eligible to receive acceptable wage replacements for time away from work they may feel less stress in deciding to spend time with their infants. This early involvement may also increase their chances of establishing routine practices of being a hands-on caregiver for their child, including being more responsive to the child's health-care needs.

Presumably children benefit when both parents are attentive to their health care during transitional periods and beyond. Parent education and counseling efforts are therefore needed to enhance resident and nonresident fathers' and mothers' ability to parent and coparent effectively during health-care decisionmaking.[53] This training and skill building should target parents involved in making relatively standard health decisions as well as those who face more difficult challenges in caring for special needs children. Ideally, fathers and mothers should have ready access to preventive-care education that enables them to gain confidence and move smoothly into and navigate new situations of a general nature or those involving children with more unusual health conditions.[54]

Specialized interventions such as the Fathers and Sons Program, which is designed to enhance nonresident African American fathers' ability to prevent their preadolescent sons' future risky health behaviors, could be modified for other types of nonresident fathers.[55] The program improved fathers' monitoring of their sons and their communication with their sons about sex. Apparently it also inspired a number of the fathers to ask for professional help to stop drinking. The participants in this highly focused intervention had lived apart from their eight- to twelve-year-old sons for varying amounts of time. A revised program might recruit father-son pairs experiencing a recent change in their living arrangement and accentuate strategies that take into account aspects of this critical transition. Similar programs could also be developed for father-daughter pairs.

Most fathers with special needs children have little or no time to prepare their reaction to the news or diagnosis that their child has a serious health problem such as autism, cancer, Crohn's disease, diabetes, or mental disabilities.[56] Fathers of children with either behavioral problems or some developmental disability are likely to cobble together an understanding of their circumstances more gradually. In either case, these fathers can best be served by programs that reach out to them quickly to shape their understanding of their children's health issues and provide them with options for helping their children. Granted, programs should still look to enroll fathers whenever the fathers are inclined to seek assistance.[57] Many already established parenting programs can benefit fathers, yet some observers contend that programs are likely to be most effective for fathers when they are tailored to their unique needs.[58]

The most challenging and politically controversial initiatives are those that focus on fathers who have engaged in intimate partner violence, child abuse, or both. Estimates from the late 1990s reveal that 30 to 60 percent of children whose mothers have been abused experience abuse themselves.[59] Children can suffer emotionally, mentally, and physically if they witness their fathers' violent behavior or are actually abused.[60] From a programmatic perspective, the men who perpetrate family violence are not particularly cooperative clients. They are usually forced by courts and other agencies to seek help, and the professionals who work with them must ultimately be concerned for the safety of the children and mothers. "The challenge facing anyone who wishes to intervene with men who batter as fathers is how to do it all—protect and respect, trust and suspect, empathize and criticize."[61]

In recent years, despite these difficulties, policymakers, practitioners, and researchers interested in family violence have increasingly sought to develop and implement programs that include fathers. Many of these programs prioritize children's healing. The philosophy, content, and tone of family violence programs as well as their timing may determine how much of a difference they make in people's lives. Numerous studies indicate that most mothers who have experienced partner abuse still want their children to have contact with the fathers and have meaningful relationships with them.[62] Some fathers with a history of abuse are still living with their partners and children when they participate in a program.

The level of professionals' sensitivity to transitions central to family life and men's identities is likely to influence the effectiveness of interventions for abusive men and fathers. Transitions may affect how fathers handle a divorce and the accompanying physical separation from children, or how they respond to court-mandated enrollment in an intervention program for batterers that only allows supervised father-child visits, or how they deal with an identity transformation that leaves them appalled at their destructive behavior.

Because there is limited evaluation research on violent men with children, specialists in this area can only suggest "promising practices and strategies," not "empirically supported practices," for deciding when and how courts, the criminal justice system, and therapeutic services should try to deal with violent men or alter their fathering style.[63] Increasingly, experienced social workers and psychologists stress the value of distinguishing between "minor and isolated acts versus acts that occur as part of a pattern of abuse that engenders fear and harm for victims and children exposed to this behavior."[64] Confirmed and alleged instances of domestic violence are very much a part of the controversial process of adjudicating child custody disputes and parenting plans when parents divorce or separate.

Child custody disputes often underscore a critical transition period for fathers, especially when they are dealing with accurate, exaggerated, or fabricated accusations of intimate violence or child abuse. Ultimately, judges who encounter fathers who have abused or have been accused of abuse will choose from a wide range of options: no contact, supervised visitation, supervised exchanges, exchanges in public places, unsupervised visitation, liberal and regular visitation, and shared custody and parenting.[65] Those working with fathers directly in a therapeutic context also have different treatment options that are connected to various sites:

child mental health centers, batterers' intervention programs, after-care programs for abusive men, supervised visitation centers, and adult mental health centers.[66]

One example of a broad therapeutic approach is the seventeen-week group intervention model, Caring Dads: Helping Fathers Value Their Children, first launched in 2002 in London, Ontario, and Boston.[67] This program is designed to "help men end the use of abusive parenting strategies; recognize attitudes, beliefs, and behaviors that support healthy and unhealthy father-child relationships; and understand the impact of child maltreatment and domestic violence on children."[68] Although this program has only been evaluated in a preliminary fashion, its accountability guidelines and intervention goals are informative for those interested in creating father-friendly programs that are also responsive to the need to protect children and their mothers.[69] This program and others seek to enhance fathers' human capital by improving their ability to reflect, empathize, and resolve interpersonal conflicts nonviolently.

Transitions Through Complex Family Relationships

Programs such as Caring Dads that seek to reconnect violent fathers with their children in healthy ways exemplify the reactive approach associated with most fatherhood initiatives. For such programs the challenge is that it is difficult to enhance fathers' human capital when fathers are in the midst of risky transitions, often accompanied by family disruptions of one sort or another. Getting and keeping men involved in ways that positively alter the father-child relationship requires political will, varied resources, devoted professionals, and creative planning. It would be ideal to have systems in place that provide men opportunities to acquire the resources that would decrease their likelihood of ever being abusive or experiencing other outcomes that adversely affect or challenge their fathering. Not all family disruptions can be avoided, of course, but fathers and their families can be better equipped to handle them.

Efforts to deal with abusive fathers are not fundamentally different from initiatives designed to help fathers manage the other challenges we've discussed. Fathers are embedded in a complex, layered social context, their experiences often framed by elements of time and place. Because fathering is ultimately a social arrangement, numerous social forces relating to family, work, schools, and the community can either hinder or help fathers negotiate critical transitions. Potential support systems tied to families, community institutions, and social policies can encourage fathers to persevere and remain generative through family crises and to promote nurturance even when men struggle to live up to their ideal image of fathering. Understanding fathers' complicated lives while mobilizing and integrating multiple support networks can help fathers deal with critical transitions. Managing transitions effectively means that men will feel self-confident and invested as fathers, have nurturing relations with their children, and participate in meaningful parenting exchanges with their partners or former partners. Their ability to draw on the parenting skills they have learned and their own human capital help them remain resilient in the face of risks and challenges.[70]

When we examine transitions in some detail, we recognize that fathering is a series of transitions and trajectories that encompass men's experiences over their lifetimes.[71] Many men develop and alter close relationships with romantic partners and children, change residences, and switch jobs repeatedly as they age into their fourth, fifth, and even sixth decades.[72] Such changes typically complicate men's family life and test the limits of trust between fathers, children, and other adults—family members mostly, but others, too, such as bosses, teachers, and coaches. Men cohabit, marry, divorce, and remarry; develop parenting arrangements with multiple partners; and become fathers, stepfathers, and, eventually, grandfathers. Romantic partners sometimes exit and return to work, and some fathers assume more responsibility for their children's care. Some relationships between fathers and children are disrupted by military deployment or incarceration, then reestablished after long periods of absence. Amid this complexity, how can fathers undergoing significant transitions use their human capital to remain engaged or even repair damaged father-child bonds?

It is difficult to design policies and programs aimed at helping fathers improve their human capital effectively during these transitions. We contribute to the discussion by exploring when transitions occur (timing) and how they occur (sequencing). Unfortunately, many of the systems set up to manage these transitions—family court, child support, and child welfare—are legal systems whose representatives struggle to recognize and respond to the nature and level of family complexity. These systems too often operate on ill-informed assumptions about deadbeat dads or poor fathers, producing a "typology" of fathers that drives policymaking. Understanding the context of transitions related to fathering creates greater flexibility in programs that can help individual fathers tap into resources such as skills training and courtroom advocacy tailored to the needs of unique family configurations.

═ Chapter 8 ═

Promoting Nurturance

NURTURANCE is at the heart of our social-change agenda.[1] Throughout this book we have used men's firsthand accounts to communicate the realities and possibilities for fathers' nurturance. These
stories also show how fathering is a social arrangement. We focus on
the cultural, social, and physical contexts in which nurturance occurs, the
interpersonal and organizational processes that shape how it unfolds
over time, with an emphasis on trust building, and the meanings individuals assign to nurturance. Our goal is to inspire and help fathers in diverse
settings to develop healthier bonds and more positive involvements with
their children.

Unfortunately, the legacy of traditional gender ideology makes it difficult to realize the full effect of such a transformation. By reinforcing the
idea that care work inside and outside the home is women's work, this
ideology reinforces perceptions of nurturance as an expectation for
mothers but largely a choice for fathers.[2] In contemporary households
and policy discussions, however, more is at stake in this transformation
than symbolic issues, which we have seen in the past. What is at stake
is, rather, the necessity to forge equitable relations at home and at work
because economic restructuring and the entry of women into the labor
market have undermined men's sole-breadwinner role.[3] These and
related conditions have also produced the new male mystique whereby
more men want to do it all and more men than women are reporting
work-family conflict.[4]

We challenge the conventional image of patriarchal fatherhood, which,
we argue, is anchored too firmly in heterosexual biology, marriage, and
conventional breadwinning models. Genetic, legal, and financial ties can
define formalities of a father-child relationship, but these markers do
less to signal a father's direct and positive contribution to his child's
development than loving, practical caregiving. Although good fathering is not monolithic, and commonly includes dedicated breadwinning,
a father-child relationship tends to thrive when the father is attentive
and responsive to his child's assorted needs in ways appropriate to the
child's developmental stage. Even before a child is conceived or born,

a man can demonstrate his commitment to fathering well by taking care of his own physical health, planning a pregnancy, and being actively involved both in supporting his partner prenatally and in pursuing prenatal education.

When stakeholders envision and implement initiatives to help men become more attentive fathers, they must take into account how realities of the larger society impinge on many men's lives and dampen their motivations to be involved fathers. As we've discussed, a poor labor market, inadequate school system, urban and rural poverty, and outdated reproductive health policies "create" fathers in some measure who believe they are unready and often incapable of playing a large part in their children's lives. In particular, the mentality that underlies the prioritizing of the breadwinning role can often give fathers a convenient excuse to retreat from caregiving because of the indignity they experience as men when they are without work or a decent paying job. So, too, men's well-intentioned and exhausting efforts of working long hours to put food on the table can leave many poor and middle-class men with little time and energy to focus on child care and fatherly nurturance. In short, even when strategies to improve employment, education, poverty, and reproductive health outcomes are not aimed at fathers directly, when successful they can indirectly enhance men's chances of being involved and nurturing fathers.

We have shown what an unconditional commitment to children and subsequent shifts in gender equity would look like as a counter to the conditional commitment that undergirds the ideology of breadwinning as the main father role. Even though the gendered landscape of parenting is evolving, the vestiges of patriarchal models of fatherhood continue to shape family-relevant policies, especially those that legitimize and emphasize men's rights and obligations as fathers.[5] In our view, concerns in many policy circles about fathers' financial contributions, though important, play a disproportionately significant role in defining good fathering and, consequently, guiding policy strategies. In addition, state and local control of school policies has led to outdated sex education and restrictive reproductive health services for young people. Remarkably, the United States has the highest teen pregnancy and birth rates in the industrialized world.[6] The pattern whereby so many young American men become fathers prematurely adversely affects their prospects of being attentive, nurturing fathers and effective breadwinners.

Consequently we call for wide-ranging initiatives that enhance men's fatherhood readiness and more productively locate fathers in caring relationships with their children, other family caregivers, and youth workers in the community. As we argued previously, many of these initiatives will be most effective if they help fathers deal with difficult transitional periods, including those in which fathers' changing residential status relative to their children leads to new daily routines in family households. Interventions must address the many structural circumstances that limit fathers' options for being more involved in particular ways, including providing nurturance. Ultimately, children stand to benefit when their fathers are attentive to their developmental needs and provide responsive care.

For decades, policy and program experimentation in the United States has focused on supporting men's efforts as providers or their potential as marital partners. As we mentioned in chapter 1, recent evaluation of national programs and ongoing assessment of random trial experiments has produced mixed results at best. Some programs help coparents develop healthy relationships and others bolster men's ability to maintain employment and pay child support. However, these outcomes are indirectly related to our focus: nurturance in the father-child relationship. Only a few programs, those aimed in particular at middle-class parents, appear to enhance the quality of this relationship. What is needed is a new approach that emphasizes nurturance.

We urge stakeholders to prioritize nurturance as a goal as important as encouraging fathers' financial contributions to children and healthy relationships between coparents. Listening to the fathers describe their lives, we suspect that efforts to promote stronger bonds between fathers and children may indirectly lead to other positive outcomes. In particular, fathers who learn to nurture their children may be more conscientious in providing child support and develop more trusting relations with both resident and nonresident coparents. Although conventional approaches to fathering policies and programs largely ignore these types of effects, reinforcing and documenting patterns such as these would help to remake the way we create and fund fathering initiatives in coming decades. Thus, we call for a progressive approach that not only promotes fathers' nurturance but also incorporates rigorous research designs to evaluate how fathers' nurturance can be reinforced and what types of measurable positive outcomes fathers' nurturance brings to children and others. If stakeholders ignore the potential that nurturance has as an incentive to generate more engaged fathering, initiatives are likely to be guided by a conventional model that ultimately does little to promote meaningful and lasting change in men's parenting.

Years of observation of Scandinavian efforts to improve fathering outcomes have shown that on their own, the impact of father-friendly public policies is limited: they hardly transform what men think, feel, and do as fathers.[7] The policies of Sweden, Germany, Japan, Britain, and Australia have become more effective when public and corporate cultures reflect these policies.[8] Although the United States lags behind these countries in funding time away from work for fathers—and mothers—to bond with their kids, recent polls show wide support across political parties for paid paternity leave. As a first step, the 2011 federal budget features a State Paid Leave Fund of $10 million directed to states to create their own paternal leave programs.

Policies, and the fathers they attempt to influence, are embedded in a multilayered cultural context. Thus, the agenda we outline to achieve a more engaged, nurturing style of fathering requires a complementary set of initiatives. They include legislative and workplace policies, national and local grassroots efforts tailored to improve fathering in different settings, and a wide range of programs designed to directly and indirectly enhance men's and fathers' human capital. In addition, a pro-feminist cultural narrative reinforced by media and court procedures is needed to dismantle some of the destructive themes of conventional manhood. This narrative must also applaud males' generative spirit as fathers, youth workers, and neighbors. Although these initiatives should recognize that some fathers and other caregivers will embrace alternative models of good fathering, the kinds of efforts we support would foster nurturance as a fundamental facet of good fathering in any form.

The types of initiatives we support are tied to the diverse platforms for social change referenced throughout the book: federal and state agencies, work sites, local communities, grassroots advocacy groups, the media, state clearinghouses, and courtrooms. Stakeholders who make use of these platforms can facilitate initiatives that can shift how fathers think, feel, and act. A fathering initiative may be linked to a specific platform or to multiple platforms. As we have noted, initiatives may operate on one or more levels by targeting individual families; narrow categories of fathers in particular settings, such as prison; fathers residing in specific communities or states; as well as fathers more generally as part of a national audience.

For instance, an initiative to establish a federal paternity leave policy may initially involve stakeholders in federal agencies, research and evaluation organizations, and a national media and lobbying network (see figure 8.1). The key objectives of the relevant people and organizations associated with a particular platform affect an initiative's scope. In this case, the paternity leave initiative may result in a broad infrastructure for men to take time off for the birth of their children that includes reimbursement of forgone wages; a set of mandates for employers; and a broad media campaign on television, radio, and the Internet to encourage men to take paternity leave. Such a collaboration would be even more effective in promoting nurturance for fathers across the board if it included additional representatives from state consortiums of child support and workforce agencies, local grassroots father advocates, and community-based social service programs. Such an initiative would

Figure 8.1   Collaborations Among Platforms to Promote Paternity Leave

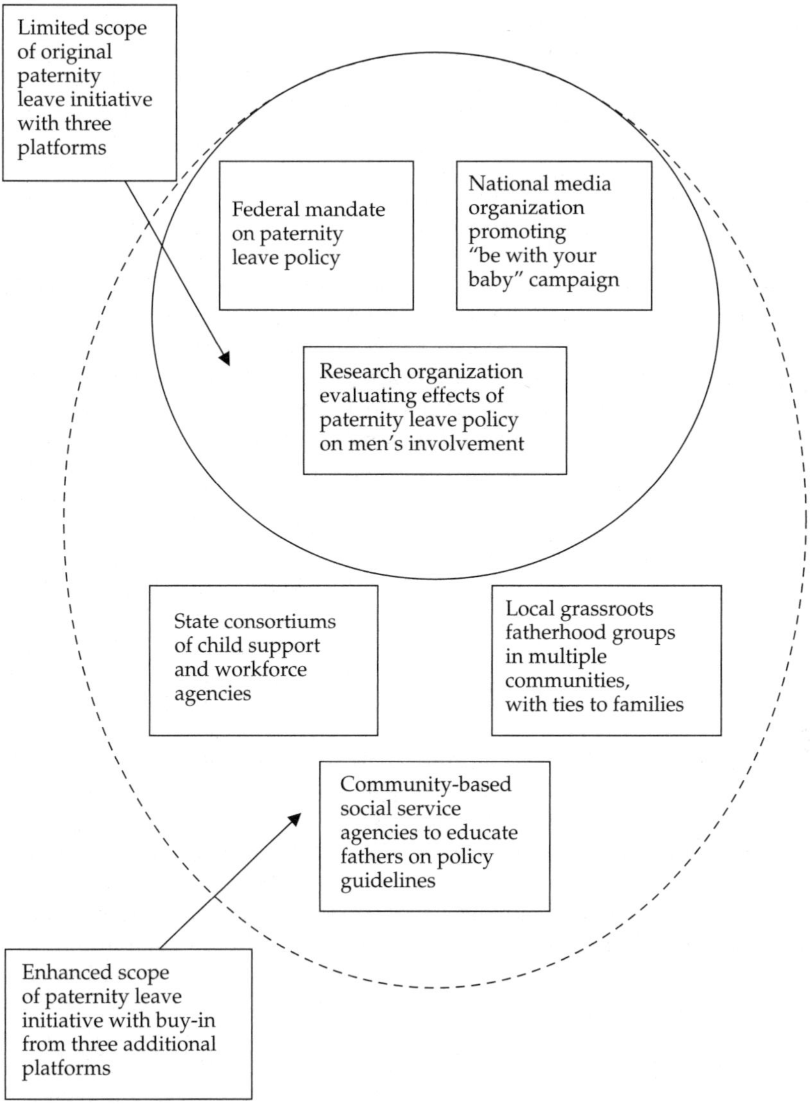

Limited scope
of original
paternity
leave initiative
with three
platforms

Federal mandate
on paternity
leave policy

National media
organization
promoting
"be with your
baby" campaign

Research organization
evaluating effects of
paternity leave policy
on men's involvement

State consortiums
of child support
and workforce
agencies

Local grassroots
fatherhood groups
in multiple
communities,
with ties to families

Community-based
social service
agencies to educate
fathers on policy
guidelines

Enhanced scope
of paternity leave
initiative with buy-in
from three additional
platforms

Source: Authors' figure.

immediately grapple with the concerns of men who are unemployed or underemployed. It would also be integrated with local services for families, including access to cash and material assistance, unemployment insurance, WIC programs, and health care.

Over time, objectives and activities can change and new collaborations can form. Although initiatives for promoting men's involvement with children may offer great promise, they can fail because of insufficient buy-in or a lack of coordination from important stakeholders of various kinds. This may be particularly relevant when local communities or businesses do not encourage nurturance to the same degree as other entities for a particular initiative.

Successful fathering initiatives are often rooted in stakeholders' hard work over many years to build relationships among diverse groups and agencies. To be effective, a social-change agenda must allow shifting alliances and fluid boundaries between organizations and entities. New understandings of what "good fathering" actually means can also emerge when policymakers work together. The early excitement of mobilizing communities for the Million Man March in 1995 has ebbed since then, but it offers a model for new generations of policymakers and stakeholders to push for men's participation in children's lives.

Currently, despite the shifting cultural tide, the value of a father being a reliable and loving presence in a child's life is too often overlooked on various fronts. For example, policies and programs have tended to assume that when a father's monetary contribution to his children was prioritized, his emotional involvement would follow automatically. This is not, however, necessarily the case. Initiatives that promote nurturance are more apt to balance the need for hands-on involvement and breadwinning.[9]

To its credit, the Department of Health and Human Services has now articulated a broad set of principles that can guide a range of initiatives to support fathers' nurturance.[10] These principles do not categorize fathers into "types" or draw attention only to problematic parenting behavior that often draws policymakers' attention. Fathers are not identified as unemployed, child support slackers, nonresident and uninvolved, incarcerated, abusive, and so forth. Resident fathers and financially stable fathers also can benefit from policies and programs that help them make the most of their fathering experience. Taken together, the principles are a starting point for organizing a diverse set of initiatives that are driven by positive contributions:

- All fathers can be important contributors to the well-being of their children.

- Parents are partners in raising their children, even when they do not live in the same household.

- The role fathers play in families is diverse and related to cultural and community norms.

- Men should receive the education and support necessary to prepare them for the responsibility of parenthood.

- Government can encourage and promote father involvement through its programs and through its workforce policies.

So how do we make policies and develop other initiatives to promote fathers' nurturance that are more responsive to fathers' everyday realities and changes in these realities over time? The initiatives will need to address the four fathering trajectories that frame our analysis (self-as-father, father-child, coparental, and copartner). Thus, a critical challenge is finding ways to compel men to become more aware of what it means to be a father long before they impregnate a woman. As we define it, a truly mindful approach toward nurturance and responsiveness anticipates children's needs prior to their conception and birth. Similarly, our approach is consistent with more progressive views that challenge the masculine codes of conduct that limit boys' and men's empathetic abilities. Yet we also need to identify strategies that move beyond those that seek to sharpen the awareness of the singular, isolated man and father. We must develop more effective approaches that focus on the interpersonal dynamics and resources critical to relationships, families, and communities. Moreover, our public initiatives must acknowledge that not only is nurturance good for children and mothers, it can also positively influence men's personal growth over the course of their lives.

Initially, we must take into account the kinds of complexities fathers reveal to us in the seven studies we tapped about their personal and family relationships. The detailed narratives we share take us inside fathers' minds and hearts as they struggle to make sense of the many changes, constraints, and supports they encounter as they try to manage various relationships over time, especially with their children and coparents. Some believe that the quality and quantity of their fathering is constrained by the limited choices they encounter because of their poor educational and job prospects, excessive work demands, lack of trust for the mother of their children, and restricted options to interact with their children. For many, their difficulties are compounded because they juggle competing expectations from multiple households and families. Our research underscores the emerging insight that multiple-partner paternity and stepfathering are no longer rare events. Viewed more broadly, we show how fathers' limited options are tied to dimensions of the larger social and cultural context.

Next, we need to understand that a man's ability to be an involved, nurturing father is often enhanced when he forges productive partnerships with other caregivers inside and outside the family. The challenge is to encourage a father to develop a strong, unmediated commitment to his child while simultaneously encouraging him to coordinate his fathering with a child's mother and other caregivers. As discussed earlier, it is essential that we develop a better understanding of the interpersonal processes that build and destroy trust between a father and other caregivers.

A father stands to benefit when professionals working on behalf of his child in diverse groups, agencies, and institutions coordinate their efforts so as to improve the father's options to be engaged with his child in a nurturing way. For example, efforts to improve a father's comfort level with a school environment can enhance the quality of the father's participation in his child's academic and social development. This is particularly true for the father who struggled in a school environment as a youth and either dropped out or barely graduated.

Federal and state agencies, court systems, activist and recreational organizations, local support groups, researchers, media, and educational and religious organizations are called upon to work collaboratively and creatively on behalf of partnerships as we have defined them. Partnerships between fathers and children, parents and professionals in the community, and representatives from different organizations will be developed most effectively if all involved are sensitive to the forces that complicate fathers' interpersonal networks and influence their approach to fathering.

Finally, as we envision a new agenda to promote fathering we must consider the distinct features and relative timing of recent cultural and behavioral trends so that attention is given to policies, programs, and public sentiment about good fathering, as well as what fathers actually do. Some initiatives and cultural narratives are out in front, progressive; others are far behind, responsible for the policy lag we describe in chapter 1. Overall, fathers' typical behavior is in the middle, trying to catch up to a new vision of engaged fathering but ahead of retrograde policies that equated fatherhood with breadwinning. Naturally, men who routinely challenge the traditional gendered norms of who cares for children are likely to believe that policy and programs haven't gone far enough to accommodate either their efforts to be engaged fathers or their complex family circumstances.

Family Complexity

As we show in our analysis, fathers from diverse backgrounds increasingly have a lot going on in their lives that makes it challenging for them to be attentive and nurturing to their children. Their narratives continue to educate those working on social initiatives to encourage nurturance. The main lesson is to recognize the complex patterns of fathering in contemporary families that actually exist—fathering with multiple partners and children, stepfathering, and social fathering.[11]

The complexity concept highlights different types of change that characterize contemporary family life and fathers' personal realities.[12] For example, fathers discuss how interaction with their children is not confined to a household with a nuclear family: it stretches across households and across multiple coparents—former spouses, on again off again girlfriends, or mothers of their children with whom they have fleeting intimate contact. These two aspects alone—fathering that unfolds in many places and couple relationships that may not be at the center of family life—dramatically alter our focus when we propose fathering initiatives.

Fathers' stories also accentuate less obvious elements of family complexity. As we saw in chapter 5, routine care of children often involves not just a mother and a father but a whole range of intergenerational kin and friends, both paternal and maternal. We learned, too, about the complexity associated with fathering dynamics over the life course. A noncustodial father may be separated from his child, then assume full-time informal custody, and then assume partial custody during holidays, all in a three-month period. Meanwhile, this estranged biological father may be a sole caregiver for the children from his second marriage. How can we measure or influence his "involvement" as a father without accounting for this increasing family complexity?

Fathers learn firsthand that what they think, feel, do, and plan for as a parent is an ongoing and often messy negotiation. They take cues from family members, friends, community members, the media, government policies, and grassroots groups about how to be a good father. They perceive that fathering is of value to them, as persons and as men, while communicating with all of these interested parties. Men do this in a world in which traditional expectations that fathers need to be the sole or primary financial provider for a family are less pervasive, even though vestiges of the sole-breadwinner role remain in certain religious and affluent communities that honor mothers' "right" to stay at home with their children. The end result: more and more fathers embrace emotional and instrumental commitments while exploring new ways to fulfill their own standards of "being there" as a nurturing, loving parent. However, as our data show, family complexity requires fathers to rework their identities on a frequent, even daily, basis. This "work" demands a great deal of time and negotiation for fathers as well as other family members. For many men, being a nurturing father on a regular basis is challenging.

Our data clearly indicate that many fathers feel constrained by social and cultural contexts. Fathers often feel that family members or government policies define them strictly as financial providers. They want to move beyond this father-as-wallet mentality. In chapter 7 we noted that many men's weak educational and employment backgrounds, as well as the circumstances associated with becoming fathers at a young age, limit their opportunities to be nurturing fathers. Unfortunately, some public and private initiatives exacerbate the constraints that men face as fathers. Reliance on worn stereotypes of fathers as irresponsible or risky can create distrust between fathers and families even though little existed beforehand.

Why is it timely to consider a broad social-change initiative to promote fathers' nurturance of children? The cultural landscape has changed considerably since 1979, when the popular movie *Kramer vs. Kramer* (starring Dustin Hoffman and Meryl Streep) took audiences into largely uncharted family territory by showcasing a devoted and caring nonresident father. In the early 1990s, the comedy *Mrs. Doubtfire* (with Robin Williams and Sally Fields) presented yet another comedic rendition of an attentive though bumbling nonresident father struggling to sustain his intimate bonds with his children.

In recent years, a flood of movies and TV shows have depicted an ever-expanding range of nontraditional family arrangements in which fathers are intimately involved with their children in productive ways. Exposure to these types of cultural materials as well as individuals' personal experiences with their networks of family, friends, neighbors, and coworkers who nurture children in nontraditional households can help sharpen individuals' sense of how fathers can navigate various types of family arrangements that include children. It can also challenge narrow conceptions of nontraditional families that view them as being outside a normative template. Perhaps these changing cultural conditions have prepared families to support a nurturing role for fathers in all types of settings. Expectations for such roles may be more established and less ambiguous than in the late 1970s. By necessity, many families have recently adapted creatively to the range of men's roles in complex families.

Contemporary social media such as Twitter and Facebook and various websites and blogs also play an increasingly important role by helping fathers connect with one another.[13] These communication resources provide stay-at-home dads, involved middle-class dads, and community and public organizations with new ways to promote learning, networking, getting information, and gaining support. As these innovations reach a larger segment of society, working-class and disadvantaged fathers, whether in typical or more complex family structures, are likely to feel less isolated.

Across our projects, we observe that men's capacity to negotiate family complexity is shaped by their own personal development. Young men generally spend little time thinking about pregnancy, childbearing, and child development. Consequently, they are often ill prepared financially, educationally, and emotionally to be nurturing, engaged fathers.[14] If a young biological father fails to commit to an intimate relationship, to secure a good job, or to engage regularly with his child, it may close the door on his future involvement with the child. His attempts to reengage his child may also continue over time, and this motivation may drive new levels of family complexity. This can include nonresident involvement from a distance that occurs alongside new partners for both parents and possibly extensive caregiving by paternal and maternal kin.

Older fathers may have the advantage over their younger counterparts of being able to draw on their maturity and life experience to understand family complexities more fully. They may be more appreciative of the repertoire of new fathering activity, including nurturance. At the same time, older fathers may be more invested in the older versions of breadwinning as constituting good fathering. In addition, whereas younger men may be less well equipped to deal with family complexity, older men are more likely to be immersed in it because they have had additional time to create multiple partnerships and children. Older fathers often struggle to balance finances, loyalties, and time with children in more than one household. With more time to accumulate wealth, possessions, and personal habits, older fathers, especially divorced fathers, may actually encounter more stress than younger fathers because they have more at stake.

Issues of family complexity entail more than dynamic family structures. Personal circumstances within complex families may color men's abilities to nurture. For a father who quits his job to care for his sick newborn, family life may grow more complex: his wife may return to work, and her parents may move in to lend a hand with care. The death of a parent may encourage a father to give back to the next generation through youth ministry or summer camps or some other mentorship role. His own children may benefit from his emerging commitment to learning about and working with youths.

If circumstances can nudge men toward nurturance, they can also thwart this behavior. Nurturance is not possible when men's decisions and activities endanger their own children, coparents, or other family members. Fathers who struggle with addictions or anger may drive their children away. And these fathers' behaviors complicate family life if they drive mothers to take their children out of the household to seek safety with other kin. Fathers suffering from illness or disability, such as soldiers returning from combat, may struggle to nurture their children in the face of coping with their own situations. In these cases, too, families may grow more complex, recruiting kin to care for children and fathers or moving children to other households to help lighten the load of stressed parents. In large part, our challenge in dealing with these complex families is to understand the "injuries" that many men cope with as they grow up and not to dismiss the fathers automatically as "sick," "bad," or "evil."[15]

Ideally, fathers should have access to a full range of initiatives that expand and enhance their choices instead of experiencing limited choices as a result of their own developmental trajectory, personal circumstances, or other social forces. So, instead of dismissing the father who failed to marry the mother of his first child, efforts should be made to engage him with his stepchildren in his new marriage. As we showed in chapter 5, some biological fathers and stepfathers can break with public stereotypes and establish an alliance to be supportive of their children and each other. If their children are their common focus of devotion, the assumption that mothers, fathers, and new partners are always pitted against each other may well be false. Although some men navigate cofathering scenarios effectively without outside assistance, others are likely to benefit from institutional and public support. Such alliances could become more common over time. Likewise, instead of casting fathers as failures because they cannot secure a full-time job in the current recession, initiatives could value the care they give on a par with providing materially for children and interaction on a par with coresidence. This orientation would acknowledge that there are multiple avenues to effect change in men's parenting. Family complexity can present opportunities to develop nurturing relationships and partnerships.

What would it take for social policy and programs to encourage activities that are effective in supporting fathers dealing with family complexity? Obviously, crafting these initiatives would not be easy. Fathers, mothers, stepparents, and other kin have their own interests apart from a commitment to their children. They also have different perspectives on how to nurture children. But initiatives can do a better job of building trust among these diverse family members. In movies, advertisements, and policy discourse, cultural narratives can promote a broad-based network of kin and friends who trust each other, which in turn enhances children's well-being. Policies and programs can move from a sole focus on individual rights and responsibilities to a deeper commitment to supporting ongoing partnerships based on trust among fathers and family members over many years.

Partnerships

How a man thinks about and expresses his masculine identity as well as his identity as a father or prospective father are relevant to how he navigates partnerships with those who are also involved in his child's life. Generally speaking, a key feature of the identity experience is that a heterosexual father is generally more likely than a mother to have a commitment to his child that is conditional on the relationship with the coparent.[16] In other words, the father's connection to his child is sometimes influenced by the quality of his romantic relationship with the child's mother. This can become a significant factor in cases of separation and divorce.

The conditional commitment pattern raises two critical questions for those wanting to effect change. First, which types of initiatives can enhance a father's ability to develop and sustain a direct commitment to his child—one not contingent on his feelings for the child's mother? Second, how can initiatives enhance the quality of a father's coparenting relationship so that he has more opportunities to nurture his children in diverse settings irrespective of the parents' status as a romantic couple?

As we noted before, much can be done to strengthen the bond a father creates with his biological, step, or adopted child. First and foremost initiatives are needed that advance more progressive messages about fatherhood throughout popular culture that elevate the status of engaged fathering and that target the everyday sites where fathering takes place. Such messages can be advanced by grassroots organizations with varied ideological credentials. The National Fatherhood Initiative (NFI) connects its organization's mission—to increase the number of children "growing up with involved, responsible, and committed fathers"—to wide-ranging practical efforts that develop and disseminate skill-building resources to fathers in diverse settings (community-based settings, health care, the military, correctional facilities, Christian settings, and the workplace).[17] The NFI tends to align itself with conservative beliefs about politics, marriage, and reproductive issues that are often at odds with those held by more liberal advocates of engaged fathering. Those associated with this initiative also tend to embrace the controversial notion that fathers are *essential*—they provide something to children's lives that is both critical and uniquely masculine.[18] Despite its conservative viewpoint, however, many of the basic messages that NFI promotes about involved fathering resonate across the political spectrum.

Some efforts have been developed without access to extensive resources but with a message of transforming men who are not considered to be sufficiently attentive parents. On Father's Day 2011, leaders from the Urban Leadership Institute, Raising Him Alone Campaign, Fathers Incorporated, Year of Responsible Men, and a variety of related national partners that focus primarily on the disengagement of men of color from low-income households declared a "Day of Amnesty for Dads."[19] These national groups, linked with community-based programs and using social media, encouraged men who were estranged from their children to "summon the courage to take steps to reconnect" with their children. They noted that fathers could pick up a phone, write a letter to break the ice, or contact a child's mother to arrange a visit. Ironically, the groups' decision to co-opt the masculine ideal of "courage" challenges men to hold their traditional masculine ego in check in order to do "relationship work" by confronting their fears and vulnerabilities.

More focused national grassroots efforts are led by fathers who try to provide support, education, and advocacy for fathers who are the primary caregivers for their children. In 2003, Mike Stillwell, Peter Steinberg, and Matt Vossler, three at-home dads living in the Washington, D.C., area, used their enjoyable experiences with a local playgroup to launch Daddyshome, Inc., the only national nonprofit organization for at-home dads. This trio offers guidance on how fathers can develop local support networks, and their organization also facilitates the Annual At-Home Convention. In April 2010 they developed an online presence, a website and Facebook page, to help individuals connect to and participate in discussion forums. In contrast to Boot Camp for New Dads (discussed in chapter 3), these online networks provide information and communication opportunities specifically for dads who stay at home with their children.[20]

In short, both broad and more focused initiatives are needed to help men embrace the value of being committed and nurturing fathers. These efforts complement attempts to re-imagine masculinity at work and at home in light of the Great Recession.[21] The mission can best be achieved when men recognize that others are judging their performance as attentive caregivers as well as breadwinners. The more men realize that their respected male peer groups are socially supportive of their nurturing style of fathering, the more inclined they will be to adopt it. As it becomes increasingly more normative for males of all ages and family circumstances to be confident and skilled nurturers, the peer pressure for fathers to be nurturers will be ingrained more fully into their everyday lives.

The man who becomes a nurturing father typically is not alone on his fathering journey. The heterosexual father usually has to consider the mother and possibly other romantic partners at various points in his life. Depending on how he enters into fatherhood, the gay father may also have a former romantic partner—the mother of his child—to contend with, another gay man who acts as a stepfather, or a gay man who jointly became part of a parenting team. Add to these individuals any number of relatives on either side of the parental equation and a father has numerous potential partnerships to take into account. The resident father, and in many instances the nonresident one as well, has various options to establish partnerships with individuals in the community who are involved in his child's life away from home.

With others in the childrearing mix, concerns about establishing and negotiating trust are critical to how men experience themselves as fathers. Typically, men are confronted with their most significant trust issues when they form and sustain coparenting arrangements with a romantic partner. Negotiating trust is likely to become even more complicated in the aftermath of a severed romantic tie. To a lesser extent, trust issues can also affect how fathers relate to their own and a partner's kin.

Left entirely to their own devices fathers can try to figure out how to deal with any or all of these people. Sometimes they will succeed; other times, not. In many instances, though, initiatives that target this larger network of individuals can complement fathers' efforts to be more involved with their children in productive ways. Counseling resources, skill-building programs, and mediation sessions may be the most salient organized responses to help fathers forge constructive partnerships within or across households. Such partnerships can give men a better chance to navigate their fathering trajectories effectively as they experience the stress of unplanned births, divorce and remarriage, unemployment, poverty, deployment, incarceration or reentry to civilian life, migration, poor health, and other notable transitions.

To date, policymakers have generally tailored fathering initiatives in a manner that focuses on men in committed heterosexual relationships. Clearly, more needs to be done to acknowledge and respond to the varied circumstances and processes that define fathers' partnerships that lead to or result from paternal commitments to children. Designing policies and programs that enable two parents to establish a trusting alliance is often a daunting task because the strategies for building healthy romantic relationships are so elusive. To the extent that programs effectively teach couple-based relationship skills, they can help decrease conflict, enhance trust, and create more coparental support in the process. In addition, the more trusting fathers feel toward their children's mothers, the easier they will find it to be nurturing toward their children. For all these reasons, more public and private investment in such programs is needed. Programs that enable young unwed fathers and fathers returning to families from prison and deployment to secure a foothold in the world of work and make decent wages may also help specific couples build trust and solidify their romantic and coparental relationships. These financial conditions can indirectly enhance fathers' chances of nurturing their children.

When couples with children go their separate ways, the emotional strain, breach of trust, and practical realities of uncoupling can fundamentally alter nonresident fathers' opportunities to be involved with their children in particular ways. One of the most contentious issues affecting many nonresident fathers involves child support. We take an unconventional stance by advocating that child support accountability measures be implemented. Our goal is to limit the uncertainty associated with child support payments and the use of such funds. In the short term, the types of accountability measures we propose would most likely create concrete situations that could lead to confrontations, especially when resident parents misuse funds. For the foreseeable future, and because a sizable majority of single resident parents are mothers, those who disproportionately feel constrained by this type of fiscal monitoring will be women, but the long-term aim is to remove some of the suspicion and grounds for mistrust among coparents who are no longer romantic partners. If that occurs, then two parents who are no longer together will be more inclined to participate in responsible coparenting.

Although most current initiatives focus on creating fathers' human capital or assisting fathers with coparenting issues, it may be possible to capitalize on fathers' kin-work experiences and their connection to an intergenerational family legacy to enhance their chances to be nurturing fathers. Whether it's with fathers involved in parenting outside of a romantic relationship, or young unwed fathers trying to gain a place in their children's lives, or some other unconventional family arrangement, policymakers and professionals committed to children's well-being should create programs that facilitate opportunities to build partnerships. These involve fathers and their maternal and paternal kin, extended family members, and even close friends. For example, many states have established a procedure by which putative (or presumed) fathers can register in order to gain constitutional protection of parental rights. However, some fathers are not informed about registration, and other states do not have this option. If nonresident fathers are not recognized as having rights and responsibilities as parents, they can be disregarded if their children are considered for adoption through the child welfare system. There may be options for courts to work with families to recognize men's potential contribution as a parent and to build trust in a kin network.

Looking beyond family and kin to fathers' full care network, partnerships with community youth workers offer fathers additional nurturing opportunities. Fathers typically are far less involved than mothers in coordinating their children's activities away from home, yet this arena offers opportunities for many to become more assertive and develop meaningful relationships with youth workers. By reaching out to youth workers, fathers can learn more about their children and share valuable information with others who are invested in the children's well-being.

Taking a long view, one critical way to enhance fathers' facility in developing social capital for their children is to encourage males at an early age to take an interest in volunteering and working with kids in the community. Men who have interacted with kids in public settings are better positioned to understand how they as fathers can capitalize on interactions with the individuals responsible for their children's care in public settings.

Not only can fathers get more involved in promoting relations with youth workers, but organizations, too, need to develop strategies to reach out to fathers and accommodate them. Youth workers may perceive some fathers as uninterested or too risky, but many well-intentioned fathers may simply have limited flexibility to juggle their work schedules or they may be caught up in family conflicts that make it difficult for them to be more involved. Organizations' program development staff need to adjust their services to accommodate fathers if they hope to realize the good that can come from more engaged fathering.

Youth workers could contribute to fathers' efforts to be more nurturing toward their children in various ways and in all sorts of contexts, including corrections, education, health care, recreation, and religion. Research on programs such as Head Start indicates that fathers' more attentive involvement can make a difference in children's lives. Men's engagement with children through Early Head Start programs seems to affect children's language development directly and positively.[22] When fathers are encouraged to talk to their children more, good things happen.

Collaborative Social Services

Some policies and programs generate benefits for fathers and children even when fathers are largely unaware of their existence. But many programs require fathers to be proactive and to intentionally access a service or remain active once they begin to participate. Professionals who seek to improve men's reproductive health and family planning, child preparation and infant-care skills, abusive behavior, involvement as nonresident fathers, participation in children's early education, and so forth, search for ways to reach out to men to offer their programming and to keep them involved. An expansive agenda to foster more nurturing fathering must get more men to participate in father-relevant programming. The agenda should also entice more men to work with fathers in a professional capacity.

Programs that involve fathers are organized according to diverse models that deliver services to fathers en masse or individual fathers, but the latter case is relatively rare. A few programs also train service providers to work with fathers.[23] The most common programs include educational groups and workshops, skill-building groups, support and self-help groups, group retreats, individual models, mixed models that include group and individual strategies, and father-child formats. Unfortunately, there is scarce research that systematically evaluates the many types of programs that target fathers or the providers who serve them.[24] The limited evaluations and commentaries that do exist tend to focus on unique aspects of particular programs as well as fathers' personal and family circumstances. Consequently, little is known about the impacts of fatherhood programming or what can be done to strengthen men's commitment to these activities as either participants or service providers.

Although our observations are not based on rigorous evaluation research, we highlight eight insights that should make programs more father friendly.

- Men tend to respond better if providers recruit them directly and convince them that their participation is critical to their children's well-being.

- If fathers recognize that they can personally benefit in various ways by participating in a program they may be more apt to invest their time and effort.

- For many fathers, a program's inconvenience in terms of time and location can drastically affect their level of involvement. Thus, programs need to plan around men's work schedules whenever possible and develop outreach strategies to engage men where they either work or play.

- Having another family member (partner or child) or friend involved in the program can provide fathers with an additional incentive to participate.

- Some programs should be strongly geared to providing practical, information-based resources rather than emotional support. Male peer support tends to be highly valued in conventional fatherhood responsibility programs focusing on nonresident and poor fathers, yet practical knowledge and resources may be valued more by many fathers grappling with challenging circumstances such as a delinquent or special needs child, fathering while in prison or deployed in the military, and fathering after a divorce.[25]

- Whenever possible programs should use male facilitators because some males may feel more at ease with them than with females and may be more likely to stay involved.

- Some programs may have greater success in sustaining their efforts if they recruit and train the most capable participants to become facilitators or serve on steering committees.

- An evaluation component should be built into programming so that results can be shared with current and future participants as well as the community of practitioners who work with fathers.[26]

Irrespective of their particular focus, policies and programs must enhance fathers' access to critical and diverse resources that enable them to adapt effectively to difficult circumstances and become more resilient, cope with stress and manage their interpersonal relations, accumulate human capital through education and work experience, and build hope. In practical terms, fathers' chances of expressing nurturance will be enhanced if they have more flexible work schedules, quality time with children, mediation support to deal with contentious coparental relations, and opportunities to learn developmentally appropriate parenting skills.

Collaborative Systemic Resources

In some instances, motivated fathers can be active fathers without relying on specific interventions. Other times, fathers' ability to be nurturing is driven by contexts and activities external to their day-to-day lives such as legislative initiatives; program components; or policies that provide specific resources that indirectly help them as fathers, such as job training, parenting classes, or loans for education. Sometimes fathers' fortunes may also be tied to the extent and quality of coordination between organizations that affect fathers' lives.

For example, although policymakers regularly criticize nonresident fathers who fail to pay child support, some recognize the value of augmenting poor fathers' child support contributions. Young fathers interested in being involved with their nonresident children can therefore benefit if child support compliance officials, welfare workers, and staff at GED and jobs-training programs work collaboratively to assess and respond to young fathers' needs. In the long run, policies that give poor young fathers incentives both to develop meaningful coparental relations and to bond and stay involved in loving ways with their child may help lay the foundation for lasting relationships—and more stable child support payments.

The recent historical record of top-down fatherhood policy has been one of long-promised changes to get fathers to pay more and do more for their kids. But there have been limited collaborations to make it happen. The Bill Clinton administration encouraged the first explicit and wide-ranging projects to both promote and understand fathers' involvement with their children. This administration teamed with state and local public and private funders to seed programs for responsible fatherhood in low-income communities. Clinton directed the staff of the Federal Interagency Forum on Child and Family Statistics to create the Fatherhood Research Initiative to gather information on the demographics of fathers and the effect of father involvement on children.[27] Ultimately, both of these efforts were tied to the 1996 welfare reform legislation, which created a federal structure for child support and paternity establishment. The Temporary Assistance for Needy Families program (TANF) also contained specific programs aimed at poor men and women to promote two-parent families, to reduce out-of-wedlock pregnancies, and to support a wide range of work activities.

By 2002, the George W. Bush administration began to build on the successful initiatives of the Clinton era by allocating additional funding to TANF for marriage education programs, technical assistance to local programs, and research on marriage. In tandem with TANF, the Healthy Marriage Initiative moved on many levels to address poverty, nonmarital fertility, cohabitation, and nonresidential parenting. In addition, a Fathers Count bill was passed in 1999, at the tail end of the Clinton presidency, to give poor fathers job training, parenting education, and support for marriage. With additional funding from the Bush administration, this set of grants to community-based groups became known as the Promoting Responsible Fatherhood Initiative. States have applied to the Department of Health and Human Services Administration for Children and Families (ACF), which implements the Promoting Responsible Fatherhood programs. ACF has also sponsored a model intervention, Building Strong Families, which was designed explicitly to evaluate services that promote healthy marriages for low-income expectant or new unwed parents.

In its first few years, the Barack Obama administration has changed course on a few issues that affect fatherhood policy.[28] It has deemphasized the promotion of marriage, a decision that was based in part on results from the Building Strong Families program, in which a random-assignment policy showed that couples with a young child who wished to marry did not have more stable or higher quality relationships than couples who did not receive Building Strong Families services. Instead, Obama has emphasized the value of collaboration and evidence-based evaluations of existing programs. In the 2011 budget, the administration eliminated funding for Bush-era programs and replaced them with a Fatherhood, Marriage, and Families Innovation Fund.[29] This fund would support state initiatives—those that rely on collaboration with community-based organizations and that offer evidence of "what works"—to remove employment barriers and to increase family functioning along with parenting capacity. These best practices could be replicated by TANF, child support enforcement, and other programs at the local or state level.

Yet the plans from the Obama administration do not suggest decisive departures from the past two decades of federal initiatives. Nor do they address the real conflicts that may keep effective collaborations from emerging. The federal initiatives have not led to dramatic shifts toward fathers' nurturance, healthy couple relationships, or better child outcomes. In part, they have floundered because stakeholders are at odds with each other. A top-down initiative may promote a "best" definition of fathering, which may grow to be in conflict with other notions of fathering at state or community levels, between women's and men's rights groups, or within families themselves. In some ways, these fathering initiatives have left community groups and families reacting to federal goals that may be out of sync with men's own experiences.

Even well-intended organizations that truly desire to promote father involvement disagree on "what the problems are" that keep men from becoming involved parents. For the past two decades, well-established organizations such as the NFI and the National Center on Fathering (NCF) have been at the forefront of educating fathers directly and training those who work with fathers in social service agencies, prisons, rehabilitation programs, government organizations, military, and churches. NCF messages tend to focus on a father's impact on children, practical tips on fathering, and stages of fathering over the life course.

Other efforts are more controversial. NFI has placed "fatherlessness" at the center of recent media campaigns whose purpose is to "serve as a catalyst for engaging America in a public and forthright discussion about the necessity of reversing" the increase of "children living in father-absent homes."[30] Without examining factors related to fatherlessness, however, such a media campaign can be based on unfounded assumptions about nonresident fathers. In a similar way, collaborations designed to implement the Healthy Marriage Initiative may be committed to a definition of fathers as husbands that is unrealistic for millions of families. Such assumptions may lead to clear disconnections between most fatherhood scholars and organizations like the NCF and NFI at both the local and national level. As a result, there is less coordination between the research, program development, and advocacy communities, with the result that fatherhood initiatives are increasingly likely to be fragmented, politicized, and inadequately informed by research.

A few prominent examples exist of collaborations in which everyone comes to the table to coordinate power and resources, but they are not in the United States. Stakeholders in the United States who are interested in promoting fathers' nurturance should review the Canadian Father Involvement Research Alliance (FIRA), highlighted in chapter 1. A key feature of the alliance is its commitment to participatory action research that encourages researchers and interested parties in the community to develop research agendas collaboratively. This grassroots approach can better account for local conditions and unique concerns. Researchers, community organizers, and fathers jointly work to translate research findings into practical solutions that involve assessment tools, resources, and training. As a result, the call for more "community-based strategies rather than top-down ones" can be answered.[31]

One way to think about a truly collaborative fathering initiative is to involve stakeholders at all levels. The primary policy domains of federal initiatives—welfare, child support, custody, workplace policies—have been made possible by federal funding and goal setting, with occasional input from researchers to help define critical issues. In other words, these are limited to legislative and workplace efforts.[32] A more effective collaboration might involve local programs, grassroots groups, and media that compose cultural narratives in a comprehensive effort to encourage child support, or to help men establish paternity, or to address complicated custody issues. A comprehensive effort might also be more sustainable over a long period of time, as it sets in motion a partnership that could outlast political administrations and the vagaries of funding for different visions of family life.

A promising step toward such full-fledged collaborations might be the state-level programs on fatherhood first funded by the Department of Health and Human Services under the Promoting Responsible Fatherhood federal initiative of the Bush administration.[33] Primarily operated by state employment, welfare, and child support agencies, these state programs take resources one step closer to families in local communities.[34] These programs could potentially foster dialogue between federal actors with specific interests (child support and paternity establishment), local programs that benefit from federal funding, and fathers and families themselves who could suggest ways to package resources so as to recognize the value of men's care. Without an open approach to families in communities, however, these programs may only serve to convey federally mandated goals that may be out of step with families' real-world needs and desires.

In the current policy and economic environment shaped by the Great Recession and limited budgets, initiatives cannot come packaged with a high price tag. From an organizational and public finance perspective, collaborations can be cost effective. At the very least, programs that streamline case management efforts to help fathers stay involved and eventually make financial contributions to their children should address issues related to housing, education, job training and placement, child care, and risky behaviors like criminal behavior and drug use. In recent decades, some stakeholders working with fathers have shared this sentiment, but more needs to be done to make it a reality.[35] With state and federal governments hesitant to make large commitments of resources to promote fathering, local groups and grassroots networks will need to contribute to such initiatives. Working together in collaboration is a tall order, but diverse stakeholders must target which resources can support fathers during specific transitions and then agree to leverage human capital to do so.

Important social initiatives with multiple actors will always feature interests that conflict and change. Resources are scarce, and children's rights, like those of women and men, are subject to negotiation. But more common ground exists now after twenty-plus years of disconnection between federal initiatives and local grassroots efforts organized around new visions of fatherhood. Everyone should recognize that men can play a vital role in providing and caring for their children, especially during a critical economic downturn that has hit families hard. Initiatives need to catch up with the changing realities of family life and focus on men's contributions as adults who nurture their children. So, what would a future with extensive social support for a nurturing style of fathering look like?

Finding Common Ground

Few would disagree that fatherhood has been a hot topic in scholarly, policy, and everyday settings for some time. Our society, as well as others, has generated plenty of research networks, organizations, activist groups, conferences, commissions, support groups, magazines, blogs, media products, and slogans that focus on fathering in some form or fashion.[36] What is less clear is the extent to which and in what ways this heightened attention has persuaded recent cohorts of fathers to relate differently to their children. For sure, the mix of cultural narratives encouraging fathers to be more active, attentive, responsive, and nurturing toward their sons and daughters is more visible and viable in some circles today than it was, say, twenty-five years ago. No doubt, too, various social forces continue to push for a more progressive social-change agenda relating to fathering. However, as we've shown, the relatively recent cultural narratives of the nurturing "good dad" exist alongside outdated policies, cultural stereotypes, and practical impediments that limit how deeply those messages penetrate the fabric of everyday family life in its many forms. Matters are further complicated, for instance, because messages steeped in competing ideologies diverge on the acceptable circumstances of gay fathering and stepfatherhood, as well as what good fathering entails.

Much has been written in the academic community since 1980 concerning the lag between cultural messages about the modern father and what fathers actually do with and for their children.[37] Even though many fathers do not in practice live up to recent images of good fathering, it has become increasingly difficult to be deaf to the frustrations of so many resident and nonresident fathers who want to be more involved and involved in more nurturing ways with their children. These fathers feel constrained by social forces they do not readily control.

We suspect, then, that the cumulative effect of fathers' everyday joys and everyday struggles of doing more child care, as well as organized grassroots efforts, will gradually exert pressure on the relevant instruments of social change. Eventually it will become sufficiently commonplace for fathers to attend to their children's many needs. In a process similar to the way public sentiment has shifted in response to individuals' increased opportunities to interact with gays and lesbians in assorted settings, public appreciation for how fathers are involved with their children will continue to grow. The general public as well as professionals who work with children will have little choice but to notice fathers' heightened commitments and child-care efforts. As a result, new initiatives may be launched in the spirit of long overdue gestures to meet fathers' and mothers' demands that men need more opportunities to nurture their children. This becomes increasingly likely as the sentiment takes hold that getting fathers to be more nurturing is in everyone's best interest—fathers', children's, mothers', and society's more generally.

What is needed to push stakeholders to do more to support fathers' efforts to bond with and nurture their children in ways that transcend breadwinning? Stakeholders need to recognize that fathering is not limited to a personal choice or a change of heart. Fathers' nurturance is inherently a social arrangement, one intimately tied to what men think, feel, and do in concert with other actors. As noted, the Canadian FIRA provides some direction on how interested parties can develop more effective collaborations to meet children's and families' needs. Just as professionals need to develop strategies that build trust between fathers and those who are involved in their children's lives, researchers, activists, professionals working with youth, and policymakers must identify common ground to foster productive collaborations.

Creating meaningful collaborations is likely to go more smoothly in some areas than others. Collaborating on issues associated with welfare, child support, custody, paternity establishment, work policies, children's health, and public education tends to be shaped by how politically complicated they are. For instance, it may be relatively easy to develop cooperation between different national fatherhood organizations, educational outlets, and media representatives with the intent of shaping public-service announcements or to inject a message about fathers' nurturance into TV programming. Eclectic coalitions are foreseeable that would work to produce effective messages about engaged, nurturing fathers. They might include such ideologically varied groups as fathers' rights organizations, the politically conservative NFI or NCF organizations, and more liberal Hollywood production companies. Setting aside ideological differences to craft a powerful message trumpeting fathers who nurture their children seems doable. The National Campaign to Prevent Teen and Unplanned Pregnancy provides a useful model for this type of collaborative work with media, although it focuses very little on fatherhood and was not explicitly trying to make peace with other groups that promoted different values or strategic visions.[38]

Feminist and men's rights groups, however, would have to strike a significant compromise to work together to support policy or programmatic efforts to include nonresident fathers more fully into their children's everyday lives.[39] These groups tend to have different interpretations of how mothers' concerns should be incorporated into initiatives. Similar tensions are likely to exist between politicians and advocacy groups that span the political spectrum. In addition, court justices with different ideological leanings about gender and caregiving will be a factor in any process that tries to ensure that nonresident fathers have a fair chance to demonstrate that they can be a regular, nurturing force in their children's lives. Attempts to design initiatives that acknowledge fathers' nurturing capabilities are apt to be framed by more general views about how a society and families in particular should do caregiving. Stakeholders will differ on how much they want to emphasize an approach that embraces gender equity, traditional family forms, or government intervention into family relations.

Collaborations are likely to flourish as the general public's views on caregiving continue to shift away from defining caregiving as women's work to an image of caregiving as more of a human experience. Furthermore, these collaborations will promote our vision of fathering most effectively when they stress how fathers' and mothers' nurturance enhances caregiving. Thus, our agenda encourages strategies that lead fathers both to provide more care for their children and to do so in more nurturing ways.

At the level of public discourse, and building on previous frameworks that incorporate broad thinking about fatherhood, we emphasize the need to develop a more compelling cultural narrative to inspire men to invest more of their time, energy, money, and goodwill into building a generative society responsive to all children's needs.[40] Such an effort necessitates that we highlight the critical ties between images of men as gendered persons and images of men as fathers. In a gendered world where men's quest for masculine capital is disproportionately influenced by the perceived judgments of other men, attempts to build a broad fatherhood campaign must rely heavily on strategies that men embrace and discuss with their male friends, acquaintances, and family. Obviously, no singularly tailored message will resonate with all men or fathers, but more can be done to rally men collectively and on an individual basis to advocate for a cohesive set of messages about fathering in which men, both fathers and nonfathers, value children more highly.

As a related undertaking, more needs to be done to recruit and support men's involvement with children in day-care facilities, elementary schools, and other youth-work settings conventionally viewed as feminine domains. These efforts might be embedded within a more general initiative that restructures the wide range of caregiving professions. Such an initiative would build training, certification and licensure, livable wages, and career development into the experiences of women and men who care for others. Although many will applaud efforts to incorporate men more fully into female-dominated professions involving children, doing so will generate greater competition between men and women for jobs, especially during an economic downturn.

Ultimately, initiatives must simultaneously engage the personal, organizational, and cultural elements of society to maximize men's potential to be nurturing fathers. Because aspects of private and public places such as homes, schools, playgrounds, health-care facilities, and prisons, among others, influence how well fathers nurture their children, fathering initiatives are more likely to succeed if they enhance fathers' ability to navigate the many spatially relevant obstacles that hinder their involvement. Initiatives not only must strengthen men's motivation to be nurturing fathers, they must also help men acquire the skills and confidence to be successful. And even this—inspiring fathers' convictions to be attentive and caring—is not enough. Initiatives need to provide fathers with timely resources to overcome the obstacles that discourage some from being more involved and nurturing, especially when their lives are in turmoil because of unemployment, divorce, incarceration, migration, military deployment, and the like.

In no small measure, public and private efforts to promote nurturance hinge on men's willingness to take all their obligations as fathers seriously. It requires fathers to move beyond a commitment to their children based on their relationship with children's mothers and to develop an unconditional relationship with children that can lead to a new and more equitable distribution of care responsibilities between men and women. Our call to elevate the significance of nurturance should in no way excuse men from taking care of their more conventional responsibilities as fathers to the best of their ability. However, fathers may negotiate their own unique mix of nurturance and more traditional tasks with other caregivers.

Fathers' negotiations will be influenced by how others close to them define their own identities as primary caregivers. Some will welcome the prospect of sharing child-care responsibilities with engaged, competent fathers, and others will resist and resent efforts that call on them to share or abdicate responsibilities that were once theirs. Although mothers' resistance is much less than in previous decades, some mothers are not eager to share or relinquish their control over domestic routines and hands-on childrearing.

To be clear, it will be quite challenging to coordinate so many organizations, special interests, and activities with ties to a fatherhood agenda that promotes nurturance. Nonetheless, we envision a social landscape in which the general public and agents of social change can find enough common ground to advocate passionately for a nurturing style of fathering.

If our vision is realized, representations in the media of fathers as capable, engaged, and nurturing will be commonplace and reflect reality. Men will be more knowledgeable and responsible about contraception, pregnancy, and various aspects of fathering—their children's health care included. Becoming a father, then, is more likely to be a planned act, and being a father is often going to entail self-assessments that involve much more than breadwinning. Educational, emotional, and practical support for men will be more readily available at diverse locations, including schools, hospitals and pediatric clinics, prisons, and all sorts of work sites. Economic support for poor fathers, including child-care facilities in settings like community colleges, will be viewed as a worthwhile investment in children's and fathers' futures. No longer will it be an oddity to see scores of fathers in a pediatrician's waiting room or men taking months of generously funded paternity leave. Professionals working with kids will be more highly committed and trained to incorporate fathers into their programs and routines. Informal support for nurturing fathers provided by networks of immediate family, kin, and friends will also be abundant and reinforced through innovative policies and programs.

As part of their collective identity as caregivers, older fathers will reach out with greater ease to younger, less experienced fathers to stress the value and skills of being a nurturing parent. The notion of caregiver may in some instances incorporate creative variations on the protector role. Ideally, men will participate more often in groups such as MAD DADS Inc. (Men Against Destruction Defending Against Drugs and Social Disorder) and align themselves more forcefully with activists who are committed to securing nutritional food for their children in schools and neighborhoods.[41] These men will be valued for recognizing children's needs and responding to them in caring ways.

When adversity strikes in any of its many forms, fathers will be given ample opportunity to prove themselves to be nurturing caregivers. A big step in that direction includes new programs for out-of-court negotiation of custody arrangements and visitation schedules that give fathers and children a reasonable chance for quality time together. Ideally, fathers with young children will have frequent and regular overnight stays to build and secure their bond. Fathers' demographic particulars—whether they are in their teens or middle years, living with or apart from their children, rich or poor, single or married, straight or gay—will matter far less than now. Fathers will have better options to enhance their human capital, and those in a position to distribute program resources will measure men's commitment to fathering more by their capacity to love and nurture on a regular basis than by their access to money. Such a shift means that programs designed to help men's parenting skills and confidence will have equal standing with efforts that seek to improve fathers' job prospects.

Achieving a society that prioritizes nurturance and care alongside breadwinning for men as well as women is only possible if fathers and other stakeholders take seriously the need to develop the types of partnerships and collaborations we highlight. What is needed is a synergy of inspired leadership at the federal, state, and local levels. Those who lead must creatively use all the potential platforms for intervention at their disposal to promote an agenda with clear expectations and adequate resources to enable men to be nurturing dads. This can best be achieved by paying attention to the concerns and complexities fathers struggle with in their everyday lives.

═ Appendix ═

Methodological Challenges in a Qualitative Multistudy Project on Fathering

FOR THOSE interested in learning more about the finer methodological details of our project, we summarize our seven qualitative data sets and then briefly describe our unique analytic approach. Although our study and sample descriptions are not meant to be exhaustive, they should provide a fairly good sense of our data sources. At the end of each data summary we provide one or more references that offer greater detail. The methodological narrative we present clarifies the novel writing process and challenges associated with two researchers integrating insights from seven data sets collected separately. The process helped us to generate the four central concepts we use to frame our book. In earlier projects we subjected our data sets to rigorous analysis, whereas for this book we used our data primarily as a way to explore critical substantive themes that enable us to highlight men's and fathers' complex lives with an emphasis on nurturance. To achieve this we used longer case studies that complement quoted material that systematically illustrates the dimensions of each theme.

Summaries of Data Sets

We drew on seven main data sets for our analysis.

Fathering in Communities (FC)

From 2003 through 2005, life-history interviews were conducted with thirty-one low-income men with family members in the Welfare, Children, and Families Three City Ethnographic Study in Chicago, or who resided in the same communities. The sample was culturally diverse, with nineteen Mexican or Puerto Rican fathers (61 percent), eleven African American fathers (35 percent), and one European American father. Fathers were recruited through a local community center and a Head Start program in two different neighborhoods. They ranged in age from nineteen to forty-eight years of age. The majority were residential and married fathers (61 percent, n = 19), and only 23 percent had children with multiple partners (n = 7). Slightly over one-third of the participants had histories of incarceration (35 percent, n = 11) or entered the program without stable jobs (35 percent, n = 11). For more details, see Roy, Buckmiller, and McDowell (2008).

Incarcerated Fathers (IF)

Life-history interviews were conducted with incarcerated men in a work-release correctional facility in Indiana, with a focus on the effects of incarceration on fathering and the reentry process into families and communities. Researchers also facilitated an 11-week life skills curriculum, meeting with fathers on a regular basis over eighteen months from 2001 to 2003. The sample consisted of twenty-eight European American, ten African American, one Native American, and one Asian American father. Fathers ranged in age from seventeen to fifty-four years of age. The average number of children per father was just over two; eight men had only one child, twenty-two men had two or three children, and six men had four or more children. Four of the fathers were expecting a child or were social fathers of their partner's biological children. These men were serving sentences of up to two years for drug or alcohol impairment or nonpayment of child support, and they were formally restricted to the facility during nonwork hours. Interviews were conducted with participants from 4 to 8 p.m. when they returned from work. For more details, see Roy (2005b) and Roy and Dyson (2005).

Male Youth Workers (MYW)

In-depth interviews lasting roughly ninety minutes were conducted with fifty-five men age nineteen to sixty-five between May 11, 2005, and July 31, 2006. At the time of the interview, all men were involved in paid work or volunteering with kids under age nineteen; some also worked with young adults. Participants included twenty-eight whites, sixteen African Americans, eight Hispanics, two Native Americans, and one Asian. Nineteen of the men reported a total household income equal to or less than $42,000, twenty-two from $40,001 to $80,000, eleven from $80,001 to $175,000, and three $175,000 or more. All of the men had earned either a high school diploma or GED, and thirty-seven had completed a college degree. Thirty-one of the men were currently married, and twenty-seven had biological children; two reported being stepfathers. Four of the men self-identified as gay. With one exception, the men resided in Florida (Gainesville, Ocala, and Miami). For more details see Marsiglio (2008a).

Responsible Fathering Program (RF)

Life-history interviews were conducted with forty African American men in a community-based fathering program in Chicago. The men ranged in age from nineteen to forty-two, and the interviews were conducted between 1997 and 1999. Fathers came to the program voluntarily, through personal references and radio advertisement, as well as through child-support court mandates. The program provided employment and parenting classes, helped men to establish paternity, and helped to untangle complicated new welfare reform laws. Twenty of the forty fathers were ex-offenders, and the same number had completed high school. Six of the fathers (15 percent) were employed at the time of the interview, with the large majority unemployed (60 percent, n = 24) or underemployed (25 percent, n = 10) and seeking job placement services at the time of enrollment in the program. Average earnings for all fathers were $204 per week, usually in part-time, short-term jobs. Almost three-quarters of the fathers (72 percent, n = 29) had never married, 13 percent (n = 5) were married, and 15 percent (n = 6) were separated or divorced. Seven fathers (18 percent) lived with their partners and children, and thirty-three fathers (83 percent) were nonresidential parents. Nine of these nonresidential fathers were still involved in romantic relationships with the mothers of their children. The average number of children per father was 2.3, and 30 percent of the men (n = 12) had three or more children. Just over one-third of the sample (n = 14) had children in multiple households. For more details, see Roy (2004, 2006).

Social Supports for Young Fathers (SS)

This project focused on men's social networks and social support. Life-history interviews were conducted with thirty-five African American men in a community-based fathering program in Indianapolis between 2002 and 2004. The program did extensive public advertising to recruit participants, although some fathers (25 percent) were referred through correctional facilities and court mandate. Like other responsible fathering programs, men were offered an array of services, although the emphasis was on GED/educational services. Job placement was available, and well-developed couples counseling services were also available. Participants were provided with small stipends during their participation in the eighteen-week program. The research team members served as facilitators of the parenting and life skills curriculum, and interviews were conducted after completion of the program. Apart from life histories, the discussions with fathers focused on men's social networks and dynamics of social support. Men ranged in age from seventeen to twenty-nine years of age.

About half of the fathers (51 percent, n = 18) were not employed or worked less than ten hours per week, and 63 percent (n = 22) had a history of incarceration. About one-third (29 percent, n = 10) of the fathers had children with multiple partners. For more details, see Roy and Dyson (2010).

Stepfathers (SF)

In-depth interviews were conducted between 2001 and 2004 with forty-six stepfathers age twenty to fifty-four. The men had to be actively involved with their partner's children who were nineteen years of age or younger and living with the mother. Thirty-three participants were currently married and living with their partner, nine cohabited with their partner but were not married, and four lived in a separate residence from their partner. Six men had legally adopted the target stepchild. Nineteen of the men had completed college, sixteen had completed high school and had some college experience, and eleven had either completed high school and not attended college or had not obtained a high school degree. Thirty-five self-identified as white, ten were African American, and two white and one black man claimed some Hispanic ancestry. Twenty-seven had fathered their own biological child, and thirteen were living with at least one of their children. The average age of the oldest child living with the stepfather was ten. For more details, see Marsiglio (2004a) and Marsiglio and Hinojosa (2007).

Young Males' Procreative Identity (YMPI)

In-depth interviews with a main sample of fifty-two men age sixteen to thirty were conducted between April 1998 and December 1999, and a supplemental sample of eighteen men age eighteen to twenty-nine were interviewed in spring 2000. Among the main sample, twenty-eight had no pregnancy or fertility experience, twelve had partners who had aborted a pregnancy, seven were involved with a partner currently pregnant with their child, four had experienced a miscarriage, and nine had biological children. Some had multiple experiences. Participants included twenty-nine white, fifteen African American (one biracial), four Hispanic, two Native American, and two Native African men. The mean age was twenty-two. Three men were still in high school, three were high school dropouts, twelve had no college experience, twenty-eight had college experience, and four were college graduates. Twelve men labeled themselves "poor" and one, "nearly poor." All participants lived in Florida, primarily in Gainesville and Jacksonville. For more details, see Marsiglio and Hutchinson (2002).

Data Analyses and Interpretation

Early on we realized that our approach to analyzing data from our seven studies would be different from the conventional grounded theory strategies we had each used previously. In other words, because we had already collected and analyzed the data, we approached our joint project with numerous theoretical insights, which is atypical of grounded theory research. We recognized, too, that we would have to improvise because we were unaware of analysis models for integrating multiple qualitative data sets. From prior collaboration, we were familiar with each other's conceptual contributions as well as the samples of fathers in our respective studies. Marsiglio initially approached Roy with an eye toward supplementing his samples of young prospective fathers, stepfathers, and male youth workers (many of whom had children of their own) with low-income fathers and incarcerated fathers. We reasoned that our data could collectively speak to a diverse and critical set of policy issues even though the data would not address every fathering topic.

We began by brainstorming which fatherhood policies and fathering programs were in play for the book. Our scope was purposefully broad, including initiatives and debates about young male reproductive health and responsibility; paternity establishment and child support; paternity leave; marriage promotion; gay adoption; reentry from incarceration; welfare; and human-capital interventions, such as job training and educational opportunities. By clustering policies and programs that dealt with similar fathering domains, we structured the book into a series of working chapters: three that dealt with the social psychological and interpersonal dimensions of fathering in families and three that focused on aspects of fathering that are less directly tied to family life (community networks, life-course events, human capital). We then determined which of our seven studies could most effectively be used to illustrate men's experiences with these policies and programs. In addition, we considered which of the working themes and concepts from our prior research would be useful. For example, when we developed the chapter "Negotiating Trust as Partners and Parents," we identified the following concepts from our earlier research: trajectories, border work, provide and reside, baby-mamadrama, gatekeeping, package deal and conditional commitment, father ally, and situated fathering. In this way we began with concepts generated from prior analyses but coordinated them to extend our analyses to inform fathering policies and programs. Thus our strategy was similar to grounded theorists' use of "sensitizing concepts" that direct researchers' attention to aspects of reality that shape their line of inquiry.[1]

Considering their relevance for a wide range of initiatives, we then began to integrate examples from our research that could illustrate the contexts, meanings, and processes that shape fathers' experiences of nurturance. We repeatedly challenged each other, asking, for example, "Do your data speak to the topic of marriage promotion, or parenting programs for social fathers, or socialization to fatherhood?" or "Can we identify men with different characteristics and social backgrounds to address this topic?" This collegial dynamic became iterative as we compared and contrasted men's experiences (similar to axial coding in grounded theory approaches), identified and filled gaps in our chapters, broadened the samples for particular themes, and expanded conceptual lenses we had worked with closely in previous studies.

In some ways, the triangulation of our diverse samples, research protocols, and interviewing styles enhanced the trustworthiness of our collaborative project. Although we did not systematically review or code each other's extensive data, we individually revisited our data and selectively opened them up to the other's review. Through this process we broadened our individual perspectives, generated new insights, and synthesized our jointly constructed interpretation of fathers' experiences.

In practical terms, our iterative analysis that involved writing chapter drafts focused on specific substantive themes eventually led us to our final conceptual framework. Our countless discussions and intensive collaborative writing resulted in us choosing four concepts to serve as the key interpretive frames that shaped our thinking about the fathering landscape: fathering as a social arrangement, trajectories of fathers' lives, trust building on multiple layers, and the intersection of fathering and place. Throughout, one constant line of questioning oriented our inquiry: Are these concepts relevant for an initiative that promotes nurturance, and if so, how?

Although our data were collected between 1997 and 2006, most policy-relevant challenges that arise from men's experiences as fathers in families have not shifted dramatically since our data collection began. In addition, our intent was not to conduct an analysis of narrative resources to determine how public and private discourses around fathering have evolved in the United States over the fifteen years since 1997. In the late 1990s and early 2000s, many fathers were inspired by the Million Man March and Promise Keeper gatherings. Policy also shifted course over this time, away from fathering toward marriage promotion under the George W. Bush administration, and the child support enforcement system (alongside paternity establishment) became more effective, efficient, and commonplace for families. Even though our collective data sets do not speak to these or other social changes, the stories men share do highlight the problems, images, and policies that have not changed. Our project reinforces the notion that men's nurturance of children remains largely ignored in our communities, our programs, and our social policies at all levels.

We extended our analyses beyond our previous empirical and theoretical work in order to move toward a more nuanced appreciation for how stakeholders can promote fathers' nurturance within the complex environment of policies and programs relating to fatherhood. In particular, we located, described, and sometimes assessed programs that we did not know existed. At times we also broadened our reach by summarizing findings from other studies that targeted specific categories of fathers not included in our combined data set. Ultimately, we pieced together an action-oriented framework that hints at how collaboration and partnerships might develop at both a policy and programmatic level. We emphasize the latter task because the connections between actors in the social policy and programmatic arenas—and between community actors and families themselves—are vital but often underdeveloped.

═ Notes ═

Preface

1. Cherlin (2009).
2. Marsiglio (2011).
3. Faludi (1999); Griswold (1993); Doucet (forthcoming).

Chapter 1

1. Lupton and Barclay (1997).
2. Griswold (1993).
3. Townsend (2002). Note that Frank Furstenberg and Andrew Cherlin (1991) introduced the "package deal" phase into the academic literature to refer to men's tendency to confound marital relations with fathering commitments. Others (Tach, Mincy, and Edin 2010) have also recently used "package deal" to capture men's tendency to make their emotional connections with their children contingent on how they feel romantically about the children's mother. However, in this book we've elected to use "package deal" in a manner consistent with Townsend's usage. We use the phrase "conditional commitment" to capture Furstenberg and Cherlin's concept.
4. Griswold (1993).
5. Doucet (2006); Gerson (1993); Hansen (2005); Harrington, Van Deusen, and Humberd (2011); Harrington, Van Deusen, and Ladge (2010); Miller (2010).
6. Harrington, Van Deusen, and Humberd (2011, 5).
7. Aumann, Galinsky, and Matos (2011).
8. Friedan (1963).
9. Focusing largely on stay-at-home dads, Smith's (2009) characterization of "the daddy shift" represents a popular press account of the new ideal of fathers who are more actively involved in their children's hands-on care. See also Chesley (2011).
10. Aumann, Galinsky, and Matos (2011).
11. LaRossa (1997).

12. Coles (2009); Hamer (2001, 2005); Roy (1999, 2005b); Tamis-LeMonda and McFadden (2010); Waller (2002).

13. Gilmore (1990).

14. Kyle Pruett, for example, a child psychiatrist at the Yale Child Student Center, has done research for several decades and written sole-authored mainstream books such as *The Nurturing Father: Journey Toward the Complete Man* (1987) and *Fatherneed: Why Father Care Is as Essential as Mother Care for Your Child* (2000) and collaborated with his wife, Marsha Kline Pruett, on publishing *Partnership Parenting: How Men and Women Parent Differently— Why It Helps Your Kids and Can Strengthen Your Marriage* (2009). Although Pruett concludes that fathers can and do nurture their children, he suggests that they often do so differently than do mothers.

15. Dowd (2000).

16. Dowd (2000, 176).

17. Furstenberg and Cherlin (1991).

18. See Dermott (2008), who notes that good fathering in the United Kingdom has become more synonymous with new ideas of intimacy in an emotional father-child relationship.

19. Matta and Knudson-Martin (2006) use the concept "responsivity" in their work, but in our book we use the term "responsiveness."

20. Collier and Sheldon (2008) detail how the heightening concern about men's roles in family life has placed English law at the center of a dialogue around rights and responsibilities. They distinguish between a push for men "inside the home" to live up to the ideal of new fatherhood, and a set of competing initiatives around families, crime, and citizenship that reconfigure the "problem of men" who are deviant, dysfunctional, and potentially dangerous and live "outside the home."

21. Pleck and Masciadrelli (2004).

22. Parker (2007); Pew Research Center (2007).

23. Blankenhorn (1995); Collier and Sheldon (2008); Coltrane (2001); Crowley (2008); Daniels (1998); Gavanas (2002); Griswold (1993); Marsiglio (1995, 2004a, 2008a); Popenoe (1996); Dowd (2000); Peters et al. (2000); Tamis-LeMonda and Cabrera (2002); Townsend (2002); Wall and Arnold (2007).

24. The National Fatherhood Initiative (NFI), founded in 1994, is perhaps the most active nonprofit organization in the United States dealing with fatherhood issues. It describes its mission as improving "the well-being of children by increasing the proportion of children growing up with involved, responsible, and committed fathers" (http://www.fatherhood.org/about/mission-and-vision; accessed November 14, 2011). Although we have concerns with how it frames both the "father absence" problem and solutions to it, NFI is a good example of how an organization can develop meaningful partnerships between different groups, in some cases while mobilizing individuals, communities, and agencies to assume a more active role in working with fathers.

25. Fagan and Palm (2004); Johnson and Salter (2006); Kiselica (1995, 2008); Levine and Pitt (1995), O'Donnell et al. (2005).

26. Booth and Crouter (1998); Bzostek (2008); Lamb (2004, 2010); Marsiglio, Amato et al. (2000).

27. Marsiglio (2008a).

28. U.S. Department of Health and Human Services (2001).

29. This report to the president in 2001 also emphasizes that multiple federal agencies including the Departments of Agriculture, Education, Health and Human Services, Housing and Urban Development, Justice, and Labor have and should continue to support fatherhood programs. A range of existing policies that shape men's experiences as fathers are described, such as child support, child welfare, housing, Temporary Assistance for Needy Families and Medicaid, WIC, and fidelity bonds.

30. See Featherstone (2009) for details about how the government in the United Kingdom has institutionalized the call to pay more attention to fathers. See also Hobson (2002) and Stanley (2005).

31. Edelman, Holzer, and Offner (2006); Mincy (2006).

32. U.S. Department of Health and Human Services (2001).

33. The effects of such programs are summarized in *Building Strong Families* (Dion et al. 2008). Recent research initiatives funded by the Administration of Children and Families include the Healthy Marriage Research Initiative (2005 to 2010) and the Responsible Fatherhood and Healthy Marriage Research Initiative (2006 to 2011).

34. Turetsky (2008); see also Center for Law and Social Policy, "Responsible Fatherhood and Healthy Families Act of 2007," available at: http://www.clasp.org/publications/responsible_fatherhood_act_of_2007.pdf; accessed August 2, 2011.

35. Bronte-Tinkew, Scott, and Horowitz (2009).

36. Bronte-Tinkew, Horowitz, and Metz (2007).

37. Knox et al. (2011).

38. As of 2010, there are four model programs that await assessment (Knox et al. (2011). Each uses community-based organizations to deliver research-based curricula. The Strengthening Healthy Marriages (SHM) study is based on a nine-year project begun in 2003. It focuses on married couples, is funded by the Administration for Children and Families (ACF), and is evaluated by Manpower Demonstration and Research Corporation. SHM integrates three program components (marriage education, social activities, and family support services) to discern which services lead to better marital well-being. The Building Strong Families (BSF) project is similar to the SHM project but targets unmarried low-income couples. Also funded by ACF, the BSF project will be evaluated by Mathematica. Both projects will finish in 2012, with evaluation data forthcoming. The Supporting Father Involvement (SFI) study is based in California and

involves primarily low-income married and unmarried Latino couples. It provides therapy sessions and compares the impact of couple-based or father-based services. The Fathers, Relationships, and Marriage Education Study (FRAME) is conducted by researchers from the University of Denver and is also funded by ACF. A unique feature of this study is its random assignment of participants to couple-based, father-based, or mother-based service groups. It targets low-income parents who live together in committed relationships. See also Avellar et al. (2011) for a recent catalog and review of seventy-five studies of sixty-two fatherhood programs. This review identifies impact, implementation, and descriptive studies. Only three of the programs explicitly incorporate outcome measures of fathers' nurturance. They include one impact study (Head Start–Based Father Involvement Program—four urban elementary classrooms) and two descriptive studies (Long Distance Dads—incarcerated fathers in one prison in Pennsylvania; and Incredible Years—two Head Start centers in New York City). None of the interventions produced significant differences in fathers' self-reported levels of nurturance.

39. Ooms et al. (2006).

40. Pleck, Lamb, and Levine (1986).

41. Bird and Rieker (2008).

42. Furstenberg (1988).

43. Marsiglio (1998).

44. Featherstone and Peckover (2007); Beaton et al. (forthcoming).

45. As Lareau (2000) suggests, fathers may on average be less well informed than mothers about their children's lives and less capable of providing rich and accurate details about what is happening in their children's everyday lives. Yet many fathers can generate relatively detailed descriptions and they certainly are capable of talking about what fathering means to them and what they expect of themselves. See also Coley and Morris (2002) for a comparative statistical analysis of fathers' and mothers' parenting reports in low-income families.

46. Marsiglio (2004a, 2008a); Marsiglio and Hutchinson (2002).

47. Schrock and Schwalbe (2009).

48. See Marsiglio and Pleck (2005) and Pleck (2010a) for detailed discussions highlighting various connections between fatherhood and masculinity. In his fatherhood-masculinity model, Pleck (2010a) differentiates between two ways the masculinity concept has been typically used in fatherhood studies. It represents one of the two socially constructed gender statuses (male versus female) or it refers to a type of orientation that depicts the extent to which men either hold particular beliefs and attitudes or possess male gender-typed characteristics. Thus, Pleck's model treats masculinity largely as an individual phenomenon or attribute while exploring how it relates to men's paternal status and fathering behavior. Other conceptualizations of masculinity, consistent with our own, treat it as a practice or

performance that is part of a larger system of gender relations (Connell 1995; Connell and Messerschmidt 2005). As such, it involves practices and meanings that occur in structured social relations and interactions between people. Although this latter conceptualization is quite common in masculinities studies, in the fathering literature it has not been as widely applied as the individual-attribute model.

49. Marsiglio and Cohan (2000, 85).

50. Marsiglio, Roy, and Fox (2005).

51. Orloff and Monson (2002); Roy (1999).

52. Curran and Abrams (2000), cited in Richter and Morrell (2006, 21).

53. Palkovitz (2002); Settersten and Cancel-Tirado (2010).

54. Elder and O'Rand (1995) use the concepts of linked lives and multiple perspectives on time (ontogenetic, generational, and cohort) to introduce dimensions to the life-course approach, which provides tools to allow us to explore how social change affects human lives, "one person at a time."

55. See Marsiglio (2004a, 2008a) for a more detailed description of this model and how it has been applied to stepfathers and youth workers. To simplify our language, we sometimes use the term "paths" in place of what Marsiglio termed trajectories.

56. Marsiglio and Roy (forthcoming); see also Doucet (2009).

57. In chapter 2 we discuss more specifically how concepts related to the procreative identity framework (Marsiglio 2003; Marsiglio and Hutchinson 2002) shape our ideas about men assigning meaning to their ability to procreate and nurture children.

58. Erikson (1975).

59. Marsiglio (2008a, 93); see also de St. Aubin, McAdams, and Kim (2004).

60. Erikson (1964, 131).

61. Erikson (1963); McAdams and de St. Aubin (1992).

62. Snarey (1993, 13).

63. Kotre (1984).

64. Marsiglio (2008a).

65. Gerson (1995).

66. Roy and Lucas (2006).

67. Marsiglio, Day, and Lamb (2000).

68. Feinberg (2002, 173; 2003).

69. Dienhart (1998).

70. Marsiglio and Hinojosa (2007).

71. Berkowitz and Marsiglio (2007).

72. Allen and Hawkins (1999).

73. Roy, Buckmiller, and McDowell (2008). For a discussion about how coparenting and couple relationship processes may influence one another, see Feinberg (2002, 2003). See also Cummings, Merrilees, and George (2010) for an extensive review of the relationship between marital quality, fathering, and child outcomes.

74. Catlett and McKenry (2004).

75. Marsiglio, Roy, and Fox (2005).

76. Elder (1995) introduced the notion of reciprocal continuity to suggest how individuals are shaped by social structures and also how they act as agents to reshape these structures.

77. Cooper (2000).

78. Marsiglio, Roy, and Fox (2005).

79. Pleck (2010a, 47). Pleck provides a useful review of the empirical literature and suggests that the evidence currently does not support this hypothesis. He also notes that advocates for greater fathers' rights and involvement are quite vocal about the "essential" notion because they fear fathers will be marginalized or marginalized more if this ideology is not adopted by those in power.

80. Pleck (2010a, 48, italics in original). See also Silverstein and Auerbach (1999).

81. See http://www.fatherhood.gov/initiative.

82. Burgess (2007); see also "How Fathers' Story Week Helps Dads in Prison Reach Out to Their Children," available at: http://www.fatherhoodinstitute.org/index.php?nID=79; accessed July 31, 2011.

83. See the Fatherhood Project, "Promoting Men's Care and Protection of Children," Human Sciences Research Council, available at: http://www.hsrc.ac.za/RPP-Fatherhood-2.phtml; accessed July 31, 2011.

84. FIRA (http://www.fira.ca) has promoted conferences and communication between policymakers, program staff, and researchers and identified diverse groups of fathers with specific needs (including gay, bi, or queer fathers; immigrant fathers; indigenous fathers; divorced fathers; new and young fathers; and fathers of children with special needs).

85. Gavanas (2002); see also Edleson and Williams (2007a); Mincy and Pouncy (2002).

86. U.S. Department of Health and Human Services (2001).

87. U.S. Department of Health and Human Services (2001); Peters et al. (2000).

88. See the appendix for our discussion of how our previous work and current data analysis led us to choose these substantive themes.

89. This approach should not be confused with a style of research that would evaluate a preexisting program systematically and then provide some sort of evidence-based, best-practice recommendation. We don't draw those types of conclusions.

Chapter 2

1. Finer and Henshaw (2006).
2. Strauss and Goldberg (1999, 245); see also Markus and Nurius (1986); Oyserman and Markus (1990).
3. Marsiglio (1998, 2003); Marsiglio and Hutchinson (2002).
4. Sonenstein et al. (1997); Marsiglio (2006).
5. Sonenstein et al. (1997); Marsiglio (2006).
6. We discuss relationship issues in detail in chapter 4; here we stress the value of male responsibility programs incorporating these types of concerns. This is critical because many young men report that a previous betrayal has made them averse to trusting women. Gender distrust makes it exceedingly difficult for young men to have relaxed, meaningful conversations with partners about sex, contraception, commitment, unplanned childbearing, and fathering.
7. For a more extensive discussion of how professionals can use strategies based on self-narratives see Marsiglio (2003). These strategies can be used in same and mixed gender focus group settings or one-on-one consultations. Young men can be asked to provide their own stories or encouraged to reflect on those of others.
8. See also Bishop (2006); see http://www.bootcampfornewdads.org and http://www.dadsadventure.com.
9. Curran and Abrams (2000).
10. Marsiglio (1998).
11. Marsiglio (1998).
12. Daniels (2006).
13. Daniels (2006, 155).
14. Cabrera, Fagan, and Farrie (2008).
15. Somewhat parallel opportunities may exist for a gay man to express himself as a supportive partner, but because his partner will not be experiencing a pregnancy directly, the options will be far more limited.
16. National Gallup Poll data from 2003 indicate that 79 percent of men and 67 percent of women favored "a law requiring that the husband of a married woman be notified if she decides to have an abortion" (Pew Research Center 2005, para. 6).
17. Marsiglio (1995); Furstenberg and Cherlin (1991).
18. Marsiglio (1995).
19. Crowley (2008).
20. See Featherstone (2009) for an overview of several paternity issues from legal and political perspectives in a European context.

21. Mincy, Garfinkel, and Nepomnyaschy (2005).

22. Bishai et al. (2006).

23. Farrel, Glosser, and Gardiner (2003).

24. Crowley (2008).

25. Bozett (1989).

26. Berkowitz (2007).

27. Berkowitz and Marsiglio (2007, 372).

28. Berkowitz and Marsiglio (2007).

29. Jeffries, Marsiglio, and Berkowitz (2009).

30. Berkowitz and Marsiglio (2007).

31. Lewin (2006).

32. One important hurdle to achieving further public support for gay marriage is that African Americans are generally less comfortable with the idea of gay marriage than whites (Pew Research Center 2010).

33. Biblarz and Stacey (2010); Stacey and Biblarz (2001).

34. Rothman (2005).

35. Marsiglio (2004a).

36. Marsiglio and Hinojosa (2010).

37. See also Marsiglio (1995).

38. These include degree of identity conviction, paternal role range, solo-shared identity, timing, degree of deliberativeness, mindfulness, propriety work, naming, seeking public recognition, and biological children as benchmarks. For a full description of these properties, see Marsiglio (2004b).

39. Fine (1994); LexisNexis (2001); Marsiglio (2004a).

40. Mason et al. (2002).

41. Mason et al. (2002, 519).

42. For an extensive discussion of the possible advantages and disadvantages of this kind of innovation, see Marsiglio (2004a).

43. Jones (2008); Miller and Garfinkel (1999).

44. Connell (1995).

45. Aumann, Galinsky, and Matos (2011); LaRossa (1997); Townsend (2002).

46. Gerson (1993); Hansen (2005).

47. Newman (1999).

48. See http://www.ecodads.org.

49. Roy and Dyson (2010).

50. Griswold (1993).

Chapter 3

1. Matta and Knudson-Martin (2006).
2. Pleck, Lamb, and Levine (1986).
3. Cooley (1909, 23).
4. Psychological studies of paternal nurturance over the past three decades have measured nurturance in terms of behaviors such as showing love for children, understanding children's worries, hugging and kissing children, caring for and paying attention to children, and making children feel better (Reuter and Biller 1973; Belsky 1984). Recently, more sociological studies of nurturant paternal involvement emphasize the importance of closeness as a way to measure bonds between fathers and children (Amato 1994; Coltrane 1988). By using concepts such as nurturance and bond, we emphasize the reciprocal interaction between fathers and children and the intimacy that emerges as a result of that interaction (Brown et al. 2007; Habib and Lancaster 2006; Rane and McBride 2000).
5. Studies of children's attachment to parents have been extended in recent years to explore the consequences of early attachment behaviors. These studies suggest that young adults who exhibited healthy attachment to their own parents may also develop closer relationships with their intimate partners and, by extension, their own children (Mikulincer and Shaver 2007). In this way, men's capacity to nurture children may be related to their attachments to their own parents and partners.
6. Whatever bonds men forge with children occur without benefit of the gestational bond that women can achieve. As O'Brien (1981) observes, reproductive physiology has historically alienated men from their seed, thereby making it more of a socially constructed effort for men to establish a commitment to a child. See also Marsiglio (1998).
7. See Marsiglio (2008a) for a fuller discussion of these types of bonds and how they relate to male youth workers' involvement with children. Bonds that youth workers establish with children have many similar properties to those shared by fathers and their children, although family bonds will have some unique features. One potentially important way fathers bond with their children that we do not include in this list involves advocacy. When fathers advocate for their children, especially in their presence, it may strengthen the trust and closeness children experience with their fathers.
8. This feeling state is related to Dermott's (2008) concept of intimacy as it is expressed in father-child relationships. She argues that framing contemporary fatherhood as intimacy reflects Giddens's (1992) ideal of a "pure relationship" and captures the interests of men to express emotions to their children in exclusive, reciprocal bonds. Care for children emerges from an emotional connection, which resolves the gap between conduct and culture for fathers.
9. LaRossa (2005).

10. For practical suggestions as to how fathers can create emotionally meaningful rituals with children and coparents see Levine and Pittinsky (1997).

11. Pew Forum on Religion and Public Life (2009).

12. Marsiglio (2004b).

13. Jarrett, Roy, and Burton (2002); see also Waller (2002).

14. Zinn and Wells (2008).

15. Marsiglio (2004a, 2008a).

16. R. Padawer, "Who Knew I Was Not the Father?" *New York Times,* November 17, 2009.

17. Pleck, Lamb, and Levine (1986).

18. Doucet (2006).

19. Holden and Hawk (2003, 191); see also Hawk and Holden (2006). These authors label this parental cognitive activity "metaparenting."

20. Nicholson, Howard, and Borkowski (2008). The authors use the abbreviation RPM3 to refer to these five areas.

21. Marsiglio and Roy (forthcoming).

22. Walzer (1998).

23. Carlson and McLanahan (2004).

24. Draper (2002); Fagan et al. (2009); see also Marsiglio (2008b).

25. Mikulincer and Shaver (2007).

26. Palmer (2004) discusses the chemistry of attachment, in which levels of oxytocin, prolactin, and opioids are shaped by infant-parent interaction during the first few months of life. A father's involvement encourages subsequent interaction with his baby and with the child's mother as well. Storey et al. (2000) found that women and men had similar stage-specific differences in hormone levels, with higher concentrations of cortisol (which enhances focus and response to infants) and prolactin (which promotes caregiving and brain reorganization to favor such behavior) prior to birth and lower concentrations of testosterone or estradiol after birth. Men with more pregnancy symptoms of their own, and who appeared more sensitive to infant reactivity, tended to have higher prolactin levels and the greatest drop in testosterone. Gettler et al. (2011) have recently conducted perhaps the most rigorous study that explores the possible effects of paternity and caregiving on men's testosterone levels. Using a longitudinal design with a large community-based sample of men from the Philippines (N=624) who were twenty-six years of age, on average, in 2009, they found that men who became new fathers had the largest declines in AM and PM testosterone between 2005 and 2009. In addition, fathers who reported participating in the most physical care of their newborn and infant children showed significantly lower values of testosterone compared to men reporting no care. For a commentary on this article see Gray (2011). See also Gray

and Anderson (2010) for further discussion of recent research on how men's neuroendocrine system and biochemistry are related to aspects of fathering.

27. Paquette (2004).

28. Tamis-LeMonda et al. (2004).

29. Messner (1992); Kimmel (2008).

30. DeGarmo and Forgatch (2007).

31. Pickhardt (1997).

32. Pickhardt (1997, 113).

33. Ganong et al. (1999).

34. Swiss and Le Bourdais (2009); Whitehead and Bala (forthcoming).

35. Collier and Sheldon (2008); Crowley (2008).

36. Crowley (2008).

37. For over a decade, commentators of various political persuasions have debated whether, to what extent, and why boys may be experiencing more educational deficits than girls, especially in high school. Efforts to engage boys more fully in school at all levels can have the longer term payoff of prompting men to be more open about school-related activities with their own children. See Marsiglio (2008a) for an overview of the debate about the feminization of schools and boys' performance.

38. See chapter 6 for further discussion.

39. MacDermid et al. (2005).

40. Nelson (2010).

41. Roy (2004).

42. Hamer (2005); Letiecq and Koblinsky (2004).

43. Hamer (2005).

44. Letiecq and Koblinsky (2004).

45. Roy and Burton (2007).

46. Haas and Hwang (2008).

47. O'Brien and Moss (2010); see also Moss and Korintus (2008).

48. O'Brien and Moss (2010, 561).

49. O'Brien and Moss (2010, 561); see also Seward, Yeatts, Zottarelli, et al. (2006).

50. Tanaka and Waldfogel (2007, 420).

51. Nepomnyaschy and Waldfogel (2007).

52. Haas and Hwang (2007, 2009); McKay, Marshall, and Doucet (forthcoming).

53. Sayers and Fox (2005); Zvonkovic et al. (2005).

54. MacDermid et al. (2005); Segal and Segal (2003).

55. Arditti, Lambert-Shute, and Joest (2003); Nurse (2002); Roy and Dyson (2005).

56. Roy (2005b).

57. Marsiglio (2009a).

58. Courtenay (2000).

59. Marsiglio (2009a); Menning (2006); Menning and Stewart (2008); Wickrama et al. (1999).

60. Caldwell et al. (2004).

61. Marsiglio (2009a, 26).

62. Levine and Pittinsky (1997).

63. Garfield, Clark-Kauffman, and Davis (2006); Marsiglio (2009a); Martin et al. (2007); Sharma and Petosa (1997).

64. Committee for Integrating the Science of Early Child Development (2000).

65. One exception is the work of John Snarey (1993). Snarey used qualitative interviews with a cohort of 240 lower- and working-class fathers born in the 1920s and 1930s in Boston whose children were baby boomers. The fathers were interviewed as young adults and again at midlife about their parenting.

66. Marsiglio and Roy (forthcoming). See also Diamond (2007); Snarey (1993). A life-course approach raises questions such as, How do youth and adult children support their fathers' cognitive or social development in the later years of life? How do fathers respond to their children's attempts to nurture them? To what extent and how does reciprocal communication, physical contact, and social or cognitive stimulation influence fathers' and children's opportunities to develop closer relationships over time?

67. Gerson (1995).

68. Juby et al. (2007); Lin and McLanahan (2007); see also Mandell (2002).

69. See chapter 6 for further discussion.

70. Featherstone and Peckover (2007).

Chapter 4

1. Marsiglio (2004b).

2. That mothers often influence fathers' involvement with their children has been a well-established reality for research and theoretical models for more than twenty years (Belsky 1984; Doherty, Kouneski, and Erickson 1998).

3. Dowd (2000); Marsiglio (1995, 93–96).

4. To understand fully intimate unions among low-income women, Burton et al. (2009) move beyond primarily using general attitudes, like gender distrust, to explain trends in marriage and cohabitation. They examine the

more complex forms of trust that poor women construct and enact in relationships based on the situations in which they find themselves. They identify emergent forms of interpersonal trust, including suspended, compartmentalized, misplaced, and integrated trust. Fathers may also exhibit similar forms of situated trust and general distrust.

5. Two recent studies suggest that coparenting support at an early stage can result in enhanced father involvement in subsequent years (Fagan and Lee 2011; Fagan and Palkovitz 2011). These effects are particularly critical for adolescent fathers (when compared to older fathers) and for nonresidential nonromantic parents. They urge researchers to consider family structure, romantic involvement, and the age of fathers to better understand how father involvement changes over time.

6. For a conceptual framework outlining key domains relevant to prevention efforts see Feinberg (2002, 2003).

7. Marsiglio and Hutchinson (2002, 139–40).

8. Marsiglio and Hutchinson (2002).

9. Stanley (2001).

10. Marsiglio (2008b).

11. Fagan et al. (2009).

12. Cabrera, Fagan, and Farrie (2008).

13. Lewin (2009); Mallon (2004); Stacey (2006).

14. Lewin (2009) interviewed and profiled this couple.

15. Mallon (2004).

16. Mallon (2004). This description comes from one of the gay fathers of a non-biologically related child.

17. Stacey (2006).

18. LaRossa (1997).

19. Wilcox (2004).

20. Annie E. Casey Foundation (2010).

21. In a prominent debate in the field of family science, Doherty, Kouneski, and Erickson (1998, 2000) and Walker and McGraw (2000) openly debated "who is responsible for responsible fatherhood?" The role of mothers in securing or promoting men's role as fathers also led to a broader discussion of the need for fathers in child development, with Silverstein and Auerbach (1999) critically evaluating the essentialist view of fathers (see also Dowd 2000). A recent study by Jia and Schoppe-Sullivan (2011) suggests that men who take the first step in being an involved parent (through play or possibly caregiving) can subsequently shape more positive coparenting relationships. However, their study suggests that a strong coparenting relationship may not lead to more nurturing father behavior.

22. Seery and Crowley (2000).

23. Annie E. Casey Foundation (2010).

24. Seward, Yeatts, Amin et al. (2006); Russell and Hwang (2004).

25. Bumpass and Lu (2000).

26. Pinsof (2002).

27. Fein et al. (2003, 18) indicate the need for "more direct research on the processes that affect the development of commitment within cohabitation and decision making about marriage." See also Lichter, Qian, and Mellott (2006). The categories of cohabitation or marriage obscure the importance of understanding relationships as trajectories (Musick and Bumpass 2006).

28. Reed (2006).

29. Stanley, Rhoades, and Markman (2006) first noted these two trajectories. Similarly, in prior research, Surra and Hughes (1997) examined event-driven and relationship-driven criteria for marriage. Some of the most extensive research on cohabitation with children is from Manning and Smock (2005), who confirm Stanley, Rhoades, and Markman's findings by documenting cohabitation as a potentially uninformed, unconscious process of couple formation.

30. Hohmann-Marriott (2011).

31. Edin et al. (2007); Bronte-Tinkew, Scott, and Horowitz (2009).

32. Henshaw and Kost (2008); see also Centers for Disease Control and Prevention (2009). Given the strong association between race and social class, and the sizable difference in abortion rates by race, the more affluent will be more likely to secure an abortion if they have an unplanned pregnancy. Still, women with higher incomes experienced some of the most pronounced declines in abortion over the past few decades.

33. Jones, Darroch, and Henshaw (2002).

34. Rindfuss (1991).

35. Roy (1999, 439).

36. Even with technology that establishes a clear biological linkage between men and their children, the obligations of biological and social fathers are not clear under family law (R. Padawer, "Who Knew I Was Not the Father?" *New York Times*, November 17, 2009; Leahy 2005). In many cases of highly contested struggles between fathers and mothers, courts have ruled that social fathering may take precedence over biological fathering. When men learn that they are not the biological fathers, as they had been led to believe by children's mothers, the acrimony between fathers and mothers can effectively color the previous and ongoing relationship between fathers and their children.

37. Johnson, Levine, and Doolittle (1999).

38. Roberts (2004).

39. Lichter, Batson, and Brown (2004); Carlson and McLanahan (2006); Dion (2005); Lichter and Graefe (2007); Harris and Parisi (2005); Gibson-Davis (2009).

40. Harris and Parisi (2005).

41. Lichter, Batson, and Brown (2004).

42. Carlson and McLanahan (2006).

43. Gibson-Davis (2009).

44. Nurse (2002).

45. Allen and Hawkins (1999).

46. Pleck and Masciadrelli (2004). A recent exception is a study by Schoppe-Sullivan and colleagues (2008) in which positive gatekeeping behavior by mothers—such as encouragement of father involvement—was shown to be associated with higher father involvement in two-parent families with an infant.

47. Marsiglio, Roy, and Fox (2005).

48. Women's Divorce, "The Disneyland Dad: Advice from the Coach," available at: http://www.womansdivorce.com/disneyland-dad.html; accessed August 2, 2011.

49. Catlett and McKenry (2004); Catlett, Toews, and McKenry (2005).

50. Marsiglio and Hinojosa (2007).

51. Marsiglio (2004a).

52. Turetsky (2007).

53. Braver and O'Connell (1998); Crowley (2008).

54. The accountability concern could be taken a step further if it were determined that some fathers should be given the opportunity in well-defined situations to influence how a portion of their child support is being spent. For example, a divorced father might want his child support payments to be used to provide school tuition for his high school–age son and daughter. Through mediation efforts with both coparents, this father's preferences would be discussed as part of the larger arrangement of providing for children's well-being with limited resources.

55. On December 6, 1995, Marsiglio presented testimony to the Florida House of Representatives' Select Committee on Child Abuse and Neglect that the state should consider instituting a child support debit card system similar to what is described in the text that follows. At this time, states had not yet instituted debit cards to disburse child support awards, and some representatives present in the meeting were opposed to the idea that nonresident fathers could monitor mothers' use of child support. Some of the states that currently use a form of debit card for child support are Florida, New Jersey, New York, Massachusetts, Texas, and Virginia.

56. Some commentators have also suggested that nonresident fathers should have more liberal child visitation rights that are in some instances linked to their child support obligations, even though this strategy is contrary to the states' practice of keeping these issues separate. This position is consistent with the notion that many fathers would be more willing to pay child support if their attachment to their children could be enhanced through quality interaction. A well-defined enforcement strategy for protecting responsible fathers' visitation rights could be developed that supplements the ongoing efforts to increase the accountability associated with child support payments. At the very least, demonstration projects that experiment with provisions designed to balance the rights and obligations of fathers, mothers, and children should be evaluated. Pursuing this strategy will, of course, require vigorous efforts to enforce visitation systematically, which may prove to be counterproductive in those instances in which children would be forced to spend time with fathers they don't want to see. Moreover, having the opportunity to spend additional time with children, especially if children feel inconvenienced by visitation arrangements, does not necessarily mean that the time fathers spend with their children will be positive. The adversarial nature of many coparental relationships is an additional factor that complicates this process.

57. Sassler (2004); Binstock and Thornton (2003).

58. Rich (2001); Edin and Nelson (2001).

59. Recent court cases on paternity disestablishment have challenged the process of paternity establishment throughout the 1990s. This is particularly relevant for noncustodial parents whose child support payments have been retained to reimburse state expenditures when children and custodial mothers received welfare assistance. Most courts have argued that the state is not liable to repay retained collections, as retroactive modifications of support orders are banned. New Jersey courts denied a father's application to reopen paternity and support judgment. One father in Maine paid $22,000 over eleven years to a child later found not to be his biological child. His efforts to recoup his payments were denied due to sovereign immunity in that a state cannot award restitution to a man who, without objection, pays child support for a child who is later determined not to be his. Connecticut is one of the only states that will refund support paid if paternity is disestablished when a child receives public assistance.

60. In a survey of nine states, Sorensen, Sousa, and Schaner (2007) find that "70 percent of unpaid support in nine states was owed by obligors earning less than $10,000 per year" (3). The authors estimate that 13 to 15 percent of offenders in county jails are found in contempt of family court. As some legal advocates point out, few of these fathers understand or can anticipate and fulfill their burden of proof. In a case before the Supreme Court (Boggess 2011), a low-income father in South Carolina was incarcerated for twelve months for failure to pay child support. He was also

denied legal representation. However, as advocates pointed out, this father "did not have the keys to his cell," meaning that he was incarcerated because of his arrearages. Without a job, this father had no recourse but to accept incarceration.

61. Roy (2005b); Swisher and Waller (2008).

62. Roy, Buckmiller, and McDowell (2008).

63. Carlson and Furstenberg (2006); Guzzo and Furstenberg (2007). Tach, Mincy, and Edin (2010) find that the most critical transition that leads to decreased paternal involvement is not when "fathers swap kids" in subsequent families but when "mothers swap daddies" in women's new partnering relationships.

64. Roy and Burton (2007).

65. Edin and Lein (1997); Roy and Burton (2007).

66. Dowd (2000, 173).

Chapter 5

1. Hansen (2005); see also O'Brien's (2005) discussion of fathers in the United Kingdom, which reinforces the need to think about father involvement as being intimately connected to larger family networks.

2. Stack (1974); Dominguez and Watkins (2003); Roschelle (1997).

3. Hansen (2005); Nelson (2006).

4. Jarrett and Burton (1999); Stack (1974).

5. Stack and Burton (1993, 160); see also Crosbie-Burnett and Lewis (1999).

6. Hamer (2001); Waller (2002).

7. Aumann, Galinsky, and Matos (2011).

8. Roy (2005a, 91).

9. Burton (2007) labels this process "adultification."

10. Kimmel (2008).

11. Kimmel (1996).

12. Burton (2007).

13. Roy, Dyson, and Jackson (2010).

14. Roy, Dyson, and Jackson (2010).

15. Marsiglio (2004a); Marsiglio and Hinojosa (2007).

16. Marsiglio and Hinojosa (2007, 846). This analysis produces theoretical insights by identifying six properties associated with how the father-ally sentiment and practice is expressed among stepfathers. These properties are labeled development, purpose, awareness level, reciprocity routines, building trust and respect, and social capital.

17. Braver and O'Connell (1998).

18. Mothers were at the forefront of developing a Web-based organization (Marsiglio 2004a), Comamas, in the early 2000s as a formal response to help stepmothers and mothers develop a productive partnership and some basic pointers. (The website is no longer active.)

19. Michelle Carcrae, "Support for Stay-at-Home Dads," Parenting Resources (blog), February 26, 2008, available at: http://parentingsupportgroups.suite101.com/article.cfm/support_for_stayathome_dads; accessed August 2, 2011.

20. Hansen (2005); Thorne (2001).

21. Smith (2009).

22. Tronto (1989, 172).

23. Doucet (2006).

24. Stack (1974).

25. Hansen (2005). Roschelle (1997) finds that upper-class married Anglo families are likely to share care with friends and not kin members. As Garey (1999) suggests, if social class reflects specific constellations of resources, then families with more resources may be able to reallocate them across wider kin and friend networks to secure care for children.

26. Oswald (2002); Weston (1991).

27. See http://www.nationalcompadresnetwork.com.

28. Bourdieau (1986); Furstenberg (2005); Portes (1998). In a recent revised conceptualization of paternal involvement, Pleck (2010b) distinguishes between family financial capital (which he terms "parental financial capital") and family social capital (in which he distinguishes parental socialization social capital and parental community social capital). Our focus will be on the relationships and resources that fathers share with family and close friends.

29. Specifically, Furstenberg (2005) asserts that researchers do not distinguish between the levels of social capital that are generated in kin networks, the mobilization of such capital, and the consequences (benefits and obligations) that may be related to the possession of such capital. This perspective reflects Marsiglio and Cohan's (2000) related call to examine social capital as both a product and a process.

30. Hogan, Eggebeen, and Clogg (1993).

31. Peter et al. (2005); Conger and Conger (2002).

32. Gregory, Long, and Volk (2004).

33. Daly (1995), Hofferth, Pleck, and Vesely (forthcoming); Roy (2006).

34. Roschelle (1997).

Chapter 6

1. In the stepfathers study, Marsiglio (2004a) did supplemental interviews with thirteen partners (mothers of the stepchildren) and two stepchildren, which we have not incorporated into our methods appendix description.

2. Christiansen and Palkovitz (2001).

3. Doucet (2006); Pleck (2010b). Pleck indicates that what he refers to as parental community social capital sometimes represents a form of "indirect care" (if the children are not actually present when the activity takes place).

4. LaRossa (2005); Marsiglio (2009a); Pew Forum on Religion and Public Life (2009).

5. Doucet (2006); Pleck (2010b); Walzer (1998).

6. Marsiglio (2008a). Fathers' connections to female youth workers are also vitally important, but these ties lack the added dimension of male youth workers who have personal experience as fathers.

7. Burgess (2009); Cooper (2000).

8. Pleck (2010b).

9. Doucet (2006).

10. Doucet (2006).

11. L. Fisher, "Are Our Kids Safe? Deaths of Two Girls Bring Sex Offender Issue to Forefront," *Gainesville Sun,* June 12, 2005, 1A; L. Skenazy, "Eeek! A Male! Treating All Men as Potential Predators Doesn't Make Our Kids Safer," *Wall Street Journal,* January 12, 2011; Marsiglio (2008a); Valentine (2004).

12. Doucet (2006); Marsiglio (2008a).

13. Marsiglio (2008a).

14. Marsiglio (2008a).

15. Of course, interacting with disruptive and emotionally demanding kids can also add unwanted stress to male youth workers' lives and seep into their family life in negative ways.

16. Aumann, Galinsky, and Matos (2011); Stephenson (2010); see also Coltrane (1996); Pleck and Pleck (1997); Thorpe and Daly (1999).

17. According to one review (Cabrera 2010), the limited data on the effects of family leave policies make it difficult to evaluate their effectiveness.

18. Reed (2005); Leavitt (2009).

19. Cabrera, Fagan, and Farrie (2008).

20. Raikes, Summers, and Roggman (2005).

21. Roggman et al. (2004).

22. Fagan and Iglesias (1999).

23. McAllister, Wilson, and Burton (2004).

24. Summers, Boller, and Raikes (2004).

25. See National Center for Education Statistics, "Fathers' Involvement in Their Children's Schools," report, September 1997, NCES 98-091, available at: http://nces.ed.gov/pubs98/fathers; accessed August 2, 2011.

26. The Black Star Project (http://blackstarproject.org/action/) was founded in 1996 as a small mentoring program in two public schools in Chicago. It has grown to become involved in parent development, student engagement, and educational advocacy by eliminating the racial academic achievement gap in African American and Latino communities. In 2004 it sponsored the first Million Father March, and in 2007 it coordinated the Men in Schools program.

27. Harrison (1997) showed that parent education improved inmates' attitudes toward appropriate parenting but did not significantly change their children's self-perceptions. Wilczak and Markstrom (1999) found that there was a higher locus of control (perception of having control over personal life events rather than being subjected to external forces, such as powerful others, fate, or God) and parental satisfaction after parent education.

28. See http://www.angeltree.org.

29. Girl Scouts, " 'Troop 1500' Documentary on Texas Girl Scout Council Premieres at South by Southwest Film Festival," press release, March 3, 2005, available at: http://www.girlscouts.org/news/news_releases/2005/troop_1500.asp; accessed August 2, 2011.

30. Chicago Press Release Services, "Leving's New Virtual Visitation Law Goes into Effect Jan. 1, 2010," press release, December 30, 2009, available at: http://chicagopressrelease.com/news/levings-new-virtual-visitation-law-goes-into-effect-jan-1-2010; accessed August 2, 2011.

31. Ann Haw Holt, "Reading Family Ties for Men: Program for Incarcerated Fathers," Florida Department of Corrections website, available at: http://www.fcnetwork.org/fatherhood/holt.html; accessed August 2, 2011.

32. See http://www.fcnetwork.org/storybook.pdf.

33. Swisher and Waller (2008) find that contact with children is more likely for formerly incarcerated black and Latino fathers and less likely for those white fathers. Similar racial and ethnic differences existed regarding mothers' trust of fathers to care for children.

34. The Center for Children of Incarcerated Parents was a program from 1989 to 1998 run by Denise Johnston at Pacific Oaks College. It sponsored a program called CHICAS, or child custody advocacy services, which assisted prisoners who were searching for their children (available at: http://www.prisontalk.com/forums/archive/index.php/t-100048.html; accessed September 12, 2011). See also National Resource Center on Children and Families of the Incarcerated at Family and Corrections Network, which disseminates information to families about incarcerated parents (http://fcnetwork.org/about-us; accessed September 12, 2011).

35. Welsh (2009).

Chapter 7

1. We extend and deepen the initial statement regarding the importance of policymakers focusing on transitional periods presented in Marsiglio (1995).

2. See Roy and Lucas (2006) for a discussion of the contextual challenges of redemptive fathering for nonresidential and often unmarried fathers.

3. Palkovitz and Palm (2009).

4. Hutchison (2010, 9); Palkovitz and Palm (2009); and Cowan (1991).

5. Cowan (1991, 5).

6. Palkovitz and Palm (2009).

7. We modified Palkovitz and Palm's (2009, 6) phrasing of their first theme, "Growth is reflected by a higher level of integration and differentiation."

8. Roy and Lucas (2006); see also Maruna (2001) and Maruna and Roy (2007).

9. Kimmel (2008).

10. Kimmel (2008); Pollack (1998).

11. Furlong and Cartmel (2007) indicate that training programs for young school leavers were common throughout the 1980s in Europe. The concern over this population led to the Luxembourg Summit on Employment in 1997, where a set of common principles was established to "guarantee education, training or employment" for youths. Responsibility for providing supports for young people has shifted recently. In the United Kingdom, for example, the term NEET (not in education, employment or training) has been used to refer to at-risk youths. The implication is that it is a young person's personal choice to not be engaged in work or school.

12. Institute for Women's Policy Research (2010a). In 1960, the average male annual earnings was $38,907; by 1970 this figure was $49,576 (adjusted for 2009 dollars). Men's annual earnings peaked in 1970 at $50,875 and since dropped to $46,202 in 2008.

13. C. Mulligan, "In a First, Women Surpass Men on U.S. Payrolls," *New York Times,* February 5, 2010, Business section.

14. Settersten, Furstenberg, and Rumbaut (2005).

15. Mouw (2005). In combination with Mouw's study, Marini's (1984) earlier research indicating that 37 to 40 percent of young adults in the 1960s followed this modal sequence of transitions documents the decreasing frequency of this traditional pattern.

16. Kimmel (2008).

17. Smeeding, Garfinkel, and Mincy (2011).

18. Heinrich and Holzer (2011).

19. U.S. Census Bureau (2009); American Council on Education (2010).

20. As of January 2008, 47 percent of the nation's African American undergraduates, 55 percent of Latino undergraduates, and 57 percent of Native American undergraduates are enrolled in community colleges (Miller and Gault 2011).

21. Capella University, "The Other 85 Percent," available at: http://www.theother85percent.com; accessed July 31, 2011.

22. According to an Institute for Women's Policy Research report (Miller and Gault 2011), of more than six million students in community college, 29 percent are parents and 14 percent are single parents (more than twice the proportion at four-year colleges); 75 percent of single parents are women. This research suggests that there are about twice as many parents in community colleges as there are in four-year institutions.

23. Kalwarski (2010).

24. Kalwarski (2010), National Center for Education Statistics, Condition of Education in 2004, indicator 19, and Project on Student Debt, "Student Debt and Class of 2008."

25. Miller and Gault (2011). More than half of all single-father parents enrolled in community college work as well.

26. L. Ratner, "Generation Recession," *The Nation,* November 23, 2009.

27. U.S. Department of Labor (2010).

28. U.S. Department of Labor (2010).

29. Edelman, Greenberg, and Holzer (2009); Heinrich and Holzer (2011).

30. Rhodes and DuBois (2008).

31. Edelman, Holzer, and Offner (2006); Heinrich and Holzer (2011).

32. In 2007, 744,200 fathers were incarcerated in federal and state prisons, an increase of 77 percent since 1991 (Glaze and Maruschak 2008). In 2007, 42 percent of fathers in state prisons and 49 percent of fathers in federal prisons were African American; 20 percent in state prisons and 28 percent in federal prisons were Latino fathers. These numbers were disproportionately related to the number of men of color in both prison systems (Glaze and Maruschak 2008). Mumola (2006) estimates that 7.4 million children have a father or mother who is currently in prison, in jail, or under correctional supervision.

33. Edelman, Holzer, and Offner (2006); Heinrich and Holzer (2011).

34. Roy (2005b).

35. Mincy, Klempin, and Schmidt (2011).

36. Edelman, Greenberg, and Holzer (2009).

37. Edelman, Holzer, and Offner (2006) identify four critical features of apprenticeship programs, including (1) workplaces and other community setting are exploited as learning environments, (2) work experience is

linked to academic training, (3) youths are simultaneously workers with real responsibilities and learners, and (4) close relationships are fostered between youths and adult mentors. See also Hamilton (1990) and Hamilton and Hamilton (2004).

38. For example, the Generations program at Children's Hospital in Washington, D.C., is an intervention designed to promote the mental health of young coparenting couples. As part of the program, young fathers and mothers are given access to health-care services as well as a support group for fathers.

39. Aumann, Galinsky, and Matos (2011).

40. Conley (2010); Harrington, Van Deusen, and Humberd (2011).

41. Goodman (2010).

42. Young (2006).

43. Mincy, Klempin, and Schmidt (2011).

44. Aron-Dine and Sherman (2007).

45. Edelman et al. (2009); Mincy, Klempin, and Schmidt (2011).

46. Edelman et al. (2009); Mincy, Klempin, and Schmidt (2011).

47. Mead (2007). A recent proposal of a new round of welfare reform for low-income men (Haskins and Sawhill 2007) argued that a two-tier approach to employment would be effective. First, it would provide incentives to work through an expansion of EITC benefits for low-income noncustodial fathers and young men. Second, these men would have to go back to prison after sixty days if they did not secure employment.

48. Wong and Gerras (2010).

49. See www.militaryonesource.com.

50. Details on timelines and implications of the Affordable Health Care Act of 2010 can be found at HealthCare.gov. The actual text of the act can be accessed at http://docs.house.gov/rules/health/111_ahcaa.pdf; accessed September 8, 2011.

51. U.S. Office of Personnel Management, "Family and Medical Leave," available at: http://www.opm.gov/oca/leave/HTML/fmlafac2.asp; accessed August 2, 2011.

52. Ray, Gornick, and Schmitt (2010). In the case of the United States, some states do offer some paid leave to eligible parents (California, Hawaii, New Jersey, New York, Rhode Island, and Washington).

53. Isacco and Garfield (2010). See also Holmes et al. (2010).

54. Cowan et al. (2009).

55. Caldwell et al. (2010).

56. For a sampling of studies that examine programs that include fathers of children with different special needs and health problems, see Beaton et al.

(forthcoming); Elder et al. (2005); McNeill (2007); Pelchat, Lefebvre, and Levert (2007). For a more practical guide to special needs programs for fathers see May (2002).

57. For reviews of parent education programs for children with special needs or severe disruptive behaviors see de Graaf et al. (2008); Maughan et al. (2005); Singer, Ethridge, and Aldana (2007).

58. McBride and McBride (1993); see also Caldwell et al. (2010).

59. Edleson (1999).

60. Edleson and Williams (2007a).

61. Peled and Perel (2007, 90).

62. Atchison et al. (2002); Tubbs and Williams (2007).

63. Edelson and Williams (2007b, 5).

64. Jaffe and Crooks (2007, 60).

65. Jaffe and Crooks (2007, 60).

66. Groves, van Horn, and Lieberman (2007).

67. Program information at http://www.caringdadsprogram.com.

68. Scott and Crooks (2007, 225).

69. The main accountability guidelines focus on children's and their mothers' safety and well-being as well as the needs of fathers and community stakeholders (Scott et al. 2007).

70. Knox et al. (2011).

71. Marsiglio (2004a).

72. Roy (2005b).

Chapter 8

1. Dowd (2000); Marsiglio and Roy (forthcoming).

2. Marsiglio (2008a); Daly and Ball (forthcoming); Doucet (forthcoming).

3. Griswold (1993); Marsiglio and Pleck (2005).

4. Aumann, Galinsky, and Matos (2011).

5. Cabrera (2010); Curran and Abrams (2000).

6. Martin et al. (2010).

7. Haas and Hwang (2008).

8. Romano and Dokoupil (2010).

9. We concur with Dowd's (2000) assessment: "The policies that flow from fatherhood redefined as nurture must begin with economic support. . . . Education efforts focused on challenging the dominant masculinity and

offering another model, as well as teaching the skills of nurture, are critical companions to economic support" (231).

10. Cabrera (2010, 530).

11. Dowd (2000, 228).

12. Morgan et al. (2008).

13. For examples, see Jeremy Adam Smith's "Daddy Dialectic" blog (http://daddy-dialectic.blogspot.com) and Stevie Ray Dallimore's "Rad Dads" blog (http://www.raddadsusa.com).

14. Marsiglio and Cohan (1997); Marsiglio and Hutchinson (2002).

15. Rich (2009).

16. Marsiglio (1995).

17. See http://www.fatherhood.org.

18. Pleck (2010a).

19. See http://www.changingfatherhood.com/amnesty.shtml.

20. See http://www.daddyshome.org/history.php; http://www.AtHome Dad.org; and http://www.diyfather.com.

21. Romano and Dokoupil (2010).

22. Cabrera et al. (2010); Tamis-LeMonda et al. (2004).

23. McBride, Rane, and Bae (2001); Oritz and Stile (2002). The NFI and the National Center on Fathering provide some training relevant to fathers.

24. Avellar et al. (2011); Holmes et al. (2010); Knox et al. (2011); McBride and Lutz (2004).

25. Curran and Abrams (2000).

26. See also Cabrera (2010); Cowan, Cowan, and Knox (2010).

27. Federal Interagency Forum on Child and Family Statistics (1996).

28. Center for Law and Social Policy (2010).

29. See information on the Fatherhood, Marriage, and Families Innovation Fund through the Department of Health and Human Services, ACF (http://www.acf.hhs.gov/programs/cse/pubs; accessed August 2, 2011). The fund will follow up the Bush-era Healthy Marriage and Responsible Fatherhood program, which was funded for its final year in 2010. See http://www.cffpp.org/publications/Innov_fund.pdf; accessed September 12, 2011.

30. Ronald C. Warren (2011). A Message from the President. National Fatherhood Initiative. See http://www.fatherhood.org/Page.aspx?pid=895; accessed August 18, 2011.

31. Dowd (2000, 228).

32. Cabrera (2010).

33. Other nonprofit organizations operate as state-level actors in fatherhood initiatives as well. Many of these groups can serve as catalysts for federal, state, and local groups. However, it can be difficult to ascertain the goals of some nonprofits. The broad promotion of "responsible fatherhood" seems appropriate and productive, but these groups may not embrace a vision of fathering that places nurturance at the center of fathering. For example, some national, state, and local groups seem more concerned with raising the status of men in families, promoting social gatherings (such as golf tournaments for dads), or networking for professional men who are parents.

34. National Responsible Fatherhood Clearinghouse, "Connect with Programs," Available at: http://www.fatherhood.gov/policy-research/policy/programs-and-initiatives/(accessed November 11, 2011).

35. Roy (1999); Parra-Cardona, Wampler, and Sharp (2006); Turetsky (2000).

36. Given the widespread interest in fathering, it is not surprising that individuals and groups representing diverse interests and communication strategies shape the culture of fatherhood. In the spirit of creative collaborations, stakeholders could benefit by incorporating the ideas of individuals such as Armin Brott (http://www.arminbrott.com) and Joe Kelly (http://www.thedadman.com), who make it their business to reach out to the general public. They deal with a wide range of fathering issues through their books, webpages, and speaking engagements. Similarly, much can be gained by recruiting high-profile celebrities and athletes as spokesmen for fatherhood.

37. LaRossa (1988).

38. This campaign has successfully worked with national broadcast networks (ABC, CBS, CW, FOX, NBC) to advance its mission of educating the public about teen pregnancy issues. For a description of how the National Campaign to Prevent Teen and Unplanned Pregnancy has collaborated with Hollywood producers and has had a presence on various television shows, see http://www.thenationalcampaign.org/media/entertainment-media.aspx (accessed November 14, 2011).

39. Doucet and Hawkins (forthcoming) provide a candid and thought-provoking account of how their feminist ideals have complicated their involvement with Canada's FIRA. They illustrate how tensions within the coalition were heightened when scholars and community advocates considered what their constituencies stood to gain or lose if a particular methodology, policy proposal, or research finding was emphasized. As dissenters, they reveal the types of struggles individuals can face navigating an alliance that includes social groups with similar as well as competing identities and political commitments. Although they favored

efforts to promote active fathering, they challenged groups that did not adequately account for how men as a group benefit from the "patriarchal dividend" or that advanced the idea that fathers are "essential" for families in an absolute sense.

40. Marsiglio (2008a).

41. See http://maddads.com. This organization's mission is to "seek out, encourage, motivate, and guide committed men in the struggle to save children, communities, and ourselves from the social ills that presently plague neighborhoods."

Appendix

1. Van den Hoonard (1997).

References

Allen, Sarah M., and Alan J. Hawkins. 1999. "Maternal Gatekeeping: Mothers' Beliefs and Behaviors That Inhibit Greater Father Involvement in Family Work." *Journal of Marriage and Family* 61(1): 199–212.

Amato, Paul. 1994. "Father-Child Relations, Mother-Child Relations, and Offspring Psychological Well-Being in Early Adulthood." *Journal of Marriage and Family* 56(4): 1031–42.

American Council on Education. 2010. *Gender Equity in Higher Education.* Washington, D.C.: American Council on Education.

Annie E. Casey Foundation. 2010. "Data Across States." Kids Count Data (website). Available at: http://datacenter.kidscount.org/data/acrossstates/Rankings .aspx?ind=130; accessed August 2, 2011.

Arditti, Joyce A., Jennifer Lambert-Shute, and Karen Joest. 2003. "Saturday Morning at the Jail: Implications of Incarceration for Families and Children." *Family Relations* 52(3): 195–204.

Aron-Dine, Aviva, and Arloc Sherman. 2007. "Ways and Means Committee Chairman Charles Rangel's Proposed Expansion of the EITC for Childless Workers: An Important Step to Make Work Pay." Washington, D.C.: Center on Budget and Policy Priorities.

Atchison, Gabriel, Angela Autry, Lonna Davis, and Kelly Mitchell-Clark. 2002. *Conversations with Women of Color Who Have Experienced Domestic Violence Regarding Working with Men to End Violence.* San Francisco: Family Violence Prevention Fund.

Aumann, Kerstin, Ellen Galinsky, and Kenneth Matos. 2011. *The New Male Mystique.* New York: Families and Work Institute.

Avellar, Sharah M., Robin Dion, Andrew Clarkwest, Heather Zaveri, Subuhi Asheer, Kelley Borradaile, Megan Hague Angus, Timothy Novak, Julie Redline, and Marykate Zukiewicz. 2011. *Catalog of Research: Programs for Low-Income Fathers,* OPRE Reports #2011-20. Washington, D.C.: Office of Planning, Research, and Evaluation, Administration for Children and Families, U.S. Department of Health and Human Services.

Beaton, John, David Nicholas, Ted McNeill, and Lisa Wenger. Forthcoming. "The Experiences of Fathers of a Child with a Chronic Health Condition: Caregiving Experiences and Potential Support Interventions." In *Father Involvement in Canada: Contested Terrain,* edited by J. Ball and K. Daly. Vancouver: University of British Columbia Press.

Belsky, Jay. 1984. "The Determinants of Parenting: A Process Model." *Child Development* 55(1): 83–96.

Berkowtiz, Dana. 2007. "A Sociohistorical Analysis of Gay Men's Procreative Consciousness." *Journal of GLBT Family Studies* 3(2–3): 157–90.

Berkowitz, Dana, and William Marsiglio. 2007. "Gay Men Negotiating Procreative, Father, and Family Identities." *Journal of Marriage and Family* 69(2): 366–81.

Biblarz, Timothy, and Judith Stacey. 2010. "How Does the Gender of Parents Matter?" *Journal of Marriage and Family* 72(1): 3–22.

Binstock, Georgina, and Arland Thornton. 2003. "Separations, Reconciliations, and Living Apart in Cohabiting and Marital Unions." *Journal of Marriage and Family* 65(2): 432–43.

Bird, Chloe E., and Patricia P. Rieker. 2008. *Gender and Health: The Effects of Constrained Choice and Social Policies.* Cambridge: Cambridge University Press.

Bishai, David, Nan M. Astone, Laura M. Argys, Chris Filidoro, and Robert Gutendorf. 2006. "A National Sample of U.S. Paternity Tests: Do Demographics Predict Test Outcomes?" *Transfusion* 46(5): 849–53.

Bishop, Greg. 2006. *Hit the Ground Crawling: Lessons from 150,000 New Fathers. Crash Course for New Dads: Tools, Checklists and Cheat Sheets.* Irvine, Calif.: Dads Adventure.

Blankenhorn, David. 1995. *Fatherless America: Confronting Our Most Urgent Social Problem.* New York: Basic.

Boggess, Jacqueline. 2011. "Child Support: Ability to Pay and Incarceration. In the Interest of Parents Research Brief." Madison, Wis.: Center for Family Policy and Practice.

Booth, Alan, and Ann C. Crouter. 1998. *Men in Families: When Do They Get Involved? What Differences Does It Make?* Mahwah, N.J.: Lawrence Erlbaum.

Bourdieau, Pierre. 1986. "The Forms of Capital." In *Handbook of Theory and Research for the Sociology of Education,* edited by J. C. Richardson. New York: Greenwood.

Bozett, Fredrick W. 1989. "Gay Fathers: A Review of the Literature." In *Homosexuality and the Family,* edited by F. W. Bozett. New York: Harrington Park.

Braver, Sanford L., and Diane O'Connell. 1998. *Divorced Dads: Shattering the Myths. The Surprising Truth About Fathers, Children, and Divorce.* New York, N.Y.: Jeremy Tarcher/Putnam.

Bronte-Tinkew, Jacinta, Allison Horowitz, and Allison Metz. 2007. "What Works in Fatherhood Programs? Ten Lessons from Evidence-Based Practice." National Responsible Fatherhood Clearinghouse Practice Brief. Washington: U.S. Department of Health and Human Services.

Bronte-Tinkew, Jacinta, Mindy Scott, and Allison Horowitz. 2009. "Male Pregnancy Intendedness and Children's Mental Proficiency and Attachment Security During Toddlerhood." *Journal of Marriage and Family* 71(4): 1001–25.

Brown, Geoffrey L., Brent A. McBride, Nana Shin, and Kelly K. Bost. 2007. "Parenting Predictors of Father-Child Attachment Security: Interactive Effects of Father Involvement and Fathering Quality." *Fathering* 5(3): 197–219.

Bumpass, Larry L., and Hsien-Hen Lu. 2000. "Trends in Cohabitation and Implications for Children's Family Contexts in the United States." *Population Studies* 54(1): 29–41.

Burgess, Adrienne. 2007. "The Costs and Benefits of Active Fatherhood: Evidence and Insights to Inform the Development of Policy and Practice." Paper prepared by Fathers Direct to inform the Department for Human Services–HM Treasury Joint Policy Review on Children and Young People. London: DfHS.

————. 2009. *Fathers and Parenting Interventions: What Works? Preliminary Research Findings and Their Application.* London: Fatherhood Institute.

Burton, Linda. 2007. "Childhood Adultification in Economically Disadvantaged Families: A Conceptual Model." *Family Relations* 56(4): 329–45.

Burton, Linda, Andrew Cherlin, Donna-Marie Winn, Angela Estación, and Clara Holder-Taylor. 2009. "The Role of Trust in Low-Income Mothers' Intimate Unions." *Journal of Marriage and Family* 71(5): 1107–24.

Bzostek, Sharon H. 2008. "Social Fathers and Child's Well-Being." *Journal of Marriage and Family* 70(4): 950–61.

Cabrera, Natasha J. 2010. "Father Involvement and Public Policies." In *The Role of Father Involvement in Child Development,* edited by Michael E. Lamb. Hoboken, N.J.: Wiley.

Cabrera, Natasha, Tonia Cristofaro, Brianne Kondelis, Catherine S. Tamis-LeMonda, and Lisa Baumwell. 2010. "Low-Income Fathers' Linguistic Influence on Their Children's Language Development." Paper presented at Head Start's Tenth National Research Conference, Washington, D.C. (June).

Cabrera, Natasha J., Jay Fagan, and Danielle Farrie. 2008. "Explaining the Long Reach of Fathers' Prenatal Involvement on Later Paternal Engagement with Children." *Journal of Marriage and Family* 70(5): 1094–107.

Caldwell, Cleopatra H., Jane Rafferty, Thomas M. Reischl, E. Hill De Loney, and Cassandra L. Brooks. 2010. "Enhancing Parenting Skills Among Nonresident African American Fathers as a Strategy for Preventing Youth Risk Behaviors." *American Journal of Community Psychology* 45(1–2): 17–35.

Caldwell, Cleopatra H., Joan C. Wright, Marc A. Zimmerman, Katrina M. Walsemann, Deborah Williams, and Patrick A. C. Isichei. 2004. "Enhancing Adolescent Health Behaviors Through Strengthening Non-Resident Father-Son Relationships: A Model for Intervention with African American Families." *Health Education Research: Theory and Practice* 19(6): 644–56.

Carlson, Marcia J., and Frank F. Furstenberg, Jr. 2006. "The Prevalence and Correlates of Multipartnered Fertility Among Urban U.S. Parents." *Journal of Marriage and Family* 68(3): 718–32.

Carlson, Marcia, and Sara McLanahan. 2004. "Early Father Involvement in Fragile Families." In *Conceptualizing and Measuring Father Involvement,* edited by R. Day and M. Lamb. Mahwah, N.J.: Lawrence Erlbaum.

————. 2006. "Strengthening Unmarried Families: Could Enhancing Couple Relationships Also Improve Parenting?" *Social Service Review* 80(2): 297–321.

Catlett, Beth S., and Patrick C. McKenry. 2004. "Class-Based Masculinities: Divorce, Fatherhood, and the Hegemonic Ideal." *Fathering* 2(2): 165–90.

Catlett, Beth S., Michelle L. Toews, and Patrick C. McKenry. 2005. "Nonresidential Fathers: Shifting Identities, Roles, and Authorities." In *Situated Fathering: A Focus on Physical and Social Spaces,* edited by William Marsiglio, Kevin Roy, and Greer L. Fox. Lanham, Md.: Rowman & Littlefield.

Center for Law and Social Policy. 2010. "President Obama's FY2011 Budget Proposals Invests in Low-Income Families." Washington, D.C. Available at: http://www.clasp.org/page?id=0025; accessed October 6, 2010.

Centers for Disease Control and Prevention. 2009. "Abortion Surveillance—United States, 2006." Surveillance Summaries, Morbidity and Mortality Weekly Report 58, No. SS-8. Atlanta: CDC.

Cherlin, Andrew. 2009. *The Marriage-Go-Round: The State of Marriage and the Family Today.* New York: Knopf.

Chesley, Noelle. 2011. "Stay-at-Home Fathers and Breadwinning Mothers: Gender, Couple Dynamics, and Social Change." *Gender & Society* 25(5): 642–64.

Christiansen, Shawn L., and Rob Palkovitz. 2001. "Why the 'Good Provider' Role Still Matters." *Journal of Family Issues* 22(1): 84–106.

Coles, Roberta I. 2009. *The Best Kept Secret: Single Black Fathers.* Lanham, Md.: Rowman & Littlefield.

Coley, Rebekah L., and Jodi E. Morris. 2002. "Comparing Father and Mother Reports of Father Involvement Among Low-Income Minority Families." *Journal of Marriage and Family* 64(4): 982–97.

Collier, R., and S. Sheldon. 2008. *Fragmenting Fatherhood: A Socio-Legal Study.* Oxford: Hart.

Coltrane, Scott. 1988. "Father-Child Relationships and the Status of Women: A Cross-Cultural Study." *American Journal of Sociology* 93(5): 1060–95.

———. 1996. *Family Man: Fatherhood, Housework, and Gender Equity.* New York: Oxford University Press.

———. 2001. "Marketing the Marriage "Solution:" Misplaced Simplicity in the Politics of Fatherhood." *Sociological Perspectives* 44(4): 387–402.

Committee for Integrating the Science of Early Child Development. 2000. *From Neurons to Neighborhoods: The Science of Early Child Development.* Washington: U.S. Department of Health and Human Services.

Conger, Rand, and Katherine Conger. 2002. "Resilience in Midwestern Families: Selected Findings from the First Decade of a Prospective Longitudinal Study." *Journal of Marriage and Family* 62(2): 361–74.

Conley, Dalton. 2010. *Elsewhere, U.S.A.: How We Got from the Company Man, Family Dinners, and the Affluent Society to the Home Office, BlackBerry Moms, and Economic Anxiety.* New York: Vintage.

Connell, R. W. 1995. *Masculinities.* Berkeley: University of California Press.

Connell, R. W., and James W. Messerschmidt. 2005. "Hegemonic Masculinity: Rethinking the Concept." *Gender and Society* 19(6): 829–59.

Cooley, Charles H. 1909. *Social Organization: A Study of the Larger Mind.* New York: Charles Scribner's Sons.

Cooper, Marianne. 2000. "Being the "Go-to-Guy": Fatherhood, Masculinity, and the Organization of Work in Silicon Valley." *Qualitative Sociology* 23(4): 379–405.

Courtenay, Will H. 2000. "Constructions of Masculinity and Their Influence on Men's Well-Being: A Theory of Gender and Health." *Social Sciences and Medicine* 50(10): 1385–401.

Cowan, Philip A. 1991. "Individual and Family Life Transitions: A Proposal for a New Definition." In *Family Transitions,* edited by Philip A. Cowan and E. Mavis Hetherington. Hillsdale, N.J.: Lawrence Erlbaum.

Cowan, Philip A., Carolyn Pape Cowan, and Virginia Knox. 2010. "Marriage and Fatherhood Programs." *The Future of Children* 20(2): 205–30.

Cowan, Philip A., Carolyn Pape Cowan, Marsha K. Pruett, Kyle Pruett, and Jessie J. Wong. 2009. "Promoting Fathers' Engagement with Children: Preventive Interventions for Low-Income Families." *Journal of Marriage and Family* 71(3): 663–79.

Crosbie-Burnett, Margaret, and Edith A. Lewis. 1999. "Use of African American Family Structures and Functioning to Address the Challenges of European American Postdivorce Families." In *American Families: A Multicultural Reader,* edited by Stephanie Coontz. New York: Routledge.

Crowley, Jocelyn E. 2008. *Defiant Dads: Fathers Rights Activists in America.* Ithaca, N.Y.: Cornell University Press.

Cummings, E. Mark, Christine E. Merrilees, and Melissa Ward George. 2010. "Fathers, Marriages, and Families: Revisiting and Updating the Framework for Fathering in Family Context." In *The Role of the Father in Child Development,* 5th ed., edited by Michael E. Lamb. Hoboken, N.J.: Wiley.

Curran, Laura, and Laura Abrams. 2000. "Making Men into Dads: Fatherhood, the State, and Welfare Reform." *Gender and Society* 14(5): 662–78.

Daly, Kerry. 1995. "Reshaping Fatherhood: Finding the Models." In *Fatherhood: Contemporary Theory, Research, and Social Policy,* edited by William Marsiglio. Thousand Oaks, Calif.: Sage.

Daly, Kerry, and Jessica Ball. Forthcoming. "Looking Forward: Father Involvement and Changing Forms of Masculine Care." In *Father Involvement in Canada: Contested Terrain,* edited by Jessica Ball and Kerry Daly. Vancouver: University of British Columbia Press.

Daniels, Cynthia R. 1998. *Lost Fathers: The Politics of Fatherlessness in America.* New York: St. Martin's Press.

———. 2006. *The Science and Politics of Male Reproduction.* Oxford, U.K.: Oxford University Press.

DeGarmo, David S., and Marion S. Forgatch. 2007. "Efficacy of Parent Training for Stepfathers: From Playful Spectator and Polite Stranger to Effective Stepfathering." *Parenting: Science and Practice* 7(4): 331–35.

de Graaf, Ireen, Paula Speetjens, Filip Smit, Marianne de Wolff, and Louis Tavecchi. 2008. "Effectiveness of the Triple P Positive Parenting Program on Parenting: A Meta-Analysis." *Family Relations* 57(5): 553–66.

Dermott, Esther. 2008. *Intimate Fatherhood: A Sociological Analysis.* London: Routledge.

de St. Aubin, Ed, Dan P. McAdams, and Tae-Chang Kim. 2004. *The Generative Society: Caring for Future Generations.* Washington, D.C.: American Psychological Association.

Diamond, Michael J. 2007. *My Father Before Me: How Fathers and Sons Influence Each Other Throughout Their Lives.* New York: Norton.

Dienhart, Anne. 1998. *Reshaping Fatherhood: The Social Construction of Shared Parenting.* Thousand Oaks, Calif.: Sage.

Dion, M. Robin, Alan M. Hershey, Heather M. Zaveri, Sarah A. Avellar, Debra A. Strong, Timothy Silman, and Ravaris Moore. 2008. "Implementation of the Building Strong Families Program." Prepared by Mathematica Policy Research for the U.S. Department of Health and Human Services, Department of Children and Families. Available at: http://www.mathematica-mpr.com/publications/pdfs/bsfimplementation.pdf; accessed July 19, 2011.

Dion, Robin. 2005. "Healthy Marriage Programs: Learning What Works." *Future of Children* 15(2): 139–56.

Doherty, William J., Edward F. Kouneski, and Martha F. Erickson. 1998. "Responsible Fathering: An Overview and Conceptual Framework." *Journal of Marriage and Family* 60(2): 277–92.

———. 2000. "We Are All Responsible for Responsible Fathering: A Response to Walker and McGraw." *Journal of Marriage and Family* 62(2): 570–74.

Dominguez, Silvia, and Celeste Watkins. 2003. "Creating Networks for Survival and Mobility: Social Capital Among African Americans and Latin American Low-Income Mothers." *Social Problems* 50(1): 111–35.

Doucet, Andrea. 2006. *Do Men Mother? Fathering, Care, and Domestic Responsibility.* Toronto: University of Toronto Press.

———. 2009. "Dad and the Baby in the First Year: Gendered Responsibilities and Embodiment." *American Academy of Political and Social Sciences* 624(1): 78–98.

———. Forthcoming. "Fathering and Gender Roles." In *Handbook of Father Involvement: Multidisciplinary Perspectives* (2d. ed.), edited by Natasha Cabrera and Catherine Tamis-LaMonda. New York: Routledge.

Doucet, Andrea, and L. Hawkins. Forthcoming. "Feminist Mothers Researching Fathering: Advocates, Contributors, and Dissenters." In *Father Involvement in Canada: Contested Terrain,* edited by Jessica Ball and Kerry Daly. Vancouver: University of British Columbia Press.

Dowd, Nancy. 2000. *Redefining Fatherhood.* New York: New York University Press.

Draper, Jan. 2002. "'It Was a Real Good Show': The Ultrasound Scan, Fathers and the Power of Visual Knowledge." *Sociology of Health and Illness* 24(6): 771–95.

Edelman, Peter, Mark Greenberg, Steve Holt, and Harry Holzer. 2009. "Expanding the EITC to Help More Low-Wage Workers." Policy brief. Washington, D.C.: Georgetown University, Georgetown Center on Poverty, Inequality and Public Policy.

Edelman, Peter, Mark Greenberg, and Harry Holzer. 2009. "The Administration and Congress Should Adopt a Comprehensive Approach to Youth Education, Employment and Connection." Policy brief. Washington, D.C.: Georgetown University, Georgetown Center on Poverty, Inequality and Public Policy.

Edelman, Peter, Harry Holzer, and Paul Offner. 2006. *Reconnecting Disadvantaged Young Men.* Washington, D.C.: Urban Institute Press.

Edin, Kathryn, Paula England, Emily Shafer, and Joanna Reed. 2007. "Forming Fragile Families: Was the Baby Planned, Unplanned, or in Between?" In *Unmarried Couples with Children,* edited by Paula England and Kathryn Edin. New York: Russell Sage Foundation.

Edin, Kathryn, and Laura Lein. 1997. *Making Ends Meet: How Single Mothers Survive Welfare and Low-Wage Work.* New York: Russell Sage Foundation.

Edin, Kathryn, and Timothy Nelson. 2001. "Working Steady: Race, Low-Wage Work, and Family Involvement Among Noncustodial Fathers in Philadelphia."

In *Problem of the Century: Racial Stratification in the United States,* edited by Elijah Anderson and Douglas S. Massey. New York: Russell Sage Foundation.

Edleson, Jeffrey. 1999. "The Overlap Between Child Maltreatment and Women Battering." *Violence Against Women* 5(2): 134–54.

Edleson, Jeffrey L., and Oliver J. Williams. 2007a. *Parenting by Men Who Batter: New Directions for Assessment and Intervention.* Oxford: Oxford University Press.

———. 2007b. "Introduction: Involving Men Who Batter in Their Children's Lives." In *Parenting by Men Who Batter: New Directions for Assessment and Intervention,* edited by Jeffrey Edleson and Oliver Williams. Oxford: Oxford University Press.

Elder, Glen H., Jr. 1995. "The Life Course Paradigm: Social Change and Individual Development." In *Examining Lives in Context,* edited by Phyllis Moen, Glen H. Elder, Jr., and Kurt Luscher. Washington, D.C.: American Psychological Association.

Elder, Glen H., Jr., and Angela O'Rand. 1995. "Adult Lives in a Changing Society." In *Sociological Perspectives on Social Psychology,* edited by Karen Cook, Gary Fine, and James House. Needham Heights, Mass.: Allyn & Bacon.

Elder, Jennifer, Gregory Valcante, Hossein Yarandi, Deborah White, and Timothy H. Elder. 2005. "Evaluating In-Home Training for Fathers of Children with Autism Using Single-Subject Experimentation and Group Analysis Methods." *Nursing Research* 54(1): 22–32.

Erikson, Eric. H. 1963. *Childhood and Society.* 2d ed. New York: Norton.

———. 1964. *Insight and Responsibility.* New York: Norton.

———. 1975. *Life History and the Historical Moment.* New York. Norton.

Fagan, Jay, and Aquiles Iglesias. 1999. "Father Involvement Program Effects on Fathers, Father Figures, and Their Head Start Children: A Quasi Experimental Study." *Early Childhood Research Quarterly* 14(2): 243–69.

Fagan, Jay, and Rob Palkovitz. 2011. "Coparenting and Relationship Quality Effects on Father Involvement: Variations by Residence, Romance." *Journal of Marriage and Family* 73(3): 637–53.

Fagan, Jay, Rob Palkovitz, Kevin Roy, and Danielle Farrie. 2009. "Pathways to Paternal Engagement: Longitudinal Effects of Risk and Resilience on Non-resident Fathers." *Developmental Psychology* 45(5): 1389–405.

Fagan, Jay, and Glen Palm. 2004. *Fathers and Early Childhood Programs.* New York: Thomson Delmar Learning.

Fagan, Jay, and Yookyong Lee. 2011. "Do Coparenting and Social Support Have a Greater Effect on Adolescent Fathers Than Adult Fathers?" *Family Relations* 60(3): 247–58.

Faludi, Susan. 1999. *Stiffed: The Betrayal of the American Man.* New York: HarperPerennial.

Farrel, M., A. Glosser, and K. Gardiner. 2003. "Child Support and TANF Interaction: Literature Review." Report prepared by the Lewin Group for the U.S. Department of Health and Human Services. Washington, D.C.: Manpower Demonstration Research Corporation.

Featherstone, Brid. 2009. *Contemporary Fathering: Theory, Policy and Practice.* Bristol, U.K.: Policy Press.

Featherstone, Brid, and Sue Peckover. 2007. "Letting Them Get Away with It: Fathers, Domestic Violence and Child Protection." *Critical Social Policy* 27(2): 181–203.

Federal Interagency Forum on Child and Family Statistics. 1996. *Nurturing Fatherhood: Improving Data and Research on Male Fertility, Family Formation and Fatherhood.* Washington: Federal Interagency Forum on Child and Family Statistics.

Fein, David, Nancy R. Burstein, Greta G. Fein, and Laura D. Lindberg. 2003. "The Determinants of Marriage and Cohabitation Among Disadvantaged Americans: Research Findings and Needs." Final report, Marriage and Family Formation Data Analysis Project. Cambridge, Mass.: Abt Associates.

Feinberg, Mark E. 2002. "Coparenting and the Transition to Parenthood: A Framework for Prevention." *Clinical Child and Family Psychology Review* 5(3): 173–95.

———. 2003. "The Internal Structure and Ecological Context of Coparenting: A Framework for Research and Intervention." *Parenting: Science and Practice* 3(2): 95–131.

Fine, Mark A. 1994. "Social Policy Pertaining to Stepfamilies: Should Stepparents and Stepchildren Have the Option of Establishing a Legal Relationship?" In *Stepfamilies: Who Benefits, Who Does Not?*, edited by Alan Booth and J. Dunn. Hillsdale, N.J.: Erlbaum.

Finer, Lawrence B., and Stanley K. Henshaw. 2006. "Disparities in Rates of Unintended Pregnancy in the United States, 1994 and 2001." *Perspectives on Sexual and Reproductive Health* 38(2): 90–96.

Friedan, Betty. 1963. *The Feminine Mystique.* New York: Norton.

Furlong, Andy, and Fred Cartmel. 2007. *Young People and Social Change: New Perspectives,* 2d ed. Buckingham, U.K.: Open University Press.

Furstenberg, Frank F., Jr. 1988. "Good Dads—Bad Dads: Two Faces of Fatherhood." In *The Changing American Family and Public Policy,* edited by Andrew Cherlin. Washington, D.C.: Urban Institute.

———. 2005. "Banking on Families: How Families Generate and Distribute Social Capital." *Journal of Marriage and Family* 67(4): 809–82.

Furstenberg, Frank F. Jr., and Andrew J. Cherlin. 1991. *Divided Families: What Happens to Children When Parents Part.* Cambridge, Mass.: Harvard University Press.

Ganong, Larry H., Marilyn Coleman, Mark Fine, and Patricia Martin. 1999. "Stepparents' Affinity-Seeking and Affinity-Maintaining Strategies with Stepchildren." *Journal of Family Issues* 20(3): 299–327.

Garey, Anita. 1999. *Weaving Work and Motherhood.* Philadelphia: Temple University Press.

Garfield, Craig, Elizabeth Clark-Kauffman, and Matthew M. Davis. 2006. "Fatherhood as a Component of Men's Health." *Journal of the American Medical Association* 296(19): 2365–68.

Gavanas, Anne. 2002. "The Fatherhood Responsibility Movement: The Centrality of Marriage, Work and Male Sexuality in Reconstructions of Masculinity and Fatherhood." In *Making Men into Fathers,* edited by Barbara Hobson. Cambridge: Cambridge University Press.

Gerson, Kathleen. 1993. *No Man's Land: Men's Changing Commitments to Family and Work.* New York: Basic Books.

———. 1995. "An Institutional Perspective on Generative Fathering: Creating Social Supports for Parenting Equality." In *Generative Fathering: Beyond Deficit Perspectives,* edited by Alan J. Hawkins and David C. Dollahite. Thousand Oaks, Calif.: Sage.

Gettler, Lee T., Thomas W. McDade, Alan B. Feranil, and Christopher W. Kuzawa. 2011. "Longitudinal Evidence That Fatherhood Decreases Testosterone in Human Males." *Proceedings of the National Academy of Sciences* (early edition): 1–6.

Gibson-Davis, Christina. 2009. "Expectations and the Economic Bar to Marriage for Low-Income Couples." In *Unmarried Couples with Children,* edited by Paula England and Kathryn Edin. New York: Russell Sage Foundation.

Giddens, Anthony. 1992. *The Transformation of Intimacy.* Cambridge: Polity Press.

Gilmore, David. 1990. *Manhood in the Making: Cultural Concepts of Masculinity.* New Haven, Conn.: Yale University Press.

Glaze, Lauren E., and Laura M. Maruschak. 2008. "Parents in Prison and Their Minor Children." Bureau of Justice Statistics special report NCJ 222984. Washington: U.S. Department of Justice, Office of Justice Programs.

Goodman, Peter S. 2010. "After Training, Still Scrambling for Employment." *New York Times,* July 18, 2010, A1. Available at: http://www.nytimes.com/2010/07/19/business/19training.html; accessed September 14, 2011.

Gray, Peter B. 2011. "The Descent of a Man's Testosterone." *Proceedings of the National Academy of Sciences* (early edition): 1–2.

Gray, Peter B., and Kermyt G. Anderson. 2010. *Fatherhood: Evolution and Human Paternal Behavior.* Cambridge, Mass.: Harvard University Press.

Gregory, Eve, Susi Long, and Dinah Volk. 2004. *Many Pathways to Literacy: Young Children Learning with Siblings, Grandparents, Peers, and Communities.* New York: Routledge.

Griswold, Robert. 1993. *Fatherhood in America: A History.* New York: Basic Books.

Groves, Betsy M., Patricia van Horn, and Alicia F. Lieberman. 2007. "Deciding on Fathers' Involvement in Their Children's Treatment After Domestic Violence." In *Parenting by Men Who Batter: New Directions for Assessment and Intervention,* edited by Jeffrey L. Edleson and Oliver J. Williams. Oxford: Oxford University Press.

Guzzo, Karen, and Frank F. Furstenberg. 2007. "Multipartnered Fertility Among American Men." *Demography* 44(3): 583–601.

Haas, Linda, and C. Philip Hwang. 2007. "Gender and Organizational Culture: Correlates of Company Responsiveness to Fathers in Sweden." *Gender and Society* 21(1): 52–79.

———. 2008. "The Impact of Taking Parental Leave on Fathers' Participation in Childcare and Relationships with Children: Lessons from Sweden." *Community, Work and Family* 11(1): 85–104.

———. 2009. "Is Fatherhood Becoming More Visible at Work? Trends in Corporate Support for Fathers Taking Parental Leave in Sweden." *Fathering* 7(3): 303–21.

Habib, Cherine, and Sandra Lancaster. 2006. "The Transition to Fatherhood: Identity and Bonding in Early Pregnancy." *Fathering* 4(3): 235–53.

Hamer, Jennifer. 2001. *What It Means to Be Daddy: Fatherhood for Black Men Living away from Their Children.* New York: Columbia University Press.

———. 2005. " 'Gotta Protect My Own': Men Parenting Children in an Abandoned City." In *Situated Fathering: A Focus on Physical and Social Spaces,* edited by William Marsiglio, Kevin Roy, and Greer L. Fox. Latham, Md.: Rowman & Littlefield.

Hamilton, Stephen F. 1990. *Apprenticeship for Adulthood: Preparing Youth for the Future.* New York: Free Press.

Hamilton, Stephen F., and Mary Agnes Hamilton. 2004. *The Handbook of Youth Development: Coming of Age in American Communities.* Thousand Oaks, Calif.: Sage.

Hansen, Karen. 2005. *Not-So-Nuclear Families: Class, Gender, and Networks of Care.* New Brunswick, N.J.: Rutgers University Press.

Harrington, Brad, Fred Van Deusen, and Beth Humberd. 2011. *The New Dad: Caring, Committed, and Conflicted.* Boston: Boston College Center for Work & Family.

Harrington, Brad, Fred Van Deusen, and Jamie Ladge. 2010. *The New Dad: Exploring Fatherhood Within a Career Context.* Boston: Boston College Center for Work & Family.

Harris, Deborah A., and Domenico Parisi. 2005. "Gender Role Ideologies and Marriage Promotion: State Policy Choices and Suggestions for Improvement." *Review of Policy Research* 22(6): 841–58.

Harrison, Kim. 1997. "Parental Training for Incarcerated Fathers: Effects on Attitudes, Self-Esteem, and Children's Self-Perceptions." *The Journal of Social Psychology* 137(5): 588–93.

Haskins, Ron, and Isabel Sawhill. 2007. "Introducing the Issue." *Future of Children* 17(2): 3–16.

Hawk, Carol Kozak, and George W. Holden. 2006. "Metaparenting: An Initial Investigation into a New Parental Social Cognition Construct." *Parenting: Science and Practice* 6(4): 21–42.

Heinrich, Carolyn, and Harry Holzer. 2011. "Improving Education and Employment for Disadvantaged Young Men: Proven and Promising Strategies." *Annals of the American Academy of Political and Social Science* 635(1): 163–91.

Henshaw, Stanley K., and Kathryn Kost. 2008. *Trends in the Characteristics of Women Obtaining Abortions, 1974 to 2004.* New York: Guttmacher Institute.

Hobson, Barbara. 2002. *Making Men into Fathers: Men, Masculinities and the Social Politics of Fatherhood.* Cambridge: Cambridge University Press.

Hofferth, Sandra, Joseph H. Pleck, and Colleen Vesely. Forthcoming. "Transmission of Parenting from Fathers to Sons." *Parenting: Science and Practice.*

Hogan, Dennis, David Eggebeen, and Clifford Clogg. 1993. "The Structure of Intergenerational Exchanges in American Families." *American Journal of Sociology* 98(6): 1428–58.

Hohmann-Marriott, Bryndl. 2011. "Coparenting and Father Involvement in Married and Unmarried Coresident Couples." *Journal of Marriage and Family* 73(1): 296–309.

Holden, George W., and Carol Kozak Hawk. 2003. "Meta-Parenting in the Journey of Child Rearing: A Cognitive Mechanism for Change." In *Handbook of Dynamics in Parent-Child Relationships,* edited by Leon Kuczynski. Thousand Oaks, Calif.: Sage.

Holmes, Erin K., Adam M. Galovan, Keitaro Yoshida, and Alan J. Hawkins. 2010. "Meta-Analysis of the Effectiveness of Resident Fathering Programs: Are Family Life Educators Interested in Fathers?" *Family Relations* 59(3): 240–52.

Hutchison, Elizabeth. 2010. *Dimensions of Human Behavior: The Changing Life Course.* Thousand Oaks, Calif.: Sage.

Institute for Women's Policy Research. 2010a. "The Gender Wage Gap." IWPR Fact Sheet No. C350. Washington, D.C.: Institute for Women's Policy Research.

———. 2010b. "Child Care Support for Student Parents in Community College Is Crucial for Success, but Supply and Funding Are Inadequate." IWCPR Fact Sheet No. C375. Washington, D.C.: Institute for Women's Policy Research.

Isacco, Anthony, and Craig F. Garfield. 2010. "Child Healthcare Decision-Making: Examining "Conjointness" in Paternal Identities Among Residential Non-Residential Fathers." *Fathering* 8(1): 109–30.

Jaffe, P. G., and C. V. Crooks. 2007. "Assessing the Best Interests of the Child." In *Parenting by Men Who Batter: New Directions for Assessment and Intervention,* edited by J. L. Edleson and O. J. Williams. Oxford: Oxford University Press.

Jarrett, Robin, and Linda Burton. 1999. "Dynamic Dimensions of Family Structure in Low-Income African-American Families: Emergent Themes in Qualitative Research." *Journal of Comparative Family Studies* 30(2): 177–88.

Jarrett, Robin, Kevin Roy, and Linda Burton. 2002. "Fathers in the 'Hood': Qualitative Research on African American Men." In *Handbook of Father Involvement: Multidisciplinary Perspectives,* edited by Catherine Tamis-LeMonda and Natasha Cabrera. Hillsdale, N.J.: Lawrence Erlbaum.

Jeffries, William L., William Marsiglio, and Dana Berkowitz. 2009. "Sexual Identity and Fatherhood Desires: A National Study of Childless Men." Unpublished paper.

Jia, Rongfang, and Sarah Schoppe-Sullivan. 2011. "Relations Between Coparenting and Father Involvement in Families with Preschool-Age Children." *Developmental Psychology* 47: 106–18.

Johnson, Earl, Ann Levine, and Fred Doolittle. 1999. *Fathers' Fair Share: Helping Poor Men Manage Child Support and Fatherhood.* New York: Russell Sage Foundation.

Johnson, Waldo, and W. Salter. 2006. "Paternity Disestablishment, Father Involvement and the Best Interest of the Child: Lessons from Child Welfare and Family Law." Report prepared for the assistant secretary for planning and evaluation, Emerging Issues in Paternity Symposium. Washington: U.S. Department of Health and Human Services.

Jones, J. 2008. "Adoption Experiences of Women and Men and Demand for Children to Adopt by Women 18–44 Years of Age in the United States, 2002." *Vital Health Stats* 23(27; August): 1–36.

Jones, R., J. Darroch, and Stanley Henshaw. 2002. "Patterns in the Socioeconomic Characteristics of Women Obtaining Abortions in 2000–2001." *Perspectives on Sexual and Reproductive Health* 34(5): 226–35.

Juby, Heather, Jean-Michel Billette, Benoît Laplante, and Céline Le Bourdais. 2007. "Nonresident Fathers and Children: Parents' New Unions and Frequency of Contact." *Journal of Family Issues* 28(9): 1220–45.

Kalwarski, Tara. 2010. "The Benefits—and Costs—of College." *Numbers* report, March. *Bloomberg Business Week*. Available at: http://www.aier.org/aier/otherpublications/businessweek_numbers.pdf; accessed September 12, 2011.

Kimmel, Michael. 1996. *Manhood in America: A Cultural History*. New York: Free Press.

———. 2008. *Guyland: The Inner World of Young Men, 18–27*. New York: HarperCollins.

Kiselica, Mark S. 1995. *Multicultural Counseling with Teenage Fathers: A Practical Guide*. Thousand Oaks, Calif.: Sage.

———. 2008. *When Boys Become Parents*. Piscataway, N.J.: Rutgers University Press.

Knox, Virginia, Philip Cowan, C. Cowan, and E. Bildner. 2011. "Policies That Strengthen Fatherhood and Family Relationships: What Do We Know and What Do We Need to Know?" *Annals of the American Academy of Political and Social Science* 635(1): 216–39.

Kotre, John. 1984. *Outliving the Self: Generativity and the Interpretation of Lives*. Baltimore: Johns Hopkins University Press.

Lamb, Michael E. 2004. *The Role of the Father in Child Development*. 4th ed. Hoboken, N.J.: Wiley.

———. 2010. *The Role of the Father in Child Development*. 5th ed. Hoboken, N.J.: Wiley.

Lareau, Annette. 2000. "My Wife Can Tell Me Who I Know: Methodological and Conceptual Problems in Studying Fathers." *Qualitative Sociology* 23: 407–33.

LaRossa, Ralph. 1988. "Fatherhood and Social Change." *Family Relations* 37(4): 451–57.

———. 1997. *The Modernization of Fatherhood: A Social and Political History*. Chicago: University of Chicago Press.

———. 2005. "Until the Ball Glows in the Twilight: Fatherland Baseball, and the Game of Playing Catch." In *Situated Fathering: A Focus on Physical and Social Spaces*, edited by William Marsiglio, Kevin Roy, and G. L. Fox. Latham, Md.: Rowman & Littlefield.

Leahy, M. 2005. "Family Vacation." *Washington Post Magazine,* June 19, 2005.

Leavitt, Judith W. 2009. *Make Room for Daddy: The Journey from Waiting Room to Birthing Room*. Chapel Hill: University of North Carolina Press.

Letiecq, Bethany, and Sally Koblinsky. 2004. "Parenting in Violent Neighborhoods: African American Fathers Share Strategies to Keep Their Children Safe." *Journal of Family Issues* 25(6): 715–34.

Levine, James A., and Edward W. Pitt. 1995. *New Expectations: Community Strategies for Responsible Fatherhood*. New York: Families and Work Institute.

Levine, James, and Todd L. Pittinsky. 1997. *Working Fathers: New Strategies for Balancing Work and Family*. Reading, Mass.: Addison-Wesley.

Lewin, Ellen. 2006. "Family Values: Gay Men and Adoption in America." In *Adoptive Families in a Diverse Society,* edited by Katarina Wegar. New Brunswick, N.J.: Rutgers University Press.

———. 2009. *Gay Fatherhood: Narratives of Family and Citizenship in America.* Chicago: University of Chicago Press.

LexisNexis. 2001. "FERPA Stepparent Has FERPA Rights When Natural Parent Is Absent." *School Law Bulletin, Administrative Rulings* 5(3).

Lichter, Daniel, C. Batson, and J. Brown. 2004. "Welfare Reform and Marriage Promotion: The Marital Expectations and Desires of Single and Cohabiting Mothers." *Social Service Review* 78(1): 2–25.

Lichter, Daniel, and Deborah Graefe. 2007. "Men and Marriage Promotion: Who Married Unwed Mothers?" *Social Service Review* 37(3): 397–421.

Lichter, Daniel, Zhenchao Qian, and Leanna Mellott. 2006. "Marriage or Dissolution? Union Transitions Among Poor Cohabiting Women." *Demography* 43(2): 223–40.

Lin, I-Fen, and Sara S. McLanahan. 2007. "Parental Beliefs About Nonresidents Fathers' Obligations and Rights." *Journal of Marriage and Family* 69(2): 382–98.

Lupton, Deborah, and Lesley Barclay. 1997. *Constructing Fatherhood: Discourses and Experiences.* Thousand Oaks, Calif.: Sage.

MacDermid, Shelley, Rona Schwarz, Anthony Faber, Joyce Adkins, Matthew Mishkind, and Howard M. Weiss. 2005. "Military Fathers on the Front Lines." In *Situated Fathering: A Focus on Physical and Social Spaces,* edited by William Marsiglio, Kevin Roy, and Greer Litton Fox. Lanham, Md.: Rowman & Littlefield.

Mallon, G. P. 2004. *Gay Men Choosing Parenthood.* New York: Columbia University Press.

Mandell, D. 2002. *"Deadbeat Dads": Subjectivity and Social Construction.* Toronto: University of Toronto Press.

Manning, Wendy, and Pamela Smock. 2005. "Measuring and Modeling Cohabitation: New Perspectives from Qualitative Data." *Journal of Marriage and Family* 67(4): 989–1002.

Marini, Margaret. 1984. "The Order of Events in the Transition to Adulthood." *Sociology of Education* 37: 63–84.

Markus, Hazel, and Paula Nurius. 1986. "Possible Selves." *American Psychologist* 41: 954–69.

Marsiglio, William. 1995. "Fathers' Diverse Life Course Patterns and Roles: Theory and Social Interventions." In *Fatherhood: Contemporary Theory, Research, and Social Policy,* edited by W. Marsiglio. Thousand Oaks, Calif.: Sage.

———. 1998. *Procreative Man.* New York: New York University Press.

———. 2003. "Making Males Mindful of Their Sexual and Procreative Identities: Using Self-Narratives in Field Settings." *Perspectives on Sexual and Reproductive Health* 35(5): 229–33.

———. 2004a. *Stepdads: Stories of Love, Hope, and Repair.* Lanham, Md.: Rowman & Littlefield.

———. 2004b. "When Stepfathers Claim Stepchildren: A Conceptual Analysis." *Journal of Marriage and Family* 66(1): 22–39.

———. 2006. "Young Men and Teen Pregnancy: A Review of Sex, Contraception, and Fertility-Related Issues." In *It's a Guy Thing: Boys, Young Men, and Teen Pregnancy Prevention,* edited by William Marsiglio, A. Ries, Freya Sonenstein, F. Troccoli, and W. Whitehead. Washington, D.C.: National Campaign to Prevent Teen Pregnancy.

———. 2008a. *Men on a Mission: Valuing Youth Work in Our Communities.* Baltimore: Johns Hopkins University Press.

———. 2008b. "Understanding Men's Prenatal Experience and the Father Involvement Connection: Assessing Baby Steps." *Journal of Marriage and Family* 70(5): 1108–13.

———. 2009a. "Healthy Dads, Healthy Kids." *Contexts* 8(4): 22–27.

———. 2009b. "Men's Relations with Kids: Exploring and Promoting the Mosaic of Youth Work and Fathering." *The Annals of the American Academy of Political and Social Science* 624: 118–38.

———. 2011. "Being a Dad, Studying Fathers." In *Papa PhD: Essays on Fatherhood by Men in the Academy,* edited by Mary R. Marotte, Paige M. Reynolds, and Ralph J. Savarese. New Brunswick, N.J.: Rutgers University Press.

Marsiglio, William, Paul Amato, Randal Day, and Michael E. Lamb. 2000. "Scholarship on Fatherhood in the 1990s and Beyond." *Journal of Marriage and Family* 62(4): 1173–91.

Marsiglio, William, and Mark Cohan. 1997. "Young Fathers and Child Development." In *The Role of the Father in Child Development,* 3rd ed., edited by Michael E. Lamb. New York: Wiley.

———. 2000. "Contextualizing Father Involvement and Paternal Influence: Sociological and Qualitative Themes." *Marriage & Family Review* 29(2–3): 75–95.

Marsiglio, William, Randal Day, and Michael Lamb. 2000. "Exploring Fatherhood Diversity: Implications for Conceptualizing Father Involvement." *Marriage and Family Review* 29(4): 269–93.

Marsiglio, William, and Ramon Hinojosa. 2007. "Managing the Multifather Family: Stepfathers as Father Allies." *Journal of Marriage and Family* 69(3): 845–62.

———. 2010. "Stepfathers' Lives: Exploring Social Context and Interpersonal Complexity." In *The Role of the Father in Child Development,* 5th ed., edited by Michael E. Lamb. New York: Wiley.

Marsiglio, William, and Sally Hutchinson. 2002. *Sex, Men, and Babies: Stories of Awareness and Responsibility.* New York: New York University Press.

Marsiglio, William, and Joseph H. Pleck. 2005. "Fatherhood and Masculinities." In *The Handbook of Studies on Men and Masculinities,* edited by Michael Kimmel, Jeff Hearn, and R. W. Connell. Thousand Oaks, Calif.: Sage.

Marsiglio, William, and Kevin Roy. Forthcoming. "Fathers' Nurturance of Children over the Life Course." In *Handbook of Marriage and the Family,* edited by Gary Peterson and Kevin Bush. New York: Springer.

Marsiglio, William, Kevin Roy, and Greer L. Fox, eds. 2005. *Situated Fathering: A Focus on Physical and Social Spaces.* Lanham, Md.: Rowman & Littlefield.

Martin, Joyce A., Brady E. Hamilton, Paul D. Sutton, Stephanie J. Ventura, T. J. Matthews, Sharon Kirmeyer, and Michelle J. K. Osterman. 2010. "Births: Final Data for 2007." *National Vital Statistics Reports* 58(24). Hyattsville, Md.: National Center for Health Statistics.

Martin, Laurie T., Michelle J. McNamara, Alyssa S. Milot, Tamara Halle, and Elizabeth C. Hair. 2007. "The Effects of Father Involvement During Pregnancy on Receipt of Prenatal Care and Maternal Smoking." *Maternal Child Health Journal* 11(6): 595–602.

Maruna, Shadd. 2001. *Making Good: How Ex-Convicts Reform and Rebuild Their Lives.* Washington, D.C.: American Psychological Association Books.

Maruna, Shadd, and Kevin Roy. 2007. "Amputation or Restorative Surgery? Notes on the Concept of "Knifing Off" and Desistance from Crime." *Journal of Contemporary Criminal Justice* 23: 104–24.

Mason, Mary Anne, Sydney Harrison-Jay, Gloria M. Svare, and Nicholas H. Wolfinger. 2002. "Stepparents: De Facto Parents or Legal Strangers?" *Journal of Family Issues* 23(4): 507–22.

Matta, Dana S., and Carmen Knudson-Martin. 2006. "Father Responsivity: Couple Processes and the Coconstruction of Fatherhood." *Family Process* 45(1): 19–37.

Maughan, Denita R., Elizabeth Christiansen, William R. Jensen, Daniel Olympia, and Elaine Clark. 2005. "Behavioral Parent Training as a Treatment for Externalizing Behaviors and Disruptive Behavior Disorders: A Meta-Analysis." *School Psychology Review* 34(3): 267–86.

May, James. 2002. *Fathers of Children with Special Needs: New Horizons.* Bellevue, Wash.: Fathers Network Kindering Center.

McAdams, Dan, and Ed de St. Aubin. 1992. "A Theory of Generativity and Its Assessment Through Self-Report, Behavioral Acts, and Narrative Themes in Autobiography." *Journal of Personality and Social Psychology* 62(6): 1003–15.

McAllister, Carol, Patrick Wilson, and Jeffrey Burton. 2004. "From Sports Fans to Nurturers." *Fathering* 2(1): 31–59.

McBride, Brent A., and Rebecca J. McBride. 1993. "Parent Education and Support Programs for Fathers: Research Guiding Practice." *Childhood Education* 70: 4–9.

McBride, Brent A., and Mary M. Lutz. 2004. "Intervention: Changing the Nature and Extent of Father Involvement." In *The Role of the Father in Child Development,* 4th ed., edited by Michael E. Lamb. Hoboken, N.J.: Wiley.

McBride, Brent A., Thomas R. Rane, and Ji-Hi Bae. 2001. "Intervening with Teachers to Encourage Father/Male Involvement in Early Childhood Programs." *Early Childhood Research Quarterly* 16(1): 77–93.

McKay, Lindsey, Katherine Marshall, and Andrea Doucet. Forthcoming. "Fathers and Parental Leave in Canada: Policies and Practices." In *Father Involvement in Canada: Contested Terrain,* edited by Jessica Ball and Kerry Daly. Vancouver: University of British Columbia Press.

McNeill, Ted. 2007. "Fathers of Children with a Chronic Health Condition: Beyond Gender Stereotypes." *Men and Masculinities* 9(4): 409–24.

Mead, Lawrence. 2007. "Toward a Mandatory Work Policy for Men." *The Future of Children* 17(2): 43–72.

Menning, Chadwick L. 2006. "Nonresident Fathers' Involvement and Adolescents' Smoking." *Journal of Health and Social Behavior* 47(1): 32–46.

Menning, Chadwick L., and Susan D. Stewart. 2008. "Nonresident Father Involvement, Social Class, and Adolescent Weight." *Journal of Family Issues* 29(12): 1673–700.

Messner, Michael A. 1992. *Power at Play: Sports and the Problem of Masculinity.* Boston: Beacon Press.

Mikulincer, Mario, and Phillip Shaver. 2007. *Attachment in Adulthood: Structure, Dynamics, and Change.* New York: Guilford Press.

Miller, Cynthia, and Irwin Garfinkel. 1999. "The Determinants of Paternity Establishment and Child Support Award Rates Among Unmarried Women." *Population Research and Policy Review* 18(3): 237–60.

Miller, Kevin, and Barbara Gault. 2011. "Improving Child Care Access to Promote Postsecondary Success Among Low-Income Parents." IWPR Report. Washington, D.C.: Institute for Women's Policy Research.

Miller, Tina. 2010. " 'It's a Triangle That's Difficult to Square': Men's Intentions and Practices Around Caring, Work and First-Time Fatherhood." *Fathering* 8(3): 362–78.

Mincy, Ronald. 2006. *Black Men Left Behind.* Washington, D.C.: Urban Institute Press.

Mincy, Ronald, Irwin Garfinkel, and Lenna Nepomnyaschy. 2005. "In-Hospital Paternity Establishment and Father Involvement in Fragile Families." *Journal of Marriage and Family* 67(3): 611–26.

Mincy, Ronald, Serena Klempin, and Heather Schmidt. 2011. "Income Support Policies for Low-Income Men and Noncustodial Fathers: Tax and Transfer Programs." *Annals of the American Academy of Political and Social Science* 635(1): 240–61.

Mincy, Ronald, and Hillary Pouncy. 2002. "The Responsible Fatherhood Field: Evolution and Goals." In *Handbook of Father Involvement: Multidisciplinary Perspectives,* edited by Catherine S. Tamis-LeMonda and Natasha J. Cabrera. Mahwah, N.J.: Lawrence Erlbaum.

Morgan, S. Philip., Suzanne M. Bianchi, Thomas A. DiPrete, V. Joseph Hotz, Seth Sanders, Judith A. Seltzer, and Duncan Thomas. 2008. "Designing New Models for Explaining Family Change and Variation." Technical proposal in response to RFP NICHD 2003-03. Washington, D.C.: National Institute of Child Health and Human Development, Demographic and Behavioral Sciences Branch. Available at: http://www.soc.duke.edu/~efc/Docs/InitialProposal_4_03.pdf; accessed July 19, 2011.

Moss, Peter, and Marta Korintus. 2008. "International Review of Leave Policies and Related Research." Employment Relations Research Series No. 100. London: Department for Business Enterprise and Regulatory Reform. Available at: http://www.berr.gov.uk/files/file47247.pdf; accessed July 19, 2011.

Mouw, Ted. 2005. "Sequences of Early Adult Transitions: A Look at Variability and Consequences." In *On the Frontier of Adulthood: Theory, Research and Public Policy,* edited by Richard Settersten, Frank F. Furstenberg, and Rubén Rumbaut. Chicago: University of Chicago Press.

Mumola, Christopher J. 2006. "Parents Under Correctional Supervision: Past Estimates, New Measures." Report prepared for "Children of Parents in the Criminal Justice System: Children at Risk," NIDA Research Meeting, North Bethesda, Md. (November 6).

Musick, Kelly, and Larry Bumpass. 2006. "Cohabitation, Marriage, and Trajectories in Well-Being and Relationships." National Survey of Families and Households Working Paper No. 93. Madison: University of Wisconsin.

Nelson, Margaret. 2006. *The Social Economy of Single Mothering: Raising Children in Rural America.* New York: Routledge.

———. 2010. *Parenting Out of Control: Anxious Parents in Uncertain Times.* New York: New York University Press.

Nepomnyaschy, Lenna, and Jane Waldfogel. 2007. "Paternity Leave and Fathers' Involvement with Their Young Children: Evidence from the ECLS-B." *Community, Work and Family* 10(4): 425–51.

Newman, Katherine. 1999. *Falling from Grace: Downward Mobility in the Age of Affluence.* Berkeley: University of California Press.

Nicholson, Jody S., Kimberley S. Howard, and John G. Borkowski. 2008. "Mental Models of Parenting: Correlates of Metaparenting Among Fathers of Young Children." *Fathering: A Journal of Theory, Research, and Practice About Men as Fathers* 6(1): 39–61.

Nurse, Anne M. 2002. *Fatherhood Arrested: Parenting Within the Juvenile Justice System.* Nashville: Vanderbilt University Press.

Obama, Barack. 2004. *Dreams from My Father: A Story of Race and Inheritance.* New York: Three Rivers Press.

———. 2008. "A More Perfect Union." Speech. Democratic National Convention: National Constitution Center, Philadelphia (March 18).

O'Brien, Margaret. 2005. *Shared Caring: Bringing Fathers into the Frame.* Norwich, U.K.: University of East Anglia.

O'Brien, Margaret, and Peter Moss. 2010. "Fathers, Work, and Family Policies in Europe." In *The Role of the Father in Child Development.* 5th ed., edited by Michael E. Lamb. New York: Wiley.

O'Brien, Mary. 1981. *The Politics of Reproduction.* Boston: Routledge and Kegan Paul.

O'Donnell, John M., Waldo E. Johnson, Lisa D'Aunno, and Helen Thornton. 2005. "Fathers in Child Welfare: Caseworkers' Perspectives." *Child Welfare* 84(3): 387–414.

Ooms, Theodora, Jacqueline Boggess, Anne Menard, Mary Myrick, Paula Roberts, Jack Tweedie, and Pamela Wilson. 2006. *Building Bridges Between Healthy Marriage, Responsible Fatherhood, and Domestic Violence Programs.* Washington, D.C.: Center for Law and Social Policy.

Oritz, Robert W., and Stephen Stile. 2002. "Project DADS: Training Fathers in Early Literacy Skills Through Community-University Partnerships." *School Community Journal* 12(1): 91–106.

Orloff, Ann, and Renee Monson. 2002. "Citizens, Workers, or Fathers? Men in the History of US Social Policy." In *Making Men into Fathers: Men, Masculinities, and the Social Politics of Fatherhood,* edited by Barbara Hobson. New York: Cambridge University Press.

Oswald, Ramona. 2002. "Resilience Within the Family Networks of Lesbians and Gay Men: Intentionality and Redefinition." *Journal of Marriage and Family* 64(2): 374–83.

Oyserman, Daphna, and Hazel Markus. 1990. "Possible Selves and Delinquency." *Journal of Personality and Social Psychology* 59(1): 112–25.

Padawer, Ruth. 2009. "Who Knew I Was Not the Father?" *New York Times Magazine,* November 17. Available at: http://www.nytimes.com/2009/11/22/magazine/22Paternity-t.html?pagewanted=all; accessed September 12, 2011.

Palkovitz, Rob. 2002. *Involved Fathering and Men's Adult Development: Provisional Balances.* Mahwah, N.J.: Lawrence Erlbaum.

Palkovitz, Rob, and Glen Palm. 2009. "Transitions Within Fathering." *Fathering* 7(1): 3–22.

Palmer, Linda F. 2004. "The Chemistry of Attachment." *Attachment Parenting International News* 5(2). Available at: http://www.attachmentparenting.org/support/articles/artchemistry.php; accessed July 19, 2011.

Paquette, Daniel. 2004. "Theorizing the Father-Child Relationship: Mechanisms and Developmental Outcomes." *Human Development* 47(4): 193–219.

Parker, Kim. 2007. "Being Dad May Be Tougher These Days, but Working Moms Are Among Their Biggest Fans." Pew Social and Demographic Trends Report. Washington, D.C.: Pew Research Center, June 13.

Parra-Cardona, Jose R., Richard Wampler, and Elizabeth Sharp. 2006. "Wanting to Be a Good Father: Experiences of Adolescent Fathers of Mexican Descent in a Teen Fathers Program." *Journal of Marital and Family Therapy* 32(2): 215–31.

Pelchat, Diane, Hélène Lefebvre, and Marie-Josée Levert. 2007. "Gender Differences and Similarities in the Experience of Parenting a Child with a Health Problem: Current State of Knowledge." *Journal of Child Health Care* 11(2): 112–31.

Peled, Einat, and Guy Perel. 2007. "A Conceptual Framework for Fathering Intervention with Men Who Batter." In *Parenting by Men Who Batter: New Directions for Assessment and Intervention,* edited by Jeffrey L. Edleson and Oliver J. Williams. Oxford: Oxford University Press.

Peter, Gregory, Michael Bell, Susan Jarnagin, and Donna Bauer. 2005. "Farm Dads: Reconstructing Fatherhood, the Legacy of the Land, and Family in the Fields of the Midwest." In *Situated Fathering: A Focus on Physical and Social Spaces,* edited by William Marsiglio, Kevin Roy, and Greer L. Fox. Latham, Md.: Rowman & Littlefield.

Peters, H. Elizabeth, Gary W. Peterson, Suzanne K. Steinmetz, and Randal D. Day. 2000. *Fatherhood: Research, Interventions and Policies.* New York: Haworth Press.

Pew Forum on Religion and Public Life. 2009. "The Stronger Sex—Spiritually Speaking." Survey analysis graph. Available at: http://pewforum.org/The-Stronger-Sex—Spiritually-Speaking.aspx; accessed August 18, 2011.

Pew Research Center. 2005. "Public Opinion Supports Alito on Spousal Notification Even as It Favors Roe v. Wade." Pew Research Center Pollwatch. Available at: http://people-press.org/2005/11/02/public-opinion-supports-alito-on-spousal-notification-even-as-it-favors-iroe-v-wadei; accessed September 9, 2011.

———. 2007. "Motherhood Today: Tougher Challenges, Less Success." Social Trends Report. Available at: http://pewsocialtrends.org/2007/05/02/motherhood-today-tougher-challenges-less-success; accessed September 12, 2011.

———. 2010. "Majority Continues to Favor Gays Serving in Military; Support for Same-Sex Marriage Edges Upward." Survey Report. Washington, D.C.: Pew Research Center. Available at: http://people-press.org/report/662/same-sex-marriage; accessed July 19, 2011.

Pickhardt, Carl E. 1997. *Keys to Successful Step-Fathering.* Hauppauge, N.Y.: Barron's Educational Services.

Pinsof, William. 2002. "The Death of 'Till Death Do Us Part': The Transformation of Pair-Bonding in the 20th Century." *Family Process* 41(2): 135–57.

Pleck, Elizabeth, and Joseph H. Pleck. 1997. "Fatherhood Ideals in the United States: Historical Dimensions." In *The Role of the Father in Child Development*, edited by Michael E. Lamb. New York: Wiley.

Pleck, Joseph H. 2010a. "Fatherhood and Masculinity." In *The Role of the Father in Child Development*, 5th ed., edited by Michael E. Lamb. Hoboken: Wiley.

———. 2010b. "Paternal Involvement: Revised Conceptualization and Theoretical Linkages with Child Outcomes." In *The Role of the Father in Child Development*, 5th ed., edited by Michael E. Lamb. New York: Wiley.

Pleck, Joseph H., Michael E. Lamb, and James A. Levine. 1986. "Epilog: Facilitating Future Change in Men's Family Roles." *Marriage and Family Review* 9(3–4): 11–16.

Pleck, Joseph H., and Brian P. Masciadrelli. 2004. "Paternal Involvement by U.S. Residential Fathers: Levels, Sources, and Consequences." In *The Role of the Father in Child Development*, 4th ed., edited by Michael E. Lamb. Hoboken, N.J.: Wiley.

Pollack, William. 1998. *Real Boys: Rescuing Our Sons from the Myth of Boyhood*. New York: Henry Holt.

Popenoe, David. 1996. *Life Without Father*. New York: Free Press.

Portes, Alejandro. 1998. "Social Capital: Its Origins and Applications in Modern Sociology." *Annual Review of Sociology* 24: 1–27.

Pruett, Kyle. 1987. *The Nurturing Father: Journey Toward the Complete Man*. New York: Warner Books.

———. 2000. *Fatherneed: Why Father Care Is as Essential as Mother Care for Your Child*. New York: The Free Press.

Pruett, Kyle, and Marsha Kline Pruett. 2009. *Partnership Parenting: How Men and Women Parent Differently—Why It Helps Your Kids and Can Strengthen Your Marriage*. Cambridge, Mass.: Da Capo Press.

Raikes, Helen, Jean Ann Summers, and Lori A. Roggman. 2005. "Father Involvement in Early Head Start Programs." *Fathering* 3(1): 29–58.

Rane, Thomas R., and Brent A. McBride. 2000. "Identity Theory as a Guide to Understanding Fathers' Involvement with Their Children." *Journal of Family Issues* 21(3): 347–66.

Ray, Rebecca, Janet C. Gornick, and John Schmitt. 2010. "Who Cares? Assessing Generosity and Gender Equality in Parental Leave Policy Designs in 21 Countries." *Journal of European Social Policy* 20(3): 196–216.

Reed, Joanna. 2006. "Not Crossing the 'Extra Line': How Cohabitors with Children View Their Unions." *Journal of Marriage and Family* 68(5): 1117–31.

Reed, Richard. 2005. *Birthing Fathers: The Transformation of Men in American Rites of Birth*. New Brunswick, N.J.: Rutgers University Press.

Reuter, Mark, and Henry Biller. 1973. "Perceived Paternal Nurturance-Availability and Personality Adjustment Among College Males." *Journal of Consulting and Clinical Psychology* 40(3): 339–42.

Rhodes, Jean E., and D. L. DuBois. 2008. "Mentoring Relationships and Programs for Youth." *Current Directions in Psychological Science* 17(4): 254–58.

Rich, John A. 2009. *Wrong Place, Wrong Time: Trauma and Violence in the Lives of Young Black Men*. Baltimore: Johns Hopkins University Press.

Rich, Lauren M. 2001. "Regular and Irregular Earnings of Unwed Fathers: Implications for Child Support Practices." *Children and Youth Services Review* 23(4–5): 353–76.

Richter, Linda, and Robert Morrell, eds. 2006. *Baba: Men and Fatherhood in South Africa.* HSRC Press: Capetown, South Africa.

Rindfuss, Ronald. 1991. "The Young Adult Years: Diversity, Structural Change, and Fertility." *Demography* 28(4): 493–512.

Roberts, Paula. 2004. "Paternity Disestablishment in 2004: The Year in Review." CLASP memorandum. Washington, D.C.: Center for Law and Social Policy.

Roggman, Lori A., Lisa K. Boyce, Gina K. Cook, Katie Christiansen, and DeAnn Jones. 2004. "Playing with Daddy: Social Toy Play, Early Head Start, and Developmental Outcomes." *Fathering* 2(1): 83–108.

Romano, Andrew, and Tony Dokoupil. 2010. "Men's Lib." *Newsweek,* September 20, 42–48.

Roschelle, Anne. 1997. *No More Kin: Exploring Race, Class, and Gender in Family Networks.* Thousand Oaks, Calif.: Sage.

Rothman, Barbara Katz. 2005. *Weaving a Family: Untangling Race and Adoption.* Boston: Beacon Press.

Roy, Kevin. 1999. "Low-Income Single Fathers in an African American Community and The requirements of Welfare Reform." *Journal of Family Issues* 20(4): 432–57.

———. 2004. "Three-Block Fathers: Spatial Perceptions and Kin-Work in Low-Income Neighborhoods." *Social Problems* 51(4): 528–48.

———. 2005a. "Transitions on the Margins of Work and Family for Low-Income African American Fathers." *Journal of Family and Economic Issues* 26(1): 77–100.

———. 2005b. "Nobody Can be a Father in Here: Identity Construction and Institutional Constraints on Incarcerated Fatherhood." In *Situated Fathering: A Focus on Physical and Social Spaces,* edited by William Marsiglio, Kevin Roy, and Greer L. Fox. Lanham, Md.: Rowman & Littlefield.

———. 2006. "Father Stories: A Life Course Examination of Paternal Identity Among Low-Income African American Men." *Journal of Family Issues* 27(1): 31–54.

Roy, Kevin, Nicolle Buckmiller, and April McDowell. 2008. "Together but Not 'Together': Trajectories of Relationship Suspension for Low-Income Unmarried Parents." *Family Relations* 57(2): 197–209.

Roy, Kevin, and Linda Burton. 2007. "Mothering Through Recruitment: Kinscription of Non-Residential Fathers and Father Figures in Low-Income Families." *Family Relations* 56(1): 24–39.

Roy, Kevin, and Omari Dyson. 2005. "Gatekeeping in Context: Babymama Drama and the Involvement of Incarcerated Fathers." *Fathering: A Journal of Theory, Research, and Practice About Men as Fathers* 3(3): 289–310.

———. 2010. "Making Daddies into Fathers: Community-Based Fatherhood Programs and the Construction of Masculinity for Low-Income African American Men." *American Journal of Community Psychology* 45(3–4): 139–54.

Roy, Kevin, Omari Dyson, and Ja-Nee Jackson. 2010. "Intergenerational Support and Reciprocity Between Low-Income African American Fathers and Their Aging Mothers." In *Social Work with African American Males,* edited by W. Johnson and E. Johnson. New York: Oxford University Press.

Roy, Kevin, and Kristin Lucas. 2006. "Generativity as Second Chance: Low-Income Fathers and Transformation of the Difficult Past." *Research on Human Development* 3(2–3): 139–59.

Russell, Graeme, and Carl P. Hwang. 2004. "The Impact of Workplace Practices on Father Involvement." In *The Role of the Father in Child Development*, 4th ed., edited by Michael E. Lamb. Hoboken: Wiley.

Sassler, Sharon. 2004. "The Process of Entering into Cohabiting Unions." *Journal of Marriage and Family* 66(2): 491–505.

Sayers, Jeremy P., and Greer L. Fox. 2005. "The Haunted Hero: Fathering Profiles of Long-Haul Truckers." In *Situated Fathering: A Focus on Physical and Social Spaces*, edited by William Marsiglio, Kevin Roy, and Greer L. Fox. Lanham, Md.: Rowman & Littlefield.

Schoppe-Sullivan, Sarah J., Geoffrey L. Brown, Elizabeth A. Cannon, Sarah C. Mangelsdorf, and Margaret Szewsczyk Sokolowski. 2008. "Maternal Gatekeeping, Coparenting Quality, and Fathering Behavior in Families with Infants." *Journal of Family Psychology* 22(3): 389–39.

Schrock, Doug, and Michael Schwalbe. 2009. "Men, Masculinity, and Manhood Acts." *Annual Review of Sociology* 35: 277–95.

Scott, Katreena L., and Claire V. Crooks. 2007. "Preliminary Evaluation of an Intervention Program for Maltreating Fathers." *Brief Treatment and Crisis Intervention* 7(3): 224–38.

Scott, Katreena L., Karen J. Francis, Claire V. Crooks, Michelle Paddon, and David A. Wolfe. 2007. "Guidelines for Intervention with Abusive Fathers." In *Parenting by Men Who Batter: New Directions for Assessment and Intervention*, edited by Jeffrey L. Edleson and Oliver J. Williams. Oxford: Oxford University Press.

Seery, Brenda L., and M. Sue Crowley. 2000. "Women's Emotion Work in the Family." *Journal of Family Issues* 21(1): 100–27.

Segal, Mady W., and David R. Segal. 2003. "Implications for Military Families of Changes in the Armed Forces of the United States." In *Handbook of Sociology of the Military*, edited by Giuseppe Caforio. New York: Kluwer Academic/Plenum Publishers.

Settersten, Richard A., Jr., and Doris Cancel-Tirado. 2010. "Fatherhood as a Hidden Variable in Men's Development and Life Courses." *Research in Human Development* 7(2): 83–102.

Settersten, Richard A., Jr., Frank F. Furstenberg, Jr., and Rubén G. Rumbaut. 2005. *On the Frontier of Adulthood: Theory, Research, and Public Policy*. Chicago: University of Chicago Press.

Seward, Rudy, Dale Yeatts, Iftekhar Amin, and Amy DeWitt. 2006. "Employment Leave and Fathers' Involvement with Children." *Men and Masculinities* 8(4): 405–27.

Seward, Rudy, Dale Yeatts, Lisa Zottarelli, and Ryan Fletcher. 2006. "Fathers' Taking Parental Leave and Their Involvement with Their Children." *Community, Work, and Family* 9(1): 1–9.

Sharma, Manoj, and Rick Petosa. 1997. "Impact of Expectant Fathers in Breast-Feeding Decisions." *Journal of the American Dietetic Association* 97(11): 1311–13.

Silverstein, Louise B., and Carl F. Auerbach. 1999. "Deconstructing the Essential Father." *American Psychologist* 54(6): 397–407.

Singer, George H. S., Brandy L. Ethridge, and Sandra I. Aldana. 2007. "Primary and Secondary Effects of Parenting and Stress Management Interventions for Parents of Children with Developmental Disabilities: A Meta-Analysis." *Mental Retardation and Developmental Disabilities Research Reviews* 13(4): 357–69.

Smeeding, Timothy, Irwin Garfinkel, and Ronald Mincy. 2011. "Young Disadvantaged Men: Fathers, Families, Poverty, and Policy: An Introduction to the Issues." *Annals of the American Academy of Political and Social Science* 635(1): 6–21.

Smith, Jeremy A. 2009. *The Daddy Shift: How Stay-at-Home Dads, Breadwinning Moms, and Shared Parenting Are Transforming the American Family.* Boston: Beacon.

Snarey, John. 1993. *How Fathers Care for the Next Generation: A Four-Decade Study.* Cambridge, Mass.: Harvard University Press.

Sonenstein, Freya L., Kellie Stewart, Laura Lindberg, Marta Pernas, and Sean Williams. 1997. *Involving Males in Preventing Teen Pregnancy: A Guide for Program Planners.* Washington, D.C.: Urban Institute.

Sorensen, Elain, Liliana Sousa, and Simon Schaner. 2007. *Assessing Child Support Arrears in Nine Large States and the Nation.* Washington, D.C.: Urban Institute.

Stacey, Judith. 2006. "Gay Parenthood and the Decline of Paternity as We Knew It." *Sexualities* 9(1): 27–55.

Stacey, Judith, and Timothy J. Biblarz. 2001. "How Does the Sexual Orientation of Parents Matter?" *American Sociological Review* 66(2): 159–83.

Stack, Carol. 1974. *All Our Kin: Strategies for Survival in a Black Community.* New York: Random House.

Stack, Carol, and Linda Burton. 1993. "Kinscripts." *Journal of Comparative Family Studies* 24(1):157–70.

Stanley, Kate. 2005. *Daddy Dearest? Active Fatherhood and Public Policy.* London: Institute for Public Policy Research.

Stanley, Scott M. 2001. "Making the Case for Premarital Education." *Family Relations* 50(3): 272–80.

Stanley, Scott M., Galena Rhoades, and Howard J. Markman. 2006. "Sliding Versus Deciding: Inertia and the Premarital Cohabitation Effect." *Family Relations* 55(4): 499–509.

Stephenson, Mary-Ann. 2010. "Fathers, Families, and Work: Putting 'Working Fathers' in the Picture." *Political Quarterly* 81(2): 237–42.

Storey, Anne, Carolyn Walsh, Roma Quinton, and Katherine Wynne-Edwards. 2000. "Hormonal Correlates of Paternal Responsiveness in New and Expectant Fathers." *Evolution and Human Behavior* 21(2): 79–85.

Strauss, Rachelle, and Wendy A. Goldberg. 1999. "Self and Possible Selves During the Transition to Fatherhood." *Journal of Family Psychology* 13(2): 244–59.

Summers, Jean Ann, Kimberly Boller, and Helen Raikes. 2004. "Preferences and Perceptions About Getting Support Expressed by Low-Income Fathers." *Fathering* 2(1): 61–82.

Surra, Catherine A., and Debra K. Hughes. 1997. "Commitment Processes in Accounts of the Development of Premarital Relationships." *Journal of Marriage and Family* 59(1): 5–21.

Swisher, Raymond, and Maureen R. Waller. 2008. "Confining Fatherhood: Incarceration and Paternal Involvement Among Nonresident White, African American, and Latino Fathers." *Journal of Family Issues* 29(8): 1067–88.

Swiss, Liam, and Celine Le Bourdais. 2009. "Father-Child Contact After Separation: The Influence of Living Arrangements." *Journal of Family Issues* 30(5): 623–52.

Tach, Laura, Ronald Mincy, and Kathryn Edin. 2010. "Parenting as a 'Package Deal': Relationships, Fertility, and Nonresident Father Involvement Among Unmarried Parents." *Demography* 47(1): 181–204.

Tamis-LeMonda, Catherine, and Natasha Cabrera. 2002. *Handbook of Father Involvement: Multidisciplinary Perspectives.* Mahwah, N.J.: Lawrence Erlbaum.

Tamis-LeMonda, Catherine, and Karen E. McFadden. 2010. "Fathers from Low-Income Backgrounds: Myths and Evidence." In *The Role of the Father in Child Development*, 5th ed., edited by Michael E. Lamb. New York: Wiley.

Tamis-LeMonda, Catherine, J. Shannon, Natasha Cabrera, and Michael E. Lamb. 2004. "Resident Fathers and Mothers at Play with Their 2- and 3-Year-Olds: Contributions to Language and Cognitive Development." *Child Development* 75(6): 1806–20.

Tanaka, Sakiko, and Jane Waldfogel. 2007. "Effects of Parental Leave and Work Hours on Fathers' Involvement with Their Babies: Evidence from the Millennium Cohort Study." *Community, Work and Family* 10(4): 409–26.

Thorne, Barrie. 2001. "Pick-up Time at Oakdale Elementary School: Work and Family from the Vantage Points of Children." In *Working Families: The Transformation of the American Home*, edited by Rosanna Hertz and Nancy Marshall. Berkeley: University of California Press.

Thorpe, Kate, and Kerry Daly. 1999. "Children, Parents, and Time: The Dialectics of Control." In *Through the Eyes of the Child: Revisioning Children as Active Agents in Family Life*, edited by Constance Shehan. Stamford, Conn.: JAI Press.

Townsend, Nicholas. 2002. *The Package Deal: Marriage, Work, and Fatherhood in Men's Lives.* Philadelphia: Temple University Press.

Tronto, Joan C. 1989. "Women and Caring: What Can Feminists Learn About Morality from Caring?" In *Gender/Body/Knowledge: Feminist Reconstructions of Being and Knowing*, edited by Susan Bordo. New Brunswick, N.J.: Rutgers University Press.

Tubbs, Carolyn Y., and Oliver J. Williams. 2007. "Shared Parenting After Abuse: Battered Mothers' Perspectives on Parenting After Dissolution of a Relationship." In *Parenting by Men Who Batter: New Directions for Assessment and Intervention*, edited by Jeffrey L. Edleson and Oliver J. Williams. Oxford: Oxford University Press.

Turetsky, Vicky. 2000. "Realistic Child Support Policies for Low-Income Fathers." Kellogg Devolution Initiative Paper. Washington, D.C.: Center for Law and Social Policy.

———. 2007. "Child Support: Preserving and Expanding a Decade of Progress." Presentation briefing on S. 803 and H.R. 1386. Washington, D.C.: Center for Law and Social Policy.

———. 2008. "Responsible Fatherhood and Healthy Families Act of 2007." CLASP Legislation in Brief. Washington, D.C.: Center for Law and Social Policy. Available at: www.clasp.org/publications/responsible_fatherhood_act_of_2007.pdf; accessed July 19, 2011.

U.S. Census Bureau. 2009. "Education Attainment." Report from Current Population Survey, 2009 data. Washington: U.S. Census Bureau.

U.S. Department of Health and Human Services. 2001. "Meeting the Challenge: What the Federal Government Can Do to Support Responsible Fatherhood Efforts." Report to the President. Washington: U.S. Department of Health and Human Services.

U.S. Department of Labor. 2010. "Employment and Unemployment Among Youth Summary." Bureau of Labor Statistics, Economic News Release, August 27, 2010. Washington: U.S. Department of Labor. Available at: http://www.bls.gov/news.release/youth.nr0.htm; accessed August 24, 2011.

Valentine, Gill. 2004. *Public Space and the Cultural of Childhood.* Burlington, Vt.: Ashgate.

Van de Hoonard, Will C. 1997. *Working with Sensitizing Concepts: Analytical Field Research.* Thousand Oaks, Calif.: Sage.

Walker, Alexis J., and Lori A. McGraw. 2000. "Who Is Responsible for Responsible Fathering?" *Journal of Marriage and Family* 62(2): 563–69.

Wall, Glenda, and Stephanie Arnold. 2007. "How Involved Is Involved Fathering? An Exploration of the Contemporary Culture of Fatherhood." *Gender and Society* 21(4): 508–27.

Waller, Maureen. 2002. *My Baby's Father: Unmarried Parents and Paternal Responsibility.* Ithaca, N.Y.: Cornell University Press.

Walzer, Susan. 1998. *Thinking About the Baby: Gender and Transitions into Parenthood.* Philadelphia: Temple University Press.

Welsh, David. 2009. "Virtual Parents: How Virtual Visitation Legislation Is Shaping the Future of Custody Law." *Journal of Law and Family Studies* 11(1): 215–25.

Weston, Kath. 1991. *Families We Choose: Lesbians, Gays, Kinship.* New York: Columbia University Press.

Whitehead, Denise L., and N. Bala. Forthcoming. "The Short End of the Stick? Fatherhood in the Wake of Separation and Divorce." In *Father Involvement in Canada: Contested Terrain,* edited by Jessica Ball and Kerry Daly. Vancouver: University of British Columbia Press.

Wickrama, K. A. S., Rand D. Conger, Lora E. Wallace, and Glen H. Elder, Jr. 1999. "The Intergenerational Transmission of Health-Risk Behaviors: Adolescent Lifestyles and Gender Moderating Effects." *Journal of Health and Social Behavior* 40(3): 258–72.

Wilcox, W. Bradford. 2004. *Soft Patriarchs and New Men: How Christianity Shapes Fathers and Husbands.* Chicago: University of Chicago Press.

Wilczak, Ginger, and Carol Markstrom. 1999. "The Effects of Parent Education on Parental Locus of Control and Satisfaction of Incarcerated Fathers." *International Journal of Offender Therapy and Comparative Criminology* 43(1): 90–102.

Wong, Leonard, and Stephen Gerras. 2010. "The Effects of Multiple Deployments on Army Adolescents." Washington, D.C.: United States Army War College, Strategic Studies Institute.

Young, Alfrod. 2006. *The Minds of Marginalized Black Men: Making Sense of Mobility, Opportunity, and Future Life Chances.* Princeton Studies in Cultural Sociology. Princeton, N.J.: Princeton University Press.

Zinn, Maxine Baca, and Barbara Wells. 2008. "Diversity Within Latino Families: New Lessons for Family Social Science." In *American Families: A Multicultural Reader,* 2d ed., edited by Stephanie Coontz. New York: Routledge.

Zvonkovic, Aniga M., Catherine Richards, Aine Humble, and Margaret Manoogian. 2005. "Lessons About Family Work and Relationships from Families of Men Whose Jobs Require Travel." *Family Relations* 54(3): 411–22.

Index

Boldface numbers refer to figures and tables.